Plays of Provocation

edited by
Farley P. Richmond
The University of Georgia

KENDALL/HUNT PUBLISHING COMPANY
4050 Westmark Drive   Dubuque, Iowa 52002

Copyright © 1999 by Farley P. Richmond

ISBN 0-7872-6007-X

Kendall/Hunt Publishing Company has the exclusive rights to reproduce this work,
to prepare derivative works from this work, to publicly distribute this work,
to publicly perform this work and to publicly display this work.

All rights reserved. No part of this publication may be reproduced,
stored in a retrieval system, or transmitted, in any form or by any
means, electronic, mechanical, photocopying, recording, or otherwise,
without the prior written permission of Kendall/Hunt Publishing Company.

Printed in the United States of America
10 9 8 7 6 5 4 3 2 1

Contents

Preface	v
The American Dream 　　Edward Albee	1
Baby with the Bathwater 　　Christopher Durang	35
Execution of Justice 　　Emily Mann	81
Split Second: A Play in Two Acts 　　Dennis McIntyre	153
Wedding Band: A Love/Hate Story in Black and White 　　Alice Childress	197
What the Butler Saw 　　Joe Orton	243
Yankee Dawg You Die 　　Philip Kan Gotanda	291

Preface

Plays have the power (some might even argue the responsibility) to address issues that call into question what we think and do about matters that confront us every day. In this respect, playwrights often take risks, tackling bold and controversial subject matter that would otherwise be impossible for audiences to encounter in any other performing art. In this respect, many plays and their productions are as pertinent today as they were thousands of years ago.

The plays in this collection were chosen because they provoke debate. Each takes on one or several issues confronting contemporary society that should cause the reader or the spectator to stop and to think more deeply. Each raises fundamental question. For example, "Are all men (and women, for that matter) created equal?" "Is there equal justice for everyone under the law?" "What are the hidden barriers that exist in society for some that do not exist for others?" "Can children thrive despite seemingly insurmountable obstacles?" "What responsibilities do parents have for raising their young?" "Should one tell the truth even if by doing so you or those you love would be irreparably harmed?"

Raising questions such as these is the business of the playwright. Providing answers to the issues once raised is the business of the reader or the viewer. Although the playwrights in this collection may have deeply held feelings and beliefs about wrongs that they see in society, they leave room for the reader and the viewer to establish their own opinions about what to do to rectify the wrongs. They want us to be actively rather than passively engaged in the process of debate provoked by the issues which confront their characters.

Three of the works use comedy to project their messages. Albee's *The American Dream,* Durang's *Baby with the Bathwater,* and Orton's *What the Butler Saw* are all written with witty dialogue, humorously drawn characters, and outrageous situations even though each play has an underlying serious intent. Childress' *Wedding Band,* McIntyre's *Split Second,* and Mann's *Execution of Justice* take a serious approach employing melodrama in formulating their plots, characters, and dramatic action. Gotanda's *Yankee Dawg You Die* combines humor and fantasy to expose the social ills it exposes.

The American Dream

Edward Albee

The American Dream appeared in the early 1960s on the heels of experiments among young European playwrights who were writing works that contained absurd themes and content. Edward Albee's play provides a distinctly American response to the cartoon-like characters and bizarre situations which characterized other plays developed in Europe during this period. In addition, it shaped the future direction of Albee's subsequent efforts, particularly laying the groundwork for *Whose Afraid of Virginia Woolf?*, arguably Albee's finest play and certainly one of the best American plays of the latter half of the twentieth century.

What makes *The American Dream* as alive today as it was when it was first written is the character of Grandma, a sassy spark of a woman who sees Mommy, her vein and pretentious mother, and Daddy, Mommy's rich emasculated husband, for what they really are and calls them on it at every opportunity. Grandma also extends sincere sympathy to the handsome but vacuous young man who mysteriously appears in the household half-way through the play and eventually replaces Grandma in the family unit.

The tight, crisp dialogue, witless behavior of his characters, and the bizarre picture that Albee paints of their off-stage world is a hallmark of this and later works.

The play raises questions which are still pertinent today such as, "What is American society to do with its elderly?" "How should the young be raised?" "What values should families have and adhere to?"

Albee's play is a comedy. Grandma confirms that fact in her address directly to the audience at the end of the work. But the subtext underlying everything that happens in the play is serious providing a rich potential for analysis and debate.

Production History

The American Dream was first produced by Theatre 1961, Richard Barr, and Clinton Wilder, at the York Playhouse, New York City, on January 24, 1961. It was directed by Alan Schneider. The sets and costumes were by William Ritman. The cast was as follows:

Daddy	John C. Becher
Mommy	Jane Hoffman
Grandma	Sudie Bond
Mrs. Barker	Nancy Cushman
The Young Man	Ben Piazza

Characters

DADDY
MOMMY
GRANDMA
MRS. BARKER
THE YOUNG MAN

The American Dream by Edward Albee

Copyright © 1961, Renewed 1988 by Edward Albee. Reprinted by permission of William Morris Agency, Inc., on behalf of the Author. All rights reserved.

CAUTION: Professionals and amateurs are hereby warned that "The American Dream" is subject to a royalty. It is fully protected under the copyright laws of the United States of America and all countries covered by the International Copyright Union (including the Dominion of Canada and the rest of the British Commonwealth), the Berne Convention, the Pan-American Copyright Convention and the Universal Copyright Convention as well as all countries with which the United States has reciprocal copyright relations. All rights, including professional/amateur stage rights, motion picture, recitation, lecturing, public reading, radio broadcasting, television, video or sound recording, all other forms of mechanical or electronic reproduction, such as CD-ROM, CD-I, information storage and retrieval systems and photocopying, and the rights of translation into foreign languages, are strictly reserved. Particular emphasis is laid upon the matter of readings, permission for which must be secured from the Author's agent in writing.

Inquiries concerning rights should be addressed to:

William Morris Agency, Inc.
1325 Avenue of the Americas
New York, New York 10019
Attn: Owen Laster

THE PLAY

THE AMERICAN DREAM

A living room. Two armchairs, one toward either side of the stage, facing each other diagonally out toward the audience. Against the rear wall, a sofa. A door, leading out from the apartment, in the rear wall, far R., an archway, leading to other rooms, in the side wall, L. At the beginning, Daddy is seated in the armchair L. Curtain up. A silence, then—Mommy enters from L.

MOMMY: (*Crossing to R. arch.*) I don't know what can be keeping them.
DADDY: They're late, naturally.
MOMMY: Of course, they're late; it never fails.
DADDY: That's the way things are today, and there's nothing you can do about it.
MOMMY: You're quite right. (*Sits chair R.*)
DADDY: When we took this apartment, they were quick enough to have me sign the lease; they were quick enough to take my check for two months rent in advance . . .
MOMMY: . . . and one month's security . . .
DADDY: . . . and one month's security. They were quick enough to check my references; they were quick enough about all that. But now! But now, try to get the ice-box fixed, try to get the door bell fixed, try to get the leak in the johnny fixed! Just try it . . . they aren't so quick about *that*.
MOMMY: Of course not; it never fails. People think they can get away with anything these days . . . and, of course they can. I went to buy a new hat yesterday. (*Pause.*) I said, I went to buy a new hat yesterday.
DADDY: Oh! Yes . . . yes.
MOMMY: Pay attention.
DADDY: I *am* paying attention, Mommy:
MOMMY: Well, be sure you do.
DADDY: Oh, I am.
MOMMY: All right, Daddy; now listen.
DADDY: I'm listening, Mommy:
MOMMY: You're sure!
DADDY: Yes . . . yes, I'm sure. I'm all ears.
MOMMY: (*Giggles at the thought, then,*) All right, now. I went to buy a new

hat yesterday and I said, "I'd like a new hat, please." And so, they showed me a few hats, green ones and blue ones, and I didn't like any of them, not one bit. What did I say? What did I just say?
DADDY: You didn't like any of them, not one bit.
MOMMY: That's right; you just keep paying attention. And then they showed me one that I did like. It was a lovely little hat, and I said, "Oh, this is a lovely little hat; I'll take this hat, oh my, it's lovely. What color is it?" And they said, "Why this is beige; isn't it a lovely little beige hat?" And I said, "Oh, it's just lovely." And so, I bought it. (*Stops, looks at Daddy:*)
DADDY: (*To show he is paying attention.*) And so you bought it.
MOMMY: And so I bought it, and I walked out of the store with the hat right on my head, and I ran spang into the chairman of our women's club, and she said, "Oh, my dear, isn't that a lovely little hat? Where did you get that lovely little hat? It's the loveliest little hat; I've always wanted a wheat-colored hat *myself*." And I said, "Why, no, my dear; this hat is beige; beige." And she laughed, and said, "Why no my dear, that's a wheat colored hat; wheat. I know beige from wheat." And I said, "Well, my dear, I know beige from wheat, too." What did I say? What did I just say?
DADDY: (*Tonelessly.*) Well, my dear, I know beige from wheat, too.
MOMMY: That's right. And she laughed, and she said, "Well, my dear, they certainly put one over on you; that's wheat if I ever saw wheat. But it's lovely, just the same." And then she walked off. She's a dreadful woman, you don't know her; she has dreadful taste, two dreadful children, a dreadful house, and an absolutely adorable husband who sits in a wheelchair all the time. You don't know him. You don't know anybody, do you? She's just a dreadful woman, but she *is* chairman of our woman's club, so naturally, I'm terribly fond of her. So, I went right back into the hat shop, and I said, "Look here; what do you mean selling me a hat that you say is beige, when it's wheat all the time; wheat. I can tell beige from wheat any day in the week, but not in this artificial light of yours." They have artificial light, Daddy:
DADDY: Have they!
MOMMY: And I said, "The minute I got outside I could tell that it wasn't a beige hat at all; it was a wheat hat." And they said to me, "How could you tell that when you had the hat on the top of your head?" Well, that made me angry, and so I made a scene right there; (*Rises and crosses to Daddy:*) I screamed as hard as I could; I took my hat off, and I threw it down on the counter, and oh I made a terrible scene. I said, I made a terrible scene.
DADDY: (*Snapping to.*) Yes . . . yes . . . good for you.
MOMMY: And I made an absolutely terrible scene; and they became frightened, and they said, "Oh, Madam, oh Madam." But I kept right on, and finally they admitted that they might have made a mistake; so they took my hat into the back, and then they came out again with a hat that looked exactly like it. I took one look at it, and I said, "This hat is wheat-

colored; wheat." Well, of course, they said, "Oh, no, Madam, this hat is beige; you go outside and see." So, I went outside, and lo and behold, it *was* beige. And so I bought it. (*Crosses to arch* R.)
DADDY: (*Clearing his throat.*) I would imagine that it was the same hat they tried to sell you before.
MOMMY: (*With a little laugh.*) Well, of course it was!
DADDY: That's the way things are today; you just can't get satisfaction; you just try.
MOMMY: Well, *I* got satisfaction.
DADDY: That's right, Mommy: *You did* get satisfaction, didn't you.
MOMMY: Why are they so late? I don't know what can be keeping them.
DADDY: I've been trying for two weeks to have the leak in the johnny fixed.
MOMMY: *You* can't get satisfaction; just try. (*Sits chair* R.) *I* can get satisfaction, but you can't.
DADDY: I've been trying for two weeks and it isn't so much for my sake; I can always go to the club.
MOMMY: It isn't so much for my sake, either; I can always go shopping.
DADDY: It's really for Grandma's sake.
MOMMY: Of course it's for Grandma's sake. Grandma cries every time she goes to the johnny as it is; but now that it doesn't work it's even worse, it makes Grandma think she's getting feeble-headed.
DADDY: Grandma is getting feeble-headed.
MOMMY: Of course Grandma is getting feeble-headed, but not about her johnny-dos.
DADDY: No, that's true. I must have it fixed.
MOMMY: (*Crossing to arch* R.) Why are they so late? I don't know what can be keeping them.
DADDY: When they came here the first time, they were ten minutes early; they were quick enough about it then. (*Enter Grandma from the archway,* L. *She is loaded down with boxes, large and small, neatly wrapped and tied.*)
MOMMY: Why, Grandma; look at you! What *is* all that you're carrying?
GRANDMA: They're boxes. What do they look like?
MOMMY: Daddy! Look at Grandma; look at all the boxes she's carrying!
DADDY: My goodness, Grandma; look at all those boxes.
GRANDMA: Where'll I put them?
MOMMY: Heavens! I don't know. Whatever are they for?
GRANDMA: That's nobody's damn business.
MOMMY: Well, in that case, put them down next to Daddy, there.
GRANDMA: (*Dumping the boxes down, on and around Daddy's feet.*) I sure wish you'd get the john fixed. (*Exit archway,* L.)
DADDY: Oh, I do wish they'd come and fix it. We hear you . . . for hours . . . whimpering away. . . .
MOMMY: Daddy! What a terrible thing to say to Grandma!
GRANDMA: (*Re-entering with more boxes.*) Yeah. For shame, talking to me that way.

DADDY: I'm sorry.
MOMMY: Daddy's sorry, Grandma: (*Sits chair* R.)
GRANDMA: Well, all right. In that case I'll go get the rest of the boxes. I suppose I deserve being talked to that way, I've gotten so old. Most people think that when you get so old, you either freeze to death, or you burn up. But you don't. When you get so old, all that happens is that people talk to you that way.
DADDY: (*Contrite.*) I said I'm sorry, Grandma:
MOMMY: Daddy said he was sorry.
GRANDMA: Well, that's all that counts. People being sorry. Makes you feel better; gives you a sense of dignity, and that's all that's important; a sense of dignity. And it doesn't matter if you don't care, or not, either. You got to have a sense of dignity, even if you don't care, 'cause, if you don't have that, civilization's doomed.
MOMMY: (*Crossing to Grandma:*) You've been reading my book club selections again!
DADDY: How dare you read Mommy's book club selections, Grandma!
GRANDMA: Because I'm old! When you're old you gotta do something. When you get old, you can't talk to people because people snap at you. When you get so old, people talk to you that way. (*Mommy sits chair,* R. *Grandma crosses to her.*) That's why you become deaf, so you won't be able to hear people talking to you that way. And that's why you go and hide under the covers in the big soft bed, so you won't feel the house shaking from people talking to you that way. (*Crossing to Daddy:*) That's why old people die, eventually. People talk to them that way. I've got to go and get the rest of the boxes. (*Grandma exits,* L.)
DADDY: Poor Grandma, I didn't mean to hurt her.
MOMMY: Don't you worry about it; Grandma doesn't know what she means.
DADDY: She knows what she says, though.
MOMMY: Don't you worry about it; she won't know that soon. I love Grandma:
DADDY: I love her too. Look how nicely she wrapped these boxes.
MOMMY: Grandma has always wrapped boxes nicely. When I was a little girl, I was very poor, and Grandma was very poor, too, because Grandpa was in heaven. And every day, when I went to school Grandma used to wrap a box for me, and I used to take it with me to school; and when it was lunch time, all the little boys and girls used to take out their boxes of lunch, and they weren't wrapped nicely at all, and they used to open them and eat their chicken legs and chocolate cakes; and I used to say, "Oh, look at my lovely lunch box; it's so nicely wrapped it would break my heart to open it." And so, I wouldn't open it.
DADDY: Because it was empty.
MOMMY: Oh, no. Grandma always filled it up, because she never ate the dinner she cooked the evening before; she gave me all her food for my

lunch box the next day. After school, I'd take the box back to Grandma, and she'd open it and eat the chicken legs and chocolate cake that was inside. Grandma used to say, "I love day-old cake." That's where the expression 'day-old cake' came from. Grandma always ate everything a day late. I used to eat all the other little boys' and girls' food at school, because they thought my lunch box was empty. They thought my lunch box was empty, and that's why I wouldn't open it. They thought I suffered from the sin of pride, and since that made them better than me, they were very generous.
DADDY: You were a very deceitful little girl.
MOMMY: We were very poor! But then I married you, Daddy, and now we're very rich.
DADDY: Grandma isn't rich.
MOMMY: (*Rising, to* C.) No, but you've been so good to Grandma she feels rich. She doesn't know you'd like to put her in a nursing home.
DADDY: I wouldn't!
MOMMY: Well, heaven knows, *I* would! I can't stand it, watching her do the cooking and the housework, polishing the silver, moving the furniture. . . .
DADDY: She likes to do that. She says it's the least she can do to earn her keep.
MOMMY: Well, she's right. You can't live off people. I can live off you, because I married you. And aren't you lucky all I brought with me was Grandma: A lot of women I know would have brought their whole families to live off you. All I brought was Grandma: Grandma is all the family I have.
DADDY: I feel very fortunate.
MOMMY: You should. I have a right to live off of you because I married you, and because I used to let you get on top of me and bump your uglies; and I have a right to all your money when you die. And when you do, Grandma and I can live by ourselves . . . if she's still here. Unless you have her put away in a nursing home.
DADDY: I have no intention of putting her in a nursing home.
MOMMY: (*Crossing to arch* R.) Well, I wish somebody would do something with her.
DADDY: At any rate, you're very well provided for.
MOMMY: (*Crosses to Daddy:*) You're my sweet Daddy; that's very nice.
DADDY: I love my Mommy: (*Enter Grandma again* L., *laden with more boxes.*)
GRANDMA: (*Dumping the boxes on and around Daddy's feet.*) There; that's the lot of them.
DADDY: They're wrapped so nicely.
GRANDMA: (*To Daddy:*) You won't get on my sweet side that way.
MOMMY: Grandma!
GRANDMA: . . . telling me how nicely I wrap boxes. Not after what you said: how I whimpered for hours. . . .

MOMMY: Grandma!
GRANDMA: (*To Mommy:*) Shut up. (*Mommy crosses to arch* R. *To Daddy:*) You don't have any feelings, that's what's wrong with you. Old people make all sorts of noises, half of them they can't help. Old people whimper, and cry, and belch, and make great hollow rumbling sounds at table; old people wake up in the middle of the night screaming, and find out they haven't even been asleep; and when old people *are* asleep, they try to wake up, and they can't . . . not for the longest time.
MOMMY: Homilies; homilies! (*Sits chair* R.)
GRANDMA: (*To Mommy:*) And there's more, too.
DADDY: I'm really very sorry, Grandma:
GRANDMA: I know you are Daddy; it's Mommy over there makes all the trouble. (*Sits on big box* R. *of Daddy:*) If you'd listened to me you wouldn't have married her in the first place. She was a tramp and a trollop and a trull to boot, and she's no better now.
MOMMY: (*Rises.*) Grandma!
GRANDMA: (*To Mommy:*) Shut up. (*Mommy sits. To Daddy:*) When she was no more than eight years old she used to climb up on my lap and say, in a sickening little voice, "When I gwo up, I'm going to mahwy a wich old man; I'm going to set my wittle were end right down in a tub o' butter; that's what I'm going to do." And I warned you Daddy; I told you to stay away from her type. I told you to. I did. (*Mommy crosses to Grandma, pulling her up and pushing her* D. R.)
MOMMY: You stop that! You're *my* mother, not his!
GRANDMA: I am?
DADDY: That's right, Grandma, Mommy's right.
GRANDMA: Well, how would you expect somebody as old as I am to remember a thing like that? You don't make allowances for people. (*Crossing* L. *to Daddy:*) I want an allowance. I want an allowance!
DADDY: All right, Grandma; I'll see to it.
MOMMY: Grandma! I'm ashamed of you.
GRANDMA: (*Running from Mommy around to* R. *of sofa.*) Humf!! It's a fine time to say that. You should have gotten rid of me a long time ago if that's the way you feel. You should have had Daddy set me up in business somewhere . . . I could have gone into the fur business, or I could have been a singer. (*Mommy crossing after Grandma around sofa.*) But no; not you. You wanted me around so you could sleep in my room when Daddy got fresh. But now it isn't important, because Daddy doesn't want to get fresh with you anymore, and I don't blame him. (*Grandma crosses* D. L. *of Daddy:*) You'd rather sleep with me, wouldn't you Daddy?
MOMMY: (*Mommy,* R. *of Daddy:*) Daddy doesn't want to sleep with anyone. Daddy's been sick.
DADDY: I've been sick. I don't even want to sleep in the apartment.
MOMMY: You see? I told you.
DADDY: I just want to get everything over with.

MOMMY: That's right. (*Crossing to arch* R.) Why are they so late? Why can't they get here on time?
GRANDMA: (*Crossing to Mommy: An owl.*) Who? Who? . . . Who? Who?
MOMMY: You know, Grandma:
GRANDMA: No, I don't.
MOMMY: (*Sits chair* R.) Well, it doesn't really matter whether you do, or not.
DADDY: Is that true?
MOMMY: Oh, more or less. Look how pretty Grandma wrapped these boxes.
GRANDMA: (*Sits on sofa.*) I didn't really like wrapping them; it hurt my fingers, and it frightened me. But, it had to be done.
MOMMY: Why, Grandma?
GRANDMA: None of your damn business.
MOMMY: Go to bed.
GRANDMA: I don't want to go to bed. I just got up. I want to stay here and watch. Besides. . . .
MOMMY: Go to bed.
DADDY: Let her stay up, Mommy; it isn't noon yet.
GRANDMA: (*Crosses to Daddy:*) I want to watch; besides. . . .
DADDY: Let her watch, Mommy:
MOMMY: Well, all right, you can watch; but don't you dare say a word.
GRANDMA: Old people are very good at listening; old people don't like to talk; (*Mommy starts for Grandma who crosses* D. L.) old people have colitis and lavender perfume. Now I'm going to be quiet.
DADDY: She never mentioned she wanted to be a singer.
MOMMY: Oh, I forgot to tell you, but it was ages ago. (*The doorbell rings.*) Oh, goodness! Here they are!
GRANDMA: (*Crossing to Mommy,* C.) Who? Who?
MOMMY: Oh, just some people.
GRANDMA: The van people? Is it the van people? Have you finally done it? Have you called the van people to come and take me away?
DADDY: Of course not, Grandma!
GRANDMA: Oh, don't be too sure. She'd have you carted off, too, if she thought she could get away with it.
MOMMY: Pay no attention to her, Daddy: (*An aside to Grandma:*) My God, you're ungrateful! (*The doorbell rings again.*)
DADDY: (*Wringing his hands.*) Oh, dear; oh, dear.
MOMMY: (*Still to Grandma:*) Just you wait; I'll fix your wagon. (*Now, to Daddy:*) Well, go let them in, Daddy: What are you waiting for?
DADDY: I think we should talk about it some more. Maybe we've been hasty . . . a little hasty, perhaps. (*Doorbell rings again.*) I'd like to talk about it some more.
MOMMY: There's no need. You made up your mind; you were firm; you were masculine and decisive.
DADDY: We might consider the pros and the . . .

MOMMY: I won't argue with you; it has to be done; you were right. Open the door.
DADDY: But I'm not sure that. . . .
MOMMY: (*Pushing Daddy up out of his chair.*) Open the door.
DADDY: (*Crosses to arch* R., *thinks better of it, turns back to Mommy:*) Was I firm about it?
MOMMY: Oh, so firm; so firm.
DADDY: And was I decisive?
MOMMY: So decisive! Oh, I shivered.
DADDY: And masculine? Was I really masculine?
MOMMY: Oh, Daddy, you were so masculine; I shivered and fainted.
GRANDMA: (*Sits chair* L.) Shivered and fainted, did she? Humf!
MOMMY: You be quiet.
GRANDMA: Old people have a right to talk to themselves; it doesn't hurt the gums, and it's comforting. (*Doorbell rings again.*)
DADDY: (*Crosses to arch* R.) I shall now open the door.
MOMMY: What a masculine Daddy! (*To Grandma:*) Isn't he a masculine Daddy?
GRANDMA: Don't expect me to say anything. Old people are obscene.
MOMMY: Some of your opinions aren't so bad. You know that?
DADDY: (*Backing off from the door.*) Maybe we can send them away.
MOMMY: Oh, look at you! You're turning into jelly; you're indecisive; you're a woman.
DADDY: All right. Watch me now; I'm going to open the door. Watch. Watch!
MOMMY: We're watching; we're watching.
GRANDMA: (*Rises, stands* D. L.) *I'm* not.
DADDY: Watch now; it's opening! (*He opens the door.*) It's open! (*Mrs. Barker steps into the room.*) Here they are!
MOMMY: Here they are!
GRANDMA: Where?
DADDY: Come in. You're late. But, of course, we expected you to be late; we were saying that we expected you to be late.
MOMMY: (*Crossing to Mrs. Barker:*) Daddy, don't be rude! We were saying that you just can't get satisfaction these days, and we were talking about you, of course. Won't you come in?
MRS. BARKER: (*Crosses* C.) Thank you; I don't mind if I do.
MOMMY: We're very glad that you're here, late as you are. You do remember us, don't you? You were here once before. I'm Mommy, and this is Daddy, and that's Grandma, doddering there in the corner.
MRS. BARKER: Hello, Mommy; hello, Daddy; and hello there, Grandma:
DADDY: Now that you're here, I don't suppose you could go away and maybe come back some other time.
MRS. BARKER: Oh, no; we're much too efficient for that. I said, hello there, Grandma:

MOMMY: Speak to them, Grandma:
GRANDMA: I don't see them.
DADDY: For shame, Grandma; they're here.
MRS. BARKER: Yes, we're here, Grandma: I'm Mrs. Barker: I remember you; don't you remember me?
GRANDMA: I don't recall; maybe you were younger, or something.
MOMMY: Grandma! What a terrible thing to say!
MRS. BARKER: Oh, now, don't scold her, Mommy; for all she knows she may be right.
DADDY: Uh . . . Mrs. Barker, is it? Won't you sit down?
MRS. BARKER: (*Sits sofa.*) I don't mind if I do.
MOMMY: Would you like a cigarette, and a drink, and would you like to cross your legs?
MRS. BARKER: You forget yourself, Mommy; I'm a professional woman. But I will cross my legs.
DADDY: (*Sits chair* L. *Mommy sits chair* R.) Yes, make yourself comfortable.
MRS. BARKER: I don't mind if I do. (*Pause.*)
GRANDMA: Are they still here?
MOMMY: Be quiet, Grandma:
MRS. BARKER: Oh, we're still here. My, what an unattractive apartment you have.
MOMMY: Yes, but you don't know what a trouble it is. Let me tell you. . . .
DADDY: I was saying to Mommy: . . .
MRS. BARKER: Yes, I know. I was listening outside.
DADDY: About the icebox, and . . . the doorbell . . . and the . . .
MRS. BARKER: . . . and the johnny. Yes, we're very efficient; we have to know everything in our work.
DADDY: Exactly what do you do?
MOMMY: Yes, what is your work?
MRS. BARKER: Well, my dear, for one thing I'm chairman of your women's club.
MOMMY: (*Crosses to Mrs. Barker:*) Don't be ridiculous. I was talking to the chairman of my women's club just yester . . . why, so you are. (*Crosses to Daddy:*) You remember, Daddy, the lady I was telling you about? The lady with the husband who sits in the *swing*? Don't you remember?
DADDY: No . . . no . . .
MOMMY: Of course you do. I'm so sorry, Mrs. Barker: I would have known you anywhere, except in this artificial light. (*Crossing around sofa to* R.) And look! You have a hat just like the one I bought yesterday.
MRS. BARKER: (*With a little laugh.*) No, not really; this hat is cream.
MOMMY: Well, my dear, that may look like a cream hat to you, but I can . . .
MRS. BARKER: Now, now; you seem to forget who I am.
MOMMY: Yes, I do, don't I? Are you sure you're comfortable? Won't you take off your dress?

MRS. BARKER: I don't mind if I do. (*Mrs. Barker removes her dress. Mommy lays it neatly over sofa back.*)
MOMMY: (*Mommy sits chair R. Mrs. Barker sits sofa.*) There; you must feel a great deal more comfortable.
MRS. BARKER: Well, I certainly *look* a great deal more comfortable.
DADDY: I'm going to blush and giggle.
MOMMY: Daddy's going to blush and giggle.
MRS. BARKER: (*Pulling the hem of her slip above her knees. Daddy giggles.*) You're lucky to have such a man for a husband.
MOMMY: Oh, don't I know it!
DADDY: I just blushed and giggled and went sticky wet.
MOMMY: Isn't Daddy a caution, Mrs. Barker?
MRS. BARKER: Maybe if I smoked . . . ?
MOMMY: Oh, that isn't necessary.
MRS. BARKER: I don't mind if I do.
MOMMY: No; no, don't, really.
MRS. BARKER: I don't mind. . . .
MOMMY: (*Rising and crossing to Mrs. Barker:*) I won't have you smoking in my house, and that's that! You're a professional woman.
DADDY: Grandma drinks AND smokes; don't you, Grandma?
GRANDMA: No.
MOMMY: (*Crosses L. into boxes.*) Well, now, Mrs. Barker; suppose you tell us why you're here.
GRANDMA: (*As Mommy walks through the boxes.*) The boxes . . . the boxes.
MOMMY: Be quiet, Grandma:
DADDY: What did you say, Grandma?
GRANDMA: (*As Mommy steps on several of the boxes.*) The boxes, damn it!
MRS. BARKER: Boxes; she said boxes. She mentioned the boxes.
DADDY: What about the boxes, Grandma? Maybe Mrs. Barker is here because of the boxes. Is that what you meant, Grandma?
GRANDMA: I don't know if that's what I meant, or not. It's certainly not what I *thought* I meant.
DADDY: Grandma is of the opinion that . . .
MRS. BARKER: Can we assume that the boxes are for us? I mean, can we assume that you had us come here for the boxes?
MOMMY: Are you in the habit of receiving boxes?
DADDY: A very good question.
MRS. BARKER: Well, that would depend on the reason we're here. I've got my fingers in so many little pies, you know. Now, I can think of one of my little activities in which we are in the habit of receiving *baskets,* but more in a literary sense than really. We *might* receive boxes, though, under very special circumstances. I'm afraid that's the best answer I can give you.
DADDY: It's a very interesting answer.
MRS. BARKER: *I* thought so. But, does it help?

MOMMY: (*Sits chair* R.) No; I'm afraid not.
DADDY: I wonder if it might help us any if I said I feel misgivings, that I have definite qualms.
MOMMY: Where, Daddy?
DADDY: (*Unbuttoning his jacket and indicating stitches.*) Well, mostly right here, right around where the stitches were.
MOMMY: Daddy had an operation, you know.
MRS. BARKER: Oh, you poor Daddy! I didn't know; but, then how could I?
GRANDMA: (*Crossing to Mrs. Barker:*) You might have asked; it wouldn't have hurt you.
MOMMY: Dry up, Grandma:
GRANDMA: There you go. Letting your true feelings come out. Old people aren't dry enough, I suppose. My sacks are empty, the fluid in my eyeballs is all caked on the inside edges, my spine is made of sugar candy, I breathe ice; but you don't hear me complain. Nobody hears old people complain because people think that's all old people do. And *that's* because old people are gnarled and sagged and twisted into the shape of a complaint. (*Signs off.*) That's all. (*Crosses* D. L.)
MRS. BARKER: What was wrong, Daddy?
DADDY: Well, you know how it is: the doctors took out something that was there and put in something that wasn't there. An operation.
MRS. BARKER: You're very fortunate, I should say.
MOMMY: Oh, he is; he is. All his life, Daddy has wanted to be a United States Senator; but now . . . why, now he's changed his mind, and for the rest of his life he's going to want to be governor . . . it would be nearer the apartment, you know.
MRS. BARKER: You *are* fortunate, Daddy:
DADDY: Yes, indeed; except that I get these qualms now and then, definite ones.
MRS. BARKER: Well, it's just a matter of things settling; you're like an old house.
MOMMY: Why Daddy, thank Mrs. Barker:
DADDY: Thank you.
MRS. BARKER: Ambition! That's the ticket. I have a brother who's very much like you, Daddy . . . ambitious. Of course, he's a great deal younger than you; he's even younger than I am . . . if such a thing is possible. He runs a little newspaper. Just a little newspaper . . . but he runs it. He's chief cook and bottle washer of that little newspaper, which he calls The Village Idiot. He has such a sense of humor; he's so self-deprecating, so modest. And he'd never admit it himself, but he *is* The Village Idiot.
MOMMY: Oh, I think that's just grand. Don't you think so, Daddy?
DADDY: Yes, just grand.
MRS. BARKER: My brother's a dear man, and he has a dear little wife, whom he loves, dearly. He loves her so much he just can't get a sentence

out without mentioning her. He wants everybody to know he's married. He's really a stickler on that point; he can't be introduced to anybody and say "hello" without adding "of course, I'm married." As far as I'm concerned, he's the chief exponent of Woman Love in this whole country; he's even been written up in psychiatric journals because of it.
DADDY: Indeed!
MOMMY: Isn't that lovely.
MRS. BARKER: Oh I think so. There's too much woman-hatred in this country, and that's a fact.
GRANDMA: Oh, I don't know.
MOMMY: Oh, I think that's just grand. Don't you think so, Daddy?
DADDY: Yes, just grand.
GRANDMA: (*Crossing* L. C.) In case anybody's interested . . .
MOMMY: Be quiet, Grandma:
GRANDMA: Nuts! (*Turns her back on the group.*)
MOMMY: Oh, Mrs. Barker, you must forgive Grandma: She's rural.
MRS. BARKER: I don't mind if I do.
DADDY: Maybe Grandma has something to say.
MOMMY: Nonsense. Old people have nothing to say; and if old people *did* have something to say, nobody would listen to them. (*Rises. To Grandma:*) You see? I can pull that stuff just as easy as you can.
GRANDMA: Well, you got the rhythm, but you don't really have the quality. Besides, you're middle-aged.
MOMMY: I'm proud of it.
GRANDMA: Look. I'll show you how it's really done. Middle-aged people think they can do anything, but the truth is that middle-aged people can't do most things as well as they used to. Middle-aged people think they're special because they're like everybody else. We live in the age of deformity. You see? Rhythm *and* content. You'll learn. (*Crosses* D. L.)
DADDY: I do wish I weren't surrounded by women, I'd like some men around here.
MRS. BARKER: You can say that again!
GRANDMA: I don't hardly count as a woman, so can I say my piece?
MOMMY: (*Sits chair* R.) Go on. Jabber away.
GRANDMA: It's very simple; the fact is, these boxes don't have anything to do with why this good lady is come to call. Now if you're interested in knowing why these boxes *are* here. . . .
DADDY: I'm sure that must be all very true, Grandma, but what does it have to do with why . . . pardon me, what is that name again?
MRS. BARKER: Mrs. Barker:
DADDY: Exactly. What does it have to do with why . . . that name again?
MRS. BARKER: Mrs. Barker:
DADDY: Precisely. What does it have to do with why what's-her-name is here?

MOMMY: They're here because we asked them.
MRS. BARKER: Yes. That's why.
GRANDMA: Now, if you're interested in knowing why these boxes *are* here. . . .
MOMMY: Well, nobody *is* interested!
GRANDMA: (*Crossing R. To Mommy:*) You can be as snippity as you like for all the good it'll do you.
DADDY: You two will have to stop arguing.
MOMMY: (*Crossing to Daddy:*) I don't argue with her.
DADDY: It will just have to stop.
MOMMY: Well, why don't you call a van and have her taken away?
GRANDMA: Don't bother; there's no need.
DADDY: No, now, perhaps I can go away myself. . . .
MOMMY: Well, one or the other; the way things are now it's impossible. In the first place, it's too crowded in this apartment. (*To Grandma:*) And it's you that takes up all the space, with your enema bottles, and your Pekinese, and God-only-knows what else . . . and now all these boxes. . . . (*Kicking the boxes.*)
GRANDMA: These boxes are . . .
MRS. BARKER: I've never heard of enema *bottles*. . . .
GRANDMA: She means enema bags, but she doesn't know the difference. Mommy comes from extremely bad stock. And, besides, when Mommy was born . . . well, it was a difficult delivery, and she had a head shaped like a banana.
MOMMY: You ungrateful . . . Daddy? Daddy, you see how ungrateful she is after all these years, after all the things we've done for her? (*To Grandma:*) One of these days you're going away in a van; that's what's going to happen to you!
GRANDMA: Do tell!
MRS. BARKER: Like a banana?
GRANDMA: Yup, just like a banana.
MRS. BARKER: My word!
MOMMY: You stop listening to her; she'll say anything. Just the other night she called Daddy a hedgehog.
MRS. BARKER: She didn't!
GRANDMA: That's right, baby; you stick up for me.
MOMMY: I don't know where she gets the words; on the television, maybe.
MRS. BARKER: Did you really call him a hedgehog?
GRANDMA: (*Crossing D. R.*) Oh, look; what difference does it make whether I did or not?
DADDY: Grandma's right. Leave Grandma alone.
MOMMY: (*To Daddy:*) How dare you!
GRANDMA: Oh, leave her alone, Daddy; the kid's all mixed up.
MOMMY: You see? I told you. It's all those television shows. Daddy, you go

right into Grandma's room and take her television and shake all the tubes loose.

DADDY: Don't mention tubes to me.

MOMMY: Oh! Mommy forgot! (*To Mrs. Barker:*) Daddy has tubes now where he used to have tracts.

MRS. BARKER: Is that a fact!

GRANDMA: (*Crossing to Mrs. Barker:*) I know why this dear lady is here.

MOMMY: You be still.

MRS. BARKER: (*Rising. To Grandma:*) Oh, I do wish you'd tell me.

MOMMY: No! No! That wouldn't be fair at all.

DADDY: Besides, she knows why she's here; she's here because we called them.

MRS. BARKER: (*Crossing L. to Daddy:*) La! But that still leaves me puzzled. I know I'm here because you called us, but I'm such a busy girl, with this committee and that committee, and the Responsible Citizens Activities I indulge in.

MOMMY: Oh my; busy, busy.

MRS. BARKER: Yes, indeed. So, I'm afraid you'll have to give me some help.

MOMMY: Oh, no. No, you must be mistaken. I can't believe we asked you here to give you any help. With the way taxes are these days, and the way you can't get satisfaction in ANYTHING. . . . No, I don't believe so.

DADDY: And if you need help . . . why, I should think you'd apply for a Fulbright Scholarship. . . .

MOMMY: And if not that . . . why, then a Guggenheim Fellowship. . . .

GRANDMA: Oh, come on; why not shoot the works and try the Ford Foundation. (*Under her breath, to Mommy and Daddy:*) Beasts! (*Crosses* D. R.)

MRS. BARKER: Oh, what a jolly family. (*Crosses* R.) But let me think. I'm knee-deep in work these days; there's the Ladies Auxiliary Air-Raid Committee, for one thing; (*To Daddy:*) how do you feel about air-raids?

MOMMY: Oh, I'd say we're hostile.

DADDY: Yes, definitely; we're hostile.

MRS. BARKER: Then you'll be no help there. There's too much hostility in the world these days, as it is; but I'll not badger you. There's a surfeit of badgers, as well. (*Sits chair* R.)

GRANDMA: While we're at it, there's been a run on old people, too. The Department of Agriculture, or maybe it wasn't the Department of Agriculture . . . anyway, it was some department that's run by a girl, put out figures showing that ninety per cent of the adult population of the country is over eighty years old . . . or eighty per cent is over ninety years old. . . .

MOMMY: You're such a liar! You just finished saying that everyone is middle-aged.

GRANDMA: (*Crosses* C. *to Mommy:*) I'm just telling you what the government says . . . that doesn't have anything to do with what . . .

MOMMY: It's that television! Daddy, go break her television.
GRANDMA: You won't find it.
DADDY: (*Wearily getting up.*) If I must. . . . I must.
MOMMY: And don't step on the Pekinese; it's blind.
DADDY: It may be blind, but Daddy isn't. (*He exits, through the archway,* L.)
GRANDMA: (*Crossing to* L. *arch after Daddy:*) You won't find *it,* either.
MOMMY: (*Crosses to Mrs. Barker,* R.) Oh, I'm so fortunate to have such a husband. Just think: I could have had a husband who was poor, or argumentative, or a husband who sat in a wheelchair all day. (*Mrs. Barker rises.*) . . . OOOOHHHH! *What* have I said? What *have* I said?
GRANDMA: You said you could have a husband who sat in a wheel . . .
MOMMY: (*Starting after Grandma who sits chair,* L.) I'm mortified! I could die! I could cut my tongue out! I could . . .
MRS. BARKER: (*Forcing a smile.*) Oh, now . . . now . . . don't think about it. . . .
MOMMY: (*Crosses to Mrs. Barker:*) I could . . . why, I could . . .
MRS. BARKER: . . . don't think about it . . . really . . .
MOMMY: You're quite right. I won't think about it, and that way I'll forget that I ever said it, and that way it will be all right. (*Pause.*) There . . . I've forgotten. (*Pulling Mrs. Barker to sofa, both sit.*) Well, now, now that Daddy is out of the room we can have some girl talk.
MRS. BARKER: I'm not sure that I . . .
MOMMY: You *do* want to have some girl talk, don't you?
MRS. BARKER: I was going to say I'm not sure that I wouldn't care for a glass of water. I feel a little faint.
MOMMY: Grandma, go get Mrs. Barker a glass of water.
GRANDMA: —I would prefer not to.
MOMMY: Grandma loves to do little things around the house; it gives her a false sense of security.
GRANDMA: I quit! I'm through! (*Begins to stack boxes.*)
MOMMY: Now, you be a good Grandma, or you know what will happen to you. You'll be taken away in a van.
GRANDMA: (*Crossing up to Mommy:*) You don't frighten me. I'm too old to be frightened. And besides . . .
MOMMY: WELL! I'll tend to you later. I'll hide your teeth . . . I'll . . .
GRANDMA: Everything's hidden.
MRS. BARKER: I *am* going to faint. I *am.*
MOMMY: (*Rises.*) Good heavens! I'll go myself. (*As she exits, through the archway,* L.) I'll fix you Grandma: I'll take care of you later. (*She exits.*)
GRANDMA: Oh, go soak your head. (*To Mrs. Barker:*) Well, dearie, how do you feel? (*Sits next to Mrs. Barker on Sofa.*)
MRS. BARKER: A little better, I think. Yes, much better, thank you, Grandma.
GRANDMA: That's good.

MRS. BARKER: But . . . I feel so lost . . . not knowing why I'm here . . . and, on top of it, they say I was here before.
GRANDMA: Well, you were. You weren't *here*, exactly, because we've moved around a lot, from one apartment to another, up and down the social ladder like mice, if you like similes.
MRS. BARKER: I don't . . . particularly.
GRANDMA: (*Rises. Resumes stacking boxes.*) Well, then, I'm sorry.
MRS. BARKER: (*Rises. Suddenly.*) Grandma, I feel I can trust you.
GRANDMA: Don't be too sure; it's every man for himself around this place. . . .
MRS. BARKER: Oh . . . is it? Nonetheless, I really do feel that I can trust you. *Please* tell me why they called and asked us to come. I implore you!
GRANDMA: Oh my; that feels good. It's been so long since anybody implored me. Do it again. Implore me some more.
MRS. BARKER: (*Crosses* R.) You're your daughter's mother all right!
GRANDMA: (*Crossing to Mrs. Barker:*) Oh, I don't mean to be hard. If you won't implore me, then beg me, or ask me, or entreat me . . . just anything like that.
MRS. BARKER: You're a dreadful old woman!
GRANDMA: (*Resumes stacking boxes.*) You'll understand some day. Please!
MRS. BARKER: Oh, for heavens sake! . . . I implore you . . . I beg you . . . I beseech you! (*Sits chair* R.)
GRANDMA: (*Crosses* R., *to Mrs. Barker.*) Beseech! Oh, that's the nicest word I've heard in ages. You're a dear, sweet woman . . . You . . . beseech . . . me. I can't resist that.
MRS. BARKER: Well then . . . please tell me why they asked us to come.
GRANDMA: (*Checks through arch* L., *then crosses to Mrs. Barker:*) Well, I'll give you a hint. That's the best I can do, because I'm a muddle-headed old woman. Now listen, because it's important. Once upon a time, not too very long ago, but a long enough time ago . . . oh, about twenty years ago. . . . there was a man very much like Daddy, and a woman very much like Mommy, who were married to each other, very much like Mommy and Daddy are married to each other; and they lived in an apartment very much like one that's very much like this one, and they lived there with an old woman who was very much like yours truly, only younger, because it was some time ago; in fact, they were all somewhat younger.
MRS. BARKER: How fascinating!
GRANDMA: Now, at the same time, there was a dear lady very much like you, only younger then, who did all sorts of Good Works. . . . And one of the Good Works this dear lady did was in something very much like a volunteer capacity for an organization very much like the Bye-Bye Adoption Service, which is nearby and which was run by a terribly deaf old lady very much like the Miss Bye-Bye who runs the Bye-Bye Adoption Service nearby.

MRS. BARKER: How enthralling!
GRANDMA: (*Crossing* L., *then back to Mrs. Barker:*) Well, be that as it may. Nonetheless, one afternoon this man, who was very much like Daddy, and this woman who was very much like Mommy came to see this dear lady who did all the Good Works, who was very much like you, dear, and they were very sad and very hopeful, and they cried and smiled and bit their fingers, and they said all the most intimate things.
MRS. BARKER: How spellbinding! What did they say?
GRANDMA: Well, it was very sweet. The woman, who was very much like Mommy, said that she and the man, who was very much like Daddy, had never been blessed with anything very much like a bumble of joy.
MRS. BARKER: A what?
GRANDMA: A bumble; a bumble of joy.
MRS. BARKER: Oh, like a bundle.
GRANDMA: Well, yes; very much like it. Bundle, bumble; who cares? At any rate, the woman, who was very much like Mommy, said that they wanted a bumble of their own, but that the man, who was very much like Daddy, couldn't have a bumble; and the man, who was very much like Daddy, said that yes, they had wanted a bumble of their own, but that the woman, who was very much like Mommy, couldn't have one, and that now they wanted to buy something very much like a bumble.
MRS. BARKER: How engrossing!
GRANDMA: Yes. And the dear lady, who was very much like you, said something that was very much like, "Oh, what a shame; but take heart; I think we have just the bumble *for* you." And, well, the lady, who was very much like Mommy, and the man, who was very much like Daddy, cried and smiled and bit their fingers, and said some more intimate things, which were totally irrelevant, but which were pretty hot stuff, and so the dear lady, who was very much like you, and who had something very much like a penchant for pornography, listened with something very much like enthusiasm. "Whee!" she said. "Whoooopeeeee!" But that's beside the point.
MRS. BARKER: I suppose *so*. But, how gripping!
GRANDMA: Anyway . . . they *bought* something very much like a bumble, and they took it away with them. But . . . things didn't work out very well.
MRS. BARKER: You mean there was trouble?
GRANDMA: You got it. (*With a glance through the archway.*) But, I'm going to have to speed up now because I think I'm leaving soon.
MRS. BARKER: (*Rises and crosses* C.) Oh. Are you really?
GRANDMA: Yup.
MRS. BARKER: But, old people don't go anywhere; they're either taken places, or put places.
GRANDMA: Well, this old person is different. (*Both sit on sofa.*) Anyway . . . things started going badly.

MRS. BARKER: Oh, yes. Yes.
GRANDMA: Weeeeeellll . . . in the first place, it turned out the bumble didn't look like either one of it's parents. That was enough of a blow, but things got worse. One night, it cried its heart out, if you can imagine such a thing.
MRS. BARKER: Cried its heart out! Well!
GRANDMA: But that was only the beginning. Then it turned out it only had eyes for its Daddy:
MRS. BARKER: For its Daddy! Why, any self-respecting woman would have gouged those eyes right out of its head.
GRANDMA: Well, she did. That's exactly what she did. But then, it kept its nose up in the air.
MRS. BARKER: Ufggh! How disgusting!
GRANDMA: That's what they thought. But *then*, it began to develop an interest in its you-know-what.
MRS. BARKER: In its you-know-what! Well! I hope they cut its hands off at the wrists!
GRANDMA: Well, yes, they did that eventually. But first, they cut off its you-know-what.
MRS. BARKER: A much better idea!
GRANDMA: That's what they thought. But after they cut off its you-know-what, it *still* put its hands under the covers, *looking* for its you-know-what. So, finally, they *had* to cut off its hands at the wrists.
MRS. BARKER: Naturally!
GRANDMA: And it was such a resentful bumble. Why, one day it called its Mommy a dirty name.
MRS. BARKER: Well, I hope they cut its tongue out!
GRANDMA: Of course. And, then, as it got bigger, they found out all sorts of terrible things about it, like: it didn't have a head on its shoulders, it had no guts, it was spineless, its feet were made of clay . . . just dreadful things.
MRS. BARKER: Dreadful!
GRANDMA: So you can understand how they became discouraged.
MRS. BARKER: I certainly can! And what did they do?
GRANDMA: What did they do? Well, for the last straw, it finally up and died; and you can imagine how *that* made them feel, their having paid for it and all. So, they called up the lady who sold them the bumble in the first place and told her to come right over to their apartment. They wanted satisfaction; they wanted their money back. That's what they wanted.
MRS. BARKER: My, my, my.
GRANDMA: How do you like them apples?
MRS. BARKER: My, my, my.
DADDY: (*Off-stage.*) Mommy? I can't find Grandma's television, and I can't find the Pekinese, either.
MOMMY: (*Off-stage.*) Isn't that funny? And I can't find the water.

GRANDMA: (*Rises and crosses to arch* L.) Heh, heh, heh. I told them everything was hidden.
MRS. BARKER: Did you hide the water, too?
GRANDMA: (*Puzzled.*) No. No. No, I didn't do *that*.
MOMMY: (*Off-stage.*) Oh, I found the water, Daddy: It wasn't where I thought it would be at all.
DADDY: (*Off-stage.*) The truth of the matter is, I can't even find Grandma's room.
GRANDMA: (*Sits sofa.*) Heh, heh, heh.
MRS. BARKER: My! You certainly did hide things, didn't you?
GRANDMA: Sure, kid, sure.
MOMMY: (*Still off-stage.*) Did you ever hear of such a thing, Grandma? Daddy can't find your television, (*Entering* L., *crosses to Grandma:*) and he can't find the Pekinese, and the truth of the matter is he can't even find your room.
GRANDMA: I told you. I hid everything.
MOMMY: Nonsense, Grandma! Just wait until I get my hands on you. You're a trouble-maker; that's what you are.
GRANDMA: (*Rises. Crosses* R. *and sits* R. *chair.*) Well, I'll be out of here pretty soon, baby.
MOMMY: (*Following Grandma* R.) Oh, you don't know how right you are! Daddy's been wanting to send you away for a long time now but I've been restraining him. I'll tell you one thing, though. I'm getting sick and tired of this fighting, and I might just let him have his way. Then you'll see what'll happen. Away you'll go; in a van, too. I'll let Daddy call the van man.
GRANDMA: I'm way ahead of you.
MOMMY: How can you be so old and so smug at the same time? You have no sense of proportion.
GRANDMA: You just answered your own question.
MOMMY: Mrs. Barker, I'd much rather you came into the kitchen for that glass of water, what with Grandma out here, and all.
MRS. BARKER: I don't see what Grandma has to do with it; and besides, I don't think you're very polite.
MOMMY: You seem to forget that you're a guest in this house. . . .
GRANDMA: Apartment!
MOMMY: Apartment! And that you're a professional woman. (*Crosses to* L. *arch.*) So, if you'll be so good as to come into the kitchen, I'll be more than happy to show you where the water is, and where the glass is, and then you can put two and two together, if you're clever enough. (*She vanishes through* L. *arch.*)
MRS. BARKER: (*After a moment's consideration.*) I suppose she's right.
GRANDMA: (*Rises, crosses up to Mrs. Barker:*) Well, that's how it is when people call you up and ask you over to do something for them.
MRS. BARKER: I suppose you're right, too. (*Rises.*) Well, Grandma, it's been very nice talking to you.

GRANDMA: And I've enjoyed listening. (*Mrs. Barker crosses* L. *to arch, Grandma stops her.*) Say, don't tell Mommy or Daddy that I gave you that hint, will you?
MRS. BARKER: Oh, dear me, the hint! I'd forgotten about it, if you can imagine such a thing. No, I won't breathe a word of it to them.
GRANDMA: (*Crossing to Mrs. Barker* L.) I don't know if it helped you any . . .
MRS. BARKER: I can't tell yet. I'll have to . . . what *is* the word I want? I'll have to relate it . . . that's it . . . I'll have to relate it to certain things that I *know*, and . . . draw . . . conclusions . . . what I'll really have to do is to see if it applies to anything. I mean, after all, I *do* do volunteer work for an adoption service, but it isn't very much *like* the Bye-Bye Adoption Service . . . it *is* the Bye-Bye Adoption Service . . . and while I can remember Mommy and Daddy coming to see me, oh, about twenty years ago, about buying a bumble, I can't quite remember anyone very much *like* Mommy and Daddy coming to see me about buying a bumble. Don't you see? It really presents quite a problem . . . I'll have to think about it . . . mull it . . . but at any rate, it was truly first-class of you to try to help me. Oh, will you still be here after I've had my drink of water?
GRANDMA: Probably . . . I'm not as spry as I used to be.
MRS. BARKER: Oh. Well, I won't say goodbye then.
GRANDMA: No. Don't. (*Mrs. Barker exits, through the archway. Grandma sits on the sofa.*) People don't say good-bye to old people because they think they'll frighten them. Lordy! If they only knew how awful hello, and my, you're looking chipper sounded, they wouldn't say those things either. (*Rises and starts stacking rest of boxes.*) The truth is, there isn't much you *can* say to old people that doesn't sound just terrible. (*The doorbell rings.*) Come on in! (*The Young Man enters,* R. *archway. Grandma looks him over.*) Well, now aren't you a breath of fresh air!
YOUNG MAN: Hello there.
GRANDMA: My, my, my. Are you the van man?
YOUNG MAN: The what?
GRANDMA: (*Crossing to Young Man:*) The van man. The van man. Are you come to take me away?
YOUNG MAN: I don't know what you're talking about. (*Crosses to* L. *arch, looking out.*)
GRANDMA: Oh. (*Pause.*) Well. (*Pause.*) My, my, aren't you something!
YOUNG MAN: Hm?
GRANDMA: I said, my, my; aren't you something.
YOUNG MAN: (*Sits chair* L.) Oh. Thank you.
GRANDMA: You don't sound very enthusiastic.
YOUNG MAN: Oh, I'm . . . I'm used to it.
GRANDMA: (*Sits on arm of chair* L.) Yup; yup; you know, if I were about a hundred and fifty years younger, I could go for you.
YOUNG MAN: Yes, I imagine so.

GRANDMA: Unh-hunh; will you look at those muscles!
YOUNG MAN: (*Rising C. and flexing his muscles.*) Yes, they're quite good, aren't they?
GRANDMA: (*Crossing to him.*) Boy, they sure are. They natural?
YOUNG MAN: Well the basic structure was there, but I've done some work too . . . you know, in a gym. (*Sprawls on the sofa.*)
GRANDMA: I'll bet you have. (*Crossing up behind sofa.*) You ought to be in the movies, boy.
YOUNG MAN: I know.
GRANDMA: (*Leaning over back of sofa.*) Yup! Right up there on the old silver screen. But I suppose you've heard that before.
YOUNG MAN: Yes, I have.
GRANDMA: You ought to try out for them . . . the movies.
YOUNG MAN: Well, actually, I may have a career there, yet. I've lived out on the west coast almost all my life . . . and I've met a few people who . . . might be able to help me. (*Sitting up on sofa.*) I'm not in too much of a hurry, though. I'm almost as young as I look.
GRANDMA: (*Crossing R. of sofa.*) Oh, that's nice. And will you look at that face!
YOUNG MAN: Yes, it's quite good, isn't it? Clean-cut, midwest farm boy type, almost insultingly good-looking in a typically American way. Good profile, straight nose, honest eyes, wonderful smile. . . .
GRANDMA: Yup. Boy, you know what you are, don't you? You're the American Dream, that's what you are. All those other people they don't know what they're talking about. You . . . *you* are the American Dream.
YOUNG MAN: Thanks.
MOMMY: (*Off-stage.*) Who rang the doorbell?
GRANDMA: (*Shouting off-stage.*) The American Dream!
MOMMY: (*Off-stage.*) What? What was that, Grandma?
GRANDMA: (*Crossing to arch L. Shouting.*) The American Dream! The American Dream! Damn it!
DADDY: (*Off-stage.*) How's that, Mommy?
MOMMY: (*Off-stage.*) Oh, some gibberish; pay no attention. Did you find Grandma's room?
DADDY: (*Off-stage.*) I can't find anything.
MOMMY: (*Off-stage.*) All right. I can't find Mrs. Barker.
YOUNG MAN: (*Crossing to Grandma:*) What was all that?
GRANDMA: (*Taking Young Man C.*) Oh, that was just the folks, but let's not talk about them, honey; let's talk about you.
YOUNG MAN: All right.
GRANDMA: (*Sits on sofa.*) Well, let's see. If you're not the van man, what are you doing here?
YOUNG MAN: I'm looking for work.
GRANDMA: Are you! Well; what kind of work?

YOUNG MAN: Oh, almost anything . . . almost anything that pays. I'll do almost anything for money.
GRANDMA: Will you . . . will you. Hmmmm. I wonder if there's anything you could do around here?
YOUNG MAN: There might be. It looked to be a likely building.
GRANDMA: It's always looked to be a rather unlikely building to me, but I suppose you'd know better than I.
YOUNG MAN: (*Crossing behind sofa and leaning over to Grandma:*) I can sense these things.
GRANDMA: There *might* be something you could do around here. (*As she turns and sees Young Man:*) Stay there! Don't come any closer.
YOUNG MAN: (*Crosses down and sits next to Grandma:*) Sorry.
GRANDMA: I don't mean I'd *mind*. I don't know whether I'd mind, or not . . . But, it wouldn't look well; it would look just *awful*.
YOUNG MAN: (*Sprawling with his feet in front of Grandma:*) Yes, I suppose so.
GRANDMA: (*Lifting his feet away, Young Man moves to end of sofa.*) Now stay there; let me concentrate. What could you do? The folks have been in something of a quandry around here today, sort of a dilemma, and I wonder if you mightn't be some help.
YOUNG MAN: I hope so . . . if there's money in it. Do you have any money?
GRANDMA: Money! Oh, there's more money around here than you'd know what to do with.
YOUNG MAN: I'm not so sure.
GRANDMA: Well, maybe not. Besides, I've got money of my own.
YOUNG MAN: You have?
GRANDMA: Sure. Old people quite often have lots of money; more often than most people expect. Come here, so I can whisper to you . . . (*As he moves closer.*) not too close. I might faint.
YOUNG MAN: (*Back to his end of sofa.*) Oh, I'm sorry.
GRANDMA: It's all right dear. Anyway . . . have you ever heard of that big baking contest they run? The one where all the ladies get together in a big barn and bake away?
YOUNG MAN: I'm . . . not . . . sure . . .
GRANDMA: Well, it doesn't matter whether you've heard of it or not. The important thing is . . . and I don't want anybody to hear this; the folks think I haven't been out of the house in eight years . . . the important thing is that I won first prize in that baking contest this year. Oh, it was in all the papers; not under my own name, though. I used a nom de boulangere; I called myself Uncle Henry.
YOUNG MAN: Did you?
GRANDMA: Why not? I didn't see any reason not to. I look just as much like an old man as I do like an old woman. And you know what I called it . . . what I won for?

YOUNG MAN: No. What did you call it?
GRANDMA: I called it Uncle Henry's Day-Old Cake.
YOUNG MAN: That's a very nice name.
GRANDMA: And it wasn't any trouble, either. All I did was go out and get a store-bought cake, keep it around for a while, and then slip it in, unbeknownst to anybody. Simple.
YOUNG MAN: You're a very resourceful person.
GRANDMA: Pioneer stock!
YOUNG MAN: Is all this true? Do you want me to believe all this?
GRANDMA: Well, you can believe it or not; it doesn't make any difference to me. All *I* know is, Uncle Henry's Day-Old Cake won me twenty-five thousand smackerolas.
YOUNG MAN: Twenty-five thou . . .
GRANDMA: Right on the old loggerhead. Now; how do you like them apples?
YOUNG MAN: Love 'em.
GRANDMA: I thought you'd be impressed.
YOUNG MAN: Money talks.
GRANDMA: (*Pause, then, softly.*) Hey. You look familiar.
YOUNG MAN: Hm? Pardon?
GRANDMA: (*Rising and crossing* D. L., *sits* L. *chair.*) I said, you look familiar.
YOUNG MAN: Well, I've done some modeling.
GRANDMA: No; no. I don't mean that. You look familiar.
YOUNG MAN: Well, I'm a type.
GRANDMA: Yup; you sure are. Why do you say you'd do anything for money . . . if you don't mind my being nosey?
YOUNG MAN: (*Rising.*) No, no. It's part of the interview. I'll be happy to tell you. It's that I have no talents at all, except what you see . . . my person; my body, my face. In every other way I am incomplete, and I must therefore . . . compensate.
GRANDMA: What do you mean, incomplete? You look pretty complete to me.
YOUNG MAN: (*Crossing to Grandma:*) I think I can explain it to you, partially because you're very old, and very old people have perceptions they keep to themselves, because if they expose them to other people . . . well, you know what ridicule and neglect are.
GRANDMA: I do, child, I do.
YOUNG MAN: Then listen. My mother died the night that I was born, and I never knew my father; I doubt my mother did. But, I wasn't alone, because lying with me . . . in the placenta . . . there was someone else . . . my brother . . . my twin.
GRANDMA: Oh, my child.
YOUNG MAN: We were identical twins . . . he and I . . . not fraternal . . . identical; we were derived from the same ovum; and in *this*, in that we

were twins not from separate ova, but from the same one, we had a kinship such as you can not imagine. We . . . we felt each other breathe . . . his heartbeats thundered in my temples . . . mine in his . . . our stomachs ached and we cried for feeding at the same time . . . are you old enough to understand?
GRANDMA: I think so, child; I think I'm nearly old enough.
YOUNG MAN: I hope so. But we were separated when we were still very young, my brother, my twin and I . . . inasmuch as you can separate one being. We were torn apart . . . thrown to opposite ends of the continent. I don't know what became of my brother . . . to the rest of myself . . . except that, from time to time, in the years that have passed, I have suffered losses . . . that I can't explain. A fall from grace . . . a departure of innocence . . . loss . . . loss. How can I put it to you? All right; like this: once . . . , it was as if all at once my heart . . . became numb . . . almost as though I . . . almost as though . . . just like that . . . it had been wrenched from my body . . . and from that time I have been unable to love. Once . . . I was asleep at the time . . . I awoke, and my eyes were burning. And since that time I have been unable to see anything, *anything*, with pity, with affection . . . with anything but . . . cool disinterest. And my groin . . . even there . . . since one time . . . one specific agony . . . since then I have not been able to *love* anyone with my body. And even my hands . . . I can not touch another person and feel love. And there is more . . . there are more losses, but it all comes down to this; I no longer have the capacity to feel anything. I have no emotions, I have been drained; torn asunder . . . disemboweled. I have, now, only my person . . . my body . . . my face. I use what I have . . . I let people love me . . . I accept the syntax around me, for, while I know I cannot relate . . . I know I must be related *to.* I let people love me . . . I let people touch me . . . I let them draw pleasure from my groin . . . from my presence . . . from the fact of me . . . but, that is all it comes to. As I told you; I am incomplete . . . I can feel nothing. I can feel nothing. (*Sits chair L.*) And so . . . here I am . . . as you see me . . . I am . . . but this . . . what you see. And it will always be thus.
GRANDMA: Oh, my child; my child. (*Long pause, then rises and crosses to him.*) I was mistaken . . . before. I don't know you from somewhere, but I knew . . . once . . . someone very much like you . . . or, very much as perhaps you were.
YOUNG MAN: (*Rises.*) Be careful; be very careful. What I have told you may not be true. In my profession . . .
GRANDMA: Shhhhhhhhhh. (*The Young Man bows his head, in acquiescence.*) Someone . . . to be more precise . . . who might have turned out to be very much like you might have turned out to be. And . . . unless I'm terribly mistaken . . . you've found yourself a job.
YOUNG MAN: What are my duties?
MRS. BARKER: (*Off-stage.*) Yoo-hoo! Yoo-hoo!

GRANDMA: Oh-oh. You'll . . . you'll have to play it by ear, my dear . . . unless I get a chance to talk to you again. I've got to go into my act now. (*Crosses up to* L. *arch.*)
YOUNG MAN: But, I . . .
GRANDMA: Yoo-hoo!
MRS. BARKER: (*Coming through the archway.*) Yoo-hoo . . . oh, there you are, Grandma: I'm glad to see somebody; I can't find Mommy or Daddy: (*Double takes.*) Well, who's this?
GRANDMA: This? Well . . . un . . . oh, this is the . . . un . . . the van man. That's who it is; the van man.
MRS. BARKER: So! It's true! They *did* call the van man. They *are* having you carted away.
GRANDMA: (*Shrugging.*) Well, you know. It figures.
MRS. BARKER: (*To Young Man:*) How dare you cart this poor old woman away!
YOUNG MAN: (*After a quick look at Grandma, who nods.*) I do what I'm paid to do. I don't ask questions.
MRS. BARKER: (*Brief pause.*) Oh. (*Pause.*) Well, you're quite right, of course, and I shouldn't meddle.
GRANDMA: (*To the Young Man:*) Dear, will you take my things out to the van? (*She points to the boxes.*)
YOUNG MAN: (*After only the briefest hesitation.*) Why, certainly.
GRANDMA: (*As the Young Man takes up half the boxes, exits by the front door.*) Isn't that a nice young van man?
MRS. BARKER: (*Shaking her head in disbelief, watching the Young Man exit and crossing to arch* R.) Unh-hunh . . . some things have changed for the better. I remember when I had *my* mother carted off, the van man who came for her wasn't anything near as nice as this one.
GRANDMA: Oh, did you have your mother carted off, too?
MRS. BARKER: (*Cheerfully.*) Why, certainly! Didn't you?
GRANDMA: (*Puzzling.*) No. . . . No, I didn't. At least, I can't remember. (*Now back to business.*) Listen, dear; I got to talk to you for a second. (*Pulling Mrs. Barker away from arch.*)
MRS. BARKER: Why, certainly, Grandma:
GRANDMA: Now, listen.
MRS. BARKER: Yes, Grandma: Yes.
GRANDMA: Now, listen carefully. You got this dilemma here with Mommy and Daddy . . .
MRS. BARKER: Yes! I wonder where they've gone to.
GRANDMA: They'll be back in. Now, listen!
MRS. BARKER: Oh, I'm sorry.
GRANDMA: Now, you got this dilemma here with Mommy and Daddy, and I think I got the way out for you. (*The Young Man reenters the front door.*) Will you take the rest of my things out now, dear? (*To Mrs. Barker, while the*

Young Man takes the rest of the boxes, exits by the front door again.) Fine; now listen, dear. *(She begins to whisper in Mrs. Barker's ear. Mrs. Barker follows Young Man to arch* R., *Grandma with her, still whispering.)*
MRS. BARKER: Oh! Oh! Oh! I don't think I could . . . do you really think I could? Well, why not? What a wonderful idea . . . what an absolutely wonderful idea!
GRANDMA: Well, yes, I thought it was.
MRS. BARKER: And you so old!
GRANDMA: Heh, heh, heh.
MRS. BARKER: Well, I think it's absolutely marvelous, anyway. *(Crossing* L. *to arch.)* I'm going to find Mommy and Daddy right now.
GRANDMA: Good. You do that.
MRS. BARKER: Well, now. I think I will say goodbye. I can't thank you enough. *(She starts to exit through the archway.)*
GRANDMA: You're welcome. Say it!
MRS. BARKER: Huh. What?
GRANDMA: Say goodbye.
MRS. BARKER: Oh, Goodbye. *(She exits.)* Mommy! I say Mommy! Daddy!
GRANDMA: Goodbye. *(By herself now, she looks about.)* Ah, me. *(Shakes her head.)* Ah, me. *(Sits chair* L. *Takes in the room.)* Goodbye. *(The Young Man re-enters.)* Oh, hello there.
YOUNG MAN: All the boxes are outside. *(Sits on sofa.)*
GRANDMA: *(A little sadly.)* I don't know why I bother to take them with me. They don't have much in them . . . some old letters, a couple of regrets, Pekinese . . . blind at that . . . the television . . . my Sunday teeth . . . eighty-six years of living . . . some sounds . . . a few images, a little garbled by now . . . and, well, *(She shrugs.)* you know . . . the things one accumulates. *(Rises.)*
YOUNG MAN: *(Rising.)* Can I get you . . . a cab, or something?
GRANDMA: Oh, no, dear . . . thank you just the same. *(Crossing to arch* R.*)* I'll take it from here.
YOUNG MAN: And what shall I do now?
GRANDMA: Oh, you stay here, dear. It will all become clear to you. It will be explained. You'll understand.
YOUNG MAN: Very well.
GRANDMA: *(After one more look about.)* Well. . . .
YOUNG MAN: *(Crossing to Grandma:)* Let me see you to the elevator.
GRANDMA: Oh . . . that *would* be nice dear. *(They both exit, by the front door slowly. Enter Mrs. Barker, followed by Mommy and Daddy,* L.*)*
MRS. BARKER: *(Crossing* R., *gets her dress and starts putting it on.)* . . . and I'm happy to tell you that the whole thing's settled. Just like that.
MOMMY: Oh, we're so glad. We were afraid there might be a problem, what with delays, and all.
DADDY: *(Sits chair* L.*)* Yes, we're very relieved.
MRS. BARKER: Well, now. That's what professional women are for.

MOMMY: (*Looking around room.*) Why . . . where's Grandma? Grandma's not here! (*Grandma enters far* D. R., *secretively.*) Where's Grandma? And look! The boxes are gone too. Grandma's gone, and so are the boxes. She's taken off, and she's stolen something! Daddy!
MRS. BARKER: Why, Mommy, the van man was here.
MOMMY: (*Startled.*) The what?
MRS. BARKER: The van man. The van man was here.
MOMMY: (*Shakes her head.*) No, that's impossible.
MRS. BARKER: Why, I saw him with my own two eyes.
MOMMY: (*Crossing* C. *Near tears.*) No, no, that's impossible. No. There's no such thing as the van man. There is no van man. We . . . we made him up. Grandma? Grandma?
DADDY: (*Moving to Mommy and seating her in chair* L.) There, there, now.
MOMMY: Oh, Daddy . . . where's Grandma?
DADDY: There, there, now.
GRANDMA: (*To the audience.*) I want to watch this. (*Mrs. Barker tip-toes to the front door, and motions to Young Man who enters.*)
MRS. BARKER: Surprise! Surprise! Here we are!
MOMMY: What? What?
DADDY: Hm? What?
MOMMY: (*Her tears merely sniffles now.*) What surprise?
MRS. BARKER: (*Pushing Young Man* C.) Why, I told you. The surprise I told you about.
DADDY: (*Turns and sees Young Man:*) You . . . you know, Mommy:
MOMMY: Sur . . . prise?
DADDY: (*Urging her to cheerfulness.*) You remember, Mommy; why we asked . . . uh . . . what's-her-name to come here?
MRS. BARKER: Mrs. Barker, if you don't mind.
DADDY: Yes. Mommy, you remember now? About the bumble . . . about wanting satisfaction?
MOMMY: (*Sees Young Man: Her sorrow turning into delight.*) Yes. Why, yes! Of course! (*Rises and crosses to Young Man:*) Yes! Oh, how wonderful!
MRS. BARKER: (*To the Young Man:*) This is Mommy:
YOUNG MAN: How . . . do you do.
MRS. BARKER: (*Stage whisper.*) Her name is Mommy:
YOUNG MAN: How . . . how do you do, Mommy:
MOMMY: Well! Hello there!
MRS. BARKER: (*To the Young Man:*) And that is Daddy:
YOUNG MAN: (*Crossing with hand outstretched out to Daddy, who backs off* D. L.) How do you do.
DADDY: How do you do.
MOMMY: (*Pulling Young Man* C. *Herself again, circling the Young Man, feeling his arm, poking him.*) Yes, Sir! Now this is more like it Yes, Siree! Now this is a great deal more like it! Daddy? Come see. Come see if this isn't a great deal more like it.

DADDY: I . . . I can see from here, Mommy: It does look a great deal more like it.
MOMMY: Yes, Sir. Yes, Siree! Mrs. Barker, I don't know *how* to thank you.
MRS. BARKER: Oh, don't worry about that. I'll send you a bill in the mail. (*Starts to leave, crossing to arch* R.)
MOMMY: What this really calls for is a celebration. It calls for a drink.
MRS. BARKER: (*Comes back in to* R. *chair.*) Oh, what a nice idea.
MOMMY: There's some sauterne in the kitchen.
YOUNG MAN: I'll go.
MOMMY: Will you? Oh, how nice. (*Showing him to arch* L.) The kitchen's through the archway there. (*As the Young Man exits . . . to Mrs. Barker:*) He's very nice. Really top notch; much better than the other one.
MRS. BARKER: I'm glad you're pleased. And I'm glad everything's all straightened out.
MOMMY: (*Crossing to Mrs. Barker:*) Well, at least we know why we sent for you. We're glad that's cleared up. By the way, what's his name?
MRS. BARKER: Ha! Call him whatever you like. He's yours. Call him what you called the other one.
MOMMY: Daddy? What did we call the other one?
DADDY: (*Puzzles.*) Why. . . .
YOUNG MAN: (*Re-entering with a tray, on which are five glasses.*) Here we are! (*Crosses* C. *to Mommy:*)
MOMMY: Hooray! Hooray!
MRS. BARKER: Oh, good!
MOMMY: (*Moving to the tray.*) So, let's . . . five glasses! Why five? There are only four of us. Why five?
YOUNG MAN: (*Catches Grandma's eye, Grandma indicates she is not there.*) Oh, I'm sorry.
MOMMY: You must learn to count. We're a wealthy family, and you must learn to count.
YOUNG MAN: I will.
MOMMY: Well, everybody take a glass. (*They do.*) And we'll drink to celebrate. To satisfaction! Who says you can't get satisfaction these days!
MRS. BARKER: What dreadful sauterne! (*Mrs. Barker sits chair* R., *Daddy sits chair* L.)
MOMMY: Yes isn't it. (*Taking tray and putting it on table* R. *of sofa. Then pulling Young Man down with her on sofa. To Young Man, her voice already a little fuzzy from the wine.*) You don't know how happy I am to see you! Yes Siree. Listen, that time we had with . . . with the other one. I'll tell you all about it some time. (*Indicates Mrs. Barker:*) After she's gone. She was responsible for all the trouble in the first place. I'll tell you all about it. (*Places his arm around her and sidles up to him a little.*) Maybe . . . maybe later tonight.
YOUNG MAN: (*Not moving away.*) Why, yes. That would be very nice.
MOMMY: (*Puzzles.*) Something familiar about you . . . you know that? (*Pulling him up to take a better look.*) I can't quite place it . . . (*Daddy and Mrs.*

Barker turn to look at them as Grandma stops the scene. The lights dim to half and Mommy, Young Man, Daddy and Mrs. Barker are in tableau.)
GRANDMA: *(To audience.)* Well, I guess that just about wraps it up. I mean, for better or worse, this is a comedy, and I don't think we'd better go any further. No, definitely not. So, let's leave things as they are right now . . . while everybody's happy . . . while everybody's got what he wants . . . or everybody's got what he thinks he wants. Goodnight, dears.

CURTAIN

END OF PLAY

Baby with the Bathwater

Christopher Durang

When *Baby with the Bathwater* was first produced it joined a list of more than a dozen comedies by Christopher Durang focusing on some eccentricity or another in American life. Among the playwrights earlier works which take comic aim at excesses are: *The Nature and Purpose of the Universe* (his first play produced in 1971), *'dentity Crisis, Better Dead Than Sorry, The Life of Mitzi Gaynor; or, Gyp, The Marriage of Bette and Boo, The Idiots Karamazov, When Dinah Shore Ruled the Earth, A History of the American Film, The Vietnamization of New Jersey, Sister Mary Ignatius Explains It All for You, Beyond Therapy, The Actor's Nightmare,* and *Christopher Durang Explains It all for You.* All are wonderful titles hinting at what Durang happens to find amusing to explore and ultimately to hold up for ridicule.

Baby with the Bathwater singles out the American family, child care, and the public schools as the object of its derision. Each subject in its turn is satirized. Durang's method is to take perfectly normal encounters and turn them into abnormal circumstances accompanied by witty dialogue. This is the characteristic of Durang's writing style. Durang raises many fundamental questions of importance for us today. Among them are the following: "Are today's parents adequately prepared to raise children?" "Do parents teach parenting skills by example or do children actually learn by observing the mistakes of their parents?" "Who are parents to trust with their children when they can't look after them?" "Are schools administered by competent individuals?" "Can parents trust the schools to assist in the upbringing of their children?"

Production History

Baby with the Bathwater was first presented off-Broadway on November 9, 1983 by Playwrights Horizons in New York City, Andre Bishop, artistic director, Paul Daniels, managing director. The production was directed by Jerry Zaks; sets designed by Loren Sherman; costumes designed by Rita Ryack; lighting designed by Jennifer Tipton; sound designed by Jonathan Vall. Production stage manager was Esther Cohen; stage manager was Diane Ward. The cast was as follows:

Helen	Christine Estabrook
John	W.H. Macy
Nanny/Woman in the Park/Principal	Dana Ivey
Cynthia/Woman in the Park/Miss Pringle and Susan	Leslie Geraci
Young Man	Keith Reddin

In the subsequent run of the play, the role of Nanny/Woman in the Park/Principal was taken over by Kate McGregor-Stewart, then by Mary Louise Wilson, then by Cynthia Darlow. The understudies were Melodie

Somers and William Kux. During the play's final week Ms. Somers played the part of Helen.

Baby with the Bathwater had its world premiere at the American Repertory Theatre in Cambridge, Massachusetts on March 31, 1983, Robert Brustein, artistic director, Rob Orchard, managing director. The production was directed by Mark Linn-Baker; sets designed by Don Soule; costumes designed by Liz Perlman; lighting designed by Thom Palm; sound designed by Randolph Head. Production stage manager was John Grant-Phillips. The cast was as follows:

Helen	Cherry Jones
John	Tony Shalhoub
Nanny/Woman in the Park/Principal	Marianne Owen
Cynthia/Woman in the Park/Miss Pringle and Susan	Karen MacDonald
Young Man	Stephen Rowe

Characters

HELEN
JOHN
NANNY/WOMAN IN THE PARK/PRINCIPAL
CYNTHIA/WOMAN IN THE PARK/MISS PRINGLE AND SUSAN
YOUNG MAN

Baby With the Bathwater by Christopher Durang

Copyright © by Christopher Durang. Reprinted by permission.

The Play

Baby With The Bathwater

ACT ONE

Scene 1

The home of John and Helen, a couple in their late 20s or early 30s. They are standing over a bassinet.

HELEN: Hello, baby. Hello.
JOHN: It looks just like me.
HELEN: Yes it does. Smaller.
JOHN: Well, yes.
HELEN: And it looks just like me. It has my hair.
JOHN: Yes it does.
HELEN: (*Slightly worried.*) I wonder if it would have been better off having your hair?
JOHN: (*Reassuringly.*) Your hair is lovely.
HELEN: (*Touched.*) Thank you.
JOHN: You're welcome. (*They smile at one another warmly.*)
JOHN: (*Back to the bassinet.*) Hello, baby. Hello. Cooooo.
HELEN: Cooooooo. Cummmmm-quat. Cummmmm-quat!
JOHN: Hee haw. Hee haw. Daddy's little baked potato.
HELEN: Don't call the child a baked potato.
JOHN: It's a term of affection.
HELEN: It isn't. It's a *food*. No one wants to be called a baked potato.
JOHN: Well it doesn't speak English.
HELEN: The various books say that you should presume your child *can* understand you. We don't want it to have problems in kindergarten or marriage because you called it a baked potato.
JOHN: It seems to me you're losing your sense of humor.
HELEN: (*Firmly.*) I just don't want to make the child insane—that's all. Bringing up a child is a delicate thing.
JOHN: Alright, you're not a baked potato, sweet pea. (*She looks at him in horror; he senses her look.*) And you're not a sweet pea either. You're a baby. Bay-bee. Bay-bee.

HELEN: I want a divorce.
JOHN: What?
HELEN: You heard me. I want a divorce.
JOHN: Are you crazy? You've read the statistics on children from broken homes. Do you want to do that to our child?
HELEN: I don't feel ready for marriage, I didn't when we got married, I should have said no.
JOHN: But we love each other.
HELEN: You have blond hair. I don't like men with blond hair. I like men with dark hair, but I'm afraid of them. I'm not afraid of you. I hate you.
JOHN: What? Is this post-partem depression?
HELEN: Don't talk about post-partem depression, you know nothing about it. (*To baby.*) Men just don't understand things, do they, sweetie pie?
JOHN: If I can't call it a potato, you can't call it a pie.
HELEN: I didn't call it a pie.
JOHN: You did. You said sweetie pie.
HELEN: Sweetie pie is an expression, it isn't a pie. You don't go into a restaurant and order sweetie pie.
JOHN: Why do you insist on winning every argument?
HELEN: If I'm right, I'm right. It has nothing to do with winning. (*To baby.*) Men don't know how to argue. That's why they always end up hitting people.
JOHN: I don't hit people.
HELEN: Boys and men hit one another constantly. They attack one another on the street, they play football, they wrestle on television, they rape one another in prison, they rape women and children in back alleys. (*To baby.*) Beware of men, darling. Be glad you're not ever going to be a man.
JOHN: That's an awful thing to say. And is it a girl? I thought it was a boy.
HELEN: We don't know what sex it is. It's too young. The doctor said we could decide later.
JOHN: You don't decide later. Gender is a fact, it's not a decision.
HELEN: That's not what the doctor said to me. He said something about the DNA molecule. They're splitting it differently now. He said if the DNA combined one way, the child would have testosterone and then we could either have it circumsized or not, depending. Or else the DNA combines with estrogen, in which case it would be a girl. Or in some cases, the DNA combines with cobalt molecules, and then the child would be radio-active for 5000 years and we'd have to send it out into orbit.
JOHN: What are you talking about?
HELEN: Can't you speak English? I'm married to an idiot. (*To baby.*) Your father is an idiot. Oh God, please let me meet a dark haired man who's smarter than I am. (*To John.*) Oh why don't you go away? I don't like you.
JOHN: I don't understand. We were very happy yesterday.
HELEN: What are you talking about? Happy? Who was happy?
JOHN: We were. We were making plans. The child's schooling, what

playground to take it to, whether to let it play with toy guns, how to toilet train it.
HELEN: Oh God, toilet training. I can't face it. We'll have to hire someone.
JOHN: We don't have money to hire anyone.
HELEN: Well, we'll have to earn the money.
JOHN: But we can't earn money. I was let go from work.
HELEN: Well, you can find another job.
JOHN: I need rest, I really don't feel able to work right now.
HELEN: John, that's not practical.
JOHN: I want to go back to bed.
HELEN: But, John, you wanted to be responsible, don't you remember? Right after that week you stayed behind the refrigerator, you came to me and said, "The immaturities of my youth are over now, Helen. Let's make a baby." And then we did. Don't you remember?
JOHN: I need professional help. I want to go to McLains in Massachusetts. That's the institution James Taylor was in for a time. He seems so tranquil and calm when he gives his concerts. And he has a summer house on Martha's Vineyard. Maybe, when the doctor says I'm well enough, I could go to Mar . . .
HELEN: JOHN, LIVE UP TO YOUR RESPONSIBILITIES! (*Baby cries.*) Oh, God, it's crying. What should we do?
JOHN: Sing to it.
HELEN: (*Sings to baby sweetly, softly.*) There's no business like show business, like no business . . .
JOHN: A lullaby, sweetheart.
HELEN: I don't know any lullabys.
JOHN: (*Sings.*)
Hush little baby, don't you cry,
Mama's gonna give you a big black eye . . .
HELEN: Good heavens, those aren't the lyrics.
JOHN: I know they're not. I can't remember the right ones.
HELEN: Oh God. You're going to teach baby all the wrong lyrics to everything. It's going to have trouble with its peer group.
JOHN: Maybe we should hold it to stop it crying.
HELEN: We might drop it. I had a cocktail for breakfast. I'm not steady.
JOHN: Why did you have a cocktail?
HELEN: You're always picking on me! I'm sorry I married you. I'm sorry I gave birth to baby. I wish I were back at the Spence School.
JOHN: We love the baby.
HELEN: How can we love the baby? It won't stop that noise. (*To baby.*) Shut up, baby. Shut up. Oh God, please help us. Please make the baby stop. (*Enter Nanny, dressed in tweeds, wearing a ladylike hat and carrying a large cloth handbag.*)
NANNY: Hello. I'm Nanny.
HELEN: Oh thank goodness you've come. Please make it stop crying.

NANNY: (*Goes over to crib; in a high, soothing if odd voice.*) Hellooooooo, baby. Helllloooooo. Yeeeeeeees. Yeeeeeees. It's Nanny. Yesssssssssssss. (*Baby stops making noise.*) That's right. That's right. I've brought you a present. (*Takes out a jar; opens it—it's a trick jar—and a large snake pops out. Baby screams in terror. John and Helen are fairly startled also. Nanny laughs.*) Ha haha haha! That surprised you, didn't it?

JOHN: See here, who are you?

HELEN: Oh my God, it's crying again. *Please* make it stop crying.

NANNY: What? I can't hear you. Child's making so much racket.

HELEN: Please. Make it stop that awful noise.

NANNY: (*High voice again.*) Quiet, little baby. Be quiet. (*No effect; then she yells stridently.*) SHUT UP! (*Baby is abruptly quiet; Nanny is pleased.*)

JOHN: (*Looking at the baby.*) I think you've given it a heart attack.

NANNY: No, no, it's just resting.

HELEN: Oh thank goodness it stopped.

JOHN: Who are you?

NANNY: I am the ghost of Christmas Past. Hahahahaha. No just making a joke. I get a list of all the new parents from the hospital, and then I just *descend* upon them. Now, I need Wednesday evenings off, and I'm allergic to asparagus and lobster . . .

HELEN: We never have lobster.

NANNY: And I like chunky peanut butter better than the smooth kind, but if you already have the smooth kind, we'll finish that off before you buy a new jar.

JOHN: I can't afford you.

NANNY: And I don't do windows, and I don't do floors, and I don't do laundry, but I make salmon salad and tuna salad and salad niçoise and chef salad and chunky peanut butter sandwiches, and I make my own yogurt in a great big vat.

JOHN: You can't stay here.

HELEN: But I need help. I can't cope by myself. Please, John.

JOHN: But I'm on unemployment.

NANNY: Well, we'll just get you another job.

JOHN: But what can I do?

NANNY: Why don't you become an astronaut? That pays very well. Or a football player. Or a newscaster. (*To baby.*) Wouldn't you like to see your Daddy on television, baby? Baby? (*Looks into the silent bassinet.*) I think the snake scared it. (*To baby.*) WAKE UP! (*Baby cries.*) There, that's better. (*Smiles, pleased.*)

HELEN: Please don't shout at it. It's not good for it.

JOHN: Maybe I should hold it to comfort it.

HELEN: That would be very responsible, John. That's a good boy. Good boy.

JOHN: Thank you. (*Holds baby, which stops crying.*)

HELEN: John's been fired from his job, you see.
NANNY: Well, that won't put food on the table.
HELEN: I could get a job, I suppose. But what would I do?
NANNY: Well, why don't you write a novel? "The World According to Garp" sold very well recently. Why don't you write something like that?
HELEN: Oh, that's a good idea. But I need a pencil and paper.
NANNY: Oh. Well, here's a dollar. Now you go to the store and buy some paper and a nice felt tip pen.
HELEN: Now?
NANNY: No time like the present. Right, baby?
HELEN: Oh, John, please put the baby down. I'm afraid one of us might drop it. (*To Nanny.*) I had a cocktail for breakfast, and John took some Nyquil and quaaludes.
JOHN: I get tense.
NANNY: Put the baby down, John. You're spoiling it. (*Takes it from him, puts it in bassinet.*) Now, what should we call it, do you think?
HELEN: Well, John's father's name was John, and his mother's name was Joan, and my father's name was John, and my mother's name was Hillary, and my doctor's name is Dr. Arthur Hammerstein, but I really want a woman doctor who can understand me, but it's so hard to find a doctor.
NANNY: Yes, but what about a name, a name?
HELEN: Don't you get cross with me.
NANNY: All right, we won't call the baby anything.
JOHN: We could call it John after me if it's a boy, and Helen after you if it's a girl.
HELEN: No, I don't want to call it anything now. I'm going back to bed.
NANNY: I thought you were going to buy paper and pencil to start your novel.
HELEN: I don't want to. I want to sleep.
NANNY: I gave you a dollar.
HELEN: I don't care.
NANNY: Here's another dollar. Go buy yourself an ice cream soda on the way home.
HELEN: Oh, thank you nanny. I love you. (*Hugs her, runs off.*)
NANNY: We're all going to have to be very kind to her. (*To baby.*) Don't depend on mommy, baby. She's not all there. (*To John.*) So—what can I do for you?
JOHN: I really haven't hired you yet, you know.
NANNY: You want a quick one?
JOHN: Pardon?
NANNY: Us older girls have a few tricks up our sleeves, you know. I bet I know some things your wife doesn't know.
JOHN: I don't know. I had a quaalude this morning, I don't really feel up to anything.

NANNY: It's very rude to turn me down. You might hurt my feelings.
JOHN: Well, what about the baby?
NANNY: The baby doesn't have to know anything about it. Now we haven't much time, she's getting the paper and pen and the ice cream soda.
JOHN: Well, all right, but let's not do it here. I feel uncomfortable in front of the baby.
NANNY: We could distract it. We could play loud music.
JOHN: But we might hurt its eardrums. I want to be a good father.
NANNY: Well, of course you do. I have tiny little earplugs we could put in its ears.
JOHN: Well, then, what's the point of the loud music?
NANNY: (*Thinks, but can't unravel the mystery.*) I don't know.
JOHN: This is all getting too complicated.
NANNY: (*Cheerfully.*) Very well! Let's just do it in the kitchen. Come on. (*She energetically drags John off into the kitchen. After a moment, the baby starts to cry. A young woman, rather sweet-looking but dressed shabbily, enters the apartment. Her name is Cynthia. She appears to have wandered into the apartment for no apparent reason. She is very pregnant. She walks over to the bassinet and sings sweetly to the baby to comfort it. After a few lines of the song, the baby does stop crying. Cynthia keeps singing to it for a while; her voice is pleasant and soothing.*)
CYNTHIA: (*Sings.*)
Hush, little baby,
Don't say a word,
Momma's gonna buy you a mockingbird,
And if that mockingbird don't sing,
Momma's gonna buy you a golden ring,
And if that golden ring turns brass,
Momma's gonna buy you a looking glass,
And if that looking glass gets broke,
Momma's gonna buy you a billy goat.
(*Hums. Cynthia smiles that the baby has been comforted and, still humming, wanders back out of the apartment. Lights dim.*)

Scene 2

Later that night. Dark. Baby cries. Voices of "Oh God." The lights come up. The couch has been opened up to make a bed. In the bed are Helen, Nanny, and John in nightgowns and pajamas. Nanny is sound asleep.

HELEN: Baby, we're sleeping. Now go back to sleep. John, you talk to it.
JOHN: Enough of this noise, little child. Daddy and Mommy are sleeping.
HELEN: Oh God it won't stop. Nanny, wake up. Nanny!
JOHN: Nanny! (*They poke her.*)

NANNY: (*Coming out of a dream.*) Where am I? Help! Water to the right of me, water to the left of me. Ode to a Grecian urn. (*Lies back down.*)
HELEN: Nanny, baby's calling you.
NANNY: I'm sleepy.
HELEN: Nanny, you're the nanny.
NANNY: (*Pointing to John.*) What about Tiger here?
JOHN: Don't call me Tiger.
NANNY: Tiger. Ruff. Ruff. (*Gets up.*) All right, baby. Nanny's coming. (*Picks up baby.*) Helloooooo, baby. Hellllooooo, baby. That's right. Wheeeeeeeeeeee. Woooooooooooooo. Waaaaaaaaaaa. (*Keeps making these odd, if soothing, sounds softly through next dialogue. Baby does stop crying.*)
HELEN: Why did she call you Tiger?
JOHN: I don't know. She was probably dreaming.
HELEN: Oh, baby's stopped. Thank goodness for Nanny. And her Salad Niçoise was so good for dinner.
JOHN: Yes it was. Helen, I don't think this is going to work out.
HELEN: What isn't?
JOHN: Nanny.
HELEN: I think it's working out fine.
JOHN: I can't sleep three in a bed.
HELEN: John, when we're rich we'll buy a big house with an extra room for Nanny. Until then, this is fine.
JOHN: Helen, I don't think Nanny is a good person.
NANNY: I heard that.
JOHN: Nanny, please, we're trying to have a private conversation.
NANNY: Don't you talk behind my back. I'll hire a lawyer. We'll slap an injunction against you.
JOHN: Please, you deal with baby, and let Helen and me figure this out.
NANNY: I've finished comforting baby. (*Brusquely.*) Go to sleep, baby. (*Tosses it back into the bassinet.*) Now you say to my face that I'm not a good person.
JOHN: Well maybe that's too strong. But I think you're too rough with baby. I mean, you just threw it into the bassinet.
NANNY: Do you hear it crying?
JOHN: No, but maybe it's fainted or something.
NANNY: It's just resting.
JOHN: You keep saying that, but I think you have it fainting. And it has this look of panic on its face.
NANNY: Look, don't tell me how to handle children. I got it down.
HELEN: Nanny knows best, John. And she's helping me with my novel. She liked the first chapter, John.
NANNY: I did. I thought it showed real promise.
HELEN: And then when I sell my novel, if we get a good deal for the paperback rights, then we can buy a house in the country and maybe we can have another baby.

JOHN: Helen, Nanny seduced me this afternoon when you were out buying paper.
NANNY: That's a lie.
JOHN: It's the truth. I was unfaithful to you, Helen. (*Helen looks hurt in earnest.*) I'm sorry.
HELEN: I don't know how to cope with this.
JOHN: So you can see why I don't feel comfortable all three of us in the bed.
HELEN: (*Near tears.*) I don't know how to cope.
JOHN: I'm really sorry. It was Nanny's fault.
NANNY: He raped me!
JOHN: I didn't. That's a lie, Helen.
HELEN: I don't want to talk about this anymore! I'm going to work on my novel in the kitchen, and I'm going to pretend that I live alone. (*Exits.*)
JOHN: Well, things are in a fine mess.
NANNY: You told her, I didn't.
JOHN: What we did was wrong.
NANNY: Oh for God's sake, it didn't mean anything. It would've been fine if you hadn't told her.
JOHN: I felt guilty. It's wrong to cheat on your wife.
NANNY: You're such a dullard. There is no right or wrong, there's only *fun!*
JOHN: That can't be true. I mean, there are certain things that are intrinsically wrong, and when we figure out what these things are, then we are said to have values.
NANNY: Haven't you read "The Brothers Karamazov"? Ivan Karamazov realizes that because there is no God, everything is permitted.
JOHN: I don't understand.
NANNY: Everything is permitted. (*Hits the back of his head hard.*)
JOHN: Why did you do that?
NANNY: I *felt* like it. Everything is permitted. (*Laughs. Re-enter Helen, in raincoat and rainhat, holding a sheaf of papers.*)
HELEN: I'm taking my coat and the first chapter of my novel and the baby, and I'm leaving you.
JOHN: Helen, I'm sorry, it won't happen again.
HELEN: You obviously prefer Nanny to me, and so as far as I'm concerned, you can just go to hell.
NANNY: (*Genuinely meaning it.*) Oh I love arguments.
JOHN: Helen, we have to stay together for the baby.
HELEN: No, I'm taking the baby and the novel, and you won't get any of the paperback rights at all. Goodbye.
JOHN: The baby's asleep.
HELEN: Or fainted, as you said, Nanny bats it around so. (*Picks up baby.*) Mommy's going to save you now, sweetie pie.
JOHN: I have rights to the baby too.

HELEN: Baby will thank me later.
JOHN: But where will you go at this hour?
HELEN: (*At a loss.*) We'll go to . . . Marriott's Essex House.
JOHN: Our credit cards have been cancelled.
HELEN: All right. We'll sleep in the park, I don't care, I just have to leave here! Don't touch me!
JOHN: But it's freezing out. Baby will catch pneumonia.
HELEN: Well I can't help it. You don't *die* from pneumonia.
JOHN: But you do, you do die from pneumonia!
HELEN: Don't tell me what to do. I KNOW WHAT I'M DOING! (*Exits with baby.*)
JOHN: Helen!
NANNY: Let her go, she'll be back in a few minutes. I know these hysterical mothers.
JOHN: They're going to get very ill, it's very cold outside.
NANNY: It's bad to fuss too much as a parent, your child will grow up afraid. Let baby discover some things for itself. You want a quick one?
JOHN: What?
NANNY: You heard me.
JOHN: But it's wrong. Sexual infidelity is *wrong*.
NANNY: Wrong, right, I don't know where you pick up these phrases. Didn't they teach you about Darwin in public school? The fish came out of the water, covered with a viscous substance, and then bones and vertebrae were evolved, and then male and female, and then the egg and the ovum and the testicles and the semen, and then reproduction, and then dinosaurs, or maybe dinosaurs before that, and then local governments, and then the space program, and then nuclear power plants and now cable television and Home Box Office. *Where* do you find right and wrong in all that??? Tell me. (*Re-enter Helen, wet, with baby, wet.*)
HELEN: I fell in a puddle. I'm all wet.
NANNY: Well, if it isn't Nora five minutes after the end of "A Doll's House."
HELEN: I thought you were going to help me, and now all you do is pick on me.
JOHN: Good God, the baby's soaking wet.
HELEN: Of course, it's wet. I told you I fell in a puddle.
NANNY: Helen is the worst mother, isn't she, baby?
HELEN: Don't you say that. John, hit her for me.
JOHN: (*Very forceful suddenly.*) Now enough of all this arguing! We're going to get baby in some dry clothes, and Helen in some dry clothes, and then we're going to take Nyquil and quaaludes and get some sleep! And we will discuss all these problems in the morning. Is that clear?
HELEN: Yes, John.
NANNY: Yes, John.

JOHN: Very well. Now no more talking. (*John puts baby in bassinet and changes its clothes; Helen starts to take off her things, sneezing occasionally. Nanny exits, re-enters.*)
NANNY: I've got the Nyquil.
JOHN: Thank God.
NANNY: You have its feet in the armholes.
JOHN: The point is that it's dry, right?
NANNY: The point is to do things right.
HELEN: You said no more talking. I want to go to sleep.
JOHN: All right. But in the morning, we're going to kill Nanny. (*Nanny looks at John with suspicion.*)
HELEN: Let's just have our Nyquil and not argue anymore.
JOHN: Should we give baby Nyquil?
HELEN: Oh I don't know. What does it say on the label?
JOHN: I don't know. I can't read the small print. I need glasses.
HELEN: Well if you can't read, then there's no solution, is there?
NANNY: Why don't we just ask baby? Do you want some Nyquil, honey? Do you? Huh? (*Pause.*) It won't say. It's just staring back, hostilely.
HELEN: Oh why can't it be a happy baby? (*Notices.*) John, you've dressed it all wrong. It can barely move that way.
JOHN: I'm going to sleep now. I don't want to hear any more complaints! (*John, Helen, and Nanny get into bed.*)
NANNY: Good night everybody.
HELEN: Good night, Nanny. (*Kisses her.*) I love you. (*To John.*) I hate you.
JOHN: Good night, Helen. (*They lie down to sleep. After a moment Cynthia enters. She goes to the bassinet.*)
CYNTHIA: Hello, baby. Hellooooooo. (*The three in bed sit up and stare at her.*)
HELEN: Who are you?
CYNTHIA: I'm just so upset. I'm very poor, and I gave birth in the hospital to a darling little boy, or girl, and when I came home from the hospital, there's no heat in my apartment and there's no furniture, there's just my German shepherd. And, of course, I hadn't fed it in about a week, since I went into the hospital, so I went out to buy some baby food and some dog food. But there's no furniture, so I left the baby on the floor, and when I came back, the dog had eaten the baby. And now I don't know what to do.
NANNY: Have you told this story to the *New York Post*?
CYNTHIA: No.
NANNY: Well, I'd start out by doing that.
CYNTHIA: But I'm so tired now.
JOHN: What is the matter with you? Why did you leave your baby on the floor?
CYNTHIA: Please don't yell at me. I don't have any furniture!
NANNY: There, there, you poor thing. We'll get you another baby. You'll adopt.
CYNTHIA: But I'm not a fit mother.

NANNY: Everyone's allowed one mistake.
HELEN: (*Suspiciously.*) Where's the dog?
CYNTHIA: I have it right outside in the hallway. Would you like to keep it? (*She goes to the door; John springs up and blocks the door.*)
JOHN: Don't you bring that dog in here!
NANNY: Now there's no reason to hold this woman's stupidity against her dog. That's unfair. (*To Cynthia.*) Of course, we want the dog. It sounds like a good watch dog.
CYNTHIA: Well actually it's always been vicious, but you see normally I feed it. It's just that when I was in the hospital, they wouldn't let me leave.
NANNY: Administrative red tape. It's really behind so much evil and suffering in the world.
HELEN: I don't know. I think she's a terrible woman.
CYNTHIA: Oh, please, I feel so guilty. Don't hate me. I really just don't know any better. I didn't listen to anything they taught me in school. Something about equal sides of an isosceles triangle. And I don't have any furniture at home. And you have lovely furniture. Do you mind if I lie down and sleep for a moment. I'm really exhausted. (*She lies down on the sofa bed and falls asleep immediately.*)
NANNY: Poor child.
HELEN: Why is she here? We don't want her here.
NANNY: Where is your charity? The poor child is going to have to live with her stupidity all the rest of her life. Maybe she'll even have to go to prison when the police hear of it all. Surely you wouldn't begrudge her one night's sleep of safety and peace?
HELEN: Well, maybe not. But can we make her go in the morning?
NANNY: We'll see. Come, John, come to bed. Tomorrow's going to be a busy day. (*Nanny, Helen, and John lie down next to the sleeping Cynthia. Lights dim.*)

Scene 3

> Sound of dog barking viciously; baby crying. Lights up on the four of them in the sofa bed.

HELEN: Someone make that noise stop.
JOHN: Be quiet, baby.
HELEN: Is baby barking?
JOHN: Oh God, that dog. (*To Cynthia.*) Hey, you, wake up. Shut up your dog somehow.
CYNTHIA: I was having such a pleasant dream.
JOHN: Make your dog be quiet.
CYNTHIA: What dog?
JOHN: Your dog is barking.
CYNTHIA: (*Pleasantly.*) Oh yes, I hear it now. It must smell baby.

HELEN: Oh dear God.
CYNTHIA: Don't be alarmed. It's just hungry. Do you have any red meat?
JOHN: Maybe there's some red meat in the refrigerator.
CYNTHIA: Well go give it some, and then it'll stop barking. (*Smiles.*) Don't let it get your hand though. (*John exits to kitchen.*)
HELEN: Where did you get the dog?
CYNTHIA: Oh, some terrible people were beating it in the park, and I felt sorry for it, so I asked them if I could have it.
HELEN: And so they gave it to you?
CYNTHIA: Yes. They beat me up for quite a while. Twenty minutes, it seemed, maybe it was shorter, it's hard to judge time that way. And then the dog and I crawled to my apartment, and we've just been together ever since. (*John returns from the kitchen with package of chopped meat, goes into the hall to the barking dog. Barking gets worse, then ferocious eating noises occur; John comes back.*)
JOHN: It took the meat.
CYNTHIA: It really *loves* meat. I'm a vegetarian myself. I tried to make the dog eat bean sprouts and broccoli once for a while, but it didn't work out.
JOHN: Someone should really change baby. I think it's made a mess.
HELEN: Oh, I don't want to. Let Nanny do it.
NANNY: (*Not moving.*) I'm sleeping.
CYNTHIA: Oh, I'll do it. I love babies. (*Goes to baby.*) I had the most wonderful dream last night. I dreamt that I kidnapped your baby, and that the dog, baby and myself took a bus to Florida and had a wonderful time on the beach. (*On the word "kidnapped," the three in bed sit up and look at her with varying degrees of concern.*) I'm afraid we all got seriously sunburned in the dream, but I don't know if we died from it or not because then I woke up with the dog barking. Oh, your baby's so grumpy looking. What's the matter, baby? Don't you like me?
HELEN: It's a very grouchy baby. We're not very happy with it.
CYNTHIA: I know. I have a little toy it will like. The nurses gave it to me at the hospital. (*Holds up little red toy that jingles when she shakes it.*) Hey? It's a little red thingamajig. Isn't it cute? I don't think baby likes me. Why don't you like me, baby?
NANNY: (*With great disinterest.*) Why don't you read to it then? Baby loves to be read to. (*Exits to get into her Nanny clothes.*)
CYNTHIA: Oh all right. (*Meanders about, looking for a book.*)
HELEN: John, you better get up and go look for work.
JOHN: I just want to sleep. Leave me alone. (*Hides under pillow.*)
HELEN: John, you have responsibilities. Look at me.
CYNTHIA: Here's a book. Now if I read to you, will you promise to smile at me, baby?
JOHN: Let's get a divorce. You wanted one yesterday. Let's get one now.
HELEN: It's not practical now. Baby needs a father, and I need financial support until I finish my novel.

CYNTHIA: Chapter Seven. Shortly after Mommie Dearest won her Oscar for "Mildred Pierce," she would burst into Christopher and my room at 3 in the morning screaming, "Fire drill! Fire drill!" (*John and Helen look at Cynthia for a moment, then return to their argument.*)
JOHN: Helen, this novel idea is a pipe dream. Don't you know that?
HELEN: It is not. Nanny said my first chapter was brilliant.
NANNY: (*Off-stage.*) Well, not brilliant perhaps. But quite commercial, I'd say.
CYNTHIA: Then she'd pour gasoline on the curtains and set them on fire, while we'd scream and scream. (*Makes playful scream noises.*) Aaaaggh! Aaaaggh!
JOHN: But you can't write, don't you know that?
HELEN: What do you know? I can too! (*Nanny re-enters with Helen's still soggy sheaf of papers.*)
NANNY: Read him your first chapter then, that'll show him.
CYNTHIA: I would try to untie Christopher from his bed, but Mommie wouldn't let me.
HELEN: (*Proudly.*) Chapter One. I am born. I was born in a workhouse in London in 1853. (*Cynthia returns to reading to the baby as Helen continues to read from her novel. Nanny and John do their best to give Helen their attention, but find their focus hopelessly caught between the two novel readings. Eventually John and Nanny begin to look discouraged and disoriented by how difficult it is to follow either story.*)
HELEN: My mother, whoever she may have been, had left me at the doorstep of a wealthy man named Mr. Squire of Squireford Manor. However, wicked travelling gypsies came by the Squire's doorstep and snatched me up and left me at the workhouse. My first conscious memory is of little Nell, the cobbler's daughter, being run over by a coach and four.
CYNTHIA: As the burning curtains came closer and closer to Christopher's bed, he cried aloud, "God in heaven, save me from Mommie!" Then Mommie took out a fire extinguisher and sprayed the curtains as well as Christopher and myself. And then with tears streaming down her cheeks, Mommie screamed, "Clean up your rooms! Bad Christina! Bad Christopher! Look at this dirt!
HELEN: (*Unable to stand it anymore.*) WILL YOU BE QUIET???? I am *trying* to read from my novel.
CYNTHIA: I am reading to baby.
HELEN: I don't care what you're doing. You're a guest in this house.
CYNTHIA: Baby will grow up with no love of literature if you don't read to it.
HELEN: It's my baby, and I'll raise it as I see fit.
CYNTHIA: No, it's my baby! (*Snatches it up.*) I can see that my dream was a sign I should have it!
HELEN: Give it back to me at once!
CYNTHIA: No, I won't! You're not fit parents. I know I'm guilty of

negligence with my baby, but it was an honest mistake. And I love babies. But you three are heartless. You don't hold the baby when it cries, you dress it wrong so it can't move in its pajamas, and you're both so inconsistent as people changing from one mood to another that you'll obviously make it crazy. That's why it never smiles. I may be forgetful, but baby has a chance with me!

HELEN: Give it back to me! (*Runs toward her.*)

CYNTHIA: Don't come near me, or I'll throw it out the window!

JOHN: Good Lord, she's insane. (*Everyone stands very still. Cynthia starts to move slowly to the door.*)

CYNTHIA: Now I'm going to leave here with baby and with the dog, and we're going to go to Florida, and you're not to follow us.

NANNY: Now let the dream be a warning. Don't stay in the sun too long. Babies have light skin.

CYNTHIA: I know what I'm doing. Come on, baby, you'll be safe with me. (*Runs out door, dog barks.*) Come on, doggie, it's just me and baby. (*Sound of dog barking, baby crying.*)

HELEN: John, what should we do?

NANNY: You could have another baby.

HELEN: John, we have to go after her.

JOHN: I need amphetamines.

HELEN: John, we haven't time.

JOHN: I told you we shouldn't have let her stay here.

HELEN: You said no such thing. And that's not the point now anyway. We've got to run after her.

JOHN: We're not dressed.

HELEN: Oh you're impossible. (*She runs out.*)

JOHN: You're right. I'm coming. (*He runs out too.*)

NANNY: (*To audience, friendly.*) Well, time to move on here, I think. I've done all I can do here. So I'll just pack. (*Notices something.*) Oh, she forgot her little red toy. Oh, too bad. (*Picks toy up, reads something on it.*) "Caution. Keep away from children. Contains lead, asbestos, and red dye #2." (*Laughs.*) Well, I guess it isn't meant as a child's toy at all then. (*Looks at it with utter bafflement.*) But what would it be meant as, I wonder? (*Energized by an idea:*) Maybe it *is* a toy, and the cautionary warning is *satiric!* (*Tosses the toy into bassinet.*) Hard to tell. So many mysteries. But children can survive it all, they are sturdy creatures. They ebb and flow, children do; they have great resiliency. (*Warmly.*) They abide and they endure. (*Re-enter John and Helen, holding baby. They are giddy with relief.*)

JOHN: We got it.

NANNY: Oh, did you?

HELEN: Yes, the stupid girl ran right in front of a bus, it ran right over her.

JOHN: Squashed her.

HELEN: Baby was just lucky and fell between the wheels.

NANNY: Oh that was lucky. Children are sturdy creatures, they ebb and flow.
HELEN: The dog was still living, so John pushed it in front of an oncoming car, and now it's dead too.
JOHN: The motorist was *real* angry. But it seemed too complicated to explain, so we just grabbed baby and ran.
HELEN: Thank goodness. (*Looks at baby.*) Baby looks so startled. It's been a busy day, hasn't it? Yessss.
JOHN: Nanny, Helen and I were talking while we ran back here, and things are going to be different now. The immaturities of my youth are over and I'm going to take the responsibility of being a father, and Helen is going to be a mother. And we're not letting anymore crackpots into our home.
HELEN: That's right, John.
JOHN: And so, Nanny, I'm going to have to ask you to leave now. Helen and I have both decided that you're insane.
NANNY: (*Crosses to them.*) When it cries, you hold it. You should feed it regularly. You should keep it clean. Be consistent with it. Don't coo one minute and shout the next.
HELEN: I'm giving up my career as a novelist to care for baby. And any resentment I feel I won't ever show.
NANNY: Well that all sounds excellent. Goodbye, Helen. Goodbye, Tiger.
HELEN: Goodbye, Nanny. We love you.
JOHN: Goodbye. (*Nanny smiles fondly and waves. Then exits.*)
HELEN: (*After a moment.*) Oh, John. I feel so lonely now.
JOHN: We have each other. And baby.
HELEN: That's true. I wish I didn't have a baby and that I had written "Scruples" instead.
JOHN: Well, I wish I were in McLains, but I thought we were going to be positive about things from now on.
HELEN: You're right. I was just kidding. Let's be parents now. Hellooo, baby. (*They put baby back into bassinet.*)
JOHN: (*To baby.*) Helllooo. Baby looks so startled.
HELEN: Well, of course, it's been a terrifying day. Baby had never even seen a bus before, let alone been under one. (*Lovingly, to the baby.*) Don't worry, sweetie pie. Mommy'll protect you from now on. She'll protect you from buses, and from dogs, and from crazy people; and from everything and anything that goes bump in the night.
JOHN: (*Playfully.*) Bump, bump, bump.
HELEN: (*Fondly.*) That's right, John.
JOHN: And Daddy loves you too, my little baked potato.
HELEN: (*Suddenly absolutely furious.*) I TOLD YOU NOT TO CALL IT A BAKED POTATO!!!
JOHN: I'm sorry, I'm sorry. Jesus. You mustn't raise your voice that way around baby. You'll make it deaf or something.

HELEN: I'm sorry. I feel better now.
JOHN: Okay, we'll forget it. (*To baby.*) All over, baby. You're safe now, my little bak- . . . baby. No more shouting. Everything's fine. Can you smile for daddy?
HELEN: Or mommy?
JOHN: Can you smile for mommy and daddy? Here's a nice little red toy. (*Holds up the red toy.*) Won't that make you smile? Huh? Oh why won't it smile? SMILE, damn it, SMILE!
HELEN: Smile, baby!
BOTH: (*Angry.*) SMILE! SMILE! SMILE! SMILE!
HELEN: (*Pleased.*) Oh, John, look, it's smiling.
JOHN: That's right, baby.
HELEN: Do you think it's just pretending to smile to humor us?
JOHN: I think it's too young to be that complicated.
HELEN: Yes, but why would it smile at us when we shouted at it?
JOHN: I don't know. Maybe it's insane.
HELEN: I wonder which it is. Insane, or humoring us?
JOHN: Look, it's still smiling. Maybe it likes the toy. Do you like the toy, baby? Here, you play with it a while, baby. It makes a funny noise, doesn't it? Tingle tangle. Tingle tangle. (*The baby throws the toy out of the bassinet.*) Oh, it doesn't like the toy.
HELEN: What a fussy baby. (*Playfully.*) Fussy baby. Fussy baby.
JOHN: (*Happy.*) Oh, it's still smiling.
HELEN: Fussy baby.
JOHN: Fussy wussy wussy.
BOTH: (*Fondly.*) Fussy wussy wussy baby. Fussy wussy wussy baby. (*Lights dim.*)

ACT TWO

Scene 1

> A park bench. Three women in park playground. The sounds of children playing. On the bench are: Helen, the mother from the previous scenes; she is looking straight ahead, smoking a cigarette, and seems unhappy, hostile. Next to her, and presently not paying attention to her, are Angela, a sweet, drably dressed woman (can be played by same actress who played Cynthia in first part, though try to make her plain) and Kate, a bright, sharp-tongued woman with a scarf tied around her head (she can be played by same actress who played Nanny, but try to make her look noticeably different). Angela

and Kate are looking straight out, watching their children, who are placed (in their and our imaginations) out in the audience. Kate is knitting.

KATE: Be careful, Billy!
ANGELA: That's your son?
KATE: Yes. Billy. He has my eyes and mouth, and his father's nose.
ANGELA: (*Looking, squinting.*) Yes, I can see that. Of course, I've never seen your husband's nose, but he does have your mouth and eyes.
KATE: Don't hang upside down, Billy! You'll crack your head open. (*To Angela.*) He's reckless, just like his uncle Fred.
ANGELA: Oh. Is that his favorite uncle?
KATE: No. He's never met Fred. Fred is dead. Is that your little girl?
ANGELA: Yes. Susie. Watch your head, Susie! It's such a full time job looking after children.
KATE: Yes it is. Susie's a pretty child. (*Stares at Angela; suspiciously.*) Is her father very handsome?
ANGELA: Yes. His whole family is very nice looking.
KATE: Oh that's nice. Nobody in our family is particularly good looking. Except for Fred, sort of, though you'd never know it from the way he ended up, all squashed that way.
ANGELA: How did he die?
KATE: Part of the roller skating craze. He didn't know how, and he skated right under a crosstown bus. (*Calls out.*) Be careful, Billy! (*Back to conversation.*) I don't think there's such a thing as a homely child, do you? I mean Billy may well grow up to be *quite* homely, but right now he's really very cute. And your daughter is downright pretty.
ANGELA: Thank you. (*Calls.*) Be careful of your face, Susie. Don't fall down on it.
HELEN: I have a child too, you know.
KATE: What?
HELEN: No one has asked me about my child.
KATE: Well no one was talking to you.
HELEN: Well I'm a human being. I deserve courtesy.
KATE: Where is your child?
HELEN: That's her lying on the ground. (*Calls.*) Get up, Daisy! Stop acting like a lump.
KATE: What's the matter with her?
HELEN: She's very depressed. She falls asleep all the time. You put her in the bathtub, she falls asleep. You put her on the toilet, she falls asleep. She's a depressing child. Get up, Daisy! Maybe one of the boys would poke her for me.
ANGELA: Maybe she has narcolepsy.
HELEN: You get that from a veneral disease, don't you? You're trying to say something nasty about me, aren't you?

ANGELA: Narcolepsy is a disease. Where people fall asleep. You should take your daughter to a doctor.
HELEN: All diseases are psychological. I'm not going to waste money on some dumb doctor who can't do anything about anything. She sleeps because she doesn't want to be awake. She has no "joie de vivre." GET UP, DAISY! Hey, you, boy, the one with the stick . . . can you get my daughter up?
KATE: (*Staring; after a bit.*) Billy, don't put the stick there, that's nasty.
ANGELA: Why isn't she moving?
HELEN: She's willful. GET UP YOU LUMP OF CLAY! (*To boy.*) Tug her hair a little.
KATE: Billy, leave the little girl alone and go play on the jungle gym. (*To Helen.*) I don't want you encouraging my son to pick on women. That's not a very good thing to teach.
ANGELA: She still hasn't moved. Maybe she's fainted.
HELEN: She just does this to annoy me. It's very successful. (*Calls.*) YOU'RE VERY SUCCESSFUL; DAISY. YOU'RE GETTING THROUGH. (*Back to them.*) It's passive aggression. I do it with my husband. He says to me, did you make dinner, I lie down on the rug and don't move. He says, get up, I don't move a muscle. He gets on top of me and starts to screw me, I pretend it isn't happening. She gets it from me. (*Yells.*) DO AS I SAY NOT AS I DO, DAISY, I'VE TOLD YOU THAT!
KATE: That's no way to bring up a child.
HELEN: What do you know? Do you want a fat lip? Don't cross me, I could do something terrible to your child.
KATE: What did you say?
HELEN: (*Suddenly coy and girlish.*) Oh nothing. My bark's worse than my bite. (*Calls viciously.*) Get up, Daisy! (*Sings, to Daisy, rather sweetly.*)
Daisy, Daisy,
Give me your answer, do,
I'm half crazy,
All for the love of you . . .
(*Hostile, to Kate & Angela.*) Sing. (*They hesitate.*) SING!
ALL THREE: (*Kate & Angela, uncomfortable.*)
It won't be a stylish marriage,
I can't afford a carriage,
But you'll look sweet . . . HELEN: (*Echoing.*) Sweet.
Upon the seat . . . HELEN: Seat.
Of a bicycle built for two.
HELEN: Did she move?
ANGELA: I think her arm twitched a little.
HELEN: Oh, I bet she heard it. She loves that song. Don't you, Daisy? Well, I have to go home now. (*Sweetly.*) Goodbye. (*Calls out to Daisy.*) Get up, Daisy, we're going home, mother can't stand the park another minute. Get

up! (*Getting wild.*) Get up, damn you, get up! All right, Daisy, I'll give you til five and then I'm gonna step on your back. You listening? 1. . . . 2. . . . 3. . . .

ANGELA: Get up, Daisy.

HELEN: . . . 4. . . . 4½. . . . 4¾. . . . Oh, look, there she goes.

KATE: My God, she's running *fast*. (*They turn their heads in unison quickly, watching Daisy run out of sight.*)

HELEN: She's like that. Very inconsistent. One minute catatonic, the next minute she *moves* like a comet.

ANGELA: My God, she's running right toward that bus!

HELEN: Yes, she's always been drawn to buses. She's always running right out in front of them. Usually the driver stops in time.

KATE: My God, it's going to hit her!

HELEN: Well, it'll probably be fine. (*Kate & Angela watch horrified, then there's a shriek of brakes, and they relax, horrified but relieved.*)

KATE: Thank God.

ANGELA: It came so close.

HELEN: This happens all the time. I get quite used to it. (*Suddenly switches to real maternal feelings, gets very upset.*) Oh my God, Daisy. Oh my God, she was almost killed. Oh God. Oh God. (*Weeps.*) Daisy, I'm coming, darling, don't move, honey, mommy's coming. (*Runs off, very upset.*)

KATE: Good grief.

ANGELA: Well, at least the child's safe.

KATE: Do you think we should do something?

ANGELA: What do you mean?

KATE: I don't know. Contact social welfare or something.

ANGELA: I don't know. Maybe it's not her child. Maybe she's only babysitting.

KATE: I don't think so.

ANGELA: I don't think we should get involved.

KATE: Alright, we won't do anything about her. We'll wait until we read about the child *dead* in the newspaper.

ANGELA: I read about that child they found dismembered in the garbage cans outside the 21 Club. CBS is going to make a TV movie about it.

KATE: I don't think television should exploit the sufferings of real people like that.

ANGELA: But they've got all those hours of programming to do. They've got to fill it up with something.

KATE: I suppose.

ANGELA: I wouldn't like to be a television executive. You'd have to have ideas all the time, and then after a while if people don't like your ideas, they fire you.

KATE: This is really off the point of what we should do about that poor child.

ANGELA: I don't like to think about it.
KATE: Well, that won't help the child.
ANGELA: I don't like to concentrate on one thing for too long a period of time. It makes my brain hurt.
KATE: I don't think either the mother or the child are mentally well.
ANGELA: No, they're probably not, but who is nowadays? Everything's so outside our control. Chemical explosions in Elizabeth, New Jersey. Somebody killed Karen Silkwood. There are all these maniacs stalking Dolly Parton, the poor woman doesn't feel like *singing* anymore. John Hinkley, David Berkowitz, Ronald Reagan. It's so difficult to maintain "joie de vivre" in the face of such universal discouragement. (*Looks glum for a moment.*) I have to take a mood elevator. (*Takes a pill.*) I have this pharmacist friend, he gives me all sorts of things. I should be cheerful in a few minutes. (*Waits for pill to take effect.*)
KATE: (*Edging away.*) Well, fine. We'll do nothing then. I'll look forward to the CBS movie about the child under the bus. (*Calls.*) Come on, Billy, we're going home. *Billy!* Don't put the stick there, that's rude. Leave Susie alone. (*Shocked.*) Billy! Don't put *that* there either, that's *very* rude. Now put that back. (*To Angela.*) I'm sorry. He's just that age now.
ANGELA: Oh that's all right. He probably meant it affectionately. I always think sex and affection are somehow connected, don't you?
KATE: Well, no, not really.
ANGELA: Oh, I do. People need affection, you know. Susie, come give mommy a hug. (*Lights dim.*)

Scene 2

> Back in the home of Helen and John. The room, though, is filled with many toys, some of them broken. There is also a pile of what seems to be laundry in clear audience view. Two little legs with red sneakers are partially visible, sticking out of the laundry pile. John and Helen are talking.

JOHN: Well, I'm very upset. That's all I can say.
HELEN: I know. You've said that, you've said that. Get on with it.
JOHN: I mean, I just don't think we're good parents.
HELEN: Why do you say that? Did the bus run over the child? No. Did a bus run over her last week? No.
JOHN: Why does she keep running to buses? What's the matter with her?
HELEN: Nothing is the matter with her. She's just depressed. We have to cheer her up. (*Crosses to pile of laundry, speaks to it.*) Cheer up, Daisy! You're depressing us.
JOHN: And why does she lie in this pile of laundry all the time? Do you think that's normal?
HELEN: Daisy is just going through a phase. She thinks she's an inanimate object. She thinks she's a baked potato because of what you said to her

when she was a baby. (*To pile of laundry.*) You're not a baked potato, sweet pea. You're mommy's little darling. Mommy loves you. Mommy doesn't mind that she's not a novelist or that she's stayed in a bad marriage just for your sake. She's willing to make that sacrifice. (*Stares at laundry.*) Uh, you see how unresponsive she is. It's enough to make you want to shake and bake her.

JOHN: Helen, we can't talk about the child that way. Did you hear what you just said?

HELEN: I was making a point, John. I'm not talking about actually cooking her. You have no sense of irony. (*To Daisy.*) We're not going to eat you, Daisy. Mommy was speaking figuratively.

JOHN: Speaking of shake and bake, have you made dinner yet?

HELEN: Have I made *dinner* yet? (*Very nasty, utterly furious.*) Well, now, let me see. I can't remember. You were at unemployment, and then I was at the playground, and then Daisy tried to run in front of a bus—now I remember all these events . . . but as to dinner. I'm going to have to lie down and think. (*She lies down on the floor and won't move.*)

JOHN: Helen, don't do this again. You know it makes me furious. Helen, stop staring at the ceiling. Helen! HELEN! (*Stares; has quick fit.*) GODDAM IT! (*Takes one of Daisy's toys, smashes it.*) I've smashed one of Daisy's toys, Helen, do you want me to smash another one? Helen, get up! Look at me. All right, Helen, I'm going to smash another one of her toys . . . (*Hears himself.*) Good God, listen to me. What's happened to us? Helen, we're ruining that poor child. I'm going to take her and leave you. We've got to get away from you. (*Goes to pile of laundry.*) Get up, Daisy, Daddy loves you. Daisy, get up. (*Sings sweetly.*) Daisy, Daisy . . . GODDAM IT, GET UP! (*Starts to tie laundry and Daisy into a manageable bundle.*) Okay, Daisy, I'll just have to carry you. Helen, I'm taking Daisy and the laundry and we're leaving you. (*Slings laundry over his shoulder.*) I don't know where we're going, but we've got to get away. Helen, can you hear me? Helen, we're leaving you. Goodbye.

HELEN: (*Sits up.*) And you'll never get any of the paperback rights! (*Lies down again.*)

JOHN: There aren't any paperback rights, Helen! You live in a fool's paradise. We're leaving now. (*Starts to leave.*) I don't know where we're going, but we're going somewhere. (*Stops.*) I just need a drink first, though. Where's the vodka, Helen? Helen? (*Puts laundry down.*) Daisy, do you know where the vodka is? Daisy? Helen? Daisy? Helen? GODDAM IT, I'M TALKING TO YOU PEOPLE, ARE YOU DEAF? (*Sits on floor.*) Oh God, how did I get in this position? Where is the vodka?

HELEN: (*Sits up.*) It's in the toy duck. (*Does speech exercise.*) Toy duck, toy duck, toy duck. (*Lies down again.*)

JOHN: Oh right. Thank you. (*Goes to toy duck, reaches into it, takes out bottle of vodka.*) Why can't we have a liquor cabinet like normal people? (*Takes a big couple of swallows from the vodka.*) Want some, Helen? (*No response.*) Daisy?

Daisy? (*Bitter.*) She's not a baked potato, she's a 20 per cent cotton, 80 per cent polyester pile of . . . (*At a loss.*) pooka-poo.
HELEN: (*Sits up.*) Pooka-poo, pooka-poo. Toy duck. Toy duck. Polly wolly windbag! Polly wolly windbag! Mee, mae, mah, moh, moo. Mee, mae, mah, moh, moo.
JOHN: Oh, Helen, you're talking again. I'm sorry I asked you about dinner. Want a cocktail?
HELEN: Thanks I'm too tired. (*Lies down.*)
JOHN: (*Sings.*)
Daisy, daisy, give me your answer, do . . .
(*Next song.*)
Hush, little baby, don't you cry,
Mamma's gonna give you a big black eye . . .
HELEN: (*Lying down, but calm.*) John, those aren't the lyrics.
JOHN: I know. I just don't know the lyrics. (*Sings.*)
And if that big black eye turns purple . . .
Mama's gonna give you a . . .
(*Spoken.*) What rhymes with purple?
HELEN: (*Sits up.*) I don't know. I'm not a rhyming dictionary. Ask Daisy.
JOHN: Daisy, honey, what rhymes with purple? Daisy? Daisy, what rhymes with purple? Daisy? (*Listens; apparently hears an answer.*) She says she doesn't know.
HELEN: (*Slightly hopeful.*) Well at least she spoke today. That's *some*thing.
JOHN: (*Cheered.*) Yes, that is something. (*Drinks. Lights fade.*)

Scene 3

A desk and chair. The Principal is seated. She is dressed handsomely, but looks somewhat severe.

PRINCIPAL: (*To intercom.*) You can send Miss Pringle in now, Henry. (*Enter Miss Pringle, a sympathetic-looking teacher.*) I love having a male secretary. It makes it all worth while. (*Into intercom.*) Sharpen all the pencils please, Henry. Then check the coffee pot. Hello, Miss Pringle, how are you?
MISS PRINGLE: I'm fine, Mrs. Willoughby, but I wanted to talk to you about Daisy Dingleberry.
PRINCIPAL: Oh yes, that peculiar child who's doing so well on the track team.
MISS PRINGLE: Yes, she runs very quickly, but I felt I should . . .
PRINCIPAL: Wait a moment, would you? (*Into intercom.*) Oh, Henry, check if we have enough non-dairy creamer for the coffee, would you? Then I want you to go out and buy my husband a birthday present for me, I don't have time. Thank you, sweetie. (*Back to Pringle.*) Now, I'm sorry, what were you saying?
MISS PRINGLE: Well, I'm worried about Daisy. She's doing very well in

track, and some days she does well in her classes, and then some days she just stares, and then she's absent a lot.

PRINCIPAL: Yes. Uh huh. Uh huh. Yes, I see. Uh huh. Uh huh. Go on.

MISS PRINGLE: Well, it's her summer essay, you know . . . "What I Did Last Summer"?

PRINCIPAL: (*With great interest.*) What did you do?

MISS PRINGLE: No, no, no, it's the *topic* of the essay: what you did last summer.

PRINCIPAL: Mr. Willoughby and I went to the New Jersey sea shore. He was brought up there. It brings back fond memories of his childhood. Bouncing on his mother's knee. Being hugged, being kissed. Mmmmmm. Mmmmmm. (*Makes kissing sounds, hugs herself; into intercom.*) Henry, sweetie, I want you to buy my husband underwear. Pink. The bikini kind. Calvin Klein, or something like that. Or you could use your "Ah Men" catalog if it wouldn't take too long. Mr. Willoughby is a medium. Thank you, Henry. (*To Pringle.*) I'm sorry, what were you saying?

MISS PRINGLE: About Daisy's essay.

PRINCIPAL: What about it?

MISS PRINGLE: Well . . .

PRINCIPAL: Wait a moment, would you? (*To intercom.*) Henry, I mean Mr. Willoughby is a medium *size*, I don't mean he holds seances. (*Laughs; to Pringle.*) I didn't want there to be any misunderstanding. I don't think there was, but just in case. I myself am into black magic. (*Takes out a black candle. To intercom.*) Henry, I have taken out a black candle and I am thinking of you. (*To Pringle.*) Do you have a match?

MISS PRINGLE: No, I'm sorry. About Daisy's essay.

PRINCIPAL: I'm all ears.

MISS PRINGLE: Well . . .

PRINCIPAL: Which is a figure of speech. As you can indeed see, I am a great deal more than just ears. I have a head, a neck, a trunk, a lower body, legs and feet. (*To intercom.*) I have legs and feet, Henry. I hope you're working quickly.

MISS PRINGLE: Pay attention to me! Focus your mind on what I'm saying! I do not have all day.

PRINCIPAL: Yes, I'm sorry, I will. You're right. Oh, I *admire* strong women. I've always been afraid I might actually be a lesbian, but I've never had any opportunity to experiment with that side of myself. You're not interested, are you? You're single. Perhaps you *are* a lesbian.

MISS PRINGLE: I'm not a lesbian, thank you, anyway.

PRINCIPAL: Neither am I. I just thought maybe I was. (*Into intercom.*) Henry, you don't think I'm a lesbian, do you? (*Listens.*) The intercom only works one way, it needs to be repaired. Of course, Henry's a mute anyway.

MISS PRINGLE: Mrs. Willoughby, please, put your hand over your mouth for a moment and don't say anything.

PRINCIPAL: I'm all ears. (*Puts her hand over her mouth.*)

MISS PRINGLE: Good, thank you. I was disturbed by Daisy's essay. I want you to listen to it. "What I Did For My Summer Vacation." By Daisy Dingleberry. "Dark, dank rags. Wet, fetid towels. A large German shepherd, its innards splashed across the windshield of a car. Is this a memory? Is it a dream? I am trapped, I am trapped, how to escape. I try to kill myself, but the buses always stop. Old people and children get discounts on buses, but still no one will ever kill me. How did I even learn to speak, it's amazing. I am a baked potato. I am a summer squash. I am a vegetable. I am an inanimate object who from time to time can run very quickly, but I am not really alive. Help, help, help. I am drowning, I am drowning, my lungs fill with the summer ocean, but still I do not die, this awful life goes on and on, can no one rescue me." (*Miss Pringle and Principal stare at one another.*) What do you think I should do?

PRINCIPAL: I'd give her an A. I think it's very good. The style is good, it rambles a bit, but it's unexpected. It's sort of an intriguing combination of Donald Barthelme and Sesame Street. All that "I am a baked potato" stuff. I liked it.

MISS PRINGLE: Yes, but don't you think the child needs help?

PRINCIPAL: Well, a good editor would give her some pointers, granted, but I think she's a long way from publishing yet. I feel she should stay in school, keep working on her essays, the school track team needs her, there's no one who runs as fast. I think this is all premature, Miss Pringle.

MISS PRINGLE: I feel she should see the school psychologist.

PRINCIPAL: I am the school psychologist.

MISS PRINGLE: What happened to Mr. Byers?

PRINCIPAL: I fired him. I thought a woman would be better suited for the job.

MISS PRINGLE: But do you have a degree in psychology?

PRINCIPAL: I imagine I do. I can have Henry check if you insist. Are you sure you're not a lesbian? I think you're too forceful, it's unfeminine. And I think you're picking on this poor child. She shows signs of promising creativity, and first you try to force her into premature publishing, and now you want to send her to some awful headshrinker who'll rob her of all her creativity in the name of some awful God of normalcy. Well, Miss Pringle, here's what I have to say to you: I will not let you rob Daisy Dingleberry of her creativity, she will not see a psychologist as long as she is in this school, and you are hereby fired from your position as teacher in this school. Good day! (*To intercom.*) Henry, come remove Miss Pringle bodily from my office, sweetie, would you?

MISS PRINGLE: No need to do that. I can see myself out. Let me just say that I think you are insane, and I am sorry you are in a position of power.

PRINCIPAL: Yes, but I *am* in a position of power! (*To intercom.*) Aren't I, Henry? Now get out of here before I start to become violent.

MISS PRINGLE: I am sorry you will not let me help this child.

PRINCIPAL: Help this child! She may be the next Virginia Woolf, the next Sylvia Plath.
MISS PRINGLE: Dead, you mean.
PRINCIPAL: (*Screams.*) Who cares if she's dead as long as she publishes? Now, get out of here! (*Blackout.*)

Scene 4

>   *A blank stage, a simple white spot. From a loudspeaker at the back of the auditorium we hear a male voice—serious, sympathetic in a detached, business-like manner.*

VOICE: Come in please. (*Enter a young man in a simple, modest dress. His haircut, shoes and socks, though, are traditionally masculine. He looks out to the back of the auditorium to where the voice is originating from. The young man seems shy, polite, tentative.*) State your name please.
YOUNG MAN: Daisy.
VOICE: How old are you?
DAISY: I'm seventeen.
VOICE: I wish I had gotten your case earlier. Why are you wearing a dress?
DAISY: Oh, I'm sorry, am I? (*Looks, is embarrassed.*) I didn't realize. I know I'm a boy . . . young man. It's just I was so used to wearing dresses for so long that some mornings I wake up and I just forget. (*Thoughtfully, somewhat to himself.*) I should really just clear all the dresses out of my closet.
VOICE: Why did you used to wear dresses?
DAISY: Well that's how my parents dressed me. They said they didn't know what sex I was, but it had to be one of two, so they made a guess, and they just guessed wrong.
VOICE: Are your genitals in any way misleading?
DAISY: No, I don't believe so. I don't think my parents ever really looked. They didn't want to intrude. It was a kind of politeness on their part. My mother is sort of delicate, and my father rests a lot.
VOICE: Did you think they acted out of politeness?
DAISY: Well, probably. It all got straightened out eventually. When I was eleven, I came across this medical book that had pictures in it, and I realized I looked more like a boy than a girl, but my mother had always wanted a girl or a best seller, and I didn't want to disappoint her. But then somedays, I don't know what gets into me, I would just feel like striking out at them. So I'd wait til she was having one of her crying fits, and I took the book to her—I was twelve now—and I said, "Have you ever seen this book? Are you totally insane? Why have you named me Daisy? Everyone else has always said I was a boy, what's the *matter* with you?" And she kept crying and she said something about Judith Krantz and something

about being out of Shake-n-Bake chicken, and then she said, "I want to die"; and then she said, *Perhaps* you're a boy, but we don't want to jump to any hasty conclusions, so why don't we just wait, and we'd see if I menstruated or not. And I asked her what that word meant, and she slapped me and washed my mouth out with soap. Then she apologized and hugged me, and said she was a bad mother. Then she washed *her* mouth out with soap. Then she tied me to the kitchen table and turned on all the gas jets, and said it would be just a little while longer for the both of us. Then my father came home and he turned off the gas jets and untied me. Then when he asked if dinner was ready, she lay on the kitchen floor and wouldn't move, and he said, I guess not, and then he sort of crouched next to the refrigerator and tried to read a book, but I don't think he was really reading, because he never turned any of the pages. And then eventually, since nothing else seemed to be happening, I just went to bed. (*Fairly long pause.*)

VOICE: How did you feel about this?

DAISY: Well I knew something was wrong with them. But then they meant well, and I felt that somewhere in all that, they actually cared for me—after all, she washed *her* mouth with soap too, and he untied me. And so I forgave them because they meant well. I tried to understand them. I felt sorry for them. I considered suicide.

VOICE: That's the end of the first session. (*Lights change. In view of the audience, Daisy removes his girl's clothing and changes into men's clothing—pants and a shirt, maybe a sweater. As he changes we hear the "Hush little baby" theme played rather quickly, as on a speeded-up music box. The change should be as fast and as simple as possible. Lights come up and focus on Daisy again.*) This is your second session. How old are you?

DAISY: I'm nineteen now.

VOICE: Why have you waited two years between your first and second sessions? And you never called to cancel them. I've been waiting here for two years.

DAISY: I'm sorry. I should have called. I was just too depressed to get here. And I'm in college now, and I've owed this paper on Jonathan Swift and "Gulliver's Travels" for one and a half *years*. I keep trying to write it, but I just have this terrible problem *beginning* it.

VOICE: In problems of this sort, it's best to begin at the beginning, follow through to the middle, and continue on until the ending.

DAISY: Ah, well, I've tried that. But I don't seem to get very far. I'm still on the first sentence. Jonathan Swift's "Gulliver's Travels" is a biting, bitter work that . . ." I keep getting stuck on the "That."

VOICE: I see you're wearing men's clothing today.

DAISY: (*With a sense of decisiveness.*) I threw all my dresses away. And I'm going to change my name from Daisy. I'm considering Francis or Hilliary or Marion.

VOICE: Any other names?
DAISY: Rocky.
VOICE: Have you seen your parents lately?
DAISY: I try not to. They call me and they cry and so on, but I hold the receiver away from my ear. And then I go next to the refrigerator and I crouch for several days.
VOICE: How are you doing in school?
DAISY: I'm not even sure I'm *registered*. It's not just the Jonathan Swift paper I owe. I owe a paper comparing a George Herbert poem with a Shakespeare sonnet; I owe a paper on characterization in "The Canterbury Tales"; and an essay on the American character as seen in Henry James' "Daisy Miller." (*Daisy looks off into the distance, and sings softly.*)
Daisy, Daisy,
Give me your answer, do,
I'm half-crazy . . .
(*He looks grave, sad, repeats the line:*)
I'm half-crazy . . .
(*His sadness increases, he speaks slowly:*)
" 'I am half-sick of shadows,' said the Lady of Shallot."
VOICE: You sound like an English major.
DAISY: (*His attention returns to the voice.*) Yes. I learned a certain love of literature from my parents. My mother is a writer. She is the author of the Cliff Notes to "Scruples" and "Princess Daisy." And my father liked reading. When he was next to the refrigerator, he would often read. I like reading. I have this eerie dream, though, sometimes that I'm a baby in my crib and somebody is reading aloud to me from what I think is "Mommie Dearest," and then this great big dog keeps snarling at me, and then this enormous truck or bus or something drops down from the sky, and it kills me. (*With a half-joking, half-serious disappointment he's not dead.*) Then I always wake up.
VOICE: That's the end of our second session. (*The lights change abruptly. From now on, these abrupt light changes—probably a center spot with side lighting that switches side to side on each change—will represent time passing and finding Daisy in the midst of other sessions. There should not be blackouts, and though Daisy should speak only once the lighting shift has completed, these changes should happen quickly.*)
DAISY: Doctor, I'm so depressed I can hardly talk on the phone. It's like I can only function two hours a day at maximum. I have this enormous desire to feel absolutely nothing.
VOICE: That's the end of our third session. (*Lights change abruptly.*)
DAISY: You know, when I *do* get up, I sleep with people obsessively. I'm always checking people out on the street to see who I can sleep with.
VOICE: Eventually you'll get a lot of venereal diseases.
DAISY: I know, I already have. It's just that during the sex, there's always

10 or 20 seconds during which I forget *who I am* and *where I am*. And that's why I'm so obsessive. But it's ridiculous to spend hours and hours seeking sex just really in order to find those 10 or 20 seconds. It's so *time-consuming!* I mean, no wonder I never get that paper on "Gulliver's Travels" done.

VOICE: Oh, you still haven't done that paper?

DAISY: No. I've been a freshman for five years now. I'm never going to graduate. At registration every fall, people just laugh at me.

VOICE: That's the end of our 53rd session. See you Tuesday. (*Lights change.*)

DAISY: (*Incensed.*) I mean it's the *inconsistency* I hate them most for! One minute they're cooing and cuddling and feeding me Nyquil, and the next minute they're turning on the gas jets, or lying on the floor, or threatening to step on my back. How *dare* they treat me like that? What's the matter with them! I didn't ask to be brought into the world. If they didn't know how to raise a child, they should have gotten a dog; or a kitten—they're more independent—or a *gerbil!* But left me *unborn.*

VOICE: That's the end of our 215th session. (*Lights change.*)

DAISY: I passed this couple on the street yesterday, and they had this four year old walking between them, and the two parents were fighting and you could just *tell* that they were insane. And I wanted to snatch that child from them and . . .

VOICE: And what?

DAISY: I don't know. Hurl it in front of a car, I guess. It was too late to save it. But at least it would be dead.

VOICE: That's the end of our 377th session. (*Lights change.*)

DAISY: (*Worn out by years of talking.*) Look, I suppose my parents aren't actually evil, and maybe my plan of hiring a hit person to kill them is going too far. They're not evil, they're just disturbed. And they mean well. *But meaning well is not enough.*

VOICE: How's your "Gulliver's Travels" paper going?

DAISY: I'm too depressed.

VOICE: I'm afraid I'm going to be on vacation next week.

DAISY: (*Unwilling to discuss this.*) I'm not happy with my present name.

VOICE: I'll just be gone a week.

DAISY: I wore a dress last week.

VOICE: I won't be gone that long.

DAISY: And I slept with thirty people.

VOICE: I hope you enjoyed it.

DAISY: And I can't be responsible for what I might do next week.

VOICE: Please, *please,* I need a vacation.

DAISY: All right, all right, take your stupid vacation. I just hope it rains.

VOICE: You're trying to manipulate me.

DAISY: Yes, but I mean well. (*Lights change. Very dark, a very pessimistic anger.*) Doctor. I've been in therapy with you for *ten* years now. I have been a college freshman for six years, and a college sophomore for four years. The National Defense loan I have taken to pay for this idiotic education will take me a *lifetime* to repay. (*His voice sounds lost.*) I don't know. I just feel sort of, well, stuck.

VOICE: Yes?

DAISY: Oh. And I had another memory I'd forgotten, something else my parents did to me. It was during that period I stayed in the laundry pile.

VOICE: (*His voice betraying a tiny touch of having had enough.*) Yes?

DAISY: My mother had promised me I could have ice cream if I would just stand up for ten minutes and not lie in the laundry, and then when I did stand up for ten minutes, it turned out she had forgotten she was defrosting the refrigerator and the ice cream was all melted. (*Sighs.*) I mean, it was so typical of her. (*Suddenly starts to get heated up.*) She had a college education. *Who could forget they were defrosting the refrigerator???* I mean, don't you just hate her?

VOICE: How old are you?

DAISY: Twenty-seven.

VOICE: Don't you think it's about time you let go of all this?

DAISY: What?

VOICE: Don't you think you should move on with your life? Yes, your parents were impossible, but that's already happened. It's time to move on. Why don't you do your damn "Gulliver's Travels" paper? Why don't you decide on a name? My secretary has writer's cramp from changing your records from Rocky to Butch to Cain to Abel to Tootsie to Raincloud to Elizabeth the First to Elizabeth the Second to PONCHITTA PEARCE TO MARY BAKER EDDY! I mean, we know you had a rough start, but PULL YOURSELF TOGETHER! You're smart, you have resources, you can't blame them forever. MOVE ON WITH IT! (*Daisy has listened to the above embarrassed and uncomfortable, not certain how to respond. Then:*)

DAISY: FUCK YOU! (*Blackout.*)

Scene 5

> *The home of John and Helen. A big box with a bow on it; on top of it a smaller box with a bow on it. A large banner that says, "Happy Birthday, Ponchitta." John has two bottles of vodka, Helen is using a Vicks inhaler.*

HELEN: (*Inhaling.*) Mmmmmmm, I love this aroma. It almost makes me wish I had a cold. (*Inhales.*) Mmmmmm, delicious. Oh, there are pleasurable things in life. (*Calls off-stage.*) Daisy, dear, are you almost ready? We want to see how you look in your present.

JOHN: I thought his name was Ponchitta. (*Pronounced: Pon–cheat–a.*)

HELEN: John, we've been telling you all day, he called himself Ponchitta only for the month of March several years ago. He's been calling himself Charles Kuralt for the last several years, and now that he's turned thirty, as a gift to me, he's decided to go back to the name of Daisy. (*Calls.*) Daisy! We're waiting for you.

JOHN: I wish someone would've told me. I would've changed the banner.

HELEN: The banner's a lovely gesture, John. We all appreciate it. No one gives a fuck what's on it. I'm sorry, I don't mean to swear. No one gives a shit what's on it. Daisy, dear! Mommy and Daddy want to see you in your present. (*Enter Daisy, wearing a Scottish kilt; he looks somewhat pained, but has decided to be polite and not make waves. He holds his pants.*)

HELEN: (*Admiring the kilt.*) Ohhhhh. Do you like it, dear?

DAISY: I'm not certain.

HELEN: Now it's not a dress, I want to make that very clear. It's a Scottish *kilt*. Scottish *men* wear them in the highlands, and all that air is wonderful for your potency if you're wearing boxer shorts rather than those awful jockey shorts that destroy your semen. Isn't that so, John?

JOHN: I wasn't listening.

HELEN: (*Making the best of things.*) That's right, you weren't listening. None of us were. All our heads were elsewhere. (*To Daisy.*) Your father's become a Christian scientist, and we're all so pleased. Now when he cuts himself, we don't even put a bandaid on him, we just watch him bleed.

JOHN: (*Cheerful, telling a fun anecdote.*) Cut myself this morning. Shaving. A nasty slice on the bottom of my foot. Between the vodka and the dalmane and then the weight of the razor, I fell right over. (*Laughs.*) Then trying to get up, I sliced my foot. Mother wouldn't let me put a bandaid on because she thinks I've become a Christian scientist.

HELEN: (*Firmly.*) That's right. That's what I do think. Ponchitta, dear, I'm sorry, I mean Daisy, you're so silent. Do you like your birthday present?

DAISY: Did you give this to me because you thought I'd like it because you're insane, or did you give it to me as a sort of nasty barb to remind me that you dressed me as a girl the first fifteen years of my life?

HELEN: (*Sincerely.*) I gave it to you because I thought you'd like it. Because I'm insane. I'm insane because I stayed in a bad marriage and didn't do what I was supposed to do with my life. But I'm not bitter. And now that your father's become a Christian scientist, I'm going to become a Jehovah's Witness and go to the supermarket *forcing* people to take copies of "The Watchtower." Perhaps "The Watchtower" will publish me. Certainly somebody has to, someday.

JOHN: Your mother's going through a religious phase. Cocktail, anyone? (*Offers one of the bottles.*)

HELEN: Your father calls drinking from a bottle a cocktail. It's sort of adorable really. No, dear, but you have one. Oh, I'm enjoying life so much today. And you've turned thirty, and that means I'm getting nearer to death and have wasted my youth—oh, it cheers me up. Happy birthday, dear. (*Kisses Daisy.*)

JOHN: He hasn't opened up his other presents.

HELEN: Yes, Daisy dear, we have other presents. Here's one. (*Daisy puts his pants down on the couch and opens small box. It's a can, which when opened a large "snake" pops out of, just as happened to baby in first scene. Daisy is startled. Helen and John laugh in delight.*) Daisy always loved surprises. And now open the bigger box. (*Daisy opens bigger box—Nanny comes springing out of the box, shrieking, much like the snake did. Daisy falls over backward.*)

NANNY: AAAAAAAAAAAAAGGGGGGHHHHH!!! Whoogie! Whoogie! Whoogie! Surprise!!!!!

HELEN: Everybody sing!

HELEN, JOHN & NANNY: (*Sing, to the tune of "Frere Jacques."*)
Happy birthday, happy birthday,
Daisy dear, Daisy dear,
Happy, happy birthday,
Happy, happy birthday,
Happy birthday, happy birthday.

DAISY: *Who is this???*

NANNY: I'm your Auntie Mame! (*Laughs.*) No, just kidding. I'm the ANTICHRIST! (*Laughs.*) No, just kidding. (*Fondly.*) I'm your Auntie Nanny. (*Helen brings Daisy over to Nanny, who remains in the box.*)

HELEN: This is Nanny. Don't you remember Nanny?

DAISY: I remember something. God knows what. Why did you sing "Happy Birthday" to the wrong melody?

HELEN: Well, Nanny told us you have to pay a royalty to sing the real "Happy Birthday" melody. The selfish people who wrote the stupid melody don't have to lift a finger for the rest of their fucking lives, while I have to sweat and slave over the Cliff Notes to "The Thorn Birds." (*Pause.*) And all because your father has never been able to earn a living. (*Looks at John; says with total, grim sincerity:*) Oh why don't you just keel over and die? (*Laughs.*) Ha, ha, just kidding, I'm fine.

NANNY: (*To Daisy, in babytalk voice.*) Hellllooooo. Hellllooooo. What pwetty bwue eyes oo have. Cooooo. Cooooo. (*Suddenly.*) SHUT UP! Comin' back to you, honey?

DAISY: Slightly. I try not to remember too much. It doesn't get me anywhere.

JOHN: (*Sings drunkenly, to the correct melody.*) Happy birthday to you, ha- . . .

HELEN: SHUSH! There are spies from ASCAP everywhere. (*John turns his head with some trepidation, looking for the spies.*)

NANNY: It's so nice to see one of my babies grown up. And what a pretty dress. The plaid matches your eyes.

HELEN: It's not a dress, Nanny. It's a *kilt.*

NANNY: Well, whatever it is, it's very becoming.

JOHN: (*Sings.*) Happy birthday . . .

HELEN: Please, John, *please.* (*Starts to get tears in her voice.*) We can't afford to pay the royalty. (*Starts to cry.*)

NANNY: (*To Helen, soothingly.*) There, there. SHUT UP! Ha, ha. (*Helen looks startled; then she and Nanny laugh and embrace.*) Oh, all my babies grow up so strong and healthy, I'm so pleased. What does baby do for a living?

HELEN: He goes to college. He was a freshman for six years, and he's been in sophomore slump for seven years.

NANNY: Thirteen years of college. Baby must be very smart.

HELEN: He's been having trouble writing his Freshman expository writing paper on "Gulliver's Travels." How's that going, Rocky, I'm sorry, I mean Daisy?

DAISY: I finished it. I thought I'd read it to you.

HELEN: Oh, this will be a treat. John, are you still there? John? Daisy is going to read to us.

NANNY: Let me just put on my glasses. (*Puts on her glasses, listens attentively.*)

DAISY: (*Reads from a sheet of paper.*) "'Gulliver's Travels' is a biting, bitter work that . . . depresses me greatly."

HELEN: Oh, I like it so far.

DAISY: "By the end of the book, Gulliver has come to agree with the King of Brobdingnag's assessment that mankind is the quote 'most pernicious race of little odious vermin that nature ever suffered to crawl upon the surface of the earth,' unquote. At the end of the book, Gulliver rejects mankind and decides he prefers the company of horses to humans. We are meant to find Gulliver's disgust with humanity understandable, but also to see that he has by now gone mad. However, I find that I do not wish to write papers analyzing these things anymore as I agree with Gulliver and find most of the world, including teachers, to be less worthwhile to speak to than horses. However, I don't like horses either, so I have decided after thirteen years of schooling that I am not meant to go to college and so I am withdrawing. Fuck your degree, I am going to become a bus driver."

HELEN: Oh I think that's excellent, I think you'll get a very good grade. John, wasn't that good? And how interesting you're going to become a bus driver. You've always been drawn to buses.

NANNY: I love buses too! I adore *all* public transportation. The danger of derailing, the closeness of the people, the smells, the dirt. I'm sort of like a bacteria!—wherever I am, I thrive. (*Smiles at Daisy.*)

DAISY: I'm glad you like the paper. I should also tell you that I'm getting married.

HELEN: (*Taken aback.*) Married? How fascinating. John, I feel you're not participating in this conversation.

JOHN: How do you spell dipsomaniac, I wonder?

HELEN: John, you're too young to write your memoirs. Besides, I'm the writer in the family.

DAISY: I wasn't really intending to get married, but she's pregnant.

HELEN: (*More taken aback.*) Pregnant, how lovely.

JOHN: D-I-P . . .

HELEN: John, participate in your life now. This isn't a spelling bee, this is a parent-child discussion.
DAISY: She's the 1,756th person I've slept with, although only the 877th woman.
HELEN: (*Slight pause.*) This conversation is just so interesting I don't know what to do with it.
DAISY: I don't think I love her, but then I don't use that word; and I do think I like her. And her getting pregnant just seemed sort of a sign that we should go ahead and get married. That, and the fact that I had taken her phone number.
JOHN: S-O-M . . .
NANNY: (*Sings.*) K-E-Y, M-O-U-S-E.
JOHN: Yes, thank you.
NANNY: Well, I think it's marvelous. Congratulations, Daisy.
HELEN: Well, your father and I will have lots of advice to give you. Don't give the baby Nyquil until it's about three. We made a mistake with you.
DAISY: I don't really wish to hear your advice.
HELEN: Well, we listened to your awful paper. You can at least do us the courtesy of listening to whatever garbage we have to say.
JOHN: (*Looks out.*) Oh, dear, here comes that owl again. (*Ducks, bats at air.*)
HELEN: Oh, your father's having problems again. John, dear, try to spell delirium tremens. That's a fun word.
JOHN: Z-B-X . . .
HELEN: No, dear, that's *way* off. Oh, God, he's going to be spelling all night long now. He's impossible to talk to when he's spelling. But, Daisy, you're here, and we'll talk, won't we? I've made you a delicious dinner. I've ordered up Chinese.
DAISY: I don't really think I can stay for dinner.
HELEN: But it's your birthday. I don't like Chinese food. What should I do with it?
DAISY: I hesitate to say.
HELEN: Pardon?
DAISY: I feel I must tell you that I've decided I don't think I should speak to you or father for a few years and see if I become less angry.
HELEN: Angry? Why are you angry?
DAISY: Let me see if I can answer that. (*Thinks.*) No, I don't think I can. Sorry. So, thank you for the kilt, and I better be going.
HELEN: Going?
NANNY: Baby, dear, let me give you some advice before you go. Get a *lot* of medical check-ups. Aside from your promiscuity, your parents exposed you to lead, asbestos, and red dye #2 from this little toy you had. Also, avoid acid rain, dioxin contamination, and any capsule tablets that might have cyanide in them. Try to avoid radiation and third degree burns after the atomic explosions come. And, finally, work on having a sense of

humor. Medically, humor and laughter have been shown to physically help people to cope with the tensions of modern life that can be otherwise internalized, leading to cancer, high blood pressure, and spastic colon. (*Smiles.*) Well! It was very nice to see you, best of luck in the future; and Helen, if you'd just mail me back to Eureeka, California, at your earliest convenience, I'd much appreciate it. (*Nanny disappears back into her box.*)

DAISY: What toy was she talking about?

HELEN: Oh who knows? Nanny's memory is probably starting to go. She must be about 103 or so by now. Resilient woman.

JOHN: D-E-L . . .

HELEN: Oh, delirium. Better start, darling.

JOHN: E-R-I . . .

DAISY: Well, I must be going now.

HELEN: Oh. Oh, stay a little longer, Daisy dear.

DAISY: (*Trying to be kind.*) Very well. (*Sits for about a count of three.*) Well, that's about it. (*Stands again.*) I think I'll just give you this kilt back, and I'll call you in a few years if I feel less hostile.

HELEN: That would be lovely, thank you, Daisy. (*He gives her back the kilt. He picks up his trousers from the couch, but does not take the time to put them on, he just heads for the door. At the door he stops and looks at his mother. She looks hurt and bewildered. He looks at her with regret, and some awful combination of dislike and tenderness.*)

DAISY: (*Softly.*) Goodbye. (*Daisy leaves.*)

HELEN: (*Recites, a great sense of loss in her voice.*)
"How sharper than a serpent's tooth
It is to have an ungrateful child."
John, what's that from?

JOHN: D-E-L . . .

HELEN: What's that *from*, John?

JOHN: E-R-I, M-O-U-S-E. There! But what's delirimouse?

HELEN: God only knows, John. (*John sees the kilt Helen is holding.*)

JOHN: Oh, another kilt.

HELEN: No, dear. Daisy gave it back. He said some very rude things, and then he left.

JOHN: Oh. Maybe he was angry about the banner.

HELEN: (*Sarcastically.*) Yes. Maybe that's it. Nonetheless, "to err is human, to forgive, divine." What's that from?

JOHN: "Bartlett's Famous Quotations."

HELEN: Oh, you're just *useless*. Nanny, what's that from? Also, "how sharper than a serpent's tongue"—"tooth!"—what's that from?

NANNY: (*From within box; irritated.*) I have nothing more to say. Send me to the post office.

HELEN: Send me to the post office. What an orderly life Nanny leads. How I envy that.

JOHN: Uh oh. (*Ducks another owl.*)
HELEN: They're low-flying little beasts, aren't they, John? John, I wonder if I'm too old to have another baby? We could try again. (*John ducks again.*) But perhaps you're not in the mood tonight. Well, we can talk about it tomorrow. (*Looks sadly out, feels alone.*) "Tomorrow and tomorrow and tomorrow." (*Very sad.*) John, what's that from? Nanny? (*No response from either; she sighs.*) One loses one's classics. (*Stares out. Lights dim.*)

Scene 6

> *The bassinet from the first scene of the play in a spot. Daisy, dressed normally in men's clothing, enters with a young woman named Susan. Susan is pretty and soft and sympathetic. They stand over the bassinet.*

SUSAN: Hello, baby, hello. Coooo. Coooo. It's such a cute baby. Isn't it amazing how immediately one loves them?
DAISY: Yes, I guess so.
SUSAN: Say hello to the baby, Alexander.
DAISY: (*Somewhat stiffly.*) Hello.
SUSAN: Alexander, you're so stiff. Be more friendly to the child.
DAISY: Hello. (*He's better at it.*) Now we do know its sex, right?
SUSAN: Yes, it's a boy. Remember we sent out that card that said Alexander and Susan Nevsky are proud to announce the birth of their son, Alexander Nevsky, Jr.?
DAISY: Yes. *I* remember. I was just testing to check that you weren't insane and suddenly saying it was a girl.
SUSAN: No, I'm not insane. Hello, Alexander, Jr. (*To Daisy.*) How odd that you're called Alexander Nevsky. Do you have Russian ancestors?
DAISY: No, truthfully. I took the name myself. I liked the musical score to the movie. I've always had trouble with names.
SUSAN: Well, it's a very nice name. (*Baby starts to cry.*)
DAISY: Oh, my God, it's crying.
SUSAN: Oh dear. What should we do, I wonder?
DAISY: I'm not certain. (*They pause for a while.*) Probably we should hold it. (*Susan picks the baby up.*)
SUSAN: Instinctively that feels right. There, there. It's all right. It's all right. (*Baby stops crying.*)
DAISY: Goodness, how did you do that?
SUSAN: Here, you try. (*Hands him the baby. Daisy holds the baby rather awkwardly; the baby starts to cry.*)
DAISY: He doesn't like me.
SUSAN: Well, bounce him a little. (*Daisy does.*)
DAISY: There, there. (*Baby stops crying.*)
SUSAN: Sing to him, why don't you?

DAISY: (*Sings.*)
Hush, little baby, don't you cry,
Mama's gonna give you a big black. . . .
(*Daisy thinks, stares out quietly for a moment, changes the word.*)
. . . poodle.
SUSAN: Are those the lyrics?
DAISY: I don't know the lyrics. (*Sings.*)
And if that big black poodle should attack,
Mama's gonna step on your little . . .
(*Catches himself again, redoes the whole line, making up the lyric as he goes:*)
Mama's . . . gonna . . . teach you . . . to bite it back,
And when baby grows up, big and strong,
Baby . . . can help mama . . . rewrite this song.
SUSAN: That's very sweet, Alexander. (*Daisy looks at Susan, smiles a little. They both sing to the baby.*)
BOTH:
Hush, little baby, don't you cry,
Mama's gonna give you a big black poodle,
And if that big black poodle should attack,
Mama's gonna teach you to bite it back,
And when baby grows up, big and strong,
Baby can help mama rewrite this song . . .
(*They keep humming to the baby as the lights dim to black.*)

Author's Notes

I have gotten into the habit of writing author's notes to the acting editions of my plays. I have mostly received good feedback on doing this from people, though recently a director about to do a play of mine told me he found the notes "annoying." So I wanted to stress that these notes are not meant to declare by fiat how my plays *must* be done, but just as guidelines to indicate the kind of acting and directing tone I had in mind when I wrote the play. To quote another writer on the issue, here's Tom Stoppard quoted in the New York Times (Nov. 22, 1983) during rehearsals for *The Real Thing*:

> "For Mr. Stoppard, whose earlier plays include Travesties *and* Rosencrantz and Guildenstern are Dead, *such daily involvement [of attending rehearsal] is customary practice with a new production. 'You save people quite a lot of time,' he notes. 'You can answer things it would take time to work out, and maybe without me it would be worked out with the wrong answer. It's not a question of how it* has *to be, but you do want people to know what you meant. They can make a different choice, but it's important that they know what they're changing.'"

I can't be at rehearsals for every production of a play of mine, so these notes are my attempt to communicate what I had in mind and to offer, I hope, shortcuts on some problems. You always have to add common sense and the particular strong points and weak points of your cast, and go from there. But every script has some moments that are ambiguous or confusing alone on the page; and I also think the playing tone of my plays is not always the easiest thing to figure out. That's the reason I offer these notes. And so enough of this defensive introduction. (The director who complained about the notes, by the way, ended up directing a very successful production.)

Baby with the Bathwater has been produced twice as of these notes: its premiere at the American Repertory Theatre in Cambridge, Massachusetts in the spring of 1983, and its New York premiere at Playwrights Horizons in the fall of 1983. I saw and enjoyed the Cambridge production, but I was more involved in the New York production that followed, and so most of these notes will refer to things I learned from that production.

Jerry Zaks, who directed "Baby with the Bathwater" in New York and who has previously directed "Sister Mary Ignatius Explains It All For You" and the off-Broadway version of "Beyond Therapy," has a very good sense of how to keep genuine human feelings in my plays so they don't shoot out into the stratosphere as only surreal farces, but he also knows how to balance the "human" qualities with a good comedy director's sense of pace and appropriate exaggeration. (As the Bible, or perhaps George Abbott, says, there is a time for exaggeration, and there is a time for saying the line sincerely.)

One thing Jerry worked for from the start was that Helen and John want to be good parents, that they do, as Daisy says later in a psychiatric session, "mean well." That's probably easier to figure out about John, who is clearly less tempestuous than Helen and who does often say things that make sense and show concern for the baby. But it's important to find these sympathetic motives in Helen as well. The opening moments of the play (up through Helen's "Don't call the child a baked potato") should be filled with genuine and happy love for the child and for each other. (This love should be genuine, though it can certainly be immature: W.H. Macy and Christine Estabrook both got appropriate audience laughter when they giggled with pleasure after he compliments her hair and she says "Thank you." It felt a little bit like children playing house—sweet, but immature, uninformed.)

On the other hand, it's important that Helen's ferocity not be ducked. She "means well," but when she screams "JOHN, LIVE UP TO YOUR RESPONSIBILITIES!" or (at the end of Act I) screams "I TOLD YOU NOT TO CALL IT A BAKED POTATO!", the actress must be willing to let John have it to the fullest extent of her vocal chords. She must not worry about "being sympathetic" to the audience. Although she is not meant to be "only" a monster, on some level and at some times she really *is* a monster—an emotional bully to John, and deeply frightened. The actress must commit to her large moments fully—both so her character is fulfilled and so that the comedy will work. The Act II in-the-park scene is written for Helen to be truly awful to Daisy, and the more vicious she is in the screaming (within the bounds of a kind of comic reality; one could turn it into a kind of psychodrama which would then not be funny and not have the tone I intended; we're back to common sense and instinct again) the funnier the scene should be, and the more serious the scene's implications for Helen and Daisy.

This is one of my less "realistic" plays, and the characters change mood and attitude more abruptly than they do in, say, *Sister Mary Ignatius*. So two things on this. The first is to commit to whatever the character is saying fully. For instance, when Helen in the first scene has her "DNA" explanation speech of what the doctor said to her about how they can decide the child's sex "later," the actress should play only that she is presenting the facts as she was told them, as straight-forwardly and simply as possible. The speech is funny/effective when it sounds plausible because Helen finds it plausible; the actress should not in some way "cue" the audience that she knows the logic is cuckoo and that she is saying something funny.

The second bit of advice is somewhat connected, and has to do with the emotional switches. One moment Helen is telling Nanny not to push her around, and the next moment Helen melts into little-girlishness (on being promised an ice cream soda) and says "I love you, Nanny." Just play those different emotions and attitudes fully and don't worry about how the transitions between them occur; trust that I've done that in the work itself.

Helen and John, though exaggerated, are fairly recognizable from life. The characters of Nanny and the Principal are a bit more surreal and Alice in Wonderland-like. Nanny is conceived as a kind of cracked Mary Poppins figure. She is also inconsistency incarnate, able to soothe the child with pleasant, soothing noises ("Wheeeeee; whaaaaaaa" etc.) and then suddenly get cross and scream "Shut up!" She also does fairly inexplicable things like (in the birthday scene near the end of the play) put on her glasses in order, apparently, to "hear" Daisy's essay better. There's no logic to this; it should be just committed to. (I read an interview with Dana Ivey, who originated Nanny in New York, in which she commented on acting in "Baby": "The Durang [play] is so filled with non sequiturs that you have to do each thing with total conviction—if you try to look for a stream of consciousness like you would for any other playwright, it would just get in the way." So, to sum up, when in doubt, commit fully to whatever choice the script indicates and don't worry about the connectives if they don't seem apparent.)

When you cast Cynthia, be careful that you cast a sympathetic actress. Cynthia's story of her baby being eaten by the German shepherd is so awful that it's important that the actress' vibes be innately sweet so that it can become clear that Cynthia actually *does* love babies, it's just that she isn't very smart. The whole point of her character then becomes that her loving babies is not enough to "save" the two babies she comes in contact with. When she says to Nanny as she leaves, "I know what I'm doing," she absolutely doesn't, of course. But she's not an evil woman; she just really doesn't (as she says) "know any better."

It's also important to cast Cynthia with a sympathetic actress, because the roles of Angela, Miss Pringle, and especially Susan should also be very sympathetic. I'd like to add a stage direction regarding Susan and the last scene that I took out of the text itself because it hurt the flow of reading but which remains essential to the final scene's meaning:

> SUSAN *is pretty and soft and sympathetic. The sense of her and* DAISY *at the end of the play is that though obviously there will be problems, they may indeed be better parents than the previous people in the play.* SUSAN *is played by the same actress who plays* CYNTHIA; *however, be certain that she looks substantially different than she did when she was* CYNTHIA, *and that this be her prettiest and most normal appearance.*

Here are some miscellaneous thoughts on various issues and moments in the play.

Blond hair for John. It seems in casting the play it is preferable that John have blond hair, better for his "vibes." However, if the best person for the part doesn't have blond hair, please change Helen's lines in scene 1 to reflect this. Change it (p. 6), I think, to "You have curly hair. I don't like men with curly hair. I like men with straight hair, but I'm afraid of them. I'm not afraid of you. I hate you." (If your actor has straight, non-blond hair, then make the lines go "You have straight hair. I don't like men with straight hair." etc.)

Strength in John. John is obviously not quite Helen's match; however, let him be successfully asserting himself when the script gives him the opportunity (chiefly in his "Now enough of all this arguing!" speech on p. 15).

Cynthia's red toy that goes tingle-tangle. Make sure it's large enough to be visually recognizable to the audience at the end of the play when John and Helen offer it to baby.

Focus in the novel-reading sequence. When Cynthia is reading from (my version of) "Mommie Dearest," I found it helpful to let her reading catch John and Helen's attention when she speaks; when she finishes, they go back to their arguing. And while they have their argument lines, Cynthia can "mark" time from her reading by making friendly faces and noises to the baby.

In Act II, Scene 1, the character of Kate. Just a clarification since it hasn't been crystal clear to actresses approaching the part. Kate is sensible, logical, very opinionated. She is, in a way, a natural enemy to Helen; if they were on a women's committee together, they'd kill one another. So once Helen enters the scene, Kate finds herself disapproving of Helen quite a bit; she doesn't confront her too directly at first out of a normal politeness; later she is careful because she starts to realize how really "off" Helen is; she might be dangerous. Kate is a realist par excellence; that's why she has no trouble saying blunt things if they're true ("no one in our family is particularly good looking"), or in her most direct "confront" of Helen, "that's no way to bring up a child." When Helen leaves the scene, Kate becomes annoyed at Angela's do-nothing attitude; when she says "Alright, we won't do anything about her. We'll wait until we read about the child *dead* in the newspaper," there's a kind of irritation in her voice that implies if the child is found dead it will be all Angela's fault for not pursuing this issue, although she clearly isn't willing to pursue it on her own. And, finally, once Angela rattles on about what makes her depressed and then pops her "mood elevators," Kate realizes she has another, different kind of loony on her hand; her "Well, fine" as she edges away is meant to (comically) indicate that she thinks Angela is quite a nut.

Also in the park. Be sure to differentiate vocal levels and energy with the mothers calling out to their children, and talking to one another. Obviously Helen is quite ferocious with some of her shouting, but the other two mothers should also be louder calling to their children than they are just talking to one another.

The toy duck prop. At American Rep. the prop person constructed a wooden duck (which looked somewhat like a wooden duck decoy) that had a hinged opening on its back, and the vodka bottle fit into this "cabinet" in the duck's back. At Playwrights Horizons, the prop man hollowed out a fluffy-looking yellow duck (that looked like it would go on a child's bed) and fit it like a glove over the vodka bottle; the cap of the bottle more or less came out the duck's ass. With this version, John drank from the bottle without taking it out of its "duck holder." Before John picked up the "duck bottle," however, it just looked like a regular child's stuffed duck. Both these solutions seem fine to me.

When Helen does her vocal "exercises" ("toy duck, toy duck; polly wolly windbag, polly wolly windbag," etc.), I can barely explain to the various actresses what I am intending except to say that it's the kind of nonsense talking someone might do when they're so tired and/or fed up that they just don't want to bother articulating thoughts or words anymore. There's a bit of a punishing quality meant too, since she is speaking aloud in a room that includes John but is not saying anything that he could possible respond to. And, all that aside, the actress shouldn't "do" too much with them, just say them simply, rhythmically, and without too much emotion except a touch of "oh, if only one of us were dead." You know. You feel that way sometimes. Don't you?

The Principal scene. She has a line that goes "Yes. Uh huh. Uh huh. Yes, I see. Uh huh. Uh huh. Go on." I don't quite know how to articulate what I want to say (toy duck, toy duck, toy duck), but here goes. Each one of these phrases should be done in the exact same, unemphasized way that one would say "Yes, I see." One should not differentiate them, stress one more than the other. Their inflection is much the same as we all do on the phone listening to someone tell a long story (uh huh; uh huh; yes; hmmn), only the principal's words are odd because, of course, she's already listened to the story and is *now* giving her reaction. Dana Ivey did it this way instinctively first time out, but other people have been a bit thrown by it. Do you follow what I mean, toy duck toy duck?

I must pull myself together.

Tiny point. When Principal *does* put her hand over her mouth to listen, finally, to what Miss Pringle has to say, I find it important that she actually *does* put her hand over her mouth; she's been so talkative that otherwise I get distracted thinking she's going to speak up again. Once Miss Pringle gets past the title and into the first sentence of the essay, however, I think the Principal should shift to a more "normal" listening posture, her-hands-supporting-her-chin kind of thing. The only reason to go on about this moment is that it is very important that the actress playing the Principal cue the audience that they must give all their attention, finally, to Miss Pringle and the essay; and the Principal is so much fun (I had a great time writing this scene) that we must let the audience know not to expect anything more from the Principal during the essay.

Final point about this scene. It is written to vocally and emotionally peak from "Yes, but I *am* in a position of power!" on through til the final line ("Who cares if she's dead as long as she publishes? Now get out of here!); you mustn't pull back at any point during these final lines, and the last line must be the biggest (or at least as big as "Yes, but I *am* in a position of power!").

The Daisy/Psychiatrist Section. In both productions the Voice has been done live by the same actor who plays John, and as long as your John doesn't have an overwhelmingly recognizable voice, I think that's the best idea. I've left the voice out of the program credits so as not to tip off the audience that we have a "psychiatrist" or a "voice" sequence; and as long as the actor is willing to forego that credit, that's preferable to me. If he definitely wanted the credit, please make it say "Voice" and not "Psychiatrist."

I think I've made this clear in the text itself now, but please please don't put blackouts in the "Daisy" scene; it hurts the flow and changes the feel from it being one long scene that has time jumps to being a long series of scenes with waits between them. (This is the one major disagreement I had with the American Rep. director.) Also, Daisy's change from dress to male clothes should not be done in the dark (unless it could *really* be done on the count of 1-2, which I doubt); it's much better to let the audience see him change, so the play *continues,* than to stop the action so we don't see the mechanics of the change. Let us see the mechanics; it's theatre, we'll accept it.

I've notated in Daisy's speech a lot of the coloring that I think should be there. For a lot of it, especially the long opening part of it, it should be kind of deadpan; among other things, Daisy doesn't know that his past has been that terrible really, and he's just recounting the facts. The only other thing I'll toss in is a phrase from Edith Oliver's praise (in *The New Yorker*) for Keith Reddin who played Daisy: "Keith Reddin . . . is the perfect Durang leading man, puzzled and gravely polite', until he finally asserts himself." Keith deserved the praise, but I quote it because Ms. Oliver's phrase itself—"puzzled and gravely polite"—is a terrific description of how I feel Daisy should be played for much of his speech, and for most of the Scene 5 birthday party.

The Scene 5 birthday party. Daisy is older (30), been in analysis, and for much of the scene is going along with his parents politely because to do otherwise would make a scene and not be worth it. John, batting owls, is clearly out to lunch. Helen is tricky. I've found actresses instinctively want to make all the lines "fake cheery" which is right for a lot of it, but not for all of it. Please excuse how many "acting adjectives" I've put in the playing text, but I can for instance understand the logic of Helen saying "Oh why don't you keel over and die" with a cheery insincerity, but I know (thanks to Christine Estabrook and to Dianne Wiest at a reading) that to do it sincerely and with utter hatred of your life is funnier and adds depth to the play and to the scene. Similarly, Helen is very, very sad and lost once Daisy leaves at the end of the scene; let her be that way; let it be the end of "Three Sisters" and "if only we knew." Weird farce with one foot in reality suddenly switching to sadness with *both* feet in reality—I've been discovering, I think, that this is the approach to take with most of my plays. Don't overdo the sad moments, but don't pass by them.

I think I've gone on already too long. Whatever your set, make the changes be as fast as possible. Long blackouts are comedy's enemy.

There is more than one way to do any play, so once again my apologies to actors for giving too many specifics; but to quote from Mr. Stoppard again, if you make another choice, "at least you will know what you're changing."

Christopher Durang
May, 1984

Execution of Justice

Emily Mann

The plays of Emily Mann are unique from those of virtually any other playwright working in the American theatre today. All of Mann's works are based on actual incidents expressed in the words of the people who originally spoke them. *Execution of Justice* is no exception. The play is an episodic reenactment of the trial of Dan White. In 1978 White, an ex-police officer, fireman, and former member of San Francisco's Board of Supervisors, murdered Harvey Milk, the first publicly elected gay official in California, and George Moscone, the Mayor of San Francisco.

Laced among selected scene from White's murder trial are verbalized comments and observations drawn from newspaper clippings and interviews with friends of White, Milk, and Moscone, as well as videotaped news footage of the period taken from an Academy Award winning documentary entitled, *The Times of Harvey Milk* by Robert Epstein and Richard Schmiechen.

Mann has described her method of writing as "theatre of testimony." She began to write plays in 1974 when she created Annulla: an *Autobiography of a Survivor,* based on personal accounts of a holocaust victim. *Still Life,* her second play, deals with Vietnam war veterans. It received five Obie awards, one of which was for playwriting. *Execution of Justice,* her third work, garnered many awards, among them the Helen Hayes Award, the Bay Area Theatre Critics Circle Award, the HBO/USA Playwrights Award, a Burns Mantle Yearbook Best Plays Citation, a Playwriting Award from the Women's Committee of The Dramatists Guild for dramatizing issues of conscience and a Drama Desk nomination. *Greensboro (A Requiem)* deals with the murder of civil rights activists in Greensboro, North Carolina at the height of the civil rights movement. Her most recent work was an adaptation of *Having Our Say,* which recently appeared on Broadway.

Mann has also enjoyed a distinguished career as a director. She currently serves as Artistic Director of the McCarter Theatre of Princeton, New Jersey, a not-for-profit theatre near New York. In 1994 the McCarter was awarded the prestigious Tony Award for Outstanding Regional Theater during her tenure as head of the organization. Mann is among a growing number of women who have established successful careers as leaders in the contemporary American theatre.

Production History

Execution of Justice was originally commissioned by the Eureka Theatre Company, San Francisco in 1982. The world premiere of the play was at the Actors Theatre of Louisville in March 1984 under the direction of Oskar Eustis, dramaturg, and Anthony Taccone, artistic director.

Execution of Justice was presented on Broadway at the Virginia Theatre in March 1986. It was produced by Lester and Margorie Osterman, Mortimer Caplin and Richard C. Norton and Christopher Stark. It was directed by Emily Mann. Sets were designed by Ming Cho Lee, costumes by Jennifer Von Mayrhauser, lights by Pat Collins, and sound by Tom Morse. The Production stage manager was Frank Marino. The cast was as follows:

Dan White	John Spencer
Mary Ann White	Mary McDonnell
Cop	Stanley Tucci
Sister Boom Boom	Wesley Snipes

Chorus of Uncalled Witnesses

Jim Denman, White's Jailer	Christopher McHale
Young Mother	Lisabeth Bartlett
Milk's Friend	Adam Redfield
Gwenn Craig, Vice President of the Harvey Milk Democratic Club	Isabell Monk
Harry Britt, City Supervisor and Milk's successor	Donal Donnelly
Joseph Freitas, D.A.	Nicholas Hormann
Mourner	Nicholas Hormann

Trial Characters

The Court	Nicholas Kepros
Court Clerk	Lizabeth Bartlett
Douglas Schmidt, Defense Attorney	Peter Friedman
Thomas F. Norman, Prosecuting Attorney	Gerry Bamman
Joanna Lu, TV reporter	Freda Foh Shen
Prospective Jurors	Josh Clark, Suzy Hunt
Juror #3/Foreman	Gary Reineke
Bailiff	Jeremy O. Caplin

Witnesses for the People

Coroner Stephens	Donal Donnelly
Rudy Nothenberg, Deputy Mayor, Moscone's friend	Earle Hyman
Barbara Taylor, reporter	Marcia Jean Kurtz
Officer Byrne, Department of Records	Isabell Monk
William Melia, civil engineer	Richard Riehle
Cyr Copertini, secretary to the Mayor	Suzy Hunt

Carl Henry Carlson, aide to Harvey Milk . . . . . Nicholas Hormann
Richard Pabich, assistant to Harvey Milk . . . . . Wesley Snipes
Frank Falzon, Chief Inspector of Homicide. . . . Jon DeVries
Edward Erdelatz, inspector . . . . Stanley Tucci

Witnesses for the Defense

Denise Apcar, aide to White . . . . Lisabeth Bartlett
Fire Chief Sherratt . . . . Gary Reineke
Fireman Frediani . . . . Jeremy O. Caplin
Police Officer Sullivan. . . . . Stanley Tucci
City Supervisor Lee Dolson . . . . Richard Riehle

Psychiatrists

Dr. Jones . . . . Earle Hyman
Dr. Solomon. . . . . Marcia Jean Kurtz
Dr. Blinder. . . . . Donal Donnelly
Dr. Lunde . . . . Gary Reineke
Dr. Delman . . . . Jon DeVries

In Rebuttal for the People

Carol Ruth Silver, City Supervisor. . . . . Marcia Jean Kurtz
Dr. Levy, psychiatrist . . . . Gary Reineke
Riot Police . . . . Jeremy O. Caplin,
          Josh Clark, Jon DeVries, Richard Riehle, Stanley Tucci
Action Cameraman. . . . . Richard Howard

Time

1978 to the present.

Place

San Francisco.

Author's Note

The words come from trial transcript, interview, reportage, the street.

Characters

DAN WHITE
MARY ANN WHITE, HIS WIFE

    Cop
    Sister Boom Boom

Chorus of Uncalled Witnesses

    Jim Denman, ex-undersheriff, White's jailer immediately following the shooting
    Young Mother, late 30s, mother of three
    Moscone's Friend, old political crone, 50s
    Milk's Friend, 30s
    Gwenn Craig, black lesbian leader, 40s
    Harry Britt, City Supervisor, 40s, Milk's successor
    Joseph Freitas, Jr., ex-D.A., speaking in 1983

Trial Characters

    Court, the judge
    Clerk
    Douglas Schmidt, defense lawyer
    Thomas F. Norman, prosecuting attorney
    Joan Lu, TV reporter
    3 Prospective Jurors
    Foreman

Witnesses for the People

    Stephens, the coroner
    Rudy Nothenberg, Deputy Mayor
    Barbara Taylor, KCBS reporter
    Officer, Byrne, policewoman in charge of records
    William Melia, Jr., civil engineer
    Cyr Copertini, appointment secretary to the Mayor
    Carl Henry Carlson, aid to Milk
    Richard Pabich, assistant to Milk
    Frank Falzon, Chief Inspector of Homicide
    Edward Erdelatz, Inspector

Witnesses for the Defense

    Fire Chief Sherrat
    Police Officer Sullivan
    City Supervisor Lee Dolson
    Fireman Ferdiani
    Psychiatrists Jones, Blinder, Solomon, Lunde, Delman
    Denise Apcar, aide to White

In Rebuttal for the People

    CAROL RUTH SILVER, CITY SUPERVISOR
    DR. LEVY, PSYCHIATRIST

Characters on Tape

    DIANNE FEINSTEIN, CITY SUPERVISOR, LATE MAYOR
    GEORGE MOSCONE, MAYOR
    HARVEY MILK, CITY SUPERVISOR

People of San Francisco, Jurors, Cameramen, Mourners, Rioters, Riot Police

(The play can be performed by as few as 18 actors.)

Execution of Justice by Emily Mann

Copyright © 1983, 1985 and 1986 by Emily Mann. Reprinted by permission of William Morris Agency, Inc. on behalf of the Author. All rights reserved.

CAUTION: Professionals and amateurs are hereby warned that "Execution of Justice" is subject to a royalty. It is fully protected under the copyright laws of the United States of America and all countries covered by the International Copyright Union (including the Dominion of Canada and the rest of the British Commonwealth), the Berne Convention, the Pan-American Copyright Convention and the Universal Copyright Convention as well as all countries with which the United States has reciprocal copyright relations. All rights, including professional/amateur stage rights, motion picture, recitation, lecturing, public reading, radio broadcasting, television, video or sound recording, all other forms of mechanical or electronic reproduction, such as CD-ROM, CD-I, information storage and retrieval systems and photocopying, and the rights of translation into foreign languages, are strictly reserved. Particular emphasis is laid upon the matter of readings, permission for which must be secured from the Author's agent in writing.

Inquiries concerning rights should be addressed to:

                William Morris Agency, Inc.
                1325 Avenue of the Americas
                New York, New York 10019
                Attn: George Lane

The Play

Execution of Justice

ACT ONE

Murder

> *A bare state.*
> *A white screen overhead.*
> *On screen: images of San Francisco.*
> *Hot, fast music. Images of Milk and Moscone punctuate the visuals.*
>
> *People enter. A day in San Francisco.*
> *A maelstrom of urban activity.*
>
> *Without warning: On screen: (video, if possible)*

DIANNE FEINSTEIN: (*almost unable to stand*)
As President of the Board of Supervisors, It is my duty to make this announcement: Mayor George Moscone . . . and Supervisor Harvey Milk . . . have been shot . . . and killed. (*GASPS AND CRIES. A LONG MOMENT.*) The suspect is Supervisor Dan White.

> *(The crown in shock. They cannot move. Then they run. Out of the chaos, Dan White appears.)*
> *On screen: A church window fades up.*
> *A shaft of light.*
> *Dan White prays.*
>
> *On audio: Hyperreal sounds of mumbled Hail Marys*
> *Sounds of a woman's high heels echoing, moving fast.*
> *Sound of breathing hard, running.*
> *Mary Ann White enters, breathless.*
> *White looks up. She approaches him.*

WHITE: I shot the Mayor and Harvey.

(She crumples. Lights change.)

CLERK: This is the matter of the People versus Daniel James White.

(Amplified gavel. Lights change.)

COP: *(quiet)*
Yeah, I'm wearing a "Free Dan White" t-shirt. *(indicating on shirt "NO MAN IS AN ISLAND")* You haven't seen what I've seen
—my nose shoved into what I think stinks.
Against everything I believe in.
There was a time in San Francisco when you knew a guy
by his parish.

(SISTER BOOM BOOM enters.)

COP: Sometimes I sit in Church and I think of those disgusting drag queens dressed up as nuns
and I'm a cop,
and I'm thinkin',
there's gotta be a law, you know,
because they're makin' me think things I don't want to think
and I gotta keep my mouth shut.

(BOOM BOOM puts out cigarette.)

COP: Take a guy out of his sling—fist fucked to death—
they say it's mutual consent, it ain't murder,
and I pull this disgusting mess down, take him to the morgue,
I mean, my wife asks me, "Hey, how was your day?"
I can't even tell her.
I wash my hands before I can even look at my kids.

(They are very aware of each other, but possibly never make eye contact.)

BOOM BOOM:
God bless you one.
God bless you all.
COP: See, Danny knew—he believes in the rights of minorities. Ya know, he just knew—we are a minority, too.
BOOM BOOM:
I would like to open with a reading from the Book of Dan. *(Opens book.)*
COP: We been workin' this job three generations—my father was a cop—and then they put—Moscone, Jesus, the mayor—Jesus—Moscone put this
N-negro loving, faggot loving Chief telling us what to do—
he doesn't even come from the neighborhood,

he doesn't even come from this city!
He's tellin' us what to do in a force that knows what to do.
He makes us paint our cop cars faggot blue—
he called it "lavender gloves" for the queers,
handle 'em, treat 'em with "lavender gloves," he called it.
He's cuttin' off our balls.
The city is stinkin' with degenerates—
I mean, I'm worried about my kids, I worry about my wife,
I worry about me and how I'm feelin' mad all the time.
You gotta understand that I'm not alone—
It's real confusion.
BOOM BOOM: "As Dan came to his day of reckoning, he feared not for he went unto the lawyers and the doctors and the jurors, and they said, 'Take heart, for in this you will receive not life but three to seven with time off for good behavior.'" (*Closes book reverently.*)
COP: Take a walk with me sometime.
See what I see every day . . .
Like I'm supposed to smile when I see two bald-headed,
shaved-head men with those tight pants and muscles,
chains everywhere, French-kissin' on the street,
putting their hands all over each other's asses,
I'm supposed to smile,
walk by, act as if this is RIGHT??!!
BOOM BOOM: As gay people and as people of color and as women we all know the cycle of brutality and ignorance which pervades our culture.
COP: I got nothin' against people doin' what they want,
if I don't see it.
BOOM BOOM: And we all know that brutality only begets more brutality.
COP: I mean, I'm not makin' some woman on the streets for everyone to see.
BOOM BOOM: Violence only sows the seed for more violence.
COP: I'm not . . .
BOOM BOOM: And I hope Dan White knows that.
COP: I can't explain it any better.
BOOM BOOM: Because the greatest, most efficient information gathering and dispersal network is the Great Gay Grapevine.
COP: Just take my word for it—
BOOM BOOM: And when Dan White gets out of jail, no matter where Dan White goes, someone will recognize him.
COP: Walk into a leather bar with me some night—They—they're—
there are queers who'd agree with me—it's disgusting.
BOOM BOOM:
All over the world, the word will go out.
And we will know where Dan White is.
COP: The point is: Dan White showed you could fight City Hall.

BOOM BOOM: (*pause*)
Now we are all aware, as I said,
Of this cycle of brutality and murder.
And the only way we can break that horrible cycle is with love, understanding and forgiveness.
And there are those who were before me here today—
gay brothers and sisters
who said that we must somehow learn to
love, understand and forgive
the sins that have been committed against us
and the sins of violence
And it sort of grieves me that some of us are not
Understanding and loving and forgiving of Dan White.
And after he gets out,
after we find out where he is . . .
(*Long, wry look.*)
I mean, not, y'know,
with any malice or planning . . .
(*Long look.*)
You know, you get so depressed and your blood sugar goes up
and you'd be capable of just about *ANYTHING!*
(*Long pause. Smiles.*)
And some angry faggot or dyke who is not
understanding, loving and forgiving—
is going to perform a horrible act of violence and brutality
against Dan White.
And if we can't break the cycle before somebody gets Dan White
somebody will *get Dan White*.
and when they do,
I beg you all to
love, understand and *for-give*. (*He throws a kiss, laughs.*)

    (*Lights fade to black.*)

CLERK: This is the matter of the People vs. Daniel James White and the record will show that the Defendant is present with his counsel and the District Attorney is present and this is out of presence of the jury.

    (*Court setting up. TV lights.*)

JOANNA LU: (*On camera.*) The list of prospective witnesses that the defense has presented for the trial of the man accused of killing the liberal Mayor of San Francisco, George Moscone, and the first avowedly homosexual elected official, City Supervisor Harvey Milk, reads like a Who's Who of City Government

(*Looks at list.*)

... Judges, Congressmen, current and former Supervisors, and even a State Senator. The D.A. has charged White with two counts of first degree murder, invoking for the first time the clause in the new California capital punishment law that calls for the gas chamber for any person who has assassinated a public official in an attempt to prevent him from fulfilling his official duties. Ironically, Harvey Milk and George Moscone vigorously lobbied against the death penalty while Dan White vigorously supported it. This is Joanna Lu at the Hall of Justice.

(*Gavel. Spotlight on clerk.*)

CLERK: Ladies and gentlemen, this is the information in the case now pending before you: the People of the State of California, Plaintiff, versus Daniel James White, Defendant. Action Number: 98663, Count One.

(*Gavel.*)
(*Lights.*)
(*On screen: JURY SELECTION.*)

COURT: Mr. Schmidt, you may continue with your jury selection.
SCHMIDT: Thank you, Your Honor.
CLERK: It is alleged that Daniel James White did willfully unlawfully and with malice aforethought murder George R. Moscone, the duly elected Mayor of the City and County of San Francisco, California.
SCHMIDT: Have you ever supported controversial causes, like homosexual rights, for instance?
JUROR #1: (*woman*) I have gay friends ... I, uh ... once walked with them in a Gay Freedom Day Parade.
SCHMIDT: Your Honor, I would like to strike the juror.
JUROR #1: (*woman*) I am str ... I am heterosexual.
COURT: Agreed.

(*Gavel.*)

CLERK: The defendant Daniel James White is further accused of a crime of felony to wit: that said defendant Daniel James White did willfully, unlawfully and with malice aforethought, murder Harvey Milk, a duly elected Supervisor of the City and County of San Francisco, California.
SCHMIDT: With whom do you live, sir?
JUROR #2: (*man*) My roommate.
SCHMIDT: What does he or she do?
JUROR #2: (*man*) He works at the Holiday Inn.
SCHMIDT: Your Honor, I ask the court to strike the juror for cause.
COURT: Agreed.

(Gavel.)

CLERK: Special circumstances: it is alleged that Daniel James White in this proceeding has been accused of more than one offense of murder.
JUROR #3: I worked briefly as a San Francisco policeman, but I've spent most of my life since then as a private security guard.
SCHMIDT: As you know, serving as a juror is a high honor and responsibility.
JUROR #3: Yes, sir.
SCHMIDT: The jury serves as the conscience of the community.
JUROR #3: Yes, sir. I know that, sir.
SCHMIDT: Now, sir, as a juror you take an oath that you will apply the laws of the State of California as the Judge will instruct you. You'll uphold that oath, won't you?
JUROR #3: Yes, sir.
SCHMIDT: Do you hold any views against the death penalty no matter how heinous the crime?
JUROR #3: No, sir. I support the death penalty.
SCHMIDT: Why do you think Danny White killed Milk and Moscone?
JUROR #3: I have certain opinions. I'd say it was social and political pressures . . .
SCHMIDT: I have my jury.
COURT: Mr. Norman?

(No response. Fine with him.)
(Gavel.)

JOANNA LU: *(On camera.)* The jury has been selected quickly for the Dan White trial. It appears the prosecution and the defense want the same jury. The prosecuting attorney, Assistant D.A. Tom Norman exercised only 3 out of 27 possible peremptory challenges. By all accounts, there are no Blacks, no gays, and no Asians. One juror is an ex-policeman, another the wife of the county jailer, four of the seven women are old enough to be Dan White's mother. Most of the jurors are working and middle-class Catholics. Speculation in the press box is that the prosecution feels that it has a law-and-order jury. In any case, Dan White will certainly be judged by a jury of his peers.
(Turns.)
I have with me this morning District Attorney Joseph Freitas, Jr.
(TV lights on FREITAS.)
May we ask, sir, the prosecution's strategy in the trial of Dan White?
FREITAS: I think it's a clear case—We'll let the facts speak for themselves—
CLERK: And the Defendant, Daniel James White, has entered a plea of not guilty to each of the charges and allegations contained in this information.

(WHITE enters. MRS. WHITE enters.)

COURT: Mr. Norman, do you desire to make an opening statement at this time?
NORMAN: I do, Judge.
COURT: All right. You may proceed.

(Lights change.)
(On screen: ACT ONE MURDER.)
(Gavel.)
(All screens go to white.)

NORMAN: (*Opening statement. The prosecution.*) Your Honor, members of the jury, and you must be the judges now, (*Actor takes in audience.*) counsel for the defense:
(*To audience.*)
Ladies and gentlemen—I am Thomas F. Norman and I am the Assistant District Attorney, and I appear here as trial representative to Joseph Freitas Jr, District Attorney. Seated with me is Frank Falzon, Chief Inspector of Homicide for San Francisco.
George R. Moscone was the duly-elected Mayor of San Francisco.

(On screen: Portrait of MOSCONE.)

Harvey Milk was the duly-elected Supervisor or City Councilman of District 5 of San Francisco.

(On screen: Portrait of HARVEY MILK.)

The defendant in this case, Mr. Daniel James White, had been the duly-elected Supervisor of District 8 of San Francisco, until for personal reasons of his own he tendered his resignation in writing to the Mayor on or about November the 10th, 1978, which was approximately 17 days before this tragedy occurred.
Subsequent to tendering his resignation he had the feeling that he wanted to withdraw that resignation, and that he wanted his job back. George Moscone, it appears, had told the accused that he would give him his job back or, in other words, appoint him back to the Board if it appeared that there was substantial support in District Number 8 for that appointment.
Material was received by the Mayor in that regard, and in the meantime, Mr. Daniel James White had resorted to the courts in an effort to withdraw his written resignation.
It appears that those efforts were not met with much success.

(On screen: The defense, DOUGLAS SCHMIDT.)

SCHMIDT: Ladies and Gentlemen, the prosecutor has quite skillfully outlined certain of the facts that he believes will be supportive of his theory of first-degree murder.
I intend to present ALL the facts, including some of the background material that will show, not so much *what* happened on November 27th, but WHY those tragedies occured on November 27th.
The evidence will show, and it's not disputed, that Dan White did, indeed, shoot and kill George Moscone and I think the evidence is equally clear that Dan White did shoot and kill Harvey Milk.
Why then should there be a trial?
The issue in this trial is properly to understand WHY that happened.

(On screen: Chief Medical Examiner and Coroner for the City and County of San Francisco.)
(Lights.)
(Coroner sits.)

STEPHENS: *(Holding photo.)* In my opinion and experience, Counsel, the larger tattoo pattern at the side of the Mayor's head is compatible with a firing distance of about one foot, and the smaller tattoo pattern within the larger tattoo pattern is consistent with a firing distance of a little less than one foot.
That is: The wounds to the head were received within a distance of one foot when the Mayor was already on the floor incapacitated.

(NORMAN looks to jury.)
(On screen: Image of figure shooting man in head from a distance of one foot, leaning down "Coup De Grace.")

SCHMIDT: Why? . . . Good people, fine people, with fine backgrounds, simply don't kill people in cold blood, it just doesn't happen, and obviously some part of them has not been presented thus far. Dan White was a native of San Francisco. He went to school here, went through high school here. He was a noted athlete in high school. He was an army veteran who served in Vietnam, and was honorably discharged from the army. He became a policeman thereafter, and after a brief hiatus developed, again returned to the police force in San Francisco, and later transferred to the fire department.
He was married in December of 1976,
(HE indicates MARY ANN WHITE.)
and he fathered his son in July 1978.
Dan White was a good policeman and Dan White was a good fireman. In fact, he was decorated for having saved a woman and her child in a very dangerous fire, but the complete picture of Dan White perhaps was not

known until some time after these tragedies on November 27th. The part that went unrecognized was since his early manhood, Daniel White was suffering from a mental disease. The disease that Daniel White was suffering from is called depression, sometimes called manic depression or uni-polar depression.
NORMAN: Doctor, what kind of a wound was that in your opinion?
STEPHENS: These are gunshot wounds of entrance, Counsel.
The cause of death was multiple gunshot wounds . . . particularly the bullet that passed through the base of the Supervisor's brain. This wound would cause instant or almost instant death. I am now holding People's 30 and 29 for identification. In order for this wound to be received, Counsel . . . the Supervisor's left arm has to be relatively close to the body with the palm turned away from the body and the thumb towards the body.
NORMAN: Can you illustrate that for us?
STEPHENS: Yes, Counsel. The left arm has to be in close to the body and slightly forward with the palm up. The right hand has to be palm away with the thumb pointed towards the body and the elbow in slightly to the body with the arm raised. In this position, all of these wounds that I have just described in People's 30 and 29 line up.
NORMAN: Thank you.

(Freeze on position. Lights.)

SCHMIDT: *(To jury.)* Dan White came from a vastly different lifestyle than Harvey Milk, who was a homosexual leader and politician. Dan White was an idealistic young man, a working class young man. He was deeply endowed with and believed very strongly in the traditional American values, family and home; like the District he represented.
(Indicates jury.)
Dan White believed people when they said something. He believed that a man's word, essentially, was his bond. I don't think Dan White was particularly insightful as to what his underlying problem was, but he was an honest man, and he was fair, perhaps too fair for politics in San Francisco.

(DAN WHITE campaign speech:)
(Hear sounds of ROCKY on audio, crowd response throughout.)

DAN: Do you like my new campaign song?
(Crowd cheers.)
Yeah!

(On screen: Live video or slides of WHITE giving speech, cameras.)

DAN: *(To camera.)* For years, we have witnessed an exodus from San

Francisco by many of our family members, friends and neighbors. Alarmed by the enormous increase in crime, poor educational facilities and a deteriorating social structure, they have fled to temporary havens . . . In a few short years these malignancies of society will erupt from our city and engulf the tree-lined, sun-bathed communities which chide us for daring to live in San Francisco. That is, unless we who have remained can transcend the apathy which has caused us to lock our doors while the tumult rages unchecked through our streets. Individually we are helpless. Yet you must realize there are thousands and thousands of angry frustrated people such as yourselves waiting to unleash a fury that can and will eradicate the malignancies which blight our beautiful city. I am not going to be forced out of San Francisco by splinter groups of radicals, social deviates, and incorrigibles. UNITE AND FIGHT WITH DAN WHITE.

(Crowd cheers.)
(Lights change.)
(Screens go to white.)

SCHMIDT: I think Dan White saw the city deteriorating as a place for the average and decent people to live.
COURT: Mr. Nothenberg, please be sworn.
SCHMIDT: The irony is . . . that the young man with so much promise in seeking the job on the Board of Supervisors actually was destined to construct his own downfall. After Dan White was elected he discovered there was a conflict of interest if he was a fireman and an elected official. His wife, Mary Ann, was a school teacher and made a good salary. But after their marriage, it was discovered that the wife of Dan White had become . . . pregnant and had to give up her teaching job. So the family income plummeted from an excess of $30,000 to $9,600 which is what a San Francisco supervisor—city councilman—is paid. I believe all the stress and the underlying mental illness culminated in his resignation that he turned in to the Mayor on November 10th, 1978.

(On screen: MR. NOTHENBERG, Deputy Mayor.)
(Lights.)

NORMAN: Would you read that for us?
NOTHENBERG: Dear Mayor Moscone: I have been proud to represent the people of San Francisco from District 8 for the past ten months, but due to personal responsibilities which I feel must take precedent over my legislative duties, I am resigning my position effective today. I am sure that the next representative to the Board of Supervisors will receive as much support from the people of San Francisco as I have. Sincerely, Dan White. It is so signed.

SCHMIDT: *(To jury.)* Some days after November the 10th pressure was brought to bear on Dan White to go back to the job that he had worked so hard for, and there was a one-way course that those persons could appeal to Dan White, and that was to appeal to his sense of humor: Basically—Dan you are letting the fire department down, letting the police department down. It worked. That type of pressure worked, because of the kind of man Dan White is. He asked the Mayor for his job back.

NORMAN: Mr. Nothenberg, on or about Monday the 27th of November last year, do you know whether Mayor Moscone was going to make an appointment to the Board of Supervisors, particularly for District No. 8?

NOTHENBERG: Yes, he was.

SCHMIDT: The Mayor said: We have political differences, but you are basically a good man, and you worked for the job and I'm not going to take you to fault. That letter was returned to Dan White.

NORMAN: Do you know whom his appointee to District 8 was going to be?

NOTHENBERG: Yes, I do.

NORMAN: Who was that, please.

NOTHENBERG: It was going to be a gentleman named Don Horanzey.

NORMAN: Thank you.

SCHMIDT: As I said, Dan White believed a man's word was his bond. Mayor Moscone had said: If there was any legal problem he would simply reappoint Dan White. Thereafter it became: Dan White there is no support in District 8 and unless you can show some broad base support, the job will not be given to you, and finally, the public statement coming from the Mayor's office: it's undecided. But you will be notified, prior to the time that any decision is made. They didn't tell Dan White. But they told Barbara Taylor.

(Blackout–Audio on phone.)
(Spotlight WHITE and TAYLOR.)

TAYLOR: I'm Barbara Taylor from KCBS. I'd like to speak to Dan White.

WHITE: Yuh.

TAYLOR: I have received information from a source within the Mayor's office that you are not getting that job. I am interested in doing an interview to find out your reaction to that. Mr. White?

(Long pause.)
(Spotlight DAN WHITE.)

WHITE: I don't know anything about it.

(Click.)
(Dial tone.)
(Lights change.)

TAYLOR: (*Live.*) Well, the Mayor's office told me: "The only one in favor of the appointment of Dan White is Dan White himself."
NORMAN: Thank you, Miss Taylor.
SCHMIDT: After that phone call, Denise Apcar, Dan's aide, told Dan White that there were going to be supporters down at City Hall the next morning to show support to the Mayor's office. In one day they had collected 1100 signatures in District 8 in support of Dan White. But the next morning, Denise called Dan and told him the Mayor was unwilling to accept the petitioners.

(*On screen: DENISE APCAR, Aide to DAN WHITE.*)

APCAR: Yes. I told Danny—I don't remember my exact words—that the Mayor had "circumvented the people."
NORMAN: Did you believe at that time that the Mayor was going to appoint someone other than Dan White?
APCAR: Oh, yes.
NORMAN: At that time, were your feelings such that you were angry?
APCAR: Definitely. Well the Mayor had told him . . . and Dan always felt that a person was going to be honest when they said something. He believed that up until the end.
NORMAN: You felt and believed that Mr. Milk had been acting to prevent the appointment of Mr. Dan White to his vacated seat on the Board of Supervisors?
APCAR: Yes. I was very much aware of that.
NORMAN: Had you expressed that opinion to Mr. White?
APCAR: Yes.
NORMAN: Did Mr. White ever express that opinion also to you?
APCAR: He wasn't down at City Hall very much that week so I was basically the person that told him these things.
NORMAN: Did you call Mr. White and tell him that you had seen Harvey Milk come out of the Mayor's office after you had been informed the Mayor was not in?
APCAR: Yes, I did. Then he called me back and said, "Denise, come pick me up. I want to see the Mayor."
NORMAN: When you picked him up, did he do anything unusual?
APCAR: Well . . . he didn't look at me and normally he would turn his body alittle bit towards the driver and we would talk, you know, in a free-form way, but this time he didn't look at me at all. He was squinting hard. He was very nervous, he was agitated. He was rubbing his hands, blowing into his hands and rubbing them like he was cold, like his hands were cold. He acted very hurt. Yes. He was, he looked like he was going to cry. He was doing everything he could to restrain his emotion.
NORMAN: (*Looks to the jury.*) Did you ever describe him as acting quote "all fired up?" unquote.

APCAR: Yes, yes I—I believe I said that.
NORMAN: Did he mention at that time that he also was going to talk to Harvey Milk?
APCAR: Yes, he did.
NORMAN: Did he ever say he was going to quote "really lay it on the Mayor?" unquote.
APCAR: It's been brought to my attention I said that, yes.
NORMAN: When you were driving Mr. White downtown, was there some discussion relative to a statement you made. Quote "Anger had run pretty high all week towards the Mayor playing pool on us, dirty, you know?" unquote.
APCAR: I believe I was describing my anger. At the time I made those statements I was in shock and I spoke freely and I'm sure I've never used those terms before.
NORMAN: When you made those statements it was 2 hours and 5 minutes after the killings occurred, was it not?
APCAR: Yes.
NORMAN: Miss Apcar—When you were driving Mr. White to City Hall did you know he was carrying a loaded gun?
APCAR: No. I did not.
NORMAN: Thank you.
SCHMIDT: Yes, Dan White went to City Hall and he took a .38 caliber revolver with him, and that was not particularly unusual for Dan White. Dan White was an ex-policeman, and as a policeman one is required to carry, off-duty, a gun, and as an ex-policeman—well I think it's common practice. And as it's been mentioned Dan White's life was being threatened continuously by the White Panther party and other radical groups. And additionally, remember, there was the atmosphere of terror created by the Jonestown People's Temple Tragedy.

(Screens flood with Jonestown image.)

Only a week before the City Hall tragedy, 900 people, mostly San Franciscans—men, women, and children—died in the jungle. Rumors surfaced that hit lists had been placed on public officials in San Francisco. Assassination squads. And in hindsight, of course, we can all realize that this did not occur, but at the time there were 900 bodies laying in Guyana to indicate that indeed people were bent on murder.

(Screen: OFFICER BYRNE, Department of Records.)
(Lights.)

NORMAN: Officer Byrne, do persons who were once on the police force who have resigned their position, do they have the right to carry a concealed firearm on their person?

SCHMIDT: And I think it will be shown that Jim Jones himself was directly allied with the liberal elements of San Francisco politics and was hostile to the conservative elements.
BYRNE: No, a resigned person would not have that right.
SCHMIDT: And so, it would be important to understand that there were threats directed towards conservative persons like Dan White.
NORMAN: Officer, have you at my instance and request examined those particular records to determine whether there is an official permit issued by the Chief of Police to a Mr. Daniel James White to carry a concealed firearm?
BYRNE: Yes, I have.
NORMAN: What have you found?
BYRNE: I find no permit.
NORMAN: Thank you.

(Lights.)

SCHMIDT: Yes, it's a violation of the law to carry a firearm without a permit, but that firearm was *registered* to Dan White. And indeed, many officials at City Hall carried guns because of this violent atmosphere including ex-police Chief, Supervisor Al Nelder and the current Mayor of San Francisco, Dianne Feinstein.
COURT: Mr. Melia, please be sworn.
SCHMIDT: Upon approaching the door on polk Street, Mr. White observed a metal detection machine. Knowing that he did not know the man that was on the metal detection machine, he simply went around to the McAllister Street well door, where he expected to meet his aide. He did not find Denise Apcar there. She'd gone to put gas in her car. He waited for several moments, but knowing that it was imminent, the talk to the Mayor, he stepped through a window at the Department of Public Works.

(Screen: Slide of windows with man in front demonstrating procedure.)

Which doesn't require any physical prowess, and you can step through those windows, and the evidence will show that though now they are barred, previously it was not uncommon for people to enter and exit there. They are very large windows, and are large, wide sills,

(Screen shows windows which are the windows he stepped through. They are actually small, high off the ground: Now they are barred.)

and it's quite easy to step into the building through these windows.

(On screen: Slide of man in three piece suit trying to get leg up.)
(Screen: WILLIAM MELIA JR., Civil Engineer.)

MELIA: At approximately 10:35 I heard the window open. I heard someone jump to the floor and then running through the adjoining room. I looked up and caught a glance of a man in a suit running past the doorway of my office into the City Hall hallway.
NORMAN: What did you do?
MELIA: I got up from my desk and called after him: "Hey, wait a second."
NORMAN: Did that person wait or stop?
MELIA: Yes, they did.
NORMAN: Do you see that person here in this courtroom today?
MELIA: Yes, I do.
NORMAN: Where is that person?
MELIA: It's Dan White.
(*pause*)
He said to me: "I had to get in. My aide was supposed to come down and let me in the side door, but never showed up." I had taken exception to the way he had entered our office, and I replied: "AND YOU ARE?" And he replied: "I'm Dan White, the City Supervisor." He said, "Say, I've got to go," and with that, he turned and ran out of the office.
NORMAN: Did you say that he ran?
MELIA: Right.
NORMAN: Uh huh Mr. Melia—had you ever seen anyone else enter or exit through that window or those windows along that side?
MELIA: Yes, I had. It was common for individuals that worked in *our* office to do that.
NORMAN: Individuals who worked in your office . . . Were you alarmed when you learned that a Supervisor crawled or walked through that window, or stepped through that window?
MELIA: Was I alarmed?
NORMAN: Yes.
MELIA: Yes. I was . . . alarmed.
NORMAN: Thank you.

(*NORMAN looks to jury.*)

SCHMIDT: (*annoyed*) I think it's significant at this point—also because the fact that he crawled through the window *appears* to be important—it's significant to re-iterate that as Mr. Melia just testified people *often climb through that window,* and indeed, on the morning of the 27th, Denise had the key to the McAllister Street well door. So, Dan White stepped through the window, identified himself, traveled up to the second floor.

(*Screen: MRS. CYR COPERTINI, appointment secretary to the Mayor.*)

And then approached the desk of Cyr Copertini and properly identified himself, and asked to see the Mayor.

(Lights.)

CYR: I am the appointment secretary to Mayor Feinstein.
NORMAN: In November of last year and particularly on November 27th what was your then occupation?
CYR: I was appointment secretary to the Elected Mayor of San Francisco, George Moscone.

(WITNESS deeply moved.)

NORMAN: Mrs. Copertini—Were you aware that there was anything that was going to happen that day of November 27th of interest to the citizens of San Francisco, uh . . . I mean, such as some public announcement?
CYR: . . . There was to be a news conference to announce the new supervisor for the Eighth District, at 11:30.
NORMAN: Mrs. Copertini, at approximately 10:30 a.m. you saw Mr. Daniel White, he appeared in front of your desk . . . do you recall what he said?
CYR: He said: "Hello, Cyr. May I see the Mayor?" I said: "He has someone with him, but let me go check with him.." I went into the Mayor and told him that Supervisor White was there to see him. He was a little dismayed. He was a little uncomfortable by it and said: "Oh, all right. Tell him I'll see him, but he will have to wait a coupla minutes."
I asked the Mayor, "Shouldn't I have someone in there with him," and he said:
"No, no, I'll see him alone." And I asked him again. And he said, "No, no, I'll see him alone." And then I went back.
I said to Dan White, "it will be a few minutes."
He asked me how I was and how things were going. Was I having a nice day.
NORMAN: Was there anything unusual about his tone of voice?
CYR: No. I don't think so. He seemed nervous.
I asked him would he like to see the newspaper while he was waiting? He said: "No, he wouldn't," and I said: "Well, that's all right. There's nothing in it anyway unless you want to read about Caroline Kennedy having turned 21." And he said: "21? Is that right." He said: "Yeah, that's all so long ago. It's even more amazing when you think that John John is now 18."

(Lights change. Music "Deus Irae")
(Boy's Choir.)

DENMAN: The only comparable situation I ever remember was when JFK was killed.
CYR: It was about that time he was admitted to the Mayor's office.
NORMAN: Did you tell Mr. Daniel White that he could go in?

CYR: Yes.
DENMAN: I remember that in my bones, in my body.
NORMAN: Did he respond in any way to that?
DENMAN: Just like this one.
CYR: He said: "Good girl, Cyr."
NORMAN: Good girl, Cyr?
CYR: Right.
DENMAN: When Camelot all of a sudden turned to hell.
NORMAN: Then what did he do?
CYR: Went in.
NORMAN: After he went in there did you hear anything of an unusual nature that was coming from the Mayor's office?
CYR: After a time I heard a . . . commotion.

   (Lights change.)

YOUNG MOTHER: I heard it on the car radio, I literally gasped.
NORMAN: Explain that to us, please.
YOUNG MOTHER: I wanted to pull over to the side of the road and scream.
CYR: Well, I heard—a series of noises—first a group and then one—
YOUNG MOTHER: Just scream.
CYR: I went to the window to see if anything was happening out in the street.
YOUNG MOTHER: Then I thought of my kids.
CYR: And the street was rather extraordinarily calm.
DENMAN: I noticed when I looked outside that there was an unusual quiet.
CYR: For that hour of the day there is usually more—there wasn't really anything out there.
DENMAN: I went to the second floor and started walking toward the Mayor's office.
YOUNG MOTHER: I wanted to get them out of school and take them home,
NORMAN: Could you describe these noises for us?
YOUNG MOTHER: I wanted to take them home and (*SHE makes a hugging gesture with her arms.*) lock the door.
CYR: Well, they were dull thuds rather like—
DENMAN: And there was this strange combination of panic and silence that you rarely see,
CYR: I thought maybe it was an automobile door that somebody had tried to shut, by, you know, pushing, and then finally succeeding.
DENMAN: It was like a silent slow-motion movie of a disaster.
NORMAN: Do you have any recollection that you can report with any certainty to us as to how many sounds there were?
CYR: No. As I stood there I—I thought I ought to remember—(*WITNESS breaks down.*)

DENMAN: There was this hush and aura, people were moving with strange faces, as if the world had just come to an end.
NOTHENBERG: (*MOSCONE's friend.*) George loved this city, and felt what was wrong could be fixed.
NORMAN: Do you want a glass of water?

(*CYR sobs.*)

DENMAN: And I asked someone what had happened and he said: "The Mayor has been shot."
CYR: I ought to remember that pattern in case it is something, but I—
NOTHENBERG: (*MOSCONE's friend.*) He knew—it was a white racist town. A Catholic town. But he believed in people's basic good will.

(*CYR sobs.*)

COURT: Just a minute. Do you want a recess?
NOTHENBERG: (*MOSCONE's friend.*) He never suspected, I bet, Dan White's psychotic behavior.
NORMAN: Do you want a recess?
NOTHENBERG: (*MOSCONE's friend.*) That son of a bitch killed someone I loved. I mean, I loved the guy.
CYR: No. I'm all right.
COURT: Are you sure you are all right?
CYR: Yes.
YOUNG MOTHER: I just thought of my kids.

(*pause*)

NOTHENBERG: (*MOSCONE's friend.*) I loved his idealism. I loved his hope.
CYR: Then what happened was Rudy Nothenberg left to tell the press that the conference would start a few minutes late.
NOTHENBERG: (*MOSCONE's friend.*) I loved the guy.
CYR: And then he came back to me right away and said: "Oh, I guess we can go ahead. I just saw Dan White leave."
NOTHENBERG: (*MOSCONE's friend.*) I loved his almost naive faith in people.
CYR: So then he went into the Mayor's office and said: "Well, he's not here." And I said: "Well, maybe he went into the back room."
NOTHENBERG: (*MOSCONE's friend.*) I loved his ability to go on.
CYR: Then he just gave a shout saying: "Gary, get in here. Call an ambulance. Get the police."
NOTHENBERG: See, I got too tired to stay in politics and do it. George and I were together from the beginning. Me, Phil Burton, Willie Brown. Beatin' all the old Irishmen.
DENMAN: I heard right away that Dan White had done it.
NOTHENBERG: But George believed, as corny as this sounds, that you do

good for the people. I haven't met many of those and George was one of those. Maybe those are the guys that get killed. I don't know.

(CYR crying.)

NORMAN: All right. All this you told us about occurred in San Francisco, didn't it?
CYR: (*Deeply moved.*) Yes.
SCHMIDT: Dan White, as it was quite apparent at that point had CRACKED because of his underlying mental illness . . .

(Screen: CARL HENRY CARLSON, Aide to HARVEY MILK.)

CARLSON: I heard Peter Nardoza, Diane Feinstein's aide, say: Diane wants to see you and Dan White said: "That'll have to wait a couple of minutes, I have something to do first."
NORMAN: I have something to do first?
CARLSON: Yes.
NORMAN: Do you recall in what manner Mr. White announced himself?
SCHMIDT: There were stress factors due to the fact that he hadn't been notified,
CARLSON: He appeared at the door which was normally left open. Stuck his head in and asked: "Say, Harv, can I see you for a minute?"
SCHMIDT: And the sudden emotional surge that he had in the Mayor's office was simply too much for him
NORMAN: What did Harvey Milk do at that time if anything?
CARLSON: He turned around.
SCHMIDT: And he cracked.
CARLSON: He turned around
SCHMIDT: The man cracked.
CARLSON: And said "Sure." and got up and went across the hall . . .
SCHMIDT: He shot the Mayor,
CARLSON: To the office designated as Dan White's office on the chart.
SCHMIDT: Reloaded his gun, basically on *instinct*, because of his police training, and was about to leave the building at that point
NORMAN: After they went across the hall to Mr. White's office . . .
SCHMIDT: And he looked down the hall,
NORMAN: Would you tell us what next you heard or saw?
SCHMIDT: He saw somebody that he believed to be an aide to Harvey Milk.
CARLSON: A few seconds, probably 10, 15 seconds later, I heard a shot, or the sound of gunfire.
SCHMIDT: He went down to the Supervisor's area to *talk* to Harvey Milk.
COURT: Excuse me. Would you speak out. Your voice is fading a bit.
SCHMIDT: At that point, in the same state of rage, emotional upheaval with the stress of 10 years of mental illness having cracked this man.

CORONER: *(Demonstrates as HE speaks.)* The left arm has to be close to the body and slightly forward with the palm up.
SCHMIDT: *Ninety seconds* from the time he shot the Mayor, Dan White shot and killed Harvey Milk.
CARLSON: After the shot, I heard Harvey Milk scream. "oh, no." And then the first—the first part of the second "no" which was then cut short by the second shot.
CORONER: The right hand has to be palm away with the thumb pointed towards the body and the elbow in slightly to the body with the arm raised.
NORMAN: How many sounds of shots did you hear altogether, Mr. Carlson?
CARLSON: Five or six. I really didn't consciously count them.
CORONER: In this position all of these wounds that I have just described in Peoples's 30 and 29 line up.

(Blackout on CORONER in position.)
(Pause.)

CARLSON: A few moments later the door opened, the door opened, and Daniel White walked out, rushed out, and proceeded down the hall.
NORMAN: Now, Mr. Carlson, when Daniel White first appeared at the office of Harvey Milk and said, "Say, Harv, can I see you for a minute?", could you describe his tone of voice in any way?
CARLSON: He appeared to be very normal, usual friendly self. I didn't, I didn't feel anything out of the ordinary. It was just very typical Dan White.

(Music out, lights change.)

GWENN: I'd like to talk about when people are pushed to the wall.
SCHMIDT: Harvey Milk was against the re-appointment of Dan White.
GWENN: In order to understand the riots, I think you have to understand that the Dan White verdict did not occur in a vacuum.
SCHMIDT: Basically, it was a political decision. It was evident there was a liberal wing of the Board of Supervisors, and there was a smaller conservative wing, and Dan White was a conservative politician for San Francisco.

(Screen: RICHARD PABICH, Legislative Assistant to HARVEY MILK.)
(Lights.)

PABICH: My address is 542-A Castro Street.
GWENN: I don't think I have to say what their presence meant to us, and what their loss meant to us—
NORMAN: What did you do after you saw Dan White run down the hall and put the key in the door of his old office, Room 237?

GWENN: The assassinations of our friends Harvey Milk and George Moscone were a crime against us all.
PABICH: Well, I was struck in my head, sort of curious as to why he'd been running.
GWENN: And right here, when I say "us," I don't mean only gay people.
PABICH: And he was—it looked like he was in a hurry. I was aware of the political situation.
GWENN: I mean all people who are getting less than they deserve.
PABICH: I was aware that Harvey was taking the position to the Mayor that Mr. White shouldn't be reappointed. Harvey and I had talked earlier that day . . . that it would be a significant day.

(Lights.)
(Subliminal music.)

MILK'S FRIEND: After Harvey died, I went into a depression that lasted about a year, I guess. They called it depression, anyway. I thought about suicide, well, I more than thought about it.
SCHMIDT: Mr. Pabich, Mr. Milk had suggested a replacement for Dan White, hadn't he?
PABICH: He had, to my understanding, recommended several people, and basically took the position that Dan White should not be reappointed.
MILK'S FRIEND: I lost my job. I stayed in the hospital for, I would guess, two months or so. They put me on some kind of drug that . . . well, it helped, I guess. I mean, I loved him and it was . . .
SCHMIDT: Was he requesting that a homosexual be appointed?
PABICH: No, he was not.
MILK'S FRIEND: Well, he was gone and that couldn't change.
SCHMIDT: I have nothing further. Thank you.
MILK'S FRIEND: He'd never be here again, I knew that.
COURT: All right. Any redirect, Mr. Norman?
NORMAN: No. Thank you for coming, Mr. Pabich. *(PABICH exits.)*
GWENN: It was as if Dan White had given the go-ahead. It was a free-for-all, a license to kill.

(PABICH with JOANNA LU.)
(TV lights.)

PABICH: *(On camera.)* It's over. Already I can tell it's over. He asked me a question, a clear queer-baiting question, and the jury didn't bat an eye. *(Starts to exit, then.)* Dan White's going to get away with murder.
JOANNA LU: Mr. Pabich.
MILK'S FRIEND: I had this recurring dream. We were at the Opera, Harvey and I. I was laughing. Harvey was laughing. Then Harvey leaned over and

said to me: When you're watching Tosca, you know you're alive. That's when I'd wake up.
GWENN: I remember the moment I heard Harvey had been shot—(*SHE breaks down.*)
MILK'S FRIEND: And I'd realize—like for the first time all over again—he's dead.

(*Blackout.*)

(*Hyperreal sounds of high heels on marble, echoing, moving fast. Mumbled Hail Marys.*)
(*Fade lights up slowly on SCHMIDT, NORMAN.*)

SCHMIDT: From here I think the evidence will demonstrate that Dan White ran down to Denise's office, screamed at his aide to give him the key to her car.
And he left, went to a church, called his wife, went into St. Mary's Cathedral, prayed, and his wife got there, and he told her, the best he could, what he remembered he had done, and then they walked together to the Northern Police Station where he turned himself in; asked the officer to look after his wife, asked the officer to take possession of an Irish poster he was carrying . . .

(*Screen: Slide: Stain glass window, cover of Uris book.*)
(*IRELAND: A Terrible Beauty.*)

and then made a statement, what best he could recall had occurred. (*FALZON hands on shoulders.*)
FALZON: Why . . . I feel like hitting you in the fuckin' mouth . . . How could you be so stupid? How?
WHITE: I . . . I want to tell you about it . . . I want to, to explain.
FALZON: Do you want a lawyer, Danny?
WHITE: No, Frank I want to talk to you.
FALZON: Okay, if you want to talk to me, I'm gonna get my tape recorder and read you your rights and do it right.
NORMAN: The people at this time move the tape recorded statement into evidence.
FALZON: Today's date is Monday, November 27th, 1978. The time is presently 12:05. We're inside the Homicide Detail, Room 454, at the Hall of Justice. Present is Inspector Edward Erdelatz, Inspector Frank Falzon and for the record, sir, your full name?
WHITE: Daniel James White.
FALZON: Would you, normally in a situation like this, ah . . . we ask questions, I'm aware of your past history as a police officer and also as a San Francisco fireman. I would prefer, I'll let you do it in a narrative form

as to what happened this morning if you can lead up to the events of the shooting and then backtrack as to why these events took place. (*Looks at ERDELATZ.*)

WHITE: Well, it's just that I've been under an awful lot of pressure lately, financial pressure, because of my job situation, family pressure because of ah . . . not being able to have the time with my family. (*sob*)

FALZON: Can you relate these pressures you've been under, Dan, at this time? Can you explain it to Inspector Erdelatz and myself.

WHITE: It's just that I wanted to serve (*FALZON nods.*) the people of San Francisco well and I did that. Then when the pressures got too great, I decided to leave. After I left, my family and friends offered their support and said, whatever it would take to allow me to go back into office,—well, they would be willing to make that effort. And then it came out that Supervisor Milk and some others were working against me to get my seat back on the Board. He didn't speak to me, he spoke to the City Attorney but I was in the office and I heard the conversation.

I could see the game that was being played, they were going to use me as a *scapegoat*, whether I was a good supervisor or not, was not the point. This was a political opportunity and they were going to degrade me and my family and the job that I had tried to do an, an more or less HANG ME OUT TO DRY. And I saw more and more evidence of this during the week when the papers reported that ah . . . someone else was going to be reappointed. The Mayor told me he was going to call me before he made any decision, he never did that. I was troubled, the pressure, my family again, my, my son's out to a babysitter.

FALZON: Dan, can you tell Inspector Erdelatz and myself, what was your plan this morning? What did you have in mind?

WHITE: I didn't have any devised plan or anything, it's, I was leaving the house to talk, to see the Mayor and I went downstairs, to, to make a phone call and I had my gun down there.

FALZON: Is this your police service revolver, Dan?

WHITE: This is the gun I had when I was a policeman. It's in my room an ah . . . I don't know, I just put it on. I, I don't know why I put it on, it's just . . .

FALZON: You went directly from your residence to the Mayor's office this morning?

WHITE: Yes, my, my aide picked me up but she didn't have any idea ah . . . you know that I had a gun on me or, you know, and I went in to see him an, an he told me he wasn't going to reappoint me and he wasn't intending to tell me about it. Then ah . . . I got kind of fuzzy and then just my head didn't feel right and I,

FALZON: Was this before any threats on your part, Dan?

WHITE: I, I never made any threats.

FALZON: There were no threats at all?

WHITE: I, I . . . oh no.

FALZON: When were you, how, what was the conversation, can you explain to Inspector Erdelatz and myself the conversation that existed between the two of you at this time?

WHITE: It was pretty much just, you know, I asked, was I going to be reappointed. He said, no I am not, no you're not. And I said, why, and he told me, it's a political decision and that's the end of it, and that's it and then he could obviously see, see I was obviously distraught an then he said, let's have a drink and I, I'm not even a drinker, you know I don't, once in a while, but I'm not even a drinker. But I just kinda stumbled in the back and he was all, he was all smiles—he was talking an nothing was getting through to me. It was just like a roaring in my ears an, an then . . . it just came to me, you know, he . . .

FALZON: You couldn't hear what he was saying, Dan?

WHITE: Just small talk that, you know, it just wasn't registering. What I was going to do now, you know, and how this would affect my family, you know, an, an just, just all the time knowing he's going to go out an, an lie to the press an, an tell 'em, you know, that I, I wasn't a good supervisor and that people didn't want me an then that was it. Then I, I just shot him, that was it, it was over.

FALZON: What happened after you left there, Dan?

WHITE: Well, I, I left his office by one of the back doors an, I was going to go down the stairs and then I saw Harvey Milk's aide across the hall at the Supervisor's an then it struck me about what Harvey had tried to do an I said, well I'll go talk to him. He didn't know I had, I had heard his conversation and he was all smiles and stuff and I went in and, you know, I, I didn't agree with him on a lot of things but I was always honest, you know, and here they were devious. And then he started kinda smirking, 'cause he knew, he knew I wasn't going to be reappointed. And ah . . . I started to say you know how hard I worked for it and what it meant to me and my family and then my reputation as, as a hard worker, good honest person and he just kind of smirked at me as if to say, too bad an then, and then, I just got all flushed an, an hot, and I shot him.

FALZON: This occurred inside your room, Dan?

WHITE: Yeah, in my office, yeah.

FALZON: And when you left there did you go back home?

WHITE: No, no, no I drove to the, the Doggie Diner on, on Van Ness and I called my wife and she, she didn't know, she . . .

FALZON: Did you tell her, Dan?

(Sobbing.)

WHITE: I called up, I didn't tell her on the phone. I just said . . . she was working. I just told her to meet me at the cathedral.

FALZON: St. Mary's?

(Sobbing.)

WHITE: She took a cab, yeah. She didn't know. She knew I'd been upset and I wasn't even talking to her at home because I just couldn't explain how I felt and she had no, nothing to blame about it, she was, she always has been great to me but it was, just the pressure hitting me an just my head's all flushed and expected that my skull's going to crack. Then when she came to the church, I, I told her and she kind of slumped an she, she couldn't say anything.

FALZON: How is she now do you, do you know is she, do you know where she is?

WHITE: I don't know now. She, she came to Northern Station with me. She asked me not to do anything about myself, you know that she, she loved me and she'd stick by me and not to hurt myself.

ERDELATZ: Dan, right now are you under a doctor's care?

WHITE: No.

ERDELATZ: Are you under any medication at all?

WHITE: No.

ERDELATZ: When is the last time you had your gun with you prior to today?

WHITE: I guess it was a few months ago. I, I was afraid of some of the threats that were made an, I, I, just wanted to make sure to protect myself you know this, this city isn't safe you know and there's a lot of people running around an well I don't have to tell you fellows, you guys know that.

ERDELATZ: When you left home this morning, Dan, was it your intention to confront the Mayor, Supervisor Milk or anyone else with that gun?

WHITE: No, I, I, what I wanted to do was just, talk to him, you know, I, I ah, I didn't even know if I was going to be reappointed or not be reappointed. *Why do we do things, you know, why did I, I don't know. No,* I, I just wanted to talk to him that's all an at least have him be honest with me and tell me why he was doing it, not because I was a bad supervisor or anything but, you know, I never killed anybody before, I never shot anybody . . .

ERDELATZ: Why did . . .

WHITE: . . . . I didn't even, I didn't even know if I wanted to kill him. I just shot him, I don't know.

ERDELATZ: What type of gun is that you were carrying, Dan?

WHITE: It's a .38, a two-inch .38.

ERDELATZ: And do you know how many shots you fired?

WHITE: Uh . . . no I don't, I don't. I, I out of instinct when I, I reloaded the gun ah . . . you know, it's just the training I guess I had, you know.

ERDELATZ: Where did you reload?

WHITE: I reloaded in my office, when I was I couldn't out in the hall.

(Pause.)

ERDELATZ: When you say you reloaded, are you speaking of following the shooting in the Mayor's office?
WHITE: Yeah.
ERDELATZ: Inspector Falzon?
FALZON: No questions. Is there anything you'd like to add, Dan, before we close this statement?
WHITE: Yes. Just that I've been honest and worked hard, never cheated anybody and I wanted to do a good job, I'm trying to do a good job and I saw this city as it's going, kind of downhill and I was always just a lonely vote on the board. I was trying to do a good job for the city.
FALZON: Inspector Erdelatz and I ah . . . appreciate your cooperation and the truthfulness of your statement.

(Lights change.)
(DAN WHITE sobbing. MARY ANNE WHITE sobbing, JURORS sobbing.)
(FALZON moved.)

NORMAN: I think that is all. You may examine.
COURT: Do you want to take a recess at this time?
SCHMIDT: Why don't we take a brief recess?
COURT: Let me admonish you, ladies and gentlemen of the jury, not to discuss this case among yourselves nor with anyone else, not allow anyone to speak to you about the matter, no are you to form or express an opinion until the matter has been submitted to you.

(Gavel.)
(House light up.)
(On screen: Recess.)

INTERMISSION

ACT TWO

In Defense of Murder

> As audience enters, on screen documentary images of Milk and Moscone company/audience watch

MOSCONE: * My late father was a guard at San Quentin, and who I was visiting one day, and who showed to me, and then explained the function of, the uh, the uh death chamber. And it just seemed inconceivable to me, though I was pretty young at the time, that in this society that I had been trained to believe was the most effective and efficient of all societies, that the only way we could deal with violent crime would be to do the ultimate ourselves, and that's to governmentally sanction the taking of another person's life.

MILK: *(FALZON enters.) Two days after I was elected I got a phone call—the voice was quite young. It was from Altoona, Pennsylvania. And the person said, "Thanks." And you've got to elect gay people so that that young child, and the thousands upon thousands like that child, * know that there's hope for a better world. There's hope for a better tomorrow. Without hope, they'll only gaze at those blacks, the Asians, the disabled, the seniors, the us'es, the us'es. Without hope, the us'es give up. I know that you cannot live on hope alone. But without it, life is not worth living. And you, and you, and you, gotta give 'em hope. Thank you very much.

> (Lights up. Courtroom.)
> (FALZON on witness stand.)
> (DAN WHITE at defense table sobbing.)
> (MARY ANN WHITE behind him sobbing.)
> (On tape.)

WHITE: (*voice*) Just that I've been honest and worked hard, never cheated anybody and I wanted to do a good job, I'm trying to do a good job and I saw this city as it's going, kind of downhill and I was always just a lonely vote on the board. I was trying to do a good job for the city.
FALZON: Inspector Erdelatz and I ah . . .
appreciate your cooperation and the truthfulness of your statement.

> (FALZON SWITCHES TAPE OFF.)

NORMAN: I think that is all. You may examine. (*Lights change, company exits.*)

---

*Dialogue from *The Times of Harvey Milk*, a film by Robert Epstein and Richard Schmeichen.

(On screen: INSPECTOR FRANK FALZON, witness for the prosecution.)
(Dissolve to on screen: ACT TWO—In Defense of Murder.)

SCHMIDT: Inspector Falzon, you mentioned that you had known Dan White in the past, prior to November 27, 1978?
FALZON: Yes, sir, quite well.
SCHMIDT: About how long have you known him?
FALZON: According to Dan,
it goes way back to the days
we attended St. Elizabeth's Grammar School together,
but we went to different high schools.
I attended St. Ignatius, and he attended Riordan.
He walked up to me one day at the Jackson Playground,
with spikes over his shoulders, glove in his hand,
and asked if he could play on the team.
I told him it was the police team,
and he stated that he was a new recruit at Northern Station,
wanted to play on the police softball team,
and since that day Dan White and I
have been very good friends.
SCHMIDT: You knew him fairly well then, that is fair?
FALZON: As well as I know anybody, I believed.
SCHMIDT: Can you tell me, when you saw him first on November 27th, 1978, how did he appear physically to you?
FALZON: Destroyed. This was not the Dan White I had known, not at all.
That day I saw a shattered individual,
both mentally and physically in appearance,
who appeared to me to be shattered.
Dan White, the man I knew
prior to Monday, the 27th of November, 1978,
was a man among men.
SCHMIDT: Knowing, with regard to the shootings of Mayor Moscone and Harvey Milk, knowing Dan White as you did, is he the type of man that could have premeditatedly and deliberately shot those people?
NORMAN: Objection as calling for an opinion and conclusion.
COURT: Sustained.
SCHMIDT: Knowing him as you do, have you ever seen anything in his past that would lead you to believe he was capable of cold-bloodedly shooting somebody?
NORMAN: Same objection.
COURT: Sustained.
SCHMIDT: Your Honor, at this point I have anticipated that maybe there would be some argument with regard to opinions not only as to Inspector Falzon, but with a number of other witnesses that I intend to call, and

accordingly I have prepared a memorandum of what I believe to be the appropriate law. (*Shows memo.*)
COURT: I have no quarrel with your authorities, but I think the form of the questions that you asked was objectionable.
SCHMIDT: The questions were calculated to bring out an opinion on the state of mind and—I believe that a lay person, if he is an intimate acquaintance, surely can hazard such an opinion. I believe that Inspector Falzon, as a police officer, has an opinion.
COURT: Get the facts from this witness. I will let you get those facts, whatever they are.
SCHMIDT: All right, we will try that.
Inspector Falzon, again, you mentioned that you were quite familiar with Dan White; can you tell me something about the man's character, as to the man that you knew prior to the—prior to November 27th, 1978?
NORMAN: Objection as being irrelevant and vague.
COURT: Overruled. (*To FALZON.*) Do you understand the question?
FALZON: I do, basically, your Honor.
COURT: All right, you may answer it.
NORMAN: Well, your Honor, character for what?
COURT: Overruled. (*To FALZON.*) You may answer it.
FALZON: The Dan White that I knew prior to Monday, November 27, 1978,
was a man who seemed to excel in pressure situations,
and it seemed that the greater the pressure, the more enjoyment
that Dan had,
exceeding at what he was trying to do.

Examples would be in his sports life,
that I can relate to,
and for the first time in the history of the State of California,
there was a law enforcement softball tournament held in 1971.
The San Francisco Police Department entered
that softball tournament along with other major departments,
Los Angeles included,
and Dan White was not only named on the All Star Team
at the end of the tournament,
but named the most valuable player.

He was just outstanding under pressure situations,
when men would be on base
and that clutch hit was needed.

Another example of Dan White's
attitude toward pressure
was that when he decided to run
for the District 8 Supervisor's seat,

and I can still vividly remember the morning
he walked into the Homicide Detail and sat down to—
announce that he was going to run for City Supervisor,
I said: "How are you going to do it, Dan?
Nobody heard of Dan White.
How are you going to go out there,
win this election?

He said: "I'm going to do it the way the people
want it to be done,
knock on their doors, go inside, shake their hands,
let them know what Dan White stands for."

And he said: "Dan White is going to represent them.
There will be a voice in City Hall, you watch, I'll make it."

He did what he said he was going to do,
he ran, won the election.
SCHMIDT: Given these things that you mentioned about Dan White, outstanding under pressure, there anything in his character that you saw of him, prior to those tragedies of the 27th of November, that would have led you to believe that he would ever kill somebody cold-bloodedly?
NORMAN: Objection, irrelevant.
COURT: Overruled.
NORMAN: Let me state my grounds for the record.
COURT: Overruled.
NORMAN: Thank you, Judge.
It's irrelevant and called for his opinion and speculation.
COURT: Overruled. (*Gavel. To FALZON.*) You may answer that.
FALZON: Yes, your Honor.
I'm aware—I'm hesitating only because
there was something I saw in Dan's personality
that didn't become relevant to me
until I was assigned this case.
He had a tendency to run, occasionally,
from situations.
I saw this flaw, and I asked him about it,
and his response was that his ultimate goal
was to purchase a boat, just travel around the world,
get away from everybody,

He wanted to be helpful to people,
and yet he wanted to run away from them.
That did not make sense to me.

Otherwise, to me,
Dan White was an exemplary individual,
a man that I was proud to know
and be associated with.

SCHMIDT: Do you think he cracked? Do you think there was something wrong with him on November 27th?

NORMAN: Objection as calling for an opinion and speculation.

COURT: Sustained.

SCHMIDT: I have nothing further. (*Turns back.*) Inspector, I have one last question. Did you ever see him act out of revenge as to the whole time you have known him?

NORMAN: Objection. That calls for speculation.

COURT: No, overruled, and this is as to his observations and contacts. Overruled.

FALZON: The only time Dan White
could have acted out in revenge
is when he took the opposite procedure
in hurting himself,
by quitting the San Francisco Police Department.

SCHMIDT: Nothing further. Thank you, sir.

NORMAN: Inspector Falzon, you regard yourself as a close friend to Mr. Daniel White, don't you?

FALZON: Yes, sir.

NORMAN: Do you regard yourself as a *very* close friend of Mr. Daniel White.

FALZON: I would consider myself a close friend of yours, if that can relate to you my closeness with Dan White.

NORMAN: Of course, you haven't known me as long as you have known Mr. Daniel White, have you, Inspector?

FALZON: Just about the same length of time, Counsel.

NORMAN: Inspector Falzon, while you've expressed some shock at these tragedies, would you subscribe to the proposition that there's a first for everything?

FALZON: It's obvious in this case; yes, sir.

NORMAN: Thank you.

(*NORMAN sits.*)
(*FALZON gets up and takes his seat.*)
(*Beside NORMAN.*)

NORMAN: The Prosecution rests.

(*Blackout.*)

(*On screen: The Prosecution rests.*)
(*Commotion in court.*)

COURT: Order.

(Gavel.)
(Lights up.)
(FREITAS alone.)

FREITAS: I was the D.A.
Obviously in some respects, the trial ruined me. This trial . . .

(On screen: Dissolve into picture of DAN WHITE as fire hero.)
(Screen: THE DEFENSE. Subliminal music.)
(Lights up.)

SHERRATT: *(Fire Chief)* Dan White was an excellent fire fighter. In fact, he was commended for a rescue at Geneva Towers. The award hasn't been given to him as yet, uh . . .
FREDIANI: *(Fireman)* Dan White was the valedictorian of the Fire Department class. He was voted so by members of the class.

(On screen: DAN WHITE as Valedictorian.)

MILK'S FRIEND: When I was in the hospital, what galled me most was the picture of Dan White as the ALL American Boy.
SHERRATT: but a meritorious advisory board and fire commission were going to present Mr. White with a class C medal.

(On screen: DAN WHITE as fire hero.)

FREDIANI: Everybody liked Dan.
SCHMIDT: Did you work with Dan as a policeman?
SULLIVAN: *(Policeman)* Yes, I did.
MILK'S FRIEND: Maybe as a gay man, I understand the tyranny of the All American Boy.

(On screen: DAN WHITE as police officer.)

FREDIANI: He loved sports and I loved sports.

(On screen: DAN WHITE as golden gloves boxer.)

SULLIVAN: Dan White as a police officer,
was a very fair police officer on the street.
MILK'S FRIEND: Maybe because I am so often his victim.
GWENN: I followed the trial in the papers.
SCHMIDT: Having had the experience of being a police officer, is it unusual for persons that have been police officers to carry guns?

SULLIVAN: Uh, pardon me, Mr. Schmidt?
GWENN: I thought then something was wrong with this picture.
SCHMIDT: I say, it is uncommon that ex-police officers would carry guns?
GWENN: Something was wrong, we thought, when the Chief Inspector of Homicide became the chief character witness for the defense.
SULLIVAN: No, it is a common thing that former police officers will carry guns.
GWENN: Why didn't the Chief Inspector of Homicide ask Dan White how he got into City Hall with a loaded gun?
SCHMIDT: Without a permit?
SULLIVAN: Yes.
GWENN: Dan White reloaded after shooting the Mayor. If it was "reflex," police training, why didn't he reload again after shooting Harvey Milk?
SCHMIDT: Is there anything in his character that would have led you to believe he was capable of shooting two persons?
NORMAN: Objection.
COURT: Overruled.
SULLIVAN: No, nothing whatever.
GWENN: And what can explain the coup de grace shots
White fired into the backs of their heads as they lay there helpless on the floor?
DOLSON: (*City Supervisor*) Dan in my opinion was a person who saved lives.
GWENN: Where is the prosecution?
FREITAS: I mean, I would have remained in politics. Except for this. I was voted out of office.
SCHMIDT: (*To DOLSON.*) Supervisor Dolson, you saw him on
November 27th, 1978, did you not?
DOLSON: I did.
FREITAS: In hindsight, you know.
I would have changed a lot of things.
SCHMIDT: What did you see?
FREITAS: But hindsight is always perfect vision.

(*Slide: DAN WHITE as City Supervisor outside City Hall.*)

DOLSON: What I saw made me want to cry . . .
Dan was always so neat.
Looked like a Marine on Parade . . .
GWENN: What pressures were you under *indeed*?
DOLSON: And here he was, this kid, who was badly disheveled
and he had his hands cuffed behind him,
which was something I never expected to see.
He looked (*sobs*) absolutely *devastated*.

GWENN: As the "VICTIM" sat in the courtroom
we heard of policemen and firemen sporting
FREE DAN WHITE t-shirts
as they raised 100,000 dollars for Dan White's defense fund,
and the same message began appearing
in spray paint on walls around the city.
FREE DAN WHITE.
DOLSON: I put my arm around him, told him that everything
was going to be all right,
but how everything was going to be all right,
I don't know.

    (WITNESS deeply moved)
    (MARY ANN WHITE sobs.)

GWENN: And the trial was still happening.
SCHMIDT: *(Deeply moved.)* Thank you. I have nothing further.

    (DOLSON sobs.)

GWENN: But the tears at the Hall of Justice
are all for Dan White.

    (Gavel.)
    (They exit.)
    (Lights change.)

    (The ex-D.A. alone in an empty courtroom.)
    (Nervous, fidgeting.)

FREITAS: I was voted out of office.

    (On screen: JOSEPH FREITAS, JR., former D.A.)

Well, I'm out of politics and I don't know whether
I'll get back into politics
because it certainly did set back my personal ah . . .
aspirations as a public figure dramatically.
I don't know.

You know, there was an attempt to not allow our office to
prosecute the case
because I was close to Moscone myself.
And we fought against that.
I was confident—
(laughs)

I chose Tom Norman because he was the senior homicide prosecutor
for fifteen years and he was quite successful at it.
I don't know . . .

The was a great division in the city then, you know.
The city was divided all during that period.
George was a liberal Democrat and Dick Hongisto.
I was considered a liberal Democrat
and George as you'll remember was elected
Mayor over John Barbagelata who was the leader
of what was considered the Right in town.
And it was a narrow victory.
So, after his election, Barbagelata persisted in attacking them
and keeping
I thought—
keeping the city divided.

It divided on emerging constituencies like
the gay constituency.
That's the one that was used to cause
the most divisive emotions more than any other.
So the divisiveness in the city was there.

I mean that was the whole point of this political fight
between Dan White
and Moscone and Milk:
The fight was over who controlled the city.

The Right couldn't afford to lose Dan.
He was their Saving vote on the Board of Supervisors.
He blocked the Milk/Moscone agenda.
Obviously Harvey Milk didn't want Dan White on the Board.

So, it was political, the murders.

Maybe I should have,
again in hindsight, possible Tom,
even though his attempts to do that may have been
ruled inadmissible,
possible Tom should have been a little stronger in that area.
But again, at the time . . . I mean,
even the press was shocked at the outcome . . .

But—

Well, I think that what the jury had already bought was
White's background—
Now that's what was really on trial.
Dan White sat there and waved his little American flag
and they acquitted him.
They convicted George and Harvey.
Now if this had been a poor Black or a poor Chicano
or a poor white janitor who'd been fired,
or the husband of an alleged girlfriend of Moscone's
I don't think they would have bought the diminished capacity
defense.
But whereas they have a guy who was a member of a
county Board of Supervisors who left the police department,
who had served in the army, who was a fireman,
who played baseball—
I think that's what they were caught up in—
that kind of person *must* have been crazy to do this.
I would have interpreted it differently.
Not to be held to a higher standard, but uh . . .
that he had all the tools to be responsible.

One of the things people said was:
"Why didn't you talk more about
George's background, his family life, etc.?"
Well . . .
One of the reasons is that Tom Norman did know,
that had he opened up that area,

they were prepared,
yeah—
they were prepared to smear George—to bring up the incident in
Sacramento. With the Woman—
(And other things.)
It would be at best a wash,
so why get into it?
If you know they're going to bring out things that aren't positive.
We wanted to let the city heal.
We—And after Jonestown . . .
Well it would have been the city on trial.
If the jury had stuck to the facts alone,
I mean, the confession alone was enough to convict him . . .
I mean, look at this kid that shot Reagan,
it was the same thing. All they way through that,
they said, my friends—

"Well, Christ, look at what the prosecutors went through on that one, Joe.
It's tragic that that has to be the kind of experience
that will make you feel better.

And then about White being anti-gay
well . . .
White inside himself may have been anti-gay, but
that Milk was his target . . .
As I say—*Malice was there.*
Milk led the fight to keep White off the Board,
which makes the murder all the more rational.
I know the gay community thinks the murder was anti-gay:
political in that sense. But
I think, they're wrong. Y' know, some people—
in the gay community
—ah—even said I threw the trial.
Before this, I was considered a great friend to the gay community.
Why would I want to throw the trial
—this trial
in an election year?

Oh, there were accusations you wouldn't believe . . .
At the trial, a woman . . .
it may have been one of the jurors—
I can't remember . . .
Actually said—
"But what would Mary Ann White do without her husband?"
And I remember my outrage.
She never thought,
"What will Gina Moscone do without George?"

I must tell you that it's hard for me to talk about a lot
of these things,
all of this is just the—just
the tip of the iceberg.

We thought—Tommy and I—Tom Norman and I—
We thought it was an open and shut case
of first degree murder.

(Lights.)

(On screen: THE PSYCHIATRIC DEFENSE)

(Lights up on four psychiatrists in conservative dress, in either separate witness stands or a multiple stand unit.)

NORMAN: It wasn't just an automatic reaction when he fired those last two shots into George Moscone's *brains* was it, Doctor?
COURT: Let's move on Mr. Norman.
You are just arguing with the witnesses now.
NORMAN: Your Honor—
COURT: Let's move on.
SOLOMON: I think he was out of control and in an unreasonable state. And I think if the gun had held, you know, maybe more bullets, maybe he would have shot more bullets. I don't know.
LUNDE: This wasn't just some mild case of the blues.
SOLOMON: I think that, you know, maybe Mr. Moscone would have been just as dead with one bullet. I don't know.
JONES: I think he was out of control.
DELMAN: Yes.
NORMAN: George Moscone was shot four times, Doctor. The gun had five cartridges in it. Does that change your opinion in any way?
SOLOMON: No. I think he just kept shooting for awhile.

(NORMAN throws his notes down.)

SCHMIDT: Now, there is another legal term we deal with in the courtroom, and that is variously called "malice" or "malice aforethought" . . . ? And this must be present in order to convict for murder in the first degree.
JONES: Okay, let me preface this by saying I am not sure how malice is defined. I'll give you what my understanding is. In order to have malice, you would have to be able to do certain things: to be able to be intent to kill somebody unlawfully. You would have to be able to do something for a base and anti-social purpose. You would have to be aware of the duty imposed on you not to do that, not to unlawfully kill somebody or do something for a base, anti-social purpose, that involved a risk of death, and you would have to be able to act, despite having that awareness of that, that you are not supposed to do that, and so you would have to know that you were not supposed to do it, and then also act despite—keeping in mind that you are not supposed to do it. Is that your answer—your question?
SCHMIDT: I think so.
JONES: *(laughs)* I felt that he had the capacity to do the first three:
that he had the capacity to intend to kill,
but that doesn't take much, you know,
to try to kill somebody,
it's not a high-falutin' mental state.
I think he had the capacity to do something

for a base and anti-social purpose.
I think he had the capacity to know that there was a duty
imposed on him not to do that,
but *I don't think he had the capacity to hold that notion
in his mind while he was acting;*
so that I think that the depression,
plus the moment, the tremendous emotions of the moment, with the depression,
reduced his capacity for conforming conduct.
In fact, I asked him:
"Why didn't you hit them?"
And he was flabbergasted that I asked such a thing,
because it was contrary to his code of behavior,
you know, was taken aback, kind of—
hit them seemed ridiculous to him—
because it would have been so unfair,
since he could have defeated them so easily
in a fist fight.
SCHMIDT: Thank you. (*HE sits. To NORMAN.*) You may examine.
* [NORMAN: Doctor Jones, when let off at City Hall the accused was let off at the Polk Street entrance and then walked a block and a half to Van Ness Avenue. Why wouldn't he just enter City Hall through the main entrance?
JONES: He got towards the top of the stairs, then looked up, saw the metal detector and thought: "Oh, my goodness, I got that gun."
NORMAN: Doctor, why would he care whether there was a metal detector there, and that a gun would have been discovered upon his person?
JONES: Well, I would presume that would mean some degree of hassle. I mean, I presume that the metal detector would see if somebody is trying to bring a weapon in.
NORMAN: That is usually why they have it. Did he realize at that time that he was unlawfully carrying a concealable firearm?
JONES: I presume so.]
NORMAN: Dr. Jones, if it's a fact that Dan White shot George Moscone twice in the body, and that when George Moscone fell to the floor disable, he shot twice more into the right side of George Moscone's head at a distance of between 12 and 18 inches, he made a decision at that time, didn't he, to either discharge the gun into the head of George Moscone, or not discharge the gun into the head of George Moscone?
JONES: If decision means he behaved in that way, then, yes.
NORMAN: Well, didn't he have to make some kind of choice based upon some reasoning process?
JONES: Oh, no, not based on reasoning necessarily. I think—I don't think

---

* NOTE: The bracketed section was cut in the Broadway production.

that I—you know, great emotional turmoil in context of major mood disorder—he was enraged and anxious and frustrated in addition to the underlying depression. I think that after Moscone says "How's your family?" or, "What's your wife going to do?" at that point, I think that it's—it's over.
NORMAN: It's over for George Moscone.
SOLOMON: I think that if you look at the gun as a transitional object, you can see that transitional objects are clung to in—in situations of great—of anxiety and insecurity, as one sees with children.

(COURT—raises eyes, gives up.)

NORMAN: Doctor, are you telling us that a person who has lived an otherwise law-abiding life and an otherwise moral life could not premeditate and deliberate as is contemplated by the definition of first degree murder?!
SOLOMON: I'm not saying that absolutely. Obviously, it's more difficult for a person who lives a highly moral life. And this individual, Dan White, had, if you want—a hypertrophy complex. Hypertrophy meaning overdeveloped, morally, rigidly, overdeveloped. In fact, if Mr. White were to receive a light sentence I think there is a distinct possiblity he could take his own life.
But I would say in general, yes.
I don't think you'd kill Mr. Schmidt if you lost this case.
NORMAN: It's unlikely.
SOLOMON: You may be very angry, but I do't think you will do it because I think your are probably a very moral and law abiding citizen, and I think if you did it, I would certainly recommend a psychiatric examination, because I think there would be a serious possibility that you had flipped.

(pause)

It's most interesting to me how split off his feelings were at this time.
LUNDE: Dan White had classical symptoms that are described in diagnostic manuals for depression and, of course, he had characteristics of compulsive personality, which happens to be kind of a bad combination in those sorts of people.
NORMAN: *(frustrated)* Dr. Solomon you are aware that he took a gun with him when he determined to see George Moscone, a loaded gun?
SOLOMON: Yes.
NORMAN: Why did he take that gun, in your opinion, Dr. Solomon?
SOLOMON: I might say that I think there are symbolic aspects to this.
NORMAN: Symbolic aspects, now Doctor . . .
COURT: Let's move onto another question.
NORMAN: Well, Your Honor . . .

COURT: Let's move on.
NORMAN: (*frustrated*) All right. Dr. Delman, after he went in the building armed with a gun through a window and went up to see George Moscone, at the time he came in to see George Moscone, do you feel that he was angry with George Moscone?
DELMAN: Yes.
NORMAN: When George Moscone told him that he wasn't going to appoint him, do you think that that brought about and increased any more anger?
DELMAN: Yes.
NORMAN: All right. Now there was some point in there when he shot George Moscone, isn't that true?
DELMAN: Yes.
NORMAN: Do you know how many times he shot him?
DELMAN: I believe it's four.
NORMAN: Well, Doctor, do you put any significance upon the circumstances that he shot George Moscone twice in the head?
DELMAN: The question is, "Do I put any significance in it?"
NORMAN: Yes.
DELMAN: I really have no idea why that happened.
NORMAN: Well, Doctor, do you think he knew that if you shot a man twice in the head that it was likely to surely kill him?!
DELMAN: I'm sure that he knew that shooting a man in the head would kill him, Mr. Norman.
NORMAN: Thank you! (*HE sits.*)
SCHMIDT: But, it is your conclusion, Doctor, that Dan White could not premeditate or deliberate, within the meaning we have discussed here, on November 27th, 1978?
DELMAN: That is correct.

(NORMAN slaps hands to head.)
(BLINDER enters.)

SCHMIDT: Thank you.
BLINDER: I teach forensic psychiatry.
I teach about the uses and abuses
of psychiatry in the judicial system.
The courts tend to place psychiatry in a position
where it doesn't belong. Where it becomes the sole arbiter
between guilt and innocence.
There is also a tendency in the stresses of the adversary system
to polarize psychiatric testimony so that a psychiatrist finds himself trying
to put labels on normal stressful behavior,
and *everything* becomes a mental illness.
And I think that is an abuse.

(He refers to his notes.)

Dan White found City Hall rife of corruption.
With the possible exceptions of Diane Feinstein and Harvey Milk,
the supervisors seemed to make their judgments, their votes,
on the basis of what was good for them,
rather than what was good for the City.

And this was a very frustrating thing for Mr. White:
to want to do a good job for his constituents
and find he was continually defeated.

In addition to these stresses, there were
attacks by the press
and there were threats of literal attacks on Supervisors.
He told me a number of Supervisors like himself
carried a gun to scheduled meetings.
Never any relief from these tensions.

Whenever he felt things were not going right,
He would abandon his usual program of exercise and good nutrition
and start gorging himself on junk foods:
Twinkies, Coca-Cola.
Soon Mr. White was just sitting in front of the TV.
Ordinarily, he reads. (Mr. White has always been an
identifiable Jack London adventurer.)

But now, getting very depressed about the fact he would
not be reappointed,
he just sat there before the TV
binging on Twinkies.

(On screen: The Twinkie Defense.)

He couldn't sleep.
He was tossing and turning on the couch in the living room
so he wouldn't disturb his wife on the bed.

Virtually no sexual contact at this time.
He was dazed, confused, had crying spells,
became increasingly ill,
and wanted to be left alone.

He told his wife:

"Don't bother cooking any food for me.
I will just munch on these potato chips."

Mr. White stopped shaving and refused to go.
out of the house to help Denise rally support.

He started to receive information that he would not be reappointed
from unlikely sources.
This was very stressing to him.

Again, it got to be cupcakes, candy bars.
He watched the sun come up on Monday morning.

Finally, at 9:00 Denise called.
He decides to go down to City Hall.
He shaves and puts on his suit.
He sees his gun—lying on the table.
Ammunition.
He simultaneously puts these in his pocket.
Denise picks him up.
He's feeling anxious about a variety of things.
He's sitting in the car hyperventilating,
blowing on his hands, repeating:
"Let him tell me to my face why he won't reappoint me.
Did he think I can't take it?
I am a man.
I can take it."

He goes down to City Hall, and I sense that time is short
so let me bridge this by saying that as I believe
it has been testified to,
he circumvents the mental (sic) detector,
goes to the side window,
gets an appointment with the Mayor.
The Mayor almost directly tells him,
"I am not going to reappoint you."
The Mayor puts his arm around him saying;
"Let's have a drink.
What are you going to do now, Dan?
Can you get back into the Fire Department?
What about your family?
Can your wife get her job back?
What's going to happen to them now?"

Somehow this inquiry directed to his family struck a nerve.
The Mayor's voice started to fade out and Mr. White felt
"As if I were in a dream."
He started to leave and then inexplicably turned around
and like a reflex
drew his revolver.
He had no idea how many shots he fired.

The similar event occurred
in Supervisor Milk's office. (sic.)

He remembers being shocked by the sound of the gun.
going off for the second time like a cannon.

He tells me that he was aware he engaged
in a lethal act,
but tells me he gave no thought to his wrongfulness.
As he put it to me:
"I had no chance to even think about it."
He remembers running out of the building
driving, I think, to church,
making arrangements to meet his wife,
and then going from the church
to the Police Department.

   (Pause.)
   (Exhausted.)

SCHMIDT: Doctor, you have mentioned the ingestion of sugar and sweets and that sort of thing. There are certain theories with regard to sugar and sweets and the ingestion thereof, and I'd like to just touch on that briefly with the jury. Does that have any significance, or could it possibly have any significance?
BLINDER: *(Turns to jury.)* First, there is a substantial body of evidence that in susceptible individuals, large quantities of what we call junk food, high sugar content food with lots of preservatives, can precipitate anti-social and even violent behavior.

There have been studies, for example, where they have taken so-called career criminals and taken them off all their junk food and put them on meat and potatoes and their criminal records immediately evaporate.
(Pause.)
It's contradictory and ironic, but the way it works is that for such a person, the American Dream is a Nightmare. For somebody like Dan White.
SCHMIDT: Thank you, Doctor.

>*(Lights fade on psychiatrists.)*
>*(Pause.)*
>*(Lights up on MARY ANN WHITE, blazing white
>She is almost blinded.) (She comes
>forward.)*

SCHMIDT: You are married to that man, is that correct?
MARY ANN: Yes.
SCHMIDT: When did you first meet him?
MARY ANN: I met him *(WITNESS sobbing.)*
SCHMIDT: If you want to take any time// just let us know.
MARY ANN: *(Pulling herself together.)* I met him in April, 1976 . . .
SCHMIDT: And you were married// and you took a trip?
MARY ANN: Yes. Yes, we went to Ireland on our honeymoon because Danny just had this feeling that Ireland could be this place could be really peaceful for him. He just really likes—loves—everything about Ireland and so we—*(sobbing)*
SCHMIDT: Excuse me.
MARY ANN: —so we went there// for about five wee—
SCHMIDT: During that period did you notice anything// unusual about his behavior?
MARY ANN: Yes, I mean, you know, when we went I thought—went thinking it was going to kind of romantic, and when we got there, the thing that attracted me most to Danny was his vitality, energy and the fact that he always had the ability to inspire in you something that made you want to do your best like he did, and when we got there, when we got to Ireland . . . it was all of a sudden, he went into like a two-week long mood, like I had seen before, but I had never seen one, I guess, all the way through, because when we were going out, I might see him for a day, and being a fireman, he would work a day, and then I wouldn't see him, and when we got to Ireland . . . I mean, I was just newly married and I thought: "What did I do?"
SCHMIDT: After he was on the Board, did you notice these moods// become more frequent?
MARY ANN: Yes, he had talked to me about how hard the job was on him. You know, from June he started to talk about how it was. Obviously you can sense when you are not sleeping together, and you are not really growing together and he would say, "Well, I can't—I can't really think of anyone else when I don't even like myself." And I said, "It's just him. He's not satisfied with what I'm doing and I don't like myself// and so I can't . . ."
SCHMIDT: Did you see him on the morning of . . . November 27th?

(NOTE: //=Overlap . . . Next speaker starts, first speaker continues.)

MARY ANN: Yes// I did.
SCHMIDT: And at that time did he indicate what he was going to do// that day?
MARY ANN: It was just, he was going to stay *home.* He wasn't leaving the house.
SCHMIDT: Later that morning, did you receive a call//to meet him somewhere?
MARY ANN: Yes. I did. Yes, I went to St. Mary's Cathedral. I went and saw him.
I could see that he had been crying, and I, I
just kind of looked at him
and he just looked at me
and he said,
he said,
"I shot the Mayor and Harvey."
SCHMIDT: (*Looks to NORMAN as if to say, "Any questions?" NORMAN nods no.*) Thank you.

> (*DAN WHITE sobs.*)
> (*SCHMIDT puts hand on WHITE's shoulder.*)
> (*MARY ANN WHITE stumbles off the stand to her husband.*)
> (*WHITE shields his eyes.*)
> (*She looks as if she will embrace him.*)

SCHMIDT: The defense is prepared to rest at this time.

> (*MARY ANN WHITE sobs.*)
> (*Hyperreal sound of a woman's high heels on marble echoing.*)
> (*Mumbled "Hail Mary's."*)

COURT: Let me admonish you, ladies gentlemen of the jury, not to discuss this case among yourselves nor with anyone else, not to allow anyone to speak to you about the case, nor are you to form or express an opinion until the matter has been submitted to you.

> (*Gavel.*)
> (*On screen: The Defense rests*)
> (*ALL exit.*)

MILK'S FRIEND: (*Enters alone.*) *We got back from the airport the night of the 27th
And my roommate said;
There's going to be a candle-light march.

---

*Dialogue from *The Times of Harvey Milk,* a film by Robert Epstein and Richard Schmeichen.

By now, we thought it had to have reached City Hall.
So we went directly there. From the airport to City Hall.
And there were maybe 75 people there.
And I remember thinking;
My God is this all anybody . . . cared?
Somebody said: No, the march hasn't gotten here yet.
So we then walked over to Market Street
which was 2 or 3 blocks away.
And looked down it.
And Market Street runs in a straight line
out to the Castro area.
And as we turned the corner,

> *(On screen: The screens flooded with
> candles and the candle-light march
> music. Barber's "Adagio.")*

there were people as wide as this wide street
As far as you could see.

> *(The entire company enters holding
> candles.)*
> *(After awhile.)*

YOUNG MOTHER: *Thousands and thousands of people,
And that feeling of such loss.

> *(Music continues.)*

GWENN: *It was one of the most eloquent expressions of a
community's response to violence
that I have ever seen . . .
A MOURNER: *(Wearing a black arm band.)* I'd like to read
from the transcript of Harvey Milk's political will.
(reads)
This is Harvey Milk speaking on Friday, November 18.
This tape is to be played only in the event of my death
by assassination.

> *(On screen: Pictures of MILK.)*

I've given long and considerable thought to this,
and not just since the election.

---

*Dialogue from *The Times of Harvey Milk*, a film by Robert Epstein and Richard Schmeichen.

I've been thinking about this for some time
prior to the election and certainly over the years.
I fully realize that a person who stands for what I stand for—
a gay activist—
becomes the target for a person who is insecure, terrified,
afraid or very disturbed themselves.

    (DAN WHITE enters. Stops.)

Knowing that I could be assassinated at any moment
or any time,
I feel it's important that some people should understand
my thoughts.
So the following are my thoughts, my wishes, my desires,
I'd like to pass them on and have them played for the appropriate people.
The first and most obvious concern is that
if I was to be shot and killed,
the mayor has the power,
George Moscone.

    (On screen: Pictures of MOSCONE, the funeral, the mourners, the widow.)

of appointing my successor . . .
to the Board of Supervisors.
I cannot prevent some people
from feeling angry and frustrated and mad,
but I hope
that they would not demonstrate violently.
If a bullet should enter my brain,
let that bullet destroy every closet door.

    (Gavel.)
    (All MOURNERS blow out candles.)
    (DAN WHITE sits.)
    (Blackout.)

    (On screen: The People's rebuttal/Dr. Levy Psychiatrist)
    (Lights up.)

LEVY: I interviewed the defendant several hours after the shootings of November 27th.
In my opinion, one can get a more accurate diagnosis
the closer one examines the suspect
after a crime has been committed.

At that time, it appeared to me that Dan White had
no remorse for the death of George Moscone.
It appeared to me, he had no remorse
for the death of Harvey Milk.
There was nothing in my interview which would suggest to me
there was any mental disorder.
I had the feeling that there was some depression but it was not
depression that I would consider as a diagnosis.
In fact, I found him to be less depressed
than I would have expected him to be.
At that time I saw him, it seemed that he felt himself to be quite justified.
(*Looks to notes.*)
I felt he had the capacity to form malice.
I felt he had the capacity to premeditate. And . . .
I felt he had the capacity to deliberate, to arrive at a
course of conduct weighing considerations.
NORMAN: Did you review the transcript of the proceeding wherein the testimonies of Drs. Jones, Blinder, Solomon, Delman and Lunde were given?
LEVY: Yes. I found nothing in them that would cause me to revise my opinion.
NORMAN: Thank you, Dr. Levy. (*sits*)

(*SCHMIDT stands.*)

SCHMIDT: Dr. Levy, are you a full professor at the University of California?
LEVY: No. I am an associate clinical professor.

(*SCHMIDT smiles, looks to jury.*)

SCHMIDT: May I inquire of your age, sir?
LEVY: I'm 55.
SCHMIDT: Huh. (*Picking up papers.*) Doctor, your report is dated November 27, 1978, is it not?
LEVY: Yes.
SCHMIDT: And yet the report was not written on November 27, 1978?
LEVY: No. It would have been within several days// of that time.
SCHMIDT: And then it was dated November 27, 1978?
LEVY: Yes.
SCHMIDT: Well, regardless of the backdating, or whatever, when did you come to your forensic conclusions?
LEVY: I'd say the conclusions would have been on November 27th.
SCHMIDT: And that was after a two-hour talk with Dan White?
LEVY: Yes.

SCHMIDT: Doctor, would it be fair to say that you made some snap decisions?
LEVY: I don't believe// I did.
SCHMIDT: Did you consult with any other doctors?
LEVY: No.
SCHMIDT: Did you review any of the witnesses' statements?
LEVY: No.
SCHMIDT: Did you consult any of the material that was available to you, save and except for the tape of Dan White on the same date?
LEVY: No. That was all that was made available to me// at that time.
SCHMIDT: Now I don't mean to be facetious, but this is a fairly important case, is that fair?
LEVY: I would certainly think so,// yes.
SCHMIDT: But you didn't talk further with Mr. White?
LEVY: No. I was not requested to.
SCHMIDT: And you didn't request to talk to him further?
LEVY: No. I was not going to do a complete assessment.
SCHMIDT: Well, in fact, you didn't do a complete assessment, is that fair?
LEVY: I was not asked to do a complete assessment.
COURT: Doctor, you are fading away.
LEVY: *I was not asked to do a complete assessment.*
SCHMIDT: Thank you.

(Blackout.)
(Commotion in court, JOANNA tries to get interview from LEVY.)

SCHMIDT: *(In black.)* She wants to tell the story so it's not responsive to the questions.

(Lights up.)
(On screen: SUPERVISOR CAROL RUTH SILVER, for the prosecution.)

SILVER: *(Very agitated, speaking fast, heated.)*
The prosecution asked in what other case did a dispute between Dan White and Harvey Milk arise! And it was the Polk Street closing was another occasion when Harvey requested that Polk Street, which is a heavily gay area in San Francisco, I am sure everybody knows, and on Halloween had traditionally had a huge number of people in costumes and so forth down there and has// traditionally been recommended for closure by the Police Department and—
SCHMIDT: I am going to object to this, Your Honor.
SILVER: It was recommended—
COURT: Just ask the next question. Just ask the next question.

SILVER: I am sorry.
NORMAN: Did Mr. Milk and Mr. White take positions that were opposite to each other?
SILVER: Yes.
NORMAN: Was there anything that became, well, rather loud and perhaps hostile in connection or consisting between the two?
SILVER: Not loud but very hostile
You have to first understand that this street closure
was recommended by the Police Chief and had been done customarily in the years past// and is, was—came
up as a uncontested issue practically.
SCHMIDT: Your Honor, I again—
COURT: Please, just make your objection.
SCHMIDT: I'd like to.
COURT: Without going through contortions.
SCHMIDT: There is an objection.
COURT: All right. Sustained.
NORMAN: Miss Silver, did you know, or did you ever see Mr. White to appear to be depressed or to be withdrawn?
SILVER: No.
NORMAN: Thank you. (*sits*)

(*SILVER flabbergasted, upset.*)

COURT: All right. Any questions, Mr. Schmidt?
SCHMIDT: Is it *Miss* Silver?
SILVER: Yes.
SCHMIDT: Miss Silver, you never had lunch with Dan White, did you?
SILVER: Did I ever have lunch?

(*Subliminal music.*)

NOTHENBERG: George Moscone was socially brilliant in that he could find the injustice.
SCHMIDT: I mean the two of you?
SILVER: I don't recall having done so// but I—
NOTHENBERG: His mind went immediately to what can we do?
SCHMIDT: Did you socialize frequently?
NOTHENBERG: What can we practically do?
SILVER: No, when his son was born// I went to a party at his house and that kind of thing.
SCHMIDT: Did Mr. Norman contact you last week, or did you// contact him?
NOTHENBERG: I was with George registering voters in Mississippi in 1964.
SILVER: On Friday morning I called his office.

NOTHENBERG: Y'know, he'd never seen that kind of despair before, but when he saw it he said right out: "This is intolerable."
SILVER: Because I was reading the newspaper—
SCHMIDT: Yes.
SILVER: And it appeared// to me that—
COURT: Don't tell us.
NOTHENBERG: And whenever he said: "this is *intolerable*,"
SILVER: I'm sorry.
NOTHENBERG: In all the years I knew him, he always *did* something about it.
COURT: The jurors are told not to read the newspaper, and I am hoping that they haven't// read the newspapers.
SILVER: I apologize.
COURT: Okay.
SCHMIDT: Miss Silver—
COURT: I am sorry, I didn't want to cut her off—
SILVER: No, I understand.
COURT: from any other answer
SCHMIDT: I think she did complete the answer, Judge.
In any event, you contacted Mr. Norman, did you not?
SILVER: Yes, I did.
SCHMIDT: And at that time, you offered to Mr. Norman to round up people who could say that Dan White never looked depressed at City Hall, is that fair?
SILVER: That's right. Well, I offered to testify to that effect and I suggested that there were other people// who could similarly testify to that fact.
SCHMIDT: In fact, you expressed it though you haven't sat here and listened to the testimony in this courtroom?
SILVER: No, I have never been here before Friday when I was subpoenaed// and spent some time in the jury room.
SCHMIDT: But to use your words, after having read what was in the paper, you said that the defense sounded like "bullshit" to you? That's correct.
DENMAN: I thought I would be a chief witness for the prosecution.
SCHMIDT: Would that suggest then that perhaps you have a bias in this case?
DENMAN: What was left unsaid was what the trial should have been about.
SILVER: I certainly have a bias.
SCHMIDT: You are a political enemy of Dan White's is that fair?
SILVER: No, that's not true.
DENMAN: Before, y'know, there was a lot of talk about assassinating the Mayor among thuggish elements of the Police Officers Association.
SCHMIDT: Did you have any training in psychology or psychiatry?
DENMAN: And those were the cops Dan White was closest to.
SILVER: No more than some of the kind of C.E.B. courses// lawyer's psychology for lawyers kind of training.

DENMAN: I think he knew a lot of guys would think he did the right thing and yeah they would make him a hero.
SCHMIDT: I mean, would you be able to diagnois, say, *Manic depression depressed type,* or could you distinguish that from *uni-polar depression?*
SILVER: No.
DENMAN: I was Dan White's jailer for 72 hours after the assassinations.
SCHMIDT: Did you ever talk to him about his dietary habits or anything like that?
DENMAN: There were no tears.
SILVER: I remember a conversation about nutrition or something like that, but I can't remember// the substance of it.
SCHMIDT: I don't have anything further.
DENMAN: There was no shame.
COURT: Any redirect, Mr. Norman?
NORMAN: Yes.
DENMAN: You got the feeling that he knew exactly what he was doing and there was no remorse.
NORMAN: Miss Silver, you were asked if you had a bias in this case. You knew Harvey Milk very well and you liked him, didn't you?
SILVER: I did; and also George Moscone.
NORMAN: Miss Silver, speaking of a bias, had you ever heard the Defendant say anything about getting people of whom Harvey Milk numbered himself?
(*Lights up on MILK's friend.*)
SILVER: In the Polk Street debate—
MILK'S FRIEND: The night Harvey was elected, I went to bed early because it was more happiness that I had been taught to deal with.
SILVER: Dan White got up and gave—
a long diatribe—
MILK'S FRIEND: Next morning we put up signs saying "thank you."
SILVER: Just a—a very unexpected and very uncharacteristic of Dan, long hostile speech about how gays and their lifestyles had to be contained and we can't// *encourage* this kind of thing and—
SCHMIDT: I am going to object to this, your Honor.
COURT: Sustained, okay.
MILK'S FRIEND: During that, Harvey came over and told me
that he had made a political will
because he expected he'd be killed.
And then in the same breath, he said (I'll never forget it):
"It works, it works . . ."
NORMAN: All right . . . that's all.
MILK'S FRIEND: The system works// . . .
NORMAN: Thank you.
DENMAN: When White was being booked, it all seemed fraternal. One

officer gave Dan a pat on the behind when he was booked, sort of a "Hey, catch you later, Dan," pat.
COURT: Any recross?
DENMAN: Some of the officers and deputies were standing around with half-smirks on their faces. Some were actually laughing.
SCHMIDT: Just a couple.
DENMAN: The joke they kept telling was,
"Dan White's mother says to him when he comes home,
'No, dummy, I said milk and baloney, not Moscone!'"
(*pause*)
SCHMIDT: Miss Silver, you are a part of the gay community also, are you?
SILVER: Myself?
SCHMIDT: Yes.
SILVER: You mean, am I gay?
SCHMIDT: Yes.
SILVER: No, I'm not.
SCHMIDT: I have nothing further.
MOSCONE'S FRIEND: George would have said, "This is intolerable," and he'd have done something about it.
COURT: All right, Miss Silver you may leave.
COURT: Next witness, please.

    (*Lights.*)
    (SILVER *exits towards door.*)
    (JOANNA *with TV lights.*)

JOANNA LU: Miss Silver, Supervisor Silver, would you like to elaborate on Mr. White's anti-gay feelings or hostility to Harvey Milk or George Moscone?
SILVER: No comment, right now.

    (SILVER *distraught, rushes past.*)

JOANNA LU: Did you feel you were baited, did you have your say?
SILVER: (*Blows up.*) I said I have no comment at this time!!!

    (*She exits.*)

COURT: Mr. Norman? Next witness?
NORMAN: Nothing further.
Those are all the witnesses we have to present.
COURT: The People rest?
NORMAN: Yes.
COURT: Does the defense have any witnesses?
SCHMIDT: (*surprised*) Well, we can discuss it, Your Honor. I am not sure there is anything to rebut.

(Light change.)
(Commontion in court.)
(On screen: The People Rest)
(Lights up on SCHMIDT.)
(He is at a podium, a parish priest at a pulpit.)
(Dissolve to on screen: Summations)

SCHMIDT: I'm nervous. I'm very nervous. I sure hope I say all the right things. I can't marshal words the way Mr. Norman can—but—I believe strongly in things.
Lord God! I don't say to you to forgive Dan White. I don't say to you to just let Dan White walk out of here a free man. He is guilty. But, the degree of responsibility is the issue here. The state of mind is the issue here. It's not who was killed; it's why. It's not who killed them; but why. The state of mind is the issue here.
Lord God! The pressures.
Nobody can say that the things that happened to him days
or weeks preceeding wouldn't make a reasonable and ordinary man
at least mad,
angry in some way.

Surely—surely, that had to have arisen, not to kill,
not to kill, just to be mad, to act irrationally,
because if you kill, when you are angry, or under the heat of passion,
if you kill, then the law will punish you,
and you will be punished by God—
God will punish you,
but the law will also punish you.

Heat of passion fogs judgement, makes one act irrationally,
in the very least,
and my God,
that is what happened at the very least.
Forget about the mental illness,
forget about all the rest of the factors
that came into play at the same time;
Surely he acted irrationally, impulsively—out of some passion.

Now . . . you will recall at the close of the prosecution's case,
it was suggested to you this was a calm, cool, deliberating,
terrible terrible person
that had committed two crimes like these,
and these are terrible crimes,
and that he was emotionally stable at that time
and there wasn't anything wrong with him.

He didn't have any diminished capacity.
Then we played these tapes he made directly after
he turned himself in at Northern Station.

My God,
that was not a person that was calm and collected and cool
and able to weigh things out.
It just wasn't.

The tape just totally fogged me up the first time I heard it.
It was a man that was, as Frank Falzon said, broken.
Shattered.
This was not the Dan White that everybody had known.

Something happened to him and he snapped.
That's the word I used in my opening statement.
Something snapped here.

The pot had boiled over here,
and people that boil over in that fashion,
they tell the truth.

Have the tape played again, if you can't remember what was said.
He said in no uncertain terms,

"My God,
why did I do these things?
What made me do this?
How on earth could I have done this?
I didn't intend to hurt anybody.
My God,
what happened to me?
Why?"

Play the tape.
If everybody says the tape is truthful, play the tape.
I'd agree it's truthful.

With regard to the reloading and some of these little
discrepancies that appeared to come up.
I am not even sure of the discrepancies,
but if there were discrepancies,
listen to it in context.
"Where did you reload?"
"I reloaded in my office, I think."

"And then did you leave the Mayor's office?"
"Yes, then I left the Mayor's office."

That doesn't mean anything to me at all.
It doesn't mean anything to me at all.
And I don't care where the reloading took place!

But listen to the tape.
It says in no uncertain terms,
"I didn't intend to hurt anybody.
I didn't intend to do this."
Why do we do things?

I don't know.
It was a man desperately trying to grab at something . . .

"What happened to me?
How could I have done this?"

If the District Attorney concedes that what is
on the tape is truthful,
and I believe that's the insinuation we have here,
then, by golly,
there is voluntary manslaughter,
nothing more and nothing less. I say this to you in all honesty.
And if you have any doubts our law tells you,
you have to judge in favor of Dan White.

Now, I don't know what more I can say.
He's got to be punished
and he will be punished.
He's going to have to live with this for the rest of his life.
His child will live with it
and his family will live with it
and God will punish him
and the law will punish him,
and they will punish him severely.
And this is the type of case where, I suppose
I don't think Mr. Norman will do it
but you can make up a picture of a dead man
or two of them for that matter
and you can have them around and say
somebody is going to pay for this
and somebody *is* going to pay for this.
But it's not an emotional type thing.

I get emotional about it
but *you* can't
because you have to be objective about the facts.

But please, please
Just justice.
That's all.
Just justice here.

(SCHMIDT appears to break for a moment.)

Now I get one argument.
I have made it.
And I just hope that—
I just hope that you'll come to the same conclusion
that I have come to,
and thank you for listening to me.
NORMAN: Ladies and gentlemen,
I listened very carefully to the summation just given you.
It appears to me, members of the jury,
to be a very facile explanation and rationalization
as to premediation and deliberation.
The evidence that has been laid before you
screams for murder in the first degree.

What counsel for the defense has done is suggest to you
to *excuse* this kind of conduct and call it something that
it isn't,
to call it voluntary manslaughter.

Members of the jury, you are the triers of fact here.
You have been asked to hear this tape recording again.
The tape recording has been aptly described
as something very moving. We all feel a sense of sympathy,
a sense of empathy for our fellow man, but you are not to let
sympathy influence you in your judgment.

To reduce the charge of murder to something less—
to reduce it to voluntary manslaughter—
means you are saying that this was not murder.
That this was an intentional killing of a human being
upon a quarrel, or heat of passion.
But ladies and gentlemen,
that quarrel must have been so extreme,
at the time

that the defendant could not—
was incapable of forming
those qualities of thought which are
malice, premeditation and deliberation.
But the evidence in this case doesn't suggest that at all.
Not at all.
If the defendant had picked up a vase or something
that happened to be in the mayor's office
and hit the mayor over the head and killed him
you know, you know that argument for voluntary manslaughter
might be one which you could say the evidence admits
a reasonable doubt. But—

Ladies and gentlemen:
THE FACTS ARE:
It was *he*—Dan White—who brought the gun to the City Hall
The gun was not there.
It was *he* who brought the extra cartidges for the gun;
they were not found there

He went to City Hall and when he got there he went
to the Polk Street door.

There was a metal detector there.
He knew he was carrying a gun.
He knew that he had extra cartridges for it.

Instead of going through the metal detector,
he *decided* to go around the corner.
He was capable at that time of expressing anger.
He was capable of, according to the doctor—
well, parenthetically, members of the jury,
I don't know how they can look in your head and tell you
what you are able to do. But—
They even said that he was capable of knowing at that time
that if you pointed a gun at somebody and you fired that gun
that you would surely kill a person.

He went around the corner, and climbed
through a window into City Hall.

He went up to the Mayor's office.
He appeared, according to witnesses,
to act calmly in his approach, in his speech.
He chatted with Cyr Copertini; he was capable of

carrying on a conversation to the extent that he was
able to ask her how she was, after having asked to see
the Mayor.

    (Looks to audience.)

He stepped into the Mayor's office.
After some conversation,

he shot the Mayor twice in the body.
Then he shot the Mayor in the head twice
while the Mayor was disabled on the floor.
The evidence suggests that in order to shoot the Mayor
twice in the head
he had to *lean down* to do it.

    (And NORMAN does.)
    (Looks to jury.)

    Deliberation is premeditation.
    It has malice.
    I feel stultified to even bring this up.
    This is the definition of murder.

He reloaded the gun.
Wherever he reloaded the gun, it was *he* who
reloaded it!

He did see Supervisor Milk
whom he knew was acting against his appointment
and he was capable of expressing anger in that regard.

He entered the Supervisor's area (a block from the Mayor's
office across City Hall)
and was told, "Dianne wants to see you."
He said, "That is going to have to wait a moment.
I have something to do first."

Then he walked to Harvey Milk's office, put his head
in the door and said
"Can I see you a moment, Harv?"
The reply was. "Yes."

He went across the hall and put three bullets
into Harvey Milk's body,

one of which hit Harvey directly in the back.
When he fell to the floor disabled,
two more were delivered to the back of his head.

Now what do you call that but premeditation and deliberation?
What do you call that realistically
but a cold-blooded killing?
Two *cold-blooded executions.*
It occurs to me that if you don't call them that,
then you are ignoring the objective evidence
and the objective facts here.
Members of the jury, there are circumstances here
which no doubt bring about anger,
maybe even rage, I don't know,
but the manner in which that anger was felt
and was handled
is *socially something that cannot be approved.*

Ladies and gentlemen,
the quality of your service is reflected in your verdict.

> *(He sits.)*
> *(JOANNA LU at door*
> *stops SCHMIDT. TV lights.)*

JOANNA LU: Mr. Schmidt, do you
SCHMIDT: Yes.
JOANNA LU: Do you feel society would feel justice is served if the jury returns two manslaughter verdicts?
SCHMIDT: Society doesn't have anything to do with it. Only those 12 people in the jury box.

> *(Gavel.)*

COURT: Ladies and gentlemen of the jury,
Now that you have heard the evidence,
we come to that part of the trial where you are instructed
on the applicable law.

In the crime of murder of the first degree
the necessary concurrent mental states are:
Malice aforethought, premeditation and deliberation.
In the crime of murder of the second degree,
the necessary concurrent mental state is:
Malice aforethought.

In the crime of voluntary manslaughter,
the necessary mental state is:
an intent to kill.
Involuntary manslaughter is an unlawful killing
without malice aforethought
and without intent to kill.

The law does not undertake to limit or define
the kinds of passion
which may cause a person to act rashly.
Such passions as desperation,
humiliation, resentment,
anger, fear, or rage
or any other high wrought emotion . . .
can be sufficient to reduce the killings to manslaughter
so long as they are sufficient
to obscure the reason
and render the average man likely to act rashly.

There is no malice aforethought
if the killing occurred upon a sudden quarrel
or heat of passion.

There is no malice aforethought
if the evidence shows that due to diminished capacity
caused by illness, mental defect, or intoxication,
the defendant did not have the capacity
to form the mental state constituting malice aforethought,
even though the killing was intentional,
voluntary, premeditated and unprovoked.

>*(A siren begins to cover the court.)*
>*(On screen: Images of the riot at City*
>*Hall begin to appear.*
>*Broken glass*
>*images of cop cars burning, riot police, angry faces.)*
>*(On audio: Explosions*
>*it is the riot.)*

GWENN: (*On video.*) In order to understand the riots, I think you have to understand that the Dan White verdict did not occur in a vacuum—
COURT: Mr. Foreman, has the jury reached verdicts// in this case?
GWENN: that there were and are other factors which contribute to a legitimate rage that was demonstrated dramatically at our symbol of Who's Responsible, City Hall.

(*On screen: Images of City Hall being stormed.*
Line of police in front in riot gear.)

FOREMAN: Yes, it has, Your Honor.
GWENN: The verdict came down and the people rioted.
COURT: Please read the verdicts.
GWENN: The people stormed City Hall, burned police cars.

(*On screen: Image of City Hall.*
Line of police cars in flames.)

FOREMAN: (*reading*) The jury finds the defendant Daniel James White guilty of violating Section 192.1 of the penal code,
GWENN: Then the police came into our neighborhood. And the police rioted.
FOREMAN: Voluntary manslaughter, for the slaying of Mayor George Moscone.

(*MARY ANN WHITE gasps.*)
(*DAN WHITE puts head in hands.*)
(*Explosion.*)
(*Riot police enter.*)

GWENN: The police came into the Castro and assaulted gays.
They stormed the Elephant Walk Bar.
One kid had an epileptic seizure and was almost killed for it.
A cop drove a motorcycle up against a phone booth
where a lesbian woman was on the phone.
blocked her exit
and began beating her up.
COURT: Is this a unanimous verdict of the jury?
FOREMAN: Yes, it is, Judge.
GWENN: I want to talk about when people are pushed to the wall. (*Off video.*)
COURT: Will each juror say "yea"// or "nay?"
YOUNG MOTHER: What about the children?
MOSCONE'S FRIEND: I know who George offended. I know who Harvey offended.
JURORS: Yea, yea, yea// yea, yea, yea.
MOSCONE'S FRIEND: I understand the offense.
YOUNG MOTHER: What do I tell my kids?
GWENN: Were the ones who are responsible seeing these things?
YOUNG MOTHER: That in this country you serve more time for robbing a bank than for killing two people?
JURORS: Yea, yea, yea// yea, yea, yea.

GWENN: Hearing these things?
MILK'S FRIEND: I understand the offense.
GWENN: Do they understand about people being pushed to the wall?
YOUNG MOTHER: Accountability?

(Yea's end.)

MILK'S FRIEND: Assassination.
I've grown up with it.
I forget it hasn't always been this way.
YOUNG MOTHER: What do I say?
That two lives are worth seven years and eight months// in jail
MILK'S FRIEND: I remember coming home from school in second grade—
JKF was killed—
Five years later, Martin Luther King.
It's a frame of reference.

(explosion)

COURT: Will the Foreman please read the verdict for the second count?
DENMAN: It's a divided city.
FOREMAN: The jury finds the defendant Daniel James White guilty of violating Section 192.1 of the penal code, voluntary manslaughter,
in the slaying of Supervisor Harvey Milk.

(DAN WHITE gasps.)
(MARY ANN WHITE sobs.)
(NORMAN, flushed, head in hands.)
(Explosion.)
(Violence ends.)
(Riot police do terror control.)
(TV lights.)

BRITT: (*On camera.*) No—I'm optimistic about San Francisco.
COURT: Is this a unanimous decision by the jury?
FOREMAN: Yes, Your Honor.
BRITT: I'm Harry Britt. I was Harvey Milk's successor.
MOSCONE'S FRIEND: If he'd just killed George, he'd be in jail for life.
BRITT: Now this is an example I don't use often because people will misunderstand it, but when a prophet is killed, it's up to those who are left to build the community or the church.
MOSCONE'S FRIEND: Dan White believed in the death// penalty . . .
YOUNG MOTHER: To this jury Dan White// was their son.
NOTHENBERG: He should have gotten the death penalty.
YOUNG MOTHER: What are we teaching our sons?

150

BRITT: But I have hope.
MILK'S FRIEND: It was an effective assassination.
BRITT: I have hope. And as Harvey said, "you can't live// without hope."
MILK'S FRIEND: They always are.
BRITT: "And you, and you, and you—we gotta give em hope."

(Riot ends.)

JOANNA LU: *(On camera.)* Dan White was examined by the psychiatrist at the state prison. They decided against therapy. Dan White had no apparent signs of mental disorder... Dan White's parole date was January 6, 1984. When Dan White left Soledad prison on January 6, 1984, it was five years, one month, and eight days since he turned himself in at Northern Station after the assassinations of Mayor George Moscone and Supervisor Milk. Mayor Diane Feinstein, the current Mayor of San Francisco, has tried to keep Dan White out of San Francisco during his parole for fear he will be killed.
BOOM BOOM: *(enters)* Dan White! It's 1984 and Big Sister is watching you.
JOANNA LU: Dan White reportedly plans to move to Ireland after his release.
NOTHENBERG: What do you do with your feelings of revenge?
With your need for retribution?
BRITT: We will never forget.

(Riot images freeze.)

BOOM BOOM: *(enters)* I would like to close with a reading from the Book of Dan. *(Opens book.)* Take of this and eat, for this is my defense. *(Raises the Twinkie. Eats it. Exits.)*
JOANNA LU: Dan White was found dead of carbon monoxide poisoning on October 21, 1985, at his wife's home in San Francisco, California.

(Lights change.)
(DAN WHITE faces the court.)

COURT: Mr. White, you are sentenced to seven years and eight months, the maximum sentence for these two counts of voluntary manslaughter. The Court feels that these sentences for the taking of life is completely inappropriate but that was the decision of the legislature.
Again, let me repeat for the record:
Seven years and eight months is the maximum sentence for
voluntary manslaughter, and this is the law.

(Gavel.)
(Long pause.)
(WHITE turns to the audience/jury.)

DAN WHITE: I was always just a lonely vote on the board. I was just trying to do a good job for the city.

>   *(Long pause.)*
>   *(Audio: Hyperreal sounds of a woman's high heels on marble.)*
>   *(Mumbled Hail Mary's. Rustle of an embrace.)*
>   *(SISTER BOOM BOOM enters. Taunts police.)*
>   *(Police raise riot shields.)*
>   *(Blackout.)*
>   *(On screen: Execution of justice)*
>   *(Gavel echoes.)*

END OF PLAY

Split Second: A Play in Two Acts

Dennis McIntyre

Split Second is unique in that Dennis McIntyre, it's author, is a white male writing about Afro-American characters and addressing issues that are relevant to all disenfranchised minorities in America. The central character around which the plot revolves is Val Johnson, a street cop in Manhattan who prevents a petty criminal from stealing a car on a dark, deserted, and dangerous street. What might have been a routine bust ends when Val shoots the white hoodlum through the heart for verbally abusing him with racial epithets. Among the questions that haunt Val throughout the play are, "Should one tell the truth about something terrible they've done?" "Can a person afford to live with the lie and his conscience or should he tell the truth knowing full well that to do so will surely destroy his career, his family, and his reputation?" Val's encounters with his superiors in the police department, his male friend, his wife, and principally his self-righteous father literally pull his fragile existence apart forever, dashing any hope of future stability.

All of Dennis McIntyre's plays deal with individuals who struggle to gain personal dignity and self respect in a world permeated by corruption and moral decay. In *National Anthems,* his final play, a stranger enters the home of a yuppie couple surrounded by the luxury acquired during the boom years of the Regan economy in suburban Detroit. Contrary to the opulence of the vacuous young couple, the stranger's only claim to fame is that he saved a black woman from a burning tenement in Detroit's slum neighborhood.

McIntyre died an untimely death of stomach cancer in 1990. He was on the verge of what promised to be a solid career as a playwright and an educator. He taught playwriting at the University of Michigan and in New York.

Production History

Split Second was first produced by The Amistad World Theatre in co-operation with John McDonald and Gus Flemming.

Split Second was presented by Philip Rose, Gus Flemming and John McDonald at Theatre Four, New York City on June 7, 1984. The production was directed by Samuel P. Barton. Scenery was by Daniel Proett; lighting was by Leo Gambacorta, and costumes were by Judy Dearing. Original music was by Jimmy Owens. The Production stage manager was Dwight R.B. Cook. The cast was as follows:

Val Johnson. . . . . John Danelle
William H. Willis. . . . . Bill Cwikowski
Parker . . . . Helmar Augustus Cooper

Charlie . . . . Peter Jay Fernandez
Alea Johnson. Michele Shay
Rusty Johnson . . . . Norman Matlock

Setting

New York City. Manhattan.

Time

The present. The action of the play begins on the evening of July 4th and ends on the morning of July 6th.

Set

A continuous flow of action, set on various platforms with suggestions of time and place, suggestions of New York City (Manhattan), and minimum props.

Music

The music should be comparable to the sound of wind chimes, tinkling, almost trembling. Its effect should be mysterious, haunting and melancholy.

Characters

VAL JOHNSON
WILLIAM H. WILLIS
PARKER
CHARLIE
ALEA JOHNSON
RUSTY JOHNSON

Split Second by Dennis McIntyre

Split Second © 1980, 1984 by Dennis McIntyre. All inquires concerning rights to the play should be addressed to the author's agent: Howard Rosenstone, Rosenstone/Wender, 3 East 48th Street, New York, NY 10017.

The Play

Split Second

ACT ONE

Scene 1

A New York City side street, 28th and Eleventh Avenue. VAL JOHNSON, a black New York City cop, street clothes, and WILLIAM H. WILLIS, white, street clothes.

Music starts before house half—continues thru present out. After preset out, the sound of labored breathing and a man running is heard offstage.

Lights. Enter WILLIS USR from arch, XSL to chain fence, XSR to D of rail, XDSL to L of bench. Enter VAL USR from arch XSL to back of chair. WILLIS XSR to fence.

VAL: Freeze, motherfucker! Freeze it! (*VAL stands upstage, breathing hard, his service revolver drawn, holding it with both hands, pointing it at WILLIS. WILLIS stands further downstage, panting, gasping for breath, slowly raising his hands.*) You move, you even sweat, and you're wasted pal! You want two more seconds of light, start staring at the green "Caddie"! Don't take your mind off it! Start thinking about the fucking "ride," shithead! Just pretend I'm not here! Man, you should have been more picky. Going to jail for an Oldsmobile, now that's dumb, real stupid. You didn't even have to grow up to do that, did you?
WILLIS: (*Starts to turn around.*) Look—
VAL: I said "freeze," fucker, you ever want to blink again! You'd better keep your eyes on that green "Caddie"! I'd do that, if I were you, I really would! I'd start thinking about "horsepower"! I'd start thinking about "chrome"! That's what I'd do! I wouldn't want to make two mistakes in one night! No, I wouldn't want to do that, not with me behind you! (*VAL moves DS to WILLIS.*)
WILLIS: I mean, is this really necessary?
VAL: (*Moving closer to WILLIS.*) Uh, huh.

WILLIS: Can't we, like, talk it over?
VAL: (*closer to WILLIS*) Nope.
WILLIS: Have a heart, would you? It's the Fourth of July, for Christ's sake!
VAL: (*right behind WILLIS*) Just another night to me, fucker. (*VAL pushes WILLIS forward and kicks his legs apart.*)
WILLIS: You don't got to do that, do you?
VAL: (*Pushes WILLIS against fence.*) You want to bet?
WILLIS: Just where in the hell am I going to go? Tell me that.
VAL: (*Holsters his revolver.*) That's the point, asshole. (*VAL begins to frisk WILLIS.*)
WILLIS: I'm clean. Really. Hey, be a little more careful, would you? I'm a citizen.
VAL: (*Takes a large pocketknife out of WILLIS' right pants pocket.*) I'll keep that in mind.
WILLIS: You'd better keep that in mind, man. (*VAL puts the knife in a jacket pocket. He takes a wallet out of WILLIS' left back pocket, throws it SL on floor.*) I got an explanation. I do. I can explain. You got it all wrong. I wasn't messing with the "Olds." I got an explanation. Really.
VAL: Left hand! (*Removes handcuffs from his belt and snaps them on WILLIS, one at a time.*)
WILLIS: (*as his left hand is cuffed*) You don't need cuffs. I'm stranded, man. This is Eleventh Avenue. I'm not going anyplace.
VAL: Right hand!
WILLIS: (*as his right hand is cuffed*) The last cab I saw, it was two days ago. You got to go to Eighth, you want a subway. I couldn't make it to Eighth, not with you chasing me. I'm out of shape. You know that.
VAL: (*Backs away from WILLIS, removes a "Miranda" card from his pocket, reads from the card.*) You have the right to remain silent. You are not required to say anything to us at any time or to answer any questions. Anything you say can be used against you in court.
WILLIS: What do you think? I don't go to the movies? This is fucking out of sight, man! You know that? It was my cousin's car. Really.
VAL: (*Replaces the card in his pocket, squats, picks up wallet and puts it in right jacket pocket.*) We'll talk about it. As soon as we call your cousin.
WILLIS: He gave me the keys. He got a ride out to the "Shore."
VAL: It must be nice, the "Shore." I mean, if you live around here.
WILLIS: Look, he didn't need his car. I had his keys. Honest.
VAL: (*Takes out knife, opens it.*) What'd you do? Drop them?
WILLIS: Yeah, that's right. They must have fell out of my hand.
VAL: I'm real sorry about that.
WILLIS: I had them. I did. I didn't know who the fuck you were. You scared the shit out of me.
VAL: (*Closes knife, puts it in his left jacket pocket.*) You didn't even see me.
WILLIS: Right. I'll admit that. You guys are fast. Real fast. I know that. But I

heard you. That was enough. This is a shit neighborhood. I mean, I told my cousin to get a garage. I told him I'd split it with him. I use his car a lot.
VAL: Real generous, your cousin.
WILLIS: He is. He's terrific. You should meet him.
VAL: (*Takes out his two-way radio and crosses to WILLIS, pulling him off fence. As he does so.*) I won't be here. You know, when he gets back from the "Shore." (*transmitting*) Officer Johnson. "Holding one." Request "transportation." West 28th Street, off Eleventh. "500" block. (*VAL crosses USL.*)
WILLIS: (*Crosses SR to C.*) A fucking Oldsmobile? Jesus Christ, man! We could have talked things out! We still can—You? One of you guys?! Shit, no wonder I didn't see you!
VAL: Surprise.
WILLIS: Look, now we can talk. What do you say? We can make a deal. Fuckin' a, all this time, I thought you were white. You got a white voice, you know that?
VAL: No deal.
WILLIS: And you're not that dark either. Really. The right light, sunset, real early in the morning, you put a hat on your head, shit, man, no kidding, you could have come over on the fucking *Mayflower*.
VAL: You want to shove it back up your ass?
WILLIS: I was trying to compliment you, that's all I was trying to do. Ever since I was a kid, I've tried to concentrate on the positive aspects of life. You know what I mean?
VAL: (*Crosses US to arch.*) You're not going anywhere. Concentrate on that.
WILLIS: (*Crosses to VAL*) All the crime in this fucking city, and we're talking about a fucked-up car. I'll bet there's three throats being slit, just while we're standing here. That's the kind of action you should be jumping on. A lot of people, they'd be real grateful not having their throats slit. Look, man, be realistic. What'd I do? I mean, really, brother? It was a '77 Oldsmobile. Nobody misses a fucking Oldsmobile, not in this neighborhood. They left it there to lose it. It would have been doing the city a favor. You know how much it costs to tow away a piece of fucking junk like that? Of course you do. You do it. Or your pals do. Shit, the muffler was hanging out all over the street. "Spark city," brother, that's all it was. What if the guy'd tried to pass one of those propane trucks? We'd be missing twenty blocks. There would have been fingers and toes in Connecticut. And there was a puddle of oil, maybe ten feet. I'm lucky I didn't kill myself.
VAL: You are.
WILLIS: I mean, talking about an abortion. Two of the tires were skinny, and the other two needed air. One of them had seven patches on it. I've never seen seven patches on a tire. That's why I counted them. The doors were open, brother, all four of them. I don't mean unlocked. I mean OPEN. The guy was just begging me to cart it away. If he knew who I was, he probably would have sent me the registration.

VAL: We'll check it out. See what he feels about it. How's that sound?
WILLIS: Check it out? You got to speak Spanish, you want to check it out. That was a spic buggy if I ever saw one. It has Jesus doing pushups on the rear-view mirror. It had fifty-two Virgin Marys all over the dashboard, for Christ's sake! If he'd had room, it would have had a palm tree! You don't want to take me in over a spic buggy. Not you. I mean, do you? Really?
VAL: No law against decorating your dashboard.
WILLIS: You couldn't see to drive it. There's got to be a fucking law.
VAL: It was parked. Remember?
WILLIS: (*Crosses DSR.*) I don't understand it. I really don't understand it. You know what?
VAL: (*Crosses DSL.*) What's that?
WILLIS: You got no sense of fair play. That's one thing you don't have, brother. (*Gestures.*) Now, if I'd been fiddling around with the "Caddie" over there, you might have had ample cause. It's an '81. It's got respect written all over it. (*spells it*) R-e-s-p-e-c-t! But an "Olds," a '77 goddamn "Olds"—that's a one-night stand, brother. You get up the next morning, you wouldn't even wipe your ass with it.
VAL: You're a real pisser, aren't you?
WILLIS: (*Crosses US to C.*) No, see, it's like this, I'm the black sheep in the family. No offense there, "Bro," but I've been in trouble before. You're going to find out. You've got computers. I know that. But it's all been small stuff. Nothing big. Like the "Olds." That's my style. I don't beat up grandmothers, man. I don't rip off purses. I don't even own a gold chain. I never took heroin in my life. I don't even know what the shit looks like. Somebody offers me "coke," I turn it down. That knife, it's for my protection. It's a tough city. You can understand that. You carry a gun, don't you? Look at my fucking wardrobe. People don't dress like this, not when they're in the money. I mean, do I look like I'm part of the cash flow? Do I look like crime pays? (*his suit*) This is one step above "May's." The spics are breathing down my neck. They're starting to dress better than me. That car, that heap, that was to buy a new suit. So I could go to court. So I could look decent. So I could make a favorable impression. My ex, she's breaking my balls. Alimony. Child support. You might appreciate that. I've been around black chicks. Marlene, my ex, she's just like a lot of black chicks. Gorgeous in bed, real nifty, you know what I mean, right? But one step away from the sheets, all of a sudden, she's putting a bat between your legs, just for fucking practice.
VAL: (*low*) You're not helping your case.
WILLIS: (*Crosses DSC.*) Look, brother—
VAL: (*low—dangerous*) Don't call me fucking "brother."
WILLIS: What else am I supposed to call you? You and me, we're in the same category.
VAL: The fuck we are!
WILLIS: No, listen, we're deprived, that's all I'm saying. Economically

deprived. We always have been—always will be. My father was a prick. Yours just happened to be colored, right? Look, you get me to a phone booth. One block over. It's not busted. 29th. Back on Tenth. I'll give you a number. You dial it, there's a thousand bucks waiting. All you've got to do is dial 348-5745—No—It's 398-5745. My brother's place. He's got a large insomniac problem. He's always up late. He owns two dry cleaners. He keeps a lot of cash in his house. He doesn't trust the night deposit. A thousand bucks, brother! It's cheaper than bail. That's why he'll pay it. It's happened before. He always pays my bail, my brother—And then he screams at me. What do you say? Hell, it's the Fourth of July, man! Have a heart. I got kids. Two girls. Six and ten. Real cute—(*VAL stares at WILLIS.*) All right, then lets talk about your twelve fucking kids, nigger! How's that?!

VAL: (*Crosses USC. Dangerous.*) I'd be real quiet, if I were you. Real quiet. (*Crosses DSL.*)

WILLIS: (*Crosses US to VAL.*) Got you there, didn't I? Finally touched a nerve, right? I was beginning to think you didn't have no emotion, "bro." Now, your kiddies, I'll bet they could use a couple thousand real fresh bucks, couldn't they? I mean, you could probably spring at least six of them. You know, fix it up with the prosecutor, as long as he's got big lips and frizzy hair, right? You got a wife on the side, brother? A couple thousand bucks, you and the little lady, you could get (*Intentional dialect. Crosses DSC.*) "yourselves" a lifetime supply of penicillin, couldn't you? Why don't you give your foxy bitch a call? See what she thinks about it. You don't want to do that? No, I wouldn't want to do that either. Not this late. I wouldn't want to disturb her, not when her mouth's full. Or how about a two-thousand-buck transistor radio? I'll bet you've already got a hard-on just thinking about it. Five hundred fucking stations, man! Wouldn't be nobody but nobody riding the subways no more, would they? And I'll even throw in a pair of earphones. Free. No extra charge. Just call it a jigaboo bonus. How's that grab you? Wait a minute. One more thing. A real package deal. Six-foot shoes. Gold and orange. No, excuse me. Make those roller skates. Purple and green. Concentrate, brother! Get a fix on it! A 125th Street, Saturday night, and you'd be the heaviest fucking dude stomping the pavement!

VAL: You keep talking, asshole, and you won't even be able to fucking limp!

WILLIS: Is that a fucking fact?!

VAL: That's a fucking fact!

WILLIS: What's wrong, "bro"? You don't want to talk to a white man? You don't want to negotiate? William H. Willis, he's not good enough for you? No dope, no deal? No pussy, no action? Fucking nigger cops! How'd you get the job, anyway? Suck off another fucking "spearchucker" cop?! That's what they call progress, don't they? They ought to take all you nigger cops and ship you back to Africa. That's what they ought to do. Let you be jungle cops. Give you some beads and a spear. Let you direct tràffic in the jungle. Because that's where you belong, nigger! Didn't you know that? I mean, like don't you miss the smell of elephant shit?! (*VAL draws his service revolver.*) Just try it! Go on! See where it fucking gets you! (*VAL slowly holsters revolver.*) You don't got the balls, do you? Well, I can understand that. Really. Most niggers, they only come with one ball, that's what I hear. Hey, I got a joke for you. You want to hear a joke? What's the difference between a nigger cop and a pile of shit. No difference, man! Get It?! (*VAL draws his service revolver, points it at WILLIS, and pulls the trigger. An explosion from the revolver. WILLIS sags to the ground, jerks, and then lies still. VAL replaces his revolver in holster, turns away from WILLIS, takes several steps, and then stops. He turns back, stumbles to WILLIS, searches in his own pockets for the handcuff key, finds it, unlocks the handcuffs, locks them again, replaces them on his belt, takes out WILLIS' knife, opens it, wipes it with his jacket, puts the knife in WILLIS' right hand, and then begins to back away. He remembers the wallet. He takes it out, wipes it on his jacket, moves back to WILLIS, and puts it in WILLIS' back pocket. He backs away again, panting, taking deep breaths. He draws his service revolver and begins moving upstage. Blackout. Sound—music.*)

Scene 2

>*Music out. Lights. A New York City Police Precinct, an office, later that evening.*
>
>*PARKER, a black Police Captain studies VAL's report. VAL sits. He sips from a cardboard container of coffee.*

PARKER: Nice. Real clean. I'd say just about textbook. Right down the line.
VAL: What?
PARKER: (*Taps the report.*) One shot. That's all it took. You're not reckless. Not you, Johnson. Not when it comes to ammunition. Usually, it takes two shots. You know, one for good luck. Especially when it's dark. Especially when it's around 28th and Eleventh. Some of those guys, they can be fierce. It's a good policy—squeeze off two—if you're going to squeeze off anything. But you, Christ, you're some shot. You drilled him right through the heart. The perfect shot, Johnson. Hell, the guys up in sharpshooting couldn't have done it better. Practice a lot?
VAL: I used to.
PARKER: When was that?
VAL: When I was a kid.
PARKER: Pittsburgh. You grew up in Pittsburgh, right?
VAL: That's right.
PARKER: A lot of crime in Pittsburgh.

VAL: A lot of crime here.

PARKER: (*Taps the report.*) I can see that. Real serious crime, too. But we're keeping ahead of it, aren't we? Or, at least we're trying to keep ahead of it. Pittsburgh? You really had a gun in those days?

VAL: I had two guns.

PARKER: Two guns? What kind?

VAL: A "38" and a "22 Magnum."

PARKER: (*Whistles.*) Some people, they just get born into the right family, don't they? Shit, I couldn't even talk my old man into a BB pistol. I had to settle for cap guns, but my mother kept hiding the caps on me. I always got shot first. That didn't make it too much fun.

VAL: Parker, I'm tired. I'm not getting paid for this, I'm off-duty, and I've got a wife I haven't even called.

PARKER: No, you're not getting paid for this, you should have called your wife, and I'd rather be out at "Rockaway" taking a stroll along the beach. But we've got to get the facts straight, don't we? Or, at least sorted out.

VAL: (*the report*) See the blanks? They're all filled out. There isn't anything else.

PARKER: Well, there must be something else. There might just be something else. Usually, there is something else. Otherwise, I wouldn't be the investigating officer, and there wouldn't be a Departmental Hearing Friday morning, would there?

VAL: It just might be that he was white.

PARKER: It just might be. And it just might be that it's official police policy. I wonder what he was doing that far downtown—a guy from Queens. A white guy from Queens.

VAL: He was trying to steal a tan '77 Oldsmobile. Line seven, in case you missed it.

PARKER: (*Stares at the report.*) You've got real legible handwriting. That's a good trait. Every little bit helps when you're a cop, doesn't it? What color cars did they have in Pittsburgh? Black-and-whites?

VAL: Black-and-whites. What's the point?

PARKER: Good combination, black and white. We never should have dropped them. A lot more mystery, black-and-white. Green-and-white—blue-and-white—it makes crime too colorful. The same thing happened when the department issued blue pens.

VAL: I remember. It was real traumatic. But I thought we were talking about a tan, '77 Oldsmobile.

PARKER: See, the thing that bothers me, Johnson, most guys, most officers, they never have to go through it once. You know, wasting some dude. Most guys, most officers, they go thirty years, and it gets rusty in their holster. But if it does happen, if they have to take it out, it usually takes them awhile to get over it. And the first night, that's the worst night, even if the pin cushion was a real scumbag. But you, it just seems to me, you

don't give a flying fuck about what you just did. I mean, let's be realistic, Johnson, you just reduced the population by one.
VAL: He tried to kill me. What am I supposed to feel?
PARKER: Well, I guess it's no fun feeling mortal for a couple of seconds, is it? You get used to life, don't you? And I guess everybody reacts differently. Three feet, right?
VAL: Three feet.
PARKER: Look, I've got to ask. It's blocking my thoughts. How'd you ever get a permit in Pittsburgh?
VAL: You mean, how did one of us folks get a permit in Pittsburgh?
PARKER: I'm interested in the permit, that's all.
VAL: Really?
PARKER: Look at my skin.
VAL: Sweet.
PARKER: See, what I'm getting at, it was a little difficult on 110th, if not impossible, unless you knew somebody. Especially in those days. And nobody spoke much English, so I was out of my element.
VAL: My old man was a cop. He fixed it.
PARKER: Sweet. Kind of a family tradition?
VAL: He likes to think of it that way.
PARKER: You and your old man, you did a lot of shooting together?
VAL: Weekends.
PARKER: You win any prizes?
VAL: I'm not interested in prizes.
PARKER: No?
VAL: No.
PARKER: That must be true. This guy, Willis, he wasn't much of a prize. Arrested fourteen times, three convictions, small stuff. Never attacked anybody. Didn't seem to be the killer-type—
VAL: I saw his sheet.
PARKER: Looked up his background?
VAL: That's right. Wouldn't you?
PARKER: I'd probably do that. It's nice to know the facts after the fact, isn't it? Nope, he wasn't any prize. I don't think too many people are going to miss him. Maybe his brother in Queens. The guy owns two dry cleaners. You'd think he would have given him a job sorting hangers or something. Kept him off the streets. And his mother, she might miss him. He had a mother in Detroit.
VAL: I know that. And his father died in 1957, four years after Willis was born. First stretch, Jackson Prison, arrested in Lansing. He tried to hold up a "Dunkin' Donut," figured it'd be a lifelong career, so he decided to come to New York. I'm tired.
PARKER: Okay, okay, just a few more things. Christ, imagine if it was "Berkowitz" instead of this cat, Willis. Or "Chapman." What a prize! How come you called for a radio car before you cuffed him?

VAL: I didn't cuff him.
PARKER: That's right. I forgot. You didn't get a chance to cuff him. I hate nights. My mind wanders. All the details get lost. I've been thinking about a Virginia ham on whole wheat for the last five minutes. Lettuce, tomatoes, mayonnaise. Maybe a couple of pickles. (*PARKER hums "Jealousy."**) Why didn't you just call in when you spotted him jerking around with the "Olds"?
VAL: I figured I could handle it. It was one-on-one.
PARKER: Johnson, most cops in this city, me included, you call "transportation" when you've got the cat laced over a hood. Not when he's just waiting around for you to make a move. Christ, don't you ever watch television?
VAL: I had him covered. He looked docile.
PARKER: A lot of sweet-faced kids, give them a chance, and they'll take your ears home with them. Didn't your old man ever tell you that?
VAL: I chased him three blocks. He was out of shape. I didn't think he'd try anything.
PARKER: That's the trouble with being on the street too much—you begin to think you own it. "Procedure" doesn't mean shit when it's cops and robbers, one-on-one time, right? That's what I like about being in the office. You can't fuck up that much. Throw away one piece of paper, you've still got five more. Three feet?
VAL: (*the report*) That's what it says, doesn't it?
PARKER: Sure it does. That's how I know. How's the coffee?
VAL: I'd like to sleep.
PARKER: Wouldn't we all? If I didn't have a wife, two kids, a mother-in-law, and a Buick, shit, I'd never get up. I heard you were in Viet-Nam. Is that true?
VAL: You looked it up. Why ask?
PARKER: I don't believe everything I read. When was it?
VAL: Most of '68. The spring of '69.
PARKER: How was it? Intense?
VAL: Sometimes.
PARKER: You guys, you vets, you call it Nam, don't you?
VAL: That's what we called it over there.
PARKER: Sounds strange, "Nam." Sounds like half a country.
VAL: It was.
PARKER: You take a lot of risks?
VAL: What's that got to do with William H. Willis?
PARKER: I'd just like to know, that's all.

---

*Note: "Jealousy" is fully protected under copyright. Permission to produce SPLIT SECOND does not include permission to use this song in production. Such permission must be procured from the copyright owner of the song.

VAL: I did "point." You were paid to take risks.
PARKER: A scout?
VAL: Something like that.
PARKER: What'd you do? Volunteer?
VAL: That's right.
PARKER: How come?
VAL: We kept running into snipers. I thought I could do something about it.
PARKER: Did you?
VAL: Nobody got "hit" for five months.
PARKER: You must have been good.
VAL: It kept me alive.
PARKER: That's real dangerous work—being the "point man."
VAL: It could be.
PARKER: What about "close calls"?
VAL: What about them?
PARKER: Did you have any?
VAL: I didn't go looking for "close calls."
PARKER: So, most of the time, you were careful, right?
VAL: I was always careful.
PARKER: Five months—you didn't take a lot of chances.
VAL: I didn't take any chances.
PARKER: Don't go out in the rain, you don't get wet?
VAL: I just didn't want to be last in line holding my medals.
PARKER: Sure, I can understand that. It's who you know that counts. And whether or not he's white. But I still don't get it, Johnson. You're careful over there. You don't fuck around. Not once. But you come back here—
VAL: I was a target over there.
PARKER: You could have been a target tonight.
VAL: I didn't have forty men depending on me. It was a "collar." I've done it a hundred times, so I took him on "solo." This time he got stupid, real stupid, so he ended up dead. That's all we're talking about, Parker—logical progression—stupid to dead. He pulled the knife, so I pulled the trigger. Nothing else applies.
PARKER: You do much killing in Viet-Nam?
VAL: No.
PARKER: Come on. Not even one?
VAL: If I did, I didn't see him.
PARKER: It gets real easy to kill when you can't see them. I read a book on the subject. Two books.
VAL: Parker, I just shot a car thief who was coming at me with a knife. There's a six-thousand-mile difference. What do you say? Why don't we just stick to that?
PARKER: Look, I'm just trying to make an analogy.

VAL: Stretch it, it won't fit. So why don't we just drop it?
PARKER: No, let me finish, see if it gets us anywhere. I don't get homicides on a regular basis.
VAL: He had a knife. Remember?
PARKER: That's right, he did. That's why I never went into Law. I just couldn't get the terms straight. Homicide, suicide—all the "cides" began to sound the same. Anyway, the point I was trying to make, the analogy, it's real dark in the jungle, isn't it?
VAL: So what?
PARKER: I'm not trying to be an expert, Johnson. I've never been in a jungle. I don't even like walking in the woods. But I've seen enough movies about us folks to get a pretty good idea of what a jungle looks like. Real dark. Even in the daytime. All those trees growing into each other for centuries. And I remember reading something about Viet-Nam, or maybe I saw it on T.V. Guys in the jungle, they used to empty out two hundred rounds if they even heard a twig snap. Three hundred rounds if a fly landed on a branch.
VAL: They had rules about that.
PARKER: Well, we can't enforce all the rules, can we? Now, it seems to me, it's awfully dark on 29th and—
VAL: Twenty-eighth.
PARKER: That's right, excuse me, 28th. Awfully dark, there, too, being so close to 29th. And real deserted, too.
VAL: It wasn't that dark.
PARKER: Not like the jungle?
VAL: Not like the jungle.
PARKER: Well, you were there. You ought to know. I just saw the movies.
VAL: And there was a street lamp on 28th.
PARKER: Busted. That's what they told me.
VAL: It wasn't busted two hours ago.
PARKER: You didn't happen to shoot it out, did you? No, one shot, right? I keep thinking there should have been two. Maybe somebody busted it after you left. Shit, they're all busted up there. You'd think they'd turn off the electricity. Save money. It's too bad "warning shots" went out. You might have scared him. Still, two verbal warnings—Some guys, they just don't listen, do they? Three feet? You really got that close?
VAL: I got that close.
PARKER: I never liked getting "close." That's why I decided to get off the street. I just couldn't get used to touching guys I didn't know. Some cops—they really enjoy slamming a guy into a wall. That might even be the reason they join up. But not me. You were patting him down, right?
VAL: It never got that far.
PARKER: You had him "spread out," didn't you?
VAL: It never got that far either.

PARKER: He just turned around, three feet, knife out?
VAL: He turned around, one foot, knife coming out. I backed up two.
PARKER: He must have been desperate.
VAL: He must have been.
PARKER: And that's when you warned him?
VAL: I told him to "drop it." That was his second warning. The first warning, I told him to "freeze."
PARKER: Let me get this straight. He had his knife out, he was coming at you, and you had time to warn him.
VAL: "Drop it" doesn't take a whole lot of time.
PARKER: Well, it's a good thing you didn't say "Drop that fucking knife, you cocksucking bastard, or I'll put a bullet through your miserable heart!" (*Moves to VAL, turns away and counts off three feet.*) One. Two. Three. (*Turns his head toward VAL.*) Let's go through it one more time, okay?
VAL: (*not moving*) This is bullshit, Parker.
PARKER: Look, it'll save time on Friday. (*VAL slowly faces PARKER's back.*) Get rid of your coffee cup. You weren't drinking coffee, were you? (*VAL sets his coffee container on chair.*) Good. Now, point your finger at me. We don't want to get too realistic.
VAL: People pay us for this?
PARKER: Go on. Point. I just want to figure something out. (*VAL pauses, and then raises his finger, pointing it at PARKER's back. PARKER speaks without looking back.*) You pointing at me?
VAL: I'm pointing at you.
PARKER: (*The pen suddenly in his left hand, wheels around and has it against VAL's stomach. They stare at each other.*) I'm surprised he didn't cut off your balls, Johnson.
VAL: He's dead, isn't he?
PARKER: (*lowering the pen*) I didn't see your finger move.
VAL: Neither did he. (*the pen*) And he had it in his right hand.
PARKER: Yes, he did. The quality of observation, that's a nice quality to have in police work. But three feet, his height, your height, and given the fact, most cutters, they come in real low—What I'd really like to know, Johnson—What baffles the living fuck out of me—How'd you ever pump one into his heart? I mean, you should have pulled it off in his face, or, at least put it through his neck.
VAL: He wasn't very good with a knife, he didn't come in low, and he was trying to open it.
PARKER: It's real sad. They get sloppy, a lot of those guys. They stop practicing, don't they? Well, at least it was quick for William H. Willis.
VAL: He didn't go out humming, if that's what you mean.
PARKER: They usually don't. Too many other things to think about. Con Ed bills. Laundry. Season tickets. Well I suppose we should look at the

brighter side of it. A lot of doughnut shop owners, they are going to sleep a little sounder tonight, ain't they?

VAL: Is that it?

PARKER: I was doing a tour, playground on 72nd, tried to break up a fight. This Mexican kid came at me with an ice pick. He came in real low. That kid kept in shape. Right for my belly. Fast. He must have been in training for ten years. I caught him twice. Once in the nose, once in the right cheek. But, see, I had time to aim. I was standing nine feet away from the punk. That kid, that "Mex," he had it in for me. He would have cut out my heart and stuck it in his mother's enchilada. But the funny thing, the really strange thing, you'd think I would have forgotten about him. Chalked him up to good shooting. But I haven't. And I had the right to do it.

VAL: So did I.

PARKER: I hope so, Johnson. Unless you get nicked in the line of duty, you're going to be around for a long time. (*They stare at each other. Blackout. Music.*)

Scene 3

Music out. Lights—SR platform. A bar. A short time later.

VAL and CHARLIE, a black cop, street clothes, standing at bar, each drinking a mug of beer.

CHARLIE: He was ripe, Val. You didn't have any other choice. You couldn't cuff him. He pulled a blade. You're a cop. What'd he think you were going to do? Sharpen it for him? What'd he expect? I'll bet he went down looking real surprised. They always do. Dumb—some of those—mothers—fucking dumb. They go along real cool, then it gets hot out one night, or their old lady won't twist it for them, and they fucking lose it. (*He attempts to unzip VAL's jacket. As he does so.*) Hey, man, it's July. At least unzip it.

VAL: (*Pulls away from CHARLIE—slightly. They stare at each other.*) Air-conditioning, Charlie—I get colds from air-conditioning.

CHARLIE: Sure, I can understand that. I get pneumonia swimming at Jones Beach in February. Look, it's over. The guy'd been in and out of shithouses—What? Since he was a kid. You did us all a favor. If it hadn't been you, it might have been me. Or Fleming. Or Carlos. He was a mark, Val. He was wearing a card on his heart. I don't get it. They walk around just inviting us to put a hole in them. We all know that. And then, when we finally do it, we're fucking depressed. Beats me. (*Sips his beer and studies VAL.*) Look, a motherfucker's a motherfucker, no matter who started throwing him against the wall when he was six months old. And once a motherfucker, always a motherfucker, dead or alive. It was up close, that's all. If you'd shot him off a roof, you'd be home in bed asleep. (*VAL nods.*) Val, it's a well-known fact in the Department that nobody but nobody digs close-up work. It looks great in the movies, but shit, who in the fuck wants to sniff a "Big Mac" and fries just before some freak gets taken out? You want to know about "up close"? I was talking to this guy in "Burglary"—Johnny Williams. Some dude on Canal Street came at him with a cleaver. It took five shots to put him away, and this dude was still swinging on number four. Now that's up close! Drink your beer. Let it go, man. The creep was a flea. Just like the dude on Canal. A dog wouldn't have pissed on either of them. (*VAL nods and sips his beer.*) You call Alea yet?

VAL: It doesn't work over the phone.

CHARLIE: That's what I'm doing here, right?

VAL: Right.

CHARLIE: My advice, and it's worked wonders in the past—get a "leave." Get out of the city. Don't start hashing it around here. Take a couple of days—drive—relax. I'll tell you one thing—you want a leave—you sure as hell bagged that son of a bitch the right time of the month. Christ, I hate this weather. It means I must be civilized or something. The ancestors—they used to have lunch on the equator. (*He studies VAL.*) Val, would you stop fingering that glass? It drives me crazy. I can't concentrate. I keep waiting for it to break. That's why I can't stand drinking with Carlos anymore. That's all he ever does—all night—fingers his glass and comments on the diameters of every good-looking ass comes in the door. No self-control—Carlos. I don't know how they ever gave him a badge, let alone a gun, and you're starting to be his replacement.

VAL: This guy—Willis—He was white.

CHARLIE: So? He could have been black, Puerto Rican, or American Indian, for all I care. He pulled more than two inches on you. He took more than one step. If he was looking for a souvenir, well, he sure as hell got it. You've got the license. He didn't have one. You remember that. If that dude'd waltzed in my direction, I would have emptied out on him. Shit, I'd still be clicking away. I'd get real nervous knowing I might not be able to get it up anymore. Real nervous.

VAL: I keep thinking, Charlie—

CHARLIE: That's not a good trait. Not right now.

VAL: I keep thinking—if he'd been black—maybe I wouldn't have shot him.

CHARLIE: What do you mean you wouldn't have shot him? That's what they trained you to do. The color doesn't mean shit. Fleming's old man, he shot two dudes. Both black. He said he didn't know what color they were until they were dead.

VAL: I don't remember doing it, Charlie. Really doing it. Pulling the trigger. I was starting to walk away—All of a sudden he was on the ground—

CHARLIE: That's the best way to remember it—you don't remember it. You've got other people to worry about. Alea, the old man, me—Come on. I'll buy you another beer. We'll talk about all the good things we're going to do. (*Picks up the beer mugs and exits.*)
VAL: I had him cuffed, Charlie—I had him cuffed. (*Slow blackout. Music.*)

Scene 4

Music out. Lights. VAL and ALEA's apartment. A short time later.

VAL enters the apartment. ALEA is asleep on the couch (DSL bench) with test papers and red pen in hand. She wears glasses. VAL takes off his jacket and drapes it on chair USC. He moves to her and attempts to remove test papers. She wakes up.

ALEA: What time is it?
VAL: Four. A little after.
ALEA: Four? Did something happen?
VAL: It was busy, that's all. I did overtime. (*Kisses her. Gestures—the door.*) You forgot to lock the "police bar."
ALEA: (*slowly sitting up*) I thought you'd be back earlier. I dropped your father off—What? Ten-thirty? I bought him a beer. He liked the fireworks.
VAL: I'm going to put a sign up—"Bolt me."
ALEA: I'll remember. Is it really four o'clock? I didn't mean to fall asleep here—
VAL: Anybody could "jimmy" the lock. He doesn't even have to be good.
ALEA: I'll remember. I promise.
VAL: (*Crosses USC to chair, takes off gun & holster.*) Second time this week.
ALEA: I'm half-awake. Quit scolding. It's four o'clock, and I've got a class in five hours.
VAL: (*Crosses DSL to ALEA, sits and massages her feet.*) How'd you like to skip it?
ALEA: I'd like to, but I can't.
VAL: Why not?
ALEA: I've already been out twice.
VAL: We could drive upstate. Look at some land for Rusty.
ALEA: They did homework. I'm supposed to collect it.
VAL: We could find a place, have dinner, take our time—
ALEA: You've got to work tomorrow night.
VAL: I'll get Charlie to cover. Or Carlos. They're both off tomorrow. They owe me.
ALEA: We can do it Sunday.
VAL: No, tomorrow's better.
ALEA: We've got the weekend.

VAL: I need to get out of the city.
ALEA: But why tomorrow?
VAL: (*Pulls at his shirt.*) How come you didn't turn on the air-conditioner?
ALEA: I fell asleep, that's all.
VAL: It's got to be eighty-five—ninety degrees in here.
ALEA: Val?
VAL: I had a close-call tonight.
ALEA: What happened?
VAL: Some punk pulled a knife on me.
ALEA: A knife?
VAL: He dropped it.
ALEA: Where'd it happen?
VAL: (*Crosses SL.*) Twenty-eighth and Eleventh.
ALEA: Was it a kid?
VAL: A kid, right. Eighteen, nineteen. I'm not sure.
ALEA: How big was the knife?
VAL: Big enough.
ALEA: What kind of knife was it?
VAL: Kitchen.
ALEA: Did he try to use it?
VAL: He made a move. But he wasn't that fast. He was high. We found a bunch of "shit" on him.
ALEA: Eighteen years old?
VAL: Something like that.
ALEA: Those bastards!
VAL: Right.
ALEA: Was he black?
VAL: Black, right—
ALEA: He had a knife. I guess it doesn't matter, does it?
VAL: No—
ALEA: (*She moves to him, embraces him.*) Why don't we stay overnight?
VAL: We can't. I mean, I can't. I've got to be back Friday—
ALEA: I'll take Friday off, too. We'll come back late.
VAL: I've got a meeting. Friday morning.
ALEA: What kind of meeting?
VAL: Routine. Departmental.
ALEA: What time?
VAL: I've got to be back, that's all. It's early. Ten o'clock.
ALEA: I don't remember any Friday morning meetings.
VAL: I've been skipping them. Captain sent me a memo. "I'm missed"—that's what it said. I don't want to push it.
ALEA: Then we'll come back tomorrow night. Do you want anything to eat? Some tea? (*He stares straight ahead. He shakes his head "no."*) Val?

VAL: I'm telling you, the next punk who comes at me with a knife—The next punk who comes at me with anything. I'm going to pull the trigger!
ALEA: What?
VAL: I'm getting to hate it. I don't know, you knock down one jerk, four more stand up behind him.
ALEA: He really scared you, didn't he?
VAL: (*Crosses SL, sits on bench.*) He didn't scare me. I wanted to tear him apart. I almost did—No, forget it. It's over.
ALEA: Why didn't you call?
VAL: I went out for a beer. I ran into Charlie—
ALEA: (*Crosses to SC, folds jacket.*) Charlie?
VAL: Right.
ALEA: Charlie's been working "days."
VAL: He was looking for some action. He came around.
ALEA: Was it more than just a kid with a knife?
VAL: No. it was a kid with a knife, that's all. One night's worse than another. The Fourth of July—it's always nuts. It was just another incident. I should have called—
ALEA: How serious was it?
VAL: (*Stands, crosses USL of ALEA.*) Look, I don't want to talk about it right now. Really. I just don't want to go through it again. I want to get some sleep. I want to get out of this city. It'll blow over. Like it always does. Like it has to. It was automatic. It was reflexes.
ALEA: What was?
VAL: This guy—What happened—
ALEA: I thought it was a kid. A black kid.
VAL: All right, it was a kid!
ALEA: Who do I have to ask? Charlie? He's got the details, doesn't he?
VAL: Some of them.
ALEA: Who else are you going to tell? Rusty?
VAL: Look, I survive. That's all you need to know. Sometimes I get home late. Sometimes I forget to call. That's it.—
ALEA: (*Puts jacket on chair.*) That's it?!
VAL: That's it! That's enough.
ALEA: People talk about their jobs!
VAL: I talk about my job.
ALEA: I get the anecdotes. I get the laughs. That's your style.
VAL: The rest is ugly. The rest stays on the streets.
ALEA: You live here. I have a right to know.
VAL: I didn't marry you so I could tell you goddamn cop stories all night!
ALEA: No? Then what am I supposed to think about while you're gone?
VAL: You've got your kids. You've got your classes. Why mix it up with a lot of shit?!

ALEA: Then what am I supposed to think about while you're here? You don't want me to know anything about your work, except that one night's dangerous, one night's not.

VAL: You got it!

ALEA: How am I supposed to know which night is which?!

VAL: You're not supposed to know!

ALEA: Then what do you need me around for?! You come home three hours late. You don't call. But I'm not supposed to say anything. I'm not supposed to ask questions, because, no, we don't talk about your work.

VAL: (*Crosses DSL.*) Alea, leave it alone.

ALEA: We talk about my work instead, don't we? My school. The kids. Do they like me? How come they don't like me? What's so goddamn important about teaching English when they'd rather speak Spanish? But let's forget about you. Let's leave the Police Department out of it. That's the way you want it, isn't it?

VAL: That's the way I want it, yes!

ALEA: Because you've always got to be in control, right?

VAL: You lose it, you let it go for a second, you even snap your fingers, somebody else picks it up, and fast!

ALEA: Is that what Rusty taught you? Is that your father's code?

VAL: No, it's mine. I learned it early—starting at six—starting in Pittsburgh. I got dragged off the "Hill." Three white punks. I got tied to a tree. I got my clothes sliced off with a knife. I got poison ivy rubbed all over me. I hung there five hours. It got dark out. I was still there. That's when I learned it. (*Crosses DSR.*)

ALEA: You were six years old, Val.

VAL: It could have been yesterday.

ALEA: And so nothing else counts?

VAL: Not a fucking thing!

ALEA: Nothing else defines you, right?

VAL: It got me through a war, and it gets me through my job!

ALEA: And what's it do to me, Val? What's it do to you?

VAL: Let it go.

ALEA: Why?

VAL: Because you wouldn't like to hear about this one. Not this one.

ALEA: No? I'm supposed to be a partner, remember? I don't give a good goddamn if Rusty never told your mother anything. All I know is that I'm tired of watching fifty percent of you disappear every night when you come through that door, barred or not barred, and I'm tired of knowing that fifty percent of me can't function when you're around me. (*Crosses DS to C.*)

VAL: You wouldn't want to hear about this one.

ALEA: Why not?

VAL: Nobody wants to hear about this one.

ALEA: (*Crosses R to VAL.*) Try me.
VAL: You don't want to hear about it!
ALEA: Try me!
VAL: All right. Why not? Let's get involved in my job.
ALEA: Don't make fun of me.
VAL: The Fourth of July. A big night in my life. I offed a white dude. Twenty-eighth and Eleventh. I put him out of commission for good. One shot. Right through the heart.
ALEA: Oh, my God, Val.
VAL: You wanted to know, didn't you?
ALEA: I wanted to help. I want to help. (*Crosses SL to bench, sits.*)
VAL: (*Crosses US to C.*) Help? No way you can do that, baby. Morgue van picked him up four hours ago. William H. Willis. Very white. Numbers and burglary. Out of Detroit. A ten-page sheet on him. Two stretches in New York. Sing Sing and Rikers. This time it was a car. A '77 Oldsmobile. He tried to snatch it. I wasn't on a break. Unlucky for me. Unlucky for him. I happened to spot him first, and now he's laid out, courtesy of the city, 30th and First, waiting for his brother.
ALEA: Why—Why'd you shoot him? Val?
VAL: The shit pulled a knife on me, that's why! So I blew his fucking chest away! How's that sound?! Three feet away from me! No time for conversation! No time for manners! He was dead with his stomach in his mouth before he even hit the street! Hey, maybe you should have been there! (*Crosses DSR.*)
ALEA: Val!
VAL: Quite a sight, baby! Real involvement. A cop's wife, right beside him. Action. Front-line action. You could have chalked him, told your kids about it, spent a whole lesson drawing it on the blackboard—
ALEA: (*Crosses R to VAL.*) It was self-defense!
VAL: Sure it was. Of course it was. But you still should have seen it. I mean, not much up front—just a neat round hole—but check out his back, no shoulder blade. But you're right. A clear-cut case of self-defense. A cop's life on the line. A black cop's life on the line, but still a cop. I've got the badge, he had the knife, and, white or not, was that son of a bitch ever surprised when the last thing he ever saw was the look on my face!
ALEA: Val? That's not the way it happened, is it?
VAL: I had an hour left. If he'd tried to steal it an hour later, I could have looked the other way. I could have done that. I didn't need to chase him. It was a goddamn car, falling apart. He wasn't even driving it. But I had to make it important. I had to do my job. I couldn't let him get away.
ALEA: (*Sits SR platform.*) How'd it happen?
VAL: (*Crosses SL to bench.*) I had the cuffs on him. I was waiting for a radio car. I was standing seven, maybe eight feet away from him. I had my gun

on him. "Procedure" to the letter. I heard the sirens. I guess I must have jumped. It was dark. There weren't any street lamps around. Firecrackers were going off all over the place. I accidentally squeezed the trigger.
ALEA: What about the handcuffs?
VAL: I had time. I took them off.
ALEA: And the knife?
VAL: He had a knife. I opened it. I wiped off the prints. I stuck it in his hand.
ALEA: (*She moves to him, embraces him.*) Then there's nothing to worry about—Is there?
VAL: No—(*The lights begin to fade to darkness. Music. Blackout. Music out.*)

END OF ACT I

ACT II

Scene 1

> Darkness. Music. Music out—gradually.
>
> Lights—SR platform. RUSTY JOHNSON's apartment. The living room. The next evening. RUSTY sits watching the television (not seen)—a can of beer in one hand—a remote control in the other hand. He is dressed casually. VAL enters—a change of clothes—but still casual.

RUSTY: (*the television program*) Shh. (*VAL watches the program—no interest in it. RUSTY refers to the program.*) Do you believe that horseshit? Just strolls in. The door isn't even locked. Whatever happened to stakeouts? (*to VAL.*) Ever notice how the black dude always trots in second? You think they're trying to tell us something? The guys who write these shows, they ought to do a tour, find out a few things. They ought to make it mandatory. (*RUSTY pushes button on remote control—snaps off the television.*) What are you doing out tonight, son? I thought you were working.

VAL: The "Fourth"—I did overtime. I got the night off.

RUSTY: How was it last night? Jumping?

VAL: I was downtown. Nothing special.

RUSTY: I always hated holidays.

VAL: I know.

RUSTY: New Year's Eve, I'd start punching people out at eight and keep on punching till four. Did I ever tell you? I used to put lead in my gloves.

VAL: No.

RUSTY: It saved a lot of time. You want a beer?

VAL: No. (*gestures*) How's the leg?

RUSTY: (*Pats his left leg.*) Coming along. Just picked up a new pair of stirrups. Won't happen again. No more tumbles. Never should have bought cheap stirrups. Cutting corners, that's all I was doing. But it was a fifty-buck difference, and I had my eye on that Mexican saddle.

VAL: I would have bought it for you.

RUSTY: I like picking up my own accessories.

VAL: I remember. You made Father's Day tough.

RUSTY: Pick them up yourself, nobody can throw them back in your face. (*Pats his left leg.*) No, it wasn't "Stallion's" fault. Cheap stirrups, that's what did it.

VAL: Aren't you ever going to name that horse?

RUSTY: "Stallion's" fine. That's what he is, isn't he? Just taught him two more words last week. I'd like to see the bastard tries to steal that horse. Better be fluent in German, or he's going to find his ass wrapped around a couple of trees.

VAL: There aren't too many German horse thieves around anymore, Dad.

RUSTY: You never can tell. A lot of people, they end up surprising you. There was this loony in Pittsburgh. I used to arrest him all the time. Every other month. Larry Malone. Worst thief you ever saw. Incompetent. So bad it was downright embarrassing. Usually pulled his heists when he was stewed. A "brick-through-the-window" type. Or, if he couldn't find a brick, a garbage can. I picked him up one night. He was carrying a 21-inch "Admiral" portable. Right down "Forbes." Three in the morning. A streetcar almost hit him. We saved his goddamn life. Anyway, we got him in the black-and-white, stashed the portable—You remember that portable. It was in your grandmother's house.
VAL: Right.
RUSTY: Worked real well, that "Admiral." Your grandmother never had any trouble with it. Where was I? Larry Malone, right. (*Studies VAL.*) What are you doing here, son?
VAL: I had an incident last night.
RUSTY: What kind of an "incident"?
VAL: I shot a guy.
RUSTY: Dead?
VAL: Dead.
RUSTY: First time outside the army?
VAL: I didn't kill anybody in Nam.
RUSTY: Funny. You know, I always assumed you did. We never talked about it. I was always waiting for you to mention it, but you never did. A whole year, and you didn't shoot anybody?
VAL: I did "point." It didn't come up.
RUSTY: It's a real shame.
VAL: What?
RUSTY: All that free ammo, tons of it, and you didn't have anything to show for it.
VAL: Disappointed?
RUSTY: You've either got a target, or you don't. You know this guy you shot? Ever see him before?
VAL: No.
RUSTY: One of "us"?
VAL: White.
RUSTY: Well, that's one for our side, isn't it? He have a gun?
VAL: Yes.
RUSTY: Did he pull it on you? (*VAL nods "yes."*) Did you have "yours" out?
VAL: Not at first.
RUSTY: You should have had it out. Fast draws went out a long time ago. (*He studies VAL.*) He was the first one, son. Not many guys are lucky enough to pull thirty-five years without having to face it. (*He crosses SL to chair, followed by VAL.*)
VAL: No—
RUSTY: What do you mean "no"?

VAL: That's not the way it went down.
RUSTY: What isn't?
VAL: I killed him.
RUSTY: Well, Christ, yes, you killed him. What else are you going to call it? He had a gun. It was pointed at you. You squeezed first, that's all. Justifiable homicide, that's what it's called.
VAL: He didn't have a gun.
RUSTY: What do you mean "He didn't have a gun"?!
VAL: He didn't have one, that's all.
RUSTY: Then why in the hell did you tell me he did?! He had a knife, right?
VAL: He had a knife—
RUSTY: Knife can kill you, too, in case you didn't know that. What'd he do? Come at you with it?
VAL: He had a knife in his pocket. I took it off him.
RUSTY: What kind of shit is this? No gun—No knife—He lunged at you, right? He made a quick move.
VAL: (*Crosses DSL to bench.*) I had my gun on him—It accidentally went off—
RUSTY: Accidentally—Accidentally went off?!
VAL: Yes!
RUSTY: Why in the hell didn't you just cuff the son of a bitch?!
VAL: I had a radio car coming. I didn't think I needed to.
RUSTY: You didn't think you needed to?! That's why they issue handcuffs! So you put your gun away!
VAL: I know that!
RUSTY: You didn't know it last night!
VAL: I didn't want to get close.
RUSTY: They pay you to get close.
VAL: It didn't seem like he was going anywhere.
RUSTY: (*Puts beer down on chair.*) You made sure of that, didn't you?!
VAL: It was an accident!
RUSTY: You don't pull out a gun and have accidents. Kids have accidents with guns. There must have been some provocation. Something!
VAL: I can't remember—
RUSTY: (*Crosses DL to VAL.*) What do you mean, "you can't remember"?! Did he look like he was going to scatter? Did he pick up a rock? Did he put a hand inside his coat?
VAL: He was yelling!
RUSTY: He was "what"?!
VAL: Yelling!
RUSTY: Yelling?! Shit, that's not against the law! They've got a right to yell! You're putting them away! Didn't you know that?! What were you doing last night? Drinking?
VAL: I wasn't drinking.

RUSTY: You should have had him cuffed! You don't put a bullet in somebody, no reason, except he was yelling at you, getting on your nerves! The worst cops I knew, the most they'd do, maybe break a kneecap—an elbow—
VAL: Look, I remember the stories. You and Lloyd, you both carried "throwaways." Just in case you made a mistake.
RUSTY: That's right. But we never made a mistake.
VAL: What do you mean you never made a mistake? You killed three men! There had to be a mistake!
RUSTY: There wasn't any mistake! Not one! I had reason! Just cause! Provocation! All three times! Two of them had me on the ground, and the other son of a bitch was coming at me with a two-by-four!
VAL: So what?! You still carried "throwaways"! You kept the "mistake" in mind!
RUSTY: We all carried them. It was part of the ritual in those days. We used to pass them around in bars. But I only knew one cop who ever used it, and he got caught. Sure, we talked big. We carried "throwaways." We had trick holsters. We had to. We were all scared shitless. But we didn't have accidents. Guns didn't just go off. People didn't die just because we got jumpy, nervous, distracted, or whatever you want to call it. So, don't start in on me, boy! You pulled the trigger! Not me! I didn't ask you to be a goddamn cop! (*Crosses USC, picks up beer.*)
VAL: (*Crosses US to RUSTY.*) Didn't ask? What else was there? I grew up with cops. The only people who ever came over to our house were cops. Cops and cops' wives. Cops and cops' kids. And once in awhile, a real distinction—some goddamn prosecutor who should have been a cop! I mean, traffic cops, vice cops, street cops, homicide—Lloyd, Frank, Daryll, every partner you ever had!
RUSTY: That's how I kept my job! (*Crosses DSR, sits on platform.*)
VAL: The hell it was! You loved it. Being a cop, that was special. The world couldn't get along without cops. In fact, cops ruled the world. That's how society functioned. I remember, Mom and me, we must have spent two thousand hours waiting for you to change your goddamn uniform. And where in the hell were you? Drinking your "Rolling Rock" with the boys, that's where you were. Cleaning your gun, loading it, unloading it—
RUSTY: It came in handy, my gun!
VAL: (*Crosses DS to RUSTY.*) Sure it did. But where were we, Mom and me? Out front, waiting, watching the hookers get booked. Or the guy who'd just carved up his wife with a screwdriver and then blown off his six-year-old daughter's head with a shotgun. Or the broad who'd just burned down her house, except her husband and four kids just happened to be in it. What are you talking about "you didn't ask me to be a cop"?! I started being a cop at five. The first Christmas I can remember, under the tree, a fingerprint kit. A goddamn fingerprint kit. And a black-and-white, made out of tin, with your name painted on the hood, "Rusty," and the number

of your squad car, "183." I broke it Christmas Day, winding it up, listening to the siren. My God, you had me in uniform when I was ten. All those precinct blasts in "Oakland." Fake ribbons. Fake medals. All the ribbons and medals I was supposed to earn when I grew up. First in the army, and then on the force. You got me a flasher for my bike. I was eleven years old, and I was arresting every other kid on the block!

RUSTY: It was my profession! What'd you expect?! We were living on the "Hill." I was a black cop. That was something in those days—a black cop. I was proud of it. And sure, I brought it home. What else was I supposed to bring home? What else was I supposed to do? Pretend I was a goddamn surgeon? Put clamps and a scalpel under the tree? Buy you a book on anatomy? No, I'm not going to listen to this! Why in the hell am I defending myself?! I'm not about to swallow a bullet just because you were raised up in a cop's house! Just because you lost your cool last night! You're on trial, kiddo! Not me! Manslaughter, that's what you gave those bastards! (*crossing USR of C*)

VAL: I didn't give them shit!

RUSTY: (*He turns to VAL, studies him.*) I must be losing my edge. I didn't see it coming. You fixed it, didn't you?

VAL: I fixed it.

RUSTY: You planted the knife.

VAL: I planted the knife.

RUSTY: And that makes it a whole different story, doesn't it?

VAL: It makes it self-defense.

RUSTY: He came at you, right?

VAL: Right.

RUSTY: (*Crosses DSC.*) And you warned him.

VAL: I warned him twice.

RUSTY: Neat.

VAL: That's right. Neat.

RUSTY: No witnesses.

VAL: Nobody.

RUSTY: And that's it?

VAL: There's a departmental hearing. Tomorrow morning.

RUSTY: And you're going to lie again?

VAL: (*Crosses DS to RUSTY.*) When are you going to realize—When are you going to learn—It's not our fucking world! When are you
going to understand that?!

RUSTY: Then maybe you should have picked cotton for a living! There are rules!

VAL: White rules!

RUSTY: Rules, buddyboy!

VAL: And sometimes they apply, sometimes they don't, right?!

RUSTY: If you accept them, you live by them. Nobody's supposed to like you. Nobody liked me. But I still got through thirty-two years.

VAL: Thirty-two years, and you didn't even make Sergeant. Fourteen citations, and you never saw a stripe.
RUSTY: That's right. But I'm alive. I've got a pension. I've got a disability. I've got everything they promised to give me. I get to ride a lot now. I could afford the move here. I could afford your mother's funeral. I can afford this apartment, and, one of these days, I'm going to nail down a piece of land. We're talking about police money. It got me through the Depression. It got your mother through the Depression. And when you came along, you had a roof over your head. You ate. You went to school.
VAL: (*Crosses SL to bench, sits.*) Those were necessities.
RUSTY: I didn't expect anything else.
VAL: Dad, those were necessities. Everybody else took them for granted. Why in the hell do we have to be grateful?!
RUSTY: Times were different. I was grateful.
VAL: They aren't any different now. Who do you think is running this country? All of a sudden, they're setting us back fifty years. Why should I be grateful? Just because you were?
RUSTY: You listen to me! A cop back then, a black cop, they tossed him into "Hazelwood." God dropped all his rejects in "Hazelwood," and I took care of them. Me, Lloyd, Jackson, Frank, and a few other guys. And you didn't last long, not in that neighborhood, not if you were chickenshit. One sign of weakness, and they'd find you behind a garage, your throat slit, so wide they could see into your stomach. Or your head caved in, four slugs from your own gun. And do you think the Department cared? You want to know what it was like being a black cop in Pittsburgh? A nigger cop? It was the bottom of the ladder. No rungs, kiddo. You just hung on, that's all you did. You got base pay. No raises. No bonuses. No promotions. None. And if you even thought about opening your mouth, then you cleaned out your locker the same night. Don't tell me things haven't changed. You've got black-Captains today. If you thought you'd seen a black Captain in Pittsburgh—1945—they would have put you in a tight jacket and hustled your ass out a side door!
VAL: Snails crawl faster than we do.
RUSTY: But they get there. They get there.
VAL: Sure, if somebody doesn't step on them.
RUSTY: The destination, that's all that counts.
VAL: We make it to the corner, we're lucky.
RUSTY: What's the alternative? Watts? Detroit? Where in the hell did they get us?
VAL: They got us noticed.
RUSTY: And last night? Where'd that get us?
VAL: I've done enough for them! I fought their goddamn war!
RUSTY: (*Crosses SR, sits on platform.*) You couldn't even find a target. How'd that help?
VAL: You don't even have an idea, do you?

RUSTY: You wasted a lot of ammunition, that's all I know.
VAL: I had you in mind, half the time I was over there—And that's all you think? I wasted a lot of ammunition? One time—One time, I got across a paddy on "point." But all of a sudden, it seemed wrong. "Charlie" was real close. All around me. He hadn't bought the "bait." He'd let me get across. He knew what he had behind me. I couldn't get anybody on the radio, so I started back. I was doing a number on "Charlie's" trap, so I expected a bullet in the back. And the only thing that went through my mind, the one thought, waiting for that bullet, "What's Rusty going to think?" His son took a fucking bullet in the back. "What in the hell was he doing to get a bullet in the back?!" Just thinking about you, it must have made me run faster, because when "Charlie" finally squeezed, he missed me by ten feet. I didn't waste ammunition. I heard it coming at me—nine long months!
RUSTY: You never talked about it. You should have talked about it.
VAL: I didn't bring back any medals. What was I going to talk about?
RUSTY: So, what are you going to do about last night, son? Let it ride? (*VAL looks away. He nods.*) This guy you shot? You ever going to think about him?
VAL: No.
RUSTY: Then what'd you come around for? Absolution?
VAL: Maybe. (*Crosses USR.*) I'll give you a call.
RUSTY: (*difficult*) I don't want to hear from you, son. I'll read about it, or I won't hear anything at all.
VAL: (*Begins to exit, as he does so.*) I'll call you.
RUSTY: Val? (*VAL faces RUSTY.*) If it'd been a black dude, this guy, would you have shot him?
VAL: The gun went off accidentally.
RUSTY: It's too bad.
VAL: What?
RUSTY: If we were still in Pittsburgh, I might have been able to help you.
VAL: I had him cuffed.
RUSTY: I thought so. I didn't think you were that dumb. (*VAL exits RUSTY's apartment. Music. The lights slowly fade on RUSTY.*)

Scene 2

>Music out. Lights—VAL and ALEA's apartment. A short time later.

>VAL enters the apartment. ALEA, on SR platform w/dust cloth, a change of clothes, waits for him. They stand apart. ALEA studies him.

ALEA: What'd he say?
VAL: What I figured he'd say.
ALEA: He wants you to tell?
VAL: That's right.

ALEA: You're not considering it, are you? Are you?
VAL: The way it stands, it's a fucking mess.
ALEA: It was an accident, that's all it was.
VAL: It couldn't have been an accident. I had him handcuffed.
ALEA: It was an accident. Accept it.
VAL: (*Sits on chair USC.*) It was right through the heart. That's not an accident.
ALEA: It happened to be right through the heart. You didn't aim.
VAL: I'm too good at it. That's what scares me. I'm a professional. I mean, I fought a war for a whole year. I had guns in my hands every day for a year, and I never had an accident.
ALEA: You're not perfect. That's Rusty's department.
VAL: If it was an accident, then why'd I take the cuffs off? Why'd I plant the knife? Why didn't I just leave it the way it was? Tell them what really happened. Dropped the "three feet." Dropped the "knife." Dropped the "warnings."
ALEA: There would have been too many complications, that's why. You knew that, so you rearranged it.
VAL: (*Shakes his head "no."*) I fixed it. I remember fixing it.
ALEA: You altered the setting, that's all you did. You can live with that. So can I.
VAL: I tampered with evidence. That's a felony.
ALEA: I can live with that, too. So can you.
VAL: That simple?
ALEA: It has to be that simple.
VAL: Rusty doesn't figure I can live with it.
ALEA: It never came up when he was a cop. He can afford to be righteous—he's got a horse to ride.
VAL: But I'd already called for a radio car. I didn't need to have my gun out.
ALEA: (*Crosses SL to VAL.*) You were scared.
VAL: I wasn't that scared. He was eight, ten feet away. He was cuffed. He couldn't have done anything.
ALEA: You didn't know that. He could have had friends.
VAL: He was a loner. I spotted it right off.
ALEA: It was Eleventh Avenue. It was dark. It was late.
VAL: I've been alone, lots of times, worse streets, and I didn't need a gun in my hand—
ALEA: It was "the Fourth." It was crazy out.
VAL: I've worked "the Fourth" before.
ALEA: But this time you were scared. It was security. You don't think Charlie wouldn't have had his gun out? Or Carlos?
VAL: I don't know.
ALEA: I've heard them talk.
VAL: But mine went off.

ALEA: And what if Charlie's had gone off? What if Charlie'd had him handcuffed? You don't think Charlie wouldn't have planted the knife? You don't think Charlie wouldn't have wiped off the fingerprints? Charlie would have done the same thing you did. Except Charlie would have walked away from it. Charlie would have justified it. It would have been one night in Charlie's life, and he wouldn't have even thought about it the next day.
VAL: That's too easy.
ALEA: That's fact. That's reality, Val. And you know it.
VAL: I'm too good a cop. It never should have happened.
ALEA: That's Rusty talking. Not you.
VAL: (*Crosses DSL.*) I'm still a good cop, and it still shouldn't have happened.
ALEA: My God, you're looking for an excuse to tell them, aren't you?
VAL: How am I supposed to go back out on the streets?
ALEA: It was settled! He came at you, three feet, knife out. It was self-defense. That's what you told them, and that's what they wrote down. You walked out of here tonight, you just wanted to talk to Rusty. You talked to him, and, all of a sudden, you're actually thinking about letting them know what really happened. And what if you did? Do you think they'd believe you?
VAL: I don't know.
ALEA: Do you?!
VAL: They might.
ALEA: (*Crosses DSL to VAL.*) Did Rusty? (*He turns away from her—for a moment.*) What's the alternative? I don't plan on visiting you twice a month for the next ten years. There's too much at stake, Val. So, feel bad. Go ahead. Replay it in your mind, every minute, every day. Replay it to your advantage. Or don't. Think about it every time you're running after somebody on the street. Or stop running. Get a transfer. Do rescue work. Do desk work. Lock up your gun. Feel terrible. Feel dishonest. Feel like a coward. Feel like a cheat. But you're going to live with it, like it or not, and so am I. There is no decision to be made. It's made. It was made the day you were born—when you ended up black instead of white. It was made, Val! (*They stare at each other.*)
VAL: A guy like Willis, I always figured I'd be able to handle it. You know, skip the lies, tell the truth, fuck the consequences. I didn't know shit, did I?
ALEA: You're just not Rusty, that's all.
VAL: So what's that make me?
ALEA: You're alive, aren't you? Who cares about the truth anymore? Who ever did? Unless they got caught. What's the truth mean, anyway? You recited his record. He was a pimp. He was a hustler. He was a thief. He smuggled cigarettes from North Carolina. He went to prison in New York. He went to prison in Michigan. He carried a knife, and, if you'd given him

a chance, he probably would have killed you. That's your fucking truth, Val. But he was white. Don't you ever forget that. White! You tell them what really happened, and they'll crucify you. And not just you. Me. All of us. The next black man who wants to become a cop, you think they're not going to think twice about giving him a gun? The next black kid they blow away in Bed Sty, you don't think they're going to bring up your name? Because when black people pull the trigger, that's not insanity, that's spontaneity! Give a gorilla a banana, he's going to eat it! And I'll tell you one thing, Val Johnson, you go to prison, you won't survive it. The guards are going to hate you. You're the ex-cop who couldn't control himself. The whites are going to hate you. You're the ex-black cop who couldn't control himself. "Control," Val! Remember? But the blacks, they're going to hate you most of all. And do you want to know why? Out of contempt, that's why! Contempt! Why'd you have to go and let them know?!

VAL: Then where in the hell are we?

ALEA: You tell me! But keep that in mind, tomorrow morning, and keep asking yourself the other question—"Where are we going to be?!" (*They stare at each other—hard. The lights slowly fade. Music.*)

Scene 3

Music out. Lights—SR platform. A park bench. A short time later.

CHARLIE, a change of clothes, sits on the bench. He is sipping a beer, a paper bag around the can. A paper bag with another beer in it is set next to him. VAL moves to the bench and sits down beside CHARLIE. CHARLIE hands him the paper bag. VAL takes the can of beer out of the bag, opens it, and takes a sip. CHARLIE keeps glancing at VAL.

CHARLIE: What's happening? (*VAL's beer*) Better cover it up. Cop might come along. (*CHARLIE sips his beer. He watches VAL twist the beer can in his hands.*) What's up, man? You still got that asshole on your mind? (*VAL nods.*) It'll be a breeze. You'll be in and out in ten minutes. Don't eat. I'll buy you breakfast.

VAL: (*Looks up.*) You ever kill anybody, Charlie? Nam? Here? I never asked you.

CHARLIE: Nam. "Bach Ma." I got a guy up close, like you did, except I used a knife. He slipped under the wire—four satchel charges—a special delivery. It took two guys to get my hand off the handle. I must have been standing there, maybe twenty, thirty minutes, holding this "Charlie" up. My namesake. So, I know what you're going through, man. I've been there.

VAL: What about here?

CHARLIE: I haven't had the chance. But I haven't been looking for it either.

VAL: One "Charlie"? That's it? (*CHARLIE stares down at his beer. He drinks.*) That's it?

CHARLIE: (*Looks up.*) I knocked off a Corporal. Saigon. White. A real prick, this guy. He was dealing scag, low-grade stock, the pits, skipping all the directions, lacing it—No, man, you don't want to hear this—(*VAL stares at CHARLIE. CHARLIE sips his beer.*) See, the word got around, guys were getting themselves into deep shit. Convulsions, that kind of stuff. One guy, brain damage. Another guy, a kid from Alabama, real competent—a real good pool player. He O.D.ed on it. Threw himself out a window. Landed on a motorcycle. A lot of the black guys, this Corporal, he was their contact. Sold it to them cheap. Maybe ten bucks. A big bag. Made it seem like you could get through a whole tour on one bag. The white dudes, the ones into the heavy stuff, this Corporal, he took care of their bags, too. Except it was a hundred percent for them. Real Asian bliss. So, this dude, this Corporal, he was dealing two bags. A white bag, and a black bag. And the "brothers" were getting "schizo," while the whites were off dreaming the good dream. Well, we decided to take him out, this Corporal, and I got the low card. (*CHARLIE sips his beer.*)

VAL: How'd you do it?

CHARLIE: We grabbed him off the street. Two in the morning. He was making his rounds. We'd been following him for five hours.

VAL: You shot him? (*CHARLIE shakes his head "no."*) Then what?

CHARLIE: You sure you want to hear this?

VAL: I want to hear it.

CHARLIE: Put a wire around his neck. The idea was—he should go out slow. And he did. I don't know what they did when they found him. We never heard anything. I don't think they gave him a Bronze Star. He had a reputation.

VAL: What if he'd been black, Charlie?

CHARLIE: Wouldn't have happened. Everybody takes care of their own. At least we did over there. You know that.

VAL: You didn't give him a chance?

CHARLIE: No, I didn't.

VAL: No explanation?

CHARLIE: None. We had the facts.

VAL: Murder?

CHARLIE: "Enthanasia," that's what I like to call it. I lost maybe a night's sleep over it. The "Charlie" I gutted, he stayed with me a lot longer. But wasting that Corporal, it saved a lot of black boys. It saved them a lot of pain.

VAL: It was still murder, Charlie.

CHARLIE: Look, man, what do you think?! The world runs on flowers?! He was dealing bad scag to the "brothers"—turning whites into fucking lotus blossoms! There comes a time you don't take it anymore! And that's not "murder one"! No way! That's just getting it on and doing what's right when everybody else is looking the other way! (*the park*) What are you staring at, shithead?!

VAL: You took him from behind. You didn't give him a chance.
CHARLIE: He didn't deserve a chance! Certain people, they don't belong here! They don't have the credentials! And that scumbag, he happened to be one of them! All right, it wasn't pretty. It wasn't neat. It wasn't by the book. It wasn't like your caper. He didn't have a knife on me. He wasn't coming at me. I didn't have to warn him. But he was a killer, baby, just like your customer! Except he didn't need a knife. He had a chemistry set, and you tell me, what's the fucking difference?! I came out tonight—I figured you needed help. I figured I'd help you out!
VAL: I do need help.
CHARLIE: How come?
VAL: I need help, that's all—
CHARLIE: The dude from Detroit, it wasn't clean enough for you? He maybe should have stuck it in you a couple of times before you pulled the trigger? Is that what's bothering you?
VAL: It wasn't three feet—
CHARLIE: No?
VAL: It was nine feet—Maybe ten—I wasn't close—
CHARLIE: Three feet, and you could dream at night, right?
VAL: Right!
CHARLIE: Shit, I would have smoked the motherfucker at fifteen feet—I even saw the tip of a blade!
VAL: But he wasn't—He wasn't—
CHARLIE: He wasn't "what?!"
VAL: I didn't—
CHARLIE: What are you talking about, man?
VAL: I didn't—I didn't have him cuffed—
CHARLIE: Let me get this straight. It wouldn't have happened, you had him cuffed. He couldn't have reached for his knife, right?
VAL: No!
CHARLIE: What do you mean "no"?!
VAL: That's not how it happened! I put it in him!
CHARLIE: You sure as shit did! The cat's dead!
VAL: (*Stands, grabs CHARLIE by the shirt.*) I put it in him—cuffed! (*VAL releases CHARLIE and backs away from him.*)
CHARLIE: No knife coming out, right?
VAL: No knife.
CHARLIE: No fancy footwork? (*VAL shakes his head "no."*) But they don't know that, do they?
VAL: No.
CHARLIE: Then that makes us just about equals, doesn't it? How'd it go off?
VAL: The guy was a "lip," so I pulled it out. I figured it might impress him.
CHARLIE: You should have rapped on his neck. That's all it takes.
VAL: Radio car was around the corner. I didn't start out to mess him up.
CHARLIE: So you put a bullet in him instead?

VAL: It was an accident. (*They stare at each other.*)
CHARLIE: (*Crosses SL of VAL.*) If that's what it was, then fuck them. It's "street." They don't know anything about it. And the less they know, the better. (*CHARLIE rubs VAL's shoulder, but the affection is gone. As he does so.*) But they've got a shovel for people like you. My advice—don't let the mothers use it. I left it in Saigon. No regrets.
VAL: Did you?
CHARLIE: You leave it on 28th. You play good-guy cop, Johnson, you won't have a friend left in the world. Guaranteed. That's just the way it is, brother. (*CHARLIE exits. Music. VAL stares straight ahead. The lights slowly fade on VAL.*)

Scene 4

Music out. Lights—VAL and ALEA's apartment. A short time later.

ALEA, no change of clothes, stands in the middle of the room. RUSTY, change of clothes, enters the room. They stare at one another—uncomfortably.

RUSTY: We could have talked about it over the phone.
ALEA: It's too easy over the phone.
RUSTY: It's his decision.
ALEA: He's your son. He needs your help.
RUSTY: It's still his decision.
ALEA: If you don't support him, he can't make it.
RUSTY: He knows what I think.
ALEA: And that's why he can't make it.
RUSTY: There's only one decision.
ALEA: In your mind.
RUSTY: In anybody's mind.
ALEA: He already told them one story.
RUSTY: I know.
ALEA: He can't tell them another one.
RUSTY: That's up to him. He took an oath.
ALEA: And he made a mistake.
RUSTY: That's why he took an oath.
ALEA: He changed things around, that's all he did.
RUSTY: That's a crime.
ALEA: And you wouldn't have done that, right?
RUSTY: I wouldn't have taken off the cuffs. I wouldn't have planted the knife. If it was an accident, it was an accident.
ALEA: No, you wouldn't have touched the handcuffs. You wouldn't have opened the knife. You were the perfect cop, weren't you?

RUSTY: I was a tough cop. I was a good cop.
ALEA: No, the Pittsburgh Police Department, they threw away the mold the day you retired. That's what you like to think, isn't it?
RUSTY: I like to think I did a decent job. I like to think I was fair. There were some rough neighborhoods.
ALEA: But cops today, Val included, they're all second-rate, aren't they?
RUSTY: It depends.
ALEA: On what? How they stack up against you? No, you wouldn't have accidentally pulled the trigger. You weren't capable of shooting a man in handcuffs, were you? That was beyond you, wasn't it?
RUSTY: I was capable. Just like Val.
ALEA: Sure you were. But you're a bit more special, aren't you?
RUSTY: No. I just never did it. I never had the "accident."
ALEA: But it never would have come up, right?
RUSTY: No, I don't think it ever would have come up.
ALEA: There wasn't even a possibility, was there?
RUSTY: There was always a possibility. I just kept it in check, that's all.
ALEA: And that's why you can be so calm. That's why it's so easy for you to pass judgement, walk out of here, feed your horses, and start jumping fences!
RUSTY: (*Crosses DSL.*) It's not easy!
ALEA: No?! In case you didn't know it, Rusty, it's our life! It's the next ten years! The next twenty!
RUSTY: I know that.
ALEA: (*Crosses DSC.*) No, you don't! You're quoting scripture, that's all you're doing! You could be talking to anybody. Take a goddamn look! I'm your son's wife! Val could go to jail, and you could be dead before he got out! That's what you're promoting! He's your son! Where's your compassion?!
RUSTY: You don't want compassion! You want approval!
ALEA: No, I don't want interference! Your interference! I don't care if Val took off the handcuffs! I don't care if he planted the knife! We don't owe them anything! Nothing!
RUSTY: No, we don't, if we don't want to. But I don't see how that's going to improve anything.
ALEA: I'm not interested in improvement! I'm interested in Val!
RUSTY: Val joined the Police Department! He took an oath! He owes them something!
ALEA: What?! His life?! Mine?!
RUSTY: There are consequences!
ALEA: There are white consequences, and there are black consequences!
RUSTY: No, sister, you're mixing it up! There are consequences! Period!
ALEA: In your mind! Not mine!
RUSTY: What about Val's?!

ALEA: If they're there, you put them there! Why do you think he took off the handcuffs?! Why do you think he opened the knife?! He knows about consequences! Except he can't live without them! You won't let him!
RUSTY: Val knows what's right!
ALEA: Val knows what works! You know what's right! And now he wants it both ways! That's what's killing him!
RUSTY: And what's he going to think about the next time he arrests somebody?!
ALEA: Nothing! I won't let him!
RUSTY: The next time he throws somebody into a cell?!
ALEA: He'll put him in a cell, and then he'll come home!
RUSTY: You don't think there's going to be any remorse?! You don't think he's going to feel anything?!
ALEA: No! No remorse and no consequences! Staying alive, that's our responsibility! Breathing! Functioning! Nothing else matters! Nothing!
RUSTY: I always figured life was a little more complicated than just staying alive!
ALEA: There's nothing more complicated than staying alive! I can't live without that man! I won't live without that man!
RUSTY: Then get ready, girl, because you're going to be living with a goddamn stranger!
ALEA: As long as he's here, that's all that counts. (*a silence*)

(*VAL enters the apartment.*)

ALEA: (*Turns toward VAL.*) I called him. I want to get it straight. I want to make sure. I don't want any more "ifs," no more "maybes." I want it clear, absolute, what you're going to tell them tomorrow morning.
VAL: (*Crosses DS to C.*) He came at me, three feet, knife out. (*to RUSTY*) That's the way it's got to be.
RUSTY: (*nods*) You got any beer around this place?
ALEA: I'll get it. Val?
VAL: I just had one. (*ALEA exits.*)
RUSTY: (*Crosses SL to bench, sits. Toward ALEA.*) No glass. I don't like glasses. Never did. (*to VAL*) Wash 'em once, and there's no more "head."
VAL: (*Crosses SL to RUSTY, faces RUSTY.*) I can't do it. (*RUSTY nods.*) It won't change anything.
RUSTY: No, it wouldn't. It just depends on who you are.
VAL: Or who you think you should be.
RUSTY: Well, nothing goes according to plan, does it? I accepted that a long time ago.
VAL: Then how come you're disappointed?
RUSTY: I liked the plan. (*ALEA re-enters with an open can of beer and hands it to RUSTY. To ALEA.*) Thanks. (*RUSTY glances at VAL—and then ALEA. Raises the can.*) Cheers.

VAL: Cheers. (*RUSTY sips from the beer can. To RUSTY.*) Do you want a sandwich or something?
RUSTY: No, I'm fine. Too much weight on me. "Stallion" can't take the corners as fast. Got to keep trim. Cut down on the junk. Two or three beers a day, that's probably too much, but it still doesn't put me over 195. That's my riding weight. I was 205 when I got him. But then I decided to drop ten, and he took off like the wind. It surprised the hell out of me—the difference—ten pounds—what it could do. It surprised the hell out of him, too.
VAL: I've got a wife. I can't take the chance.
RUSTY: I know that, son.
VAL: I've got a job.
RUSTY: I know that, too.
VAL: I don't want to vanish.
RUSTY: Nobody does.
VAL: He was a loser.
RUSTY: Most of them are.
VAL: It was a mistake.
RUSTY: I thought it was an accident.
VAL: It was an accident.
RUSTY: Was it?
VAL: Yes.
RUSTY: I don't buy that, Val. You had him in cuffs.
VAL: (*Crosses USR.*) Then don't buy it.
RUSTY: I haven't asked for much, son, but I'm asking now. I want an answer. I want the truth. You never have to repeat it. You can lie to your wife. You can lie to your friends. You can lie tomorrow. You can lie for the rest of your goddamn life. But don't lie to me, Val. I want the truth!
ALEA: Why? It won't mean anything. The man's dead.
RUSTY: It'll mean something to me.
ALEA: You're not important! (*Indicates VAL.*) He is!
RUSTY: I want to hear it once, Val. I want to know if a little bit of me rubbed off on you. Not a lot. Just a little bit. That's all I want to know.
ALEA: (*Turns away.*) Goddamn you, Rusty.
RUSTY: You aimed, didn't you?
ALEA: Goddamn you!
RUSTY: Didn't you?!
VAL: That's right. I aimed.
ALEA: (*Crosses DSR, sits on platform.*) Of course he did. Didn't you know that? He probably even toyed with the idea of putting it between the fourth and fifth buttons. That's how good Val is. He wanted to turn it off, just once, and he had the power to do it. He didn't want to hear it anymore. "Nigger." He didn't want the spit in his face. "Nigger!" He wanted to turn it off forever. "NIGGER!" Just like you did, except you never pulled the trigger. You were afraid to do it. So you took it. And took

it. And took it! But you tell me—who gave them the right to say it?! And you tell me—why do we have to take it?! It's wrong. He shouldn't have shot him. He should have ignored him. Like you did. But it never would have happened—he never would have even thought about it—if we didn't have to spend most of our lives being tempted to do it! Val had to do it for you! He had to do it for a lot of people like you! Why'd you have to ask?! You couldn't even let him have that, could you? I believed him. The whole story. And I knew it wasn't true. Why'd you have to ask?! (*She turns away from them.*)

RUSTY: (*Crosses SR to VAL.*) You can't turn it off, son. I thought you knew that.

VAL: It seemed like a good idea at the time.

RUSTY: I figured it out early. That's why I never pulled the trigger. Everything's temporary. Most people don't stay in your life that long. Not if you're a cop. I thought I taught you that.

VAL: I suppose you did. But I remember you telling me, six years old, the day you found me tied to that tree—"Ain't no difference between a white man and a black man can't be erased by a bullet."

RUSTY: I was angry. What they'd done to you. I didn't mean it.

VAL: You never told me you didn't mean it.

ALEA: (*Turns back.*) Rusty? It could have been an accident.

RUSTY: (*Crosses SL to bench.*) It could have been.

ALEA: Why didn't you just leave it at that?

RUSTY: I was a cop. I got used to answers,

ALEA: It could have been your excuse for not asking him to change his story. It could have been your excuse for not asking him to take a chance on going to jail. (*Crosses SR to VAL.*)

RUSTY: I know. Except I always would have wondered. And that would have been worse.

ALEA: (*Crosses SL to RUSTY.*) How much worse, Rusty? Don't you think I know what I'm asking him to do? Don't you think I know him? So, what's that make me?

RUSTY: (*Nods—fiddles with his beer can.*) Beer's gone. That makes three today. Well, not really—It wasn't sixteen ounces. I've got to get up early. "Stallion's" waiting for me. He's probably short on sugar or something—And it takes a lot longer to drive in New York—I'm trying not to judge you, son. (*Crosses USC.*)

VAL: No, you're not.

RUSTY: I am. But it's hard.

VAL: It's not that hard.

RUSTY: You killed a man. You shot him point blank. What in the hell do you expect me to do?! Act like it never happened?!

VAL: No, you expect me to pay for it.

RUSTY: I expect it, yes! That's the law!

VAL: Whose law?!

RUSTY: It's the law! It's been around for a long time!
VAL: The law never did shit for us! What's so important about it now?! So why not bend it?! Like they do! When it's convenient! Like you did! When Grandmother needed a television set!
RUSTY: I bent it! You broke it!
VAL: What's the difference?! I don't see it! William H. Willis—a television set?!
RUSTY: T.V. sets don't breathe, that's the difference!
VAL: So that makes it okay, right?!
RUSTY: The sign says "60." I drive "75." We're talking about a cop who aimed!
VAL: No, we're talking about a creep who kept up his patter too long!
RUSTY: He was handcuffed, for Christ's sake!
VAL: What handcuffs? I didn't see any handcuffs. I just saw his mouth. Then I checked out his heart, and it all made sense. It was making his mouth move. All I had to do was zero in on his heart, and I wouldn't have to watch his mouth move anymore. That's all I saw—his fucking heart! And I wanted to rip it out! And no, I'm not certain I want to pay for it. I'm not real sure I want to throw it all away, just for William H. Willis, I'm not! It never happened to you!
RUSTY: I never let it happen!
VAL: And that's why you want me to pay for it!
RUSTY: You lost control, buster! You snapped! That's not why they gave you a badge!
VAL: That's right! I lost it! I finally lost my "cool." I snapped, and it was all out front. And do you want to know how long I've been waiting to do it? All my life. The "chip" just got too heavy, and I didn't want to carry it around anymore. One split second, that's all it took to knock it off, and that made him dead. No, it didn't happen to you. Not you. But let's say it did happen. One time, one night, when you'd finally heard it once too often. It was hot out. It was dark. You were alone. The scum of the earth, spitting it out at you. "Nigger!" "Coon!" "Shine!" "Jigaboo!" And you didn't want to take it anymore. You couldn't take it anymore. And then "click." Nobody heard the shot, and nobody saw him fall. Who was he, anyway? Who in the fuck was he?! What then? What would you have done? Thrown away Mom? Twenty-five years? Thrown away me? Thrown away your friends? Your job? Your reputation? Your weekends on the Allegheny teaching me how to fish? Your nights in the Poconos—after supper—teaching me how to ride? Is that what you would have done, Rusty? Just because some son of a bitch, the lowest of the low, finally screamed "nigger" at you once too often and once too loud?! Is it?!
RUSTY: (*Fiddles with his beer can.*) I'd like to think—I'd like to think I would have assumed the responsibility. That's what I'd like to think.
ALEA: Which one?
RUSTY: The more important one.

ALEA: Which one, Rusty?
VAL: He would have gone to jail.
ALEA: Is that what you would have done? Is it?
RUSTY: I think so, yes.
VAL: I could kill you for saying that!
RUSTY: I doubt it!
VAL: Mom, me—No, I could do it!
RUSTY: How?! I'm not cuffed! (*VAL slowly turns away from RUSTY.*) I didn't mean that, son.
VAL: Neither did I.
RUSTY: (*Sets his beer can down, moves to exit, stops.*) I'll be in the country, you need me. "Spence's" place again. You've got the number. I think—I think I'm going to look at some land. I'd like to have a little land. I could maybe build me a permanent stable—(*Shakes his head "no."*) There I go again. It'd probably blow over—The first winter storm—(*Starts to exit again, stops.*) If I could—If there was any way, Val—If I were still in uniform—If I could convince anyone—I'd take credit for the guy you shot. I'd claim it. I would. I'd make it mine.
VAL: I know. (*RUSTY begins to exit again.*) Rusty? (*RUSTY stops. He faces VAL.*) You keep in touch, okay?
RUSTY: Sure, son. I'll try to do that. (*RUSTY and VAL stare at each other.*) You know, the funny thing, I moved out of Pittsburgh to get closer to you. (*RUSTY exits.*)
ALEA: He's old, Val. We can't listen to him. (*No response from VAL.*) We can't afford to listen to him. (*No response from VAL.*) We've got a life. (*No response from VAL. Voice breaking.*) Val?

(*The lights slowly fade to darkness. Sound—music.*)

Scene 5

Music out—Lights—SR platform. The next morning.

VAL, a minimum change of clothes, sits in a witness chair. PARKER stands upstage in the shadows.

VAL: (*without looking up*) I spotted the said perpetrator, William H. Willis, at approximately 11:15, on the evening of July 4th. Suspect was in the process of committing grand theft auto—a tan, 1977 Oldsmobile, license number "817 Y as in yellow, V as in Victor, C as in Charlie." parked on West 27th Street and Tenth Avenue. I approached the suspect, identifying myself as a police officer. Suspect immediately fled north on Tenth Avenue turning west on West 28th Street. I pursued the suspect on foot, catching up with him approximately six minutes later on the south side of the 500 block of West 28th Street. I drew my service revolver and ordered the suspect to halt. Suspect—Suspect came to a halt between—West 28th Street—And—Eleventh Avenue—I approached the suspect—I approached the suspect—And ordered—I—Ordered him to—I called for "transportation"—

PARKER: Officer Johnson? Could you please speak up? And could you also look up, please? We can't see your face.

VAL: (*Grips his legs harder. He doesn't look up.*) I approached the suspect—William H. Willis—And I—I—I ordered him to—Suspect—

PARKER: Officer Johnson, please? We can't hear you, and we can't see your face. (*VAL grips his legs harder. He doesn't look up.*) Officer Johnson? (*VAL slowly relaxes his hands. He looks up slowly and stares straight ahead.*) Thank you, Officer Johnson. That's much better. Please continue.

VAL: I called "transportation." I approached the suspect with the specific intention of patting him down and placing him in handcuffs. When I was within three feet of him, the suspect turned on me with an open knife in his right hand. I backed up two feet and ordered the suspect to drop the knife. The suspect did not comply with my order, but instead, made a menacing movement in my direction, the knife still in his hand. I fired my service revolver once, the bullet striking the suspect in the chest and killing him instantly.

(*The lights slowly begin to fade on VAL. He remains motionless. He stares straight ahead. The life seems to have gone out of him. Blackout.*)

END OF PLAY

Wedding Band: A Love/Hate Story in Black and White

Alice Childress

Wedding Band; A Love/Hate Story in Black and White was written during the civil rights struggles of the 1960s. Although set in 1918, the play deals with issues which dominated the political and social discourse of the 60s. Among the questions it raises are these: "Is it possible for women, both black and white, to make progress in a society dominated by white males?" "How can state and federal laws be eliminated which are designed to impede the freedom of some people at the expense of others?" "Can blacks and whites ever hope to live together in harmony and mutual respect given the scarred history of their relationships?" Many of these same issues haunt us today.

When Childress wrote *Wedding Band* she was in the process of developing a second career as a playwright. Her first career had been as an actress and member of the technical staff for the American Negro Theatre during the 1940s and early 1950s. The play was initially produced while she was studying at Radcliffe's Institute for Independent Study. In the early 1970s it was produced in New York starring Ruby Dee. A television version directed by Ms. Childress was made in 1973, again starring Ruby Dee and James Broderick. ABC Television billed the production as a two-hour prime-time special although some affiliates chose not to carry it and others preferred to air it after midnight because it dealt with a taboo interracial theme.

At the core of the play is Julia, a black woman who makes her living as a seamstress. She has lived out of wedlock with a white man for ten years. The play is set in the backyards of three small cottages in a coastal city in South Carolina. It's dialogue is earthy and realistic, characteristic of many plays of the period. As with all her other works, in *Wedding Band* Childress deals with people at the lower rung of society. She said of her writing, "My writing attempts the 'ordinary' because they are not ordinary. Each individual is uniquely different. Like snowflakes, the human pattern is never cast twice. . . . I concentrate on portraying have-nots in a have society, those seldom singled out by mass media, except as source material for derogatory humor and/or condescending clinical, social analysis." (Alice Childress, "A Candle in a Gale Wind," in *Black Women Writers (1950–1980): A Critical Evaluation*, ed. Mari Evans. New York: Doubleday, 1984, 112.)

The struggles of all the finely drawn characters to find some grain of happiness in an otherwise oppressive and proscribed world in which they live mark this as a excellent example of American realism and melodrama. Few plays match it for its craftsmanship or its art.

Production History

Wedding Band was first performed by the University of Michigan in December 1966 with a cast headed by Ruby Dee, Abbey Lincoln, and Moses Gunn.

Wedding Band was first presented by the New York Shakespeare Public Theater, directed by Joseph Papp and Alice Childress on November 26, 1972. The setting was by Ming Cho Lee; costumes by Theoni V. Aldredge; lighting by Martin Aronstein; produced by Joseph Papp, with Bernard Gersten the associate producer. The cast was as follows:

Julia Augustine	Ruby Dee
Teeta	Calisse Dinwiddie
Mattie	Juanita Clark
Lula Green	Hilda Haynes
Fanny Johnson	Clarice Taylor
Nelson Green	Albert Hall
Bell Man	Brandon Maggart
Princess	Vicky Geyer
Herman	James Broderick
Annabelle	Polly Holiday
Herman's Mother	Jean David

Time

Summer 1918. Saturday morning.

Place

A city by the sea . . . South Carolina, USA

Characters

JULIA AUGUSTINE
TEETA
MATTIE
LULA GREEN
FANNY JOHNSON
NELSON GREEN
BELL MAN
PRINCESS
HERMAN
ANNABELLE
HERMAN'S MOTHER

Wedding Band by Alice Childress

Copyright © 1973 by Alice Childress. Used by permission of Flora Roberts Inc.

The Play

Wedding Band

ACT ONE

Scene 1

TIME: *Summer 1918 . . . Saturday morning. A city by the sea . . . South Carolina, U.S.A.*

SCENE: *Three houses in a backyard. The center house is newly painted and cheery looking in contrast to the other two which are weather-beaten and shabby. Center house is gingerbready . . . odds and ends of "picked up" shutters, picket railing, wrought iron railing, newel posts, a Grecian pillar, odd window boxes of flowers . . . everything clashes with a beautiful, subdued splendor; the old and new mingles in defiance of style and period. The playing areas of the houses are raised platforms furnished according to the taste of each tenant. Only one room of each house is visible.* JULIA AUGUSTINE. [*tenant of the center house*] *has recently moved in and there is still unpacking to be done. Paths are worn from the houses to the front yard entry. The landlady's house and an outhouse are off-stage. An outdoor hydrant supplies water.*

JULIA: *is sleeping on the bed in the center house.* TEETA, *a girl about eight years old, enters the yard from the Stage Right house. She tries to control her weeping as she examines a clump of grass. The muffled weeping disturbs* JULIA'S *sleep. She starts up, half rises from her pillow, then falls back into a troubled sleep.* MATTIE, TEETA'S *mother, enters carrying a switch and fastening her clothing. She joins the little girl in the search for a lost quarter. The search is subdued, intense.*

MATTIE: You better get out there and get it! Did you find it? Gawd, what've I done to be treated this way! You gon' get a whippin' too.
FANNY: (*Enters from the front entry. She is landlady and the self-appointed, fifty-year-old representative of her race.*) Listen, Mattie . . . I want some quiet out here this mornin'.

MATTIE: Dammit, this gal done lost the only quarter I got to my name. (LULA *enters from the direction of the outhouse carrying a covered slop jar. She is forty-five and motherly.*) "Teeta," I say, "Go to the store, buy three cent grits, five cent salt pork, ten cent sugar; and keep your hand closed 'roun' my money." How I'm gonna sell any candy if I got no sugar to make it? You little heifer! (*Goes after* TEETA *who hides behind* LULA.)
LULA: Gawd, help us to find it.
MATTIE: Your daddy is off sailin' the ocean and you got nothin' to do but lose money! *I'm gon' put you out in the damn street, that's what!* (TEETA *cries out.* JULIA *sits up in the bed and cries out.*)
JULIA: No . . . no . . .
FANNY: You disturbin' the only tenant who's paid in advance.
LULA: Teeta, retrace your steps. Show Lula what you did.
TEETA: I hop-hop-hop . . . (*Hops near a post-railing of* JULIA'S *porch.*)
MATTIE: What the hell you do that for?
LULA: There 'tis! That's a quarter . . . down in the hole . . . Can't reach it . . . (JULIA *is now fully awake. Putting on her house-dress over her camisole and petticoat.* MATTIE *takes an axe from the side of the house to knock the post out of the way.*) Aw, move, move! That's all the money I got. I'll tear this damn house down and you with it!
FANNY: And I'll blow this police whistle. (JULIA *steps out on the porch. She is an attractive brown woman about thirty-five years old.*)
MATTIE: Blow it . . . blow it . . . blow it . . . hot damn—(*Near tears. She decides to tell* JULIA *off also.*) I'll tear it down—that's right. If you don't like it—come on down here and whip me.
JULIA: (*Nervous but determined to present a firm stand.*) Oh, my . . . Good mornin' ladies. My name is Julia Augustine. I'm not gonna move.
LULA: My name is Lula. Why you think we wantcha to move?
FANNY: Miss Julia, I'm sorry your first day starts like this. Some people are ice cream and others just cow-dung. I try to be ice cream.
MATTIE: Dammit, I'm ice cream too. Strawberry. (*Breaks down and cries.*)
FANNY: That's Mattie. She lost her last quarter, gon' break down my house to get it.
JULIA: (*Gets a quarter from her dresser.*) Oh my, dear heart, don't cry. Take this twenty-five cents, Miss Mattie.
MATTIE: No thank you, ma'm.
JULIA: And I have yours under my house for good luck.
FANNY: Show your manners.
TEETA: Thank you. You the kin'est person in the worl'. (LULA *enters her house.* TEETA *starts for home, then turns to see if her mother is coming.*)
MATTIE: (*To* JULIA.) I didn't mean no harm. But my husband October's in the Merchant Marine and I needs my little money. Well, thank you. (*To* TEETA.) Come on, honey bunch. (*She enters her house Stage Right.* TEETA *proudly follows.* LULA *is putting* NELSON'S *breakfast on the table at Stage Left.*)
FANNY: (*Testing strength of post.*) My poor father's turnin' in his grave. He

built these rent houses just 'fore he died . . . And he wasn't a carpenter. Shows what the race can do when we wanta. (*Feels the porch railing and tests its strength.*) That loud-mouth Mattie used to work in a white cat-house.

JULIA: A what?

FANNY: Sportin' house, house of . . . A whore house. know what she used to do?

JULIA: (*Embarrassed.*) Not but so many things *to* do, I guess. (FANNY *wants to follow her in the house but* JULIA *fends her off.*)

FANNY: Used to wash their joy-towels. Washin' joy-towels for one cent apiece. I wouldn't work in that kinda place—would you?

JULIA: Indeed not.

FANNY: Vulgarity.

JULIA: (*Trying to get away.*) I have my sewing to do now, Miss Fanny.

FANNY: I got a lovely piece-a blue serge. Six yards. (*She attempts to get into the house but* JULIA *deftly blocks the door.*)

JULIA: I don't sew for people. (FANNY *wonders why not.*) I do homework for a store . . . hand-finishin' on ladies' shirtwaists.

FANNY: You 'bout my age . . . I'm thirty-five.

JULIA: (*After a pause.*) I thought you were younger.

FANNY: (*Genuinely moved by the compliment.*) Thank you. But I'm not married 'cause nobody's come up to my high standard. Where you get them expensive-lookin', high-class shoes?

JULIA: In a store. I'm busy now, Miss Fanny.

FANNY: Doin' what?

JULIA: First one thing then another. Good-day. (*Thinks she has dismissed her. Goes in the house.* FANNY *quickly follows into the room . . . picks up a teacup from the table.*)

FANNY: There's a devil in your tea-cup . . . also prosperity. Tell me 'bout yourself, don't be so distant.

JULIA: It's all there in the tea-leaves.

FANNY: Oh, go on! I'll tell you somethin' . . . that sweet-face Lula killed her only child.

JULIA: No, she didn't.

FANNY: In a way-a speakin'. And then Gawd snatched up her triflin' husband. One nothin' piece-a man. Biggest thing he ever done for her was to lay down and die. Poor woman. Yes indeed, then she went and adopted this fella from the colored orphan home. Boy grew too big for a lone woman to keep in the house. He's a big, strappin', over-grown man now. I wouldn't feel safe livin' with a man that's not blood kin, 'doption or no 'doption. It's 'gainst nature. Oughta see the muscles on him.

JULIA: (*Wearily.*) Oh, my . . . I think I hear somebody callin' you.

FANNY: Yesterday the white-folks threw a pail-a dirty water on him. A black man on leave got no right to wear his uniform in public. The crackers don't like it. That's flauntin' yourself.

JULIA: Miss Fanny, I don't talk about people.
FANNY: Me neither. (*Giving her serious advice.*) We high-class, quality people oughta stick together.
JULIA: I really do stay busy.
FANNY: Doin' what? Seein' your beau? You have a beau haven't-cha?
JULIA: (*Realizing she must tell her something in order to get rid of her.*) Miss Johnson . . .
FANNY: Fanny.
JULIA: (*Managing to block her toward the door.*) My mother and father have long gone on to Glory.
FANNY: Gawd rest the dead and bless the orphan.
JULIA: Yes, I do have a beau . . . But I'm not much of a mixer. (*She now has* FANNY *out on the porch.*)
FANNY: Get time, come up front and see my parlor. I got a horsehair settee and a four piece, silver-plated tea service.
JULIA: Think of that.
FANNY: The first and only one to be owned by a colored woman in the United States of America. Salesman told me.
JULIA: Oh, just imagine. (MATTIE *enters wearing a blue calico dress and striped apron.*)
FANNY: My mother was a genuine, full-blooded, qualified, Seminole Indian.
TEETA: (*Calls to her mother from the doorway.*) Please . . . Mama . . . Mama . . . Buy me a hair ribbon.
MATTIE: All right! I'm gon' buy my daughter a hair-ribbon.
FANNY: Her hair is so short you'll have to nail it on. (FANNY *exits to her house.*)
MATTIE: That's all right about that, Fanny. Your father worked in a stinkin' phosphate mill . . . yeah, and didn't have a tooth in his head. Then he went and married some half Portuguese woman. I don't call that bein' in no damn society. I works for my livin'. I makes candy and I takes care of a little white girl. Hold this nickel 'til I get back. Case of emergency I don't like Teeta to be broke.
JULIA: I'll be busy today, lady.
MATTIE: (*As she exits carrying a tray of candy.*) Thank you, darlin'.
TEETA: Hey lady, my daddy helps cook food on a big war boat. He peels potatoes. You got any children?
JULIA: No . . . Grace-a Gawd. (*Starts to go in house.*)
TEETA: Hey, lady! Didja ever hear of Philadelphia? After the war that's where we're goin' to live. Philadelphia!
JULIA: Sounds like heaven.
TEETA: Jesus is the President of Philadelphia. (TEETA *sweeps in front of* JULIA'S *house. Lights come up in* LULA'S *house.* NELSON *is eating breakfast. He is a rather rough-looking muscly fellow with a soft voice and a bittersweet sense of humor. He is dressed in civilian finery and his striped silk shirt seems out of place*

in the drab little room. LULA *makes paper flowers, and the colorful bits of paper are seen everywhere as finished and partially finished flowers and stems, also a finished funeral piece. A picture of Abraham Lincoln hangs on the upstage wall.* LULA *is brushing* NELSON'S *uniform jacket.*)

LULA: Last week the Bell Man came to collect the credit payment he says . . . "Auntie, whatcha doin' with Abraham Lincoln's pitcher on the wall? He was such a poor president."

NELSON: Tell the cracker to mind his damn business.

LULA: It don't pay to get mad. Remember yesterday.

NELSON: (*Studying her face for answers.*) Mama, you supposed to get mad when somebody throw a pail-a water on you.

LULA: It's their country and their uniform, so just stay out the way.

NELSON: Right. I'm not goin' back to work in that coal-yard when I get out the army.

LULA: They want you back. A bird in the hand, y'know.

NELSON: A bird in the hand ain't always worth two in the bush.

LULA: This is Saturday, tomorrow Sunday . . . thank Gawd for Monday; back to the army. That's one thing . . . Army keeps you off the street. (*The sound of the* SHRIMP MAN *passing in the street.*)

SHRIMP MAN: (*Offstage.*) Shrimp-dee-raw . . . I got raw shrimp. (NELSON *leaves the house just as* JULIA *steps out on her porch to hang a rug over the rail.* TEETA *enters* GREEN *house.*)

NELSON: Er . . . howdy-do, er . . . beg pardon. My name is Nelson. Lula Green's son, if you don't mind. Miss . . . er . . . Mrs.?

JULIA: (*After a brief hesitation.*) Miss . . . Julia Augustine.

NELSON: Miss Julia, you the best-lookin' woman I ever seen in my life. I declare you look jus' like a violin sounds. And I'm not talkin' 'bout pretty. You look like you got all the right feelin's, you know?

JULIA: Well, thank you, Mr. Nelson.

NELSON: See, you got me talkin' all outta my head. (LULA *enters,* TEETA *follows eating a biscuit and carrying a milk pail . . . she exits toward street.*) Let's go for a walk this evenin', get us a lemon phosphate.

JULIA: Oh, I don't care for any, Mr. Nelson.

LULA: That's right. She say stay home.

JULIA: (*To* NELSON.) I'm sorry.

NELSON: Don't send me back to the army feelin' bad 'cause you turn me down. Orange-ade tonight on your porch. I'll buy the oranges, you be the sugar.

JULIA: No, thank you.

NELSON: Let's make it—say—six o'clock.

JULIA: No, I said no!

LULA: Nelson, go see your friends. (*He waves goodbye to* JULIA *and exits through the back entry.*) He's got a lady friend, her name is Merrilee Jones. And he was just tryin' to be neighborly. That's how me and Nelson do. But you go on and stay to yourself. (*Starts toward her house.*)

JULIA: Miss Lula! I'm sorry I hurt your feelin's. Miss Lula! I have a gentleman friend, that's why I said no.
LULA: I didn't think-a that. When yall plan to cut the cake?
JULIA: Not right now. You see . . . when you offend Gawd you hate for it to be known. Gawd might forgive but people never will. I mean . . . when a man and a woman are not truly married . . .
LULA: Oh, I see.
JULIA: I live by myself . . . but he visits . . . I declare I don't know how to say . . .
LULA: Everybody's got some sin, but if it troubles your heart you're a gentle sinner, just a good soul gone wrong.
JULIA: That's a kind thought.
LULA: My husband, Gawd rest the dead, used to run 'round with other women; it made me kind-a careless with my life. One day, many long years ago, I was sittin' in a neighbor's house tellin' my troubles; my only child, my little boy, wandered out on the railroad track and got killed.
JULIA: That must-a left a fifty pound weight on your soul.
LULA: It did. But if we grow stronger . . . and rise higher than what's pullin' us down . . .
JULIA: Just like Climbin' Jacob's Ladder . . . (*Sings.*) Every round goes higher and higher . . .
LULA: Yes, rise higher than the dirt . . . that fifty pound weight will lift and you'll be free, free without anybody's by-your-leave. Do something to wash out the sin. That's why I got Nelson from the orphanage.
JULIA: And now you feel free?
LULA: No, not yet. But I believe Gawd wants me to start a new faith; one that'll make our days clear and easy to live. That's what I'm workin' on now. Oh, Miss Julia, I'm glad you my neighbor.
JULIA: Oh, thank you, Miss Lula! Sinners or saints, didn't Gawd give us a beautiful day this mornin'! (*The sound of cow-bells clanking and the thin piping of a tin and paper flute.* TEETA *backs into the yard carefully carrying the can of milk. The* BELL MAN *follows humming, "Over There" on the flute. He is a poor white about thirty years old but time has dealt him some hard blows. He carries a large suitcase; the American flag painted on both sides, cowbells are attached.* THE BELL MAN *rests his case on the ground. Fans with a very tired-looking handkerchief. He cuts the fool by dancing and singing a bit of a popular song as he turns corners around the yard.*)
THE BELL MAN: (*As* LULA *starts to go in the house.*) Stay where you at, Aunty! You used to live on Thompson Street. How's old Thompson Street?
JULIA: (*A slightly painful memory.*) I moved 'bout a year ago, moved to Queen Street.
THE BELL MAN: Move a lot, don'tcha? (*Opens suitcase.*) All right, everybody stay where you at! (*Goes into a fast sales spiel.*) Lace-trim ladies' drawers! Stockin's, ladies' stockin's . . . gottem for the knock-knees and the bow-legs too . . . white, black and navy blue! All right, no fools no fun! The

joke's on me! Here we go! (*As he places some merchandise in front of the* WOMEN; *does a regular minstrel walk-around.*) Anything in the world . . . fifty cent a week and one long, sweet year to pay . . . Come on, little sister!
TEETA: (*Doing the walk-around with* THE BELL MAN.) And a-ring-ting-tang
And-a shimmy-she-bang
While the sun am a-shinin' and the sky am blue . . .
And a-ring-ting-tang
And-a shimmy-she-bang
While the sun am a-shinin' and the sky am blue . . .
LULA: (*Annoyed with* TEETA'S *dancing with* THE BELL MAN.) Stop all that shimmy she-bang and get in the house! (*Swats at* TEETA *as she passes.*)
THE BELL MAN: (*Coldly.*) Whatcha owe me, Aunty?
LULA: Three dollars and ten cent. I don't have any money today.
THE BELL MAN: When you gon' pay?
LULA: Monday, or better say Wednesday.
JULIA: (*To divert his attention from* LULA.) How much for sheets?
THE BELL MAN: For you they on'y a dollar. (JULIA *goes to her house to get the money.* THE BELL MAN *moves toward her house as he talks to* LULA.) Goin' to the Service Men's parade Monday?
LULA: Yes, sir. My boy's marchin'. (*She exits.*)
THE BELL MAN: Uh-huh, I'll getcha later. Lord, Lord, Lord, how'dja like to trot 'round in the sun beggin' the poorest people in the world to buy somethin' from you. This is nice. Real nice. (*To* JULIA.) A good friend-a mine was a nigra boy. Me 'n' him was jus' like that. Fine fella, he couldn't read and he couldn't write.
JULIA: (*More to herself than to him.*) When he learns you're gon' lose a friend.
THE BELL MAN: But talkin' serious, what is race and color? Put a paper bag over your head and who'd know the difference. Tryin' to remember me ain'tcha. I seen you one time coming out that bakery shop on Thompson Street, didn' see me.
JULIA: Is that so?
THE BELL MAN: (*Sits on the bed and bounces up and down.*) Awwww, Great Gawd-a-mighty! I haven't been on a high-built bed since I left the back woods.
JULIA: Please don't sit on my bed!
THE BELL MAN: Old country boy, that's me! Strong and healthy country boy . . . (*Not noticing any rejection.*) Sister, Um in need for it like I never been before. Will you 'comodate me? Straighten me, fix me up, will you? Wouldn't take but five minutes. Um quick like a jack rabbit. Wouldn't nobody know but you and me. (*She backs away from him as he pants and wheezes out his admiration.*) Um clean, too. Clean as the . . . Board-a Health. Don't believe in dippin' inta everything. I got no money now, but Ladies always need stockin's.

JULIA: (*Trying to keep her voice down, throws money at his feet.*) Get out of my house! Beneath contempt, that's what you are.
THE BELL MAN: Don't be lookin' down your nose at me . . . actin' like you Mrs. Martha Washington . . . Throwin' one chicken-shit dollar at me and goin' on . . .
JULIA: (*Picking up wooden clothes hanger.*) Get out! Out, before I take a stick to you.
THE BELL MAN: (*Bewildered, gathering his things to leave.*) Hell, what I care who you sleep with! It's your nooky! Give it way how you want to. I don't own no run-down bakery shop but I'm good as those who do. A baker ain' nobody . . .
JULIA: I wish you was dead, you just oughta be dead, stepped on and dead.
THE BELL MAN: Bet that's what my mama said first time she saw me. I was a fourteenth child. Damn women! . . . that's all right . . . Gawd bless you, Gawd be with you and let his light shine on you. I give you good for evil . . . God bless you! (*As he walks down the porch steps.*) She must be goin' crazy. Unfriendly, sick-minded bitch! (TEETA *enters from* LULA'S *house.* THE BELL MAN *takes a strainer from his pocket and gives it to* TEETA *with a great show of generosity.*) Here, little honey. You take this sample. You got nice manners.
TEETA: Thank you, you the kin'est person in the world. (THE BELL MAN *exits to the tune of clanking bells and* LULA *enters.*)
JULIA: I hate those kind-a people.
LULA: You mustn't hate white folks. Don'tcha believe in Jesus? He's white.
JULIA: I wonder if he believes in me.
LULA: Gawd says we must love everybody.
JULIA: Just lovin' and lovin', no matter what? There are days when I love, days when I hate.
FANNY: Mattie, Mattie, mail!
JULIA: Your love is worthless if nobody wants it. (FANNY *enters carrying a letter. She rushes over to* MATTIE'S *house.*)
FANNY: I had to pay the postman two cent. No stamp.
TEETA: (*Calls to* JULIA.) Letter from Papa! Gimmie my mama's five cents!
FANNY: (*To* TEETA.) You gon' end your days in the Colored Women's Jailhouse. (PRINCESS, *a little girl, enters skipping and jumping. She hops, runs and leaps across the yard.* PRINCESS *is six years old.* TEETA *takes money from* JULIA'S *outstretched hand and gives it to* FANNY.)
TEETA: (*To* MATTIE.) Letter from Papa! Gotta pay two cent!
FANNY: Now I owe you three cent . . . or do you want me to read the letter? (PRINCESS *gets wilder and wilder, makes Indian war whoops.* TEETA *joins the noise-making. They climb porches and play follow-the-leader.* PRINCESS *finally lands on* JULIA'S *porch after peeping and prying into everything along the way.*)
PRINCESS: (*Laughing merrily.*) Hello . . . hello . . . hello.
JULIA: (*Overwhelmed by the confusion.*) Well—Hello.

FANNY: Get away from my new tenant's porch!
PRINCESS: (*Is delighted with* FANNY'S *scolding and decides to mock her.*) My new tennis porch! (MATTIE *opens the letter and removes a ten dollar bill. Lost in thought she clutches the letter to her bosom.*)
FANNY: (*To* MATTIE.) Ought-a mind w-h-i-t-e children on w-h-i-t-e property!
PRINCESS: (*Now swinging on* JULIA'S *gate.*) . . . my new tennis porch!
FANNY: (*Chases* PRINCESS *around the yard.*) You Princess! Stop that! (JULIA *laughs but she is very near tears.*)
MATTIE: A letter from October.
FANNY: Who's gon' read it for you?
MATTIE: Lula!
PRINCESS: My new tennis porch!
FANNY: Princess! Mattie!
MATTIE: Teeta! In the house with that drat noise!
FANNY: It'll take Lula half-a day. (*Snatches letter.*) I won't charge but ten cent. (*Reads.*) "Dear, Sweet Molasses, My Darlin' Wife . . ."
MATTIE: No, I don't like how you make words sound. You read too rough. (*Sudden Offstage yells and screams from* TEETA *and* PRINCESS *as they struggle for possession of some toy.*)
PRINCESS: (*Offstage.*) Give it to me!
TEETA: No! It's mine!
MATTIE: (*Screams.*) Teeta! (*The* CHILDREN *are quiet.*)
FANNY: Dear, Sweet Molasses—how 'bout that?
JULIA: (*To* FANNY.) Stop that! Don't read her mail.
FANNY: She can't read it.
JULIA: She doesn't want to. She's gonna go on holdin' it in her hand and never know what's in it . . . just 'cause it's hers!
FANNY: Forgive 'em Father, they know not.
JULIA: Another thing, you told me it's quiet here! You call this quiet? I can't stand it!
FANNY: When you need me come and humbly knock on my *back* door. (*She exits.*)
MATTIE: (*Shouts to* FANNY.) I ain't gonna knock on no damn back door! Miss Julia, can you read? (*Offers the letter to* JULIA.) I'll give you some candy when I make it.
JULIA: (*Takes the letter.*) All right. (LULA *takes a seat to enjoy a rare social event. She winds stems for the paper flowers as* JULIA *reads.*) Dear, sweet molasses, my darlin' wife.
MATTIE: Yes, honey. (*To* JULIA.) Thank you.
JULIA: (*Reads.*) Somewhere, at sometime, on the high sea, I take my pen in hand . . . well, anyway, this undelible pencil.
LULA: Hope he didn't put it in his mouth.
JULIA: (*Reads.*) I be missin' you all the time.
MATTIE: And we miss you.

JULIA: (*Reads.*) Sorry we did not have our picture taken.
MATTIE: Didn't have the money.
JULIA: (*Reads.*) Would like to show one to the men and say this is my wife and child . . . They always be showin' pictures.
MATTIE: (*Waves the ten dollar bill.*) I'm gon' send you one, darlin'.
JULIA: (*Reads.*) I recall how we used to take a long walk on Sunday afternoon . . . (*Thinks about this for a moment.*) . . . then come home and be lovin' each other.
MATTIE: I recall.
JULIA: (*Reads.*) The Government people held up your allotment.
MATTIE: Oh, do Jesus.
JULIA: (*Reads.*) They have many papers to be sign, pink, blue and white also green. Money can't be had 'til all papers match. Mine don't match.
LULA: Takes a-while.
JULIA: (*Reads.*) Here is ten cash dollars I hope will not be stole.
MATTIE: (*Holds up the money.*) I got it.
JULIA: (*Reads.*) Go to Merchant Marine office and push things from your end.
MATTIE: Monday. Lula, let's go Monday.
LULA: I gotta see Nelson march in the parade.
JULIA: (*Reads.*) They say people now droppin' in the street, dying' from this war-time influenza. Don't get sick—buy tonic if you do. I love you.
MATTIE: Gotta buy a bottle-a tonic.
JULIA: (*Reads.*) Sometimes people say hurtful things 'bout what I am, like color and race . . .
MATTIE: Tell 'em you my brown-skin Carolina daddy, that's who the hell you are. Wish I was there.
JULIA: (*Reads.*) I try not to hear 'cause I do want to get back to your side. Two things a man can give the woman he loves . . . his name and his protection . . . The first you have, the last is yet to someday come. The war is here, the road is rocky. I am *ever* your lovin' husband, October.
MATTIE: So-long, darlin'. I wish I had your education.
JULIA: I only went through eighth grade. Name and protection. I know you love him.
MATTIE: Yes'm, I do. If I was to see October in bed with another woman, I'd never doubt him 'cause I trust him more than I do my own eyesight. Bet yall don't believe me.
JULIA: I know how much a woman can love. (*Glances at the letter again.*) Two things a man ran give . . .
MATTIE: Name and protection. That's right, too. I wouldn't live with no man. Man got to marry me. Man that won't marry you thinks nothin' of you. Just usin' you.
JULIA: I've never allowed anybody to *use* me!
LULA: (*Trying to move her away Stage Right.*) Mattie, look like rain.
MATTIE: A man can't use a woman less she let him.

LULA: (*To* MATTIE.) You never know when to stop.
JULIA: Well, I read your letter. Good day.
MATTIE: Did I hurtcha feelin's? Tell me, what'd I say.
JULIA: I—I've been keepin' company with someone for a long time and . . . we're not married.
MATTIE: For how long?
LULA: (*Half-heartedly tries to hush* MATTIE *but she would also like to know.*) Ohhh, Mattie.
JULIA: (*Without shame.*) Ten years today, ten full, faithful years.
MATTIE: He got a wife?
JULIA: (*Very tense and uncomfortable.*) No.
MATTIE: Oh, a man don't wanta get married, work on him. Cut off piece-a his shirt-tail and sew it to your petticoat. It works. Get Fanny to read the tea leaves and tell you how to move. She's a old bitch but what she sees in a tea-cup is true.
JULIA: Thank you, Mattie.
LULA: Let's pray on it, Miss Julia. Gawd bring them together, in holy matrimony.
JULIA: Miss Lula, please don't . . . You know it's against the law for black and white to get married, so Gawd nor the tea leaves can help us. My friend is white and that's why I try to stay to myself. (*After a few seconds of silence.*)
LULA: Guess we shouldn't-a disturbed you.
JULIA: But I'm so glad you did. Oh, the things I can tell you 'bout bein' lonesome and shut-out. Always movin', one place to another, lookin' for some peace of mind. I moved out in the country . . . Pretty but quiet as the graveyard; so lonesome. One year I was in such a *lovely* colored neighborhood but they couldn't be bothered with me, you know? I've lived near sportin' people . . . they were very kindly but I'm not a sporty type person. Then I found this place hid way in the backyard so quiet, didn't see another soul . . . And that's why I thought yall wanted to tear my house down this mornin' . . . 'cause you might-a heard 'bout me and Herman . . . and some people are . . . well, they judge, they can't help judgin' you.
MATTIE: (*Eager to absolve her of wrong doing.*) Oh, darlin', we all do things we don't want sometimes. You grit your teeth and take all he's got; if you don't somebody else will.
LULA: No, no, you got no use for 'em so don't take nothin' from 'em.
MATTIE: He's takin' somethin' from her.
LULA: Have faith, you won't starve.
MATTIE: Rob him blind. Take it all. Let him froth at the mouth. Let him die in the poorhouse—bitter, bitter to the gone!
LULA: A white man is somethin' else. Everybody knows how that low-down slave master sent for a different black woman every night . . . for his pleasure. That's why none of us is the same color.

MATTIE: And right now today they're mean, honey. They can't help it; their nose is pinched together so close they can't get enough air. It makes 'em mean. And their mouth is set back in their face so hard and flat . . . no roundness, no sweetness, they can't even carry a tune.
LULA: I couldn't stand one of 'em to touch me intimate no matter what he'd give me.
JULIA: Miss Lula, you don't understand. Mattie, the way you and your husband feel that's the way it is with me 'n' Herman. He loves me . . . We love each other, that's all, we just love each other. (*After a split second of silence.*) And someday, as soon as we're able, we have to leave here and go where it's right . . . Where it's legal for everybody to marry. That's what we both want . . . to be man and wife—like you and October.
LULA: Well I have to cut out six dozen paper roses today. (*Starts for her house.*)
MATTIE: And I gotta make a batch-a candy and look after Princess so I can feed me and Teeta 'til October comes back. Thanks for readin' the letter. (*She enters her house.*)
JULIA: But Mattie, Lula—I wanted to tell you why it's been ten years—and why we haven't—
LULA: Good day, Miss Julia. (*Enters her house.*)
JULIA: Well, that's always the way. What am I doing standin' in a backyard explainin' my life? Stay to yourself, Julia Augustine. Stay to yourself. (*Sweeps her front porch.*)
I got to climb my way to glory
Got to climb it by myself
Ain't nobody here can climb it for me
I got to climb it for myself.

CURTAIN

ACT ONE

Scene 2

TIME: *That evening. Cover closed Scene 1 curtain with song and laughter from* MATTIE, LULA *and* KIDS.

As curtain opens, JULIA *has almost finished the unpacking. The room now looks quite cozy. Once in a while she watches the clock and looks out of the window.* TEETA *follows* PRINCESS *out of* MATTIE'S *house and ties her sash.* PRINCESS *is holding a jump-rope.*

MATTIE: (*Offstage. Sings.*)
My best man left me, it sure do grieve my mind
When I'm laughin', I'm laughin' to keep from cryin' . . .
PRINCESS: (*Twirling the rope to one side.*) Ching, ching, China-man eat dead rat . . .
TEETA: (*As* PRINCESS *jumps rope.*) Knock him in the head with a baseball bat . . .
PRINCESS: You wanta jump?
TEETA: Yes.
PRINCESS: Say "Yes, Mam."
TEETA: No.
PRINCESS: Why?
TEETA: You too little.
PRINCESS: (*Takes bean bag from her pocket.*) You can't play with my bean-bag.
TEETA: I 'on care, play it by yourself.
PRINCESS: (*Drops rope, tosses the bag to* TEETA.) Catch. (TEETA *throws it back.* HERMAN *appears at the back-entry. He is a strong, forty year old working man. His light brown hair is sprinkled with gray. At the present moment he is tired.* PRINCESS *notices him because she is facing the back fence. He looks for a gate or opening but can find none.*) Hello.
TEETA: Mama! Mama!
HERMAN: Hello, children. Where's the gate? (HERMAN *passes several packages through a hole in the fence; he thinks of climbing the fence but it is very rickety. He disappears from view.* MATTIE *dashes out of her house, notices the packages, runs into* LULA'S *house, then back into the yard.* LULA *enters in a flurry of excitement; gathers a couple of pieces from the clothesline.* MATTIE *goes to inspect the packages.*)
LULA: Don't touch 'em, Mattie. Might be dynamite.
MATTIE: Well, I'm gon' get my head blowed off, 'cause I wanta see. (NELSON *steps out wearing his best civilian clothes; neat fitting suit, striped silk shirt and bulldog shoes in ox-blood leather. He claps his hands to frighten* MATTIE.)
MATTIE: Oh, look at him. Where's the party?
NELSON: Everywhere! The ladies have heard Nelson's home. They waitin' for me!
LULA: Don't get in trouble. Don't answer anybody that bothers you.
NELSON: How come it is that when I carry a sack-a coal on my back you don't worry, but when I'm goin' out to enjoy myself you almost go crazy.
LULA: Go on! Deliver the piece to the funeral. (*Hands him a funeral piece.* MATTIE *proceeds to examine the contents of a paper bag.*)
NELSON: Fact is, I was gon' stay home and have me some orange drink, but Massa beat me to it. None-a my business no-how, dammit. (MATTIE *opens*

another bag. HERMAN *enters through the front entry.* FANNY *follows at a respectable distance.*)

MATTIE: Look, rolls and biscuits!

LULA: Why'd he leave the food in the yard?

HERMAN: Because I couldn't find the gate. Good evening. Pleasant weather. Howdy do. Cool this evenin'. (*Silence.*) Err—I see where the Allies suffered another set-back yesterday. Well, that's the war, as they say. (*The* WOMEN *answers with nods and vague throat clearings.* JULIA *opens her door, he enters.*)

MATTIE: That's the lady's husband. He's a light colored man.

PRINCESS: What is a light colored man? (*Children exit with* MATTIE *and* NELSON. FANNY *exits by front entry,* LULA *to her house.*)

JULIA: Why'd you pick a conversation? I tell you 'bout that.

HERMAN: Man gotta say somethin' stumblin' round in a strange back yard.

JULIA: Why didn't you wear your good suit? You know how people like to look you over and sum you up.

HERMAN: Mama and Annabelle made me so damn mad tonight. When I got home Annabelle had this in the window. (*Removes a cardboard sign from the bag . . . printed with red, white and blue crayon . . .* WE ARE AMERICAN CITIZENS . . .)

JULIA: We are American Citizens. Why'd she put it in the window?

HERMAN: Somebody wrote cross the side of our house in purple paint . . . "Krauts . . . Germans live here"! I'd-a broke his arm if I caught him.

JULIA: It's the war. Makes people mean. But didn't she print it pretty.

HERMAN: Comes from Mama boastin' 'bout her German grandfather, now it's no longer fashionable. I snatched that coward sign outta the window . . . Goddamit, I says . . . Annabelle cryin', Mama hollerin' at her. Gawd save us from the ignorance, I say . . . Why should I see a sign in the window when I get home? That Annabelle got flags flyin' in the front yard, the backyard . . . and red, white and blue flowers in the grass . . . confound nonsense . . . Mama is an ignorant woman . . .

JULIA: Don't say that . . .

HERMAN: A poor ignorant woman who is mad because she is born a sharecropper . . . outta her mind 'cause she ain't high class society. We're red-neck crackers, I told her, that's what.

JULIA: Oh, Herman . . . no you didn't . . .

HERMAN: I did.

JULIA: (*Standing.*) But she raised you . . . loaned you all-a-her three thousand dollars to pour into that bakery shop. You know you care about her.

HERMAN: Of course I do. But sometimes she makes me so mad . . . Close the door, lock out the world . . . all of 'em that ain't crazy are coward. (*Looks at sign.*) Poor Annabelle—Miss War-time Volunteer . . .

JULIA: She's what you'd call a very Patriotic Person, wouldn't you say?

HERMAN: Well, guess it is hard for her to have a brother who only makes pies in time of war.

JULIA: A brother who makes pies and loves a nigger!
HERMAN: Sweet Kerist, there it is again!
JULIA: Your mama's own words . . . according to you—I'll never forget them as long as I live. Annabelle, you've got a brother who makes pies and loves a nigger.
HERMAN: How can you remember seven or eight years ago, for Gawd's sake? Sorry I told it.
JULIA: I'm not angry, honeybunch, dear heart. I just remember.
HERMAN: When you say honeybunch, you're angry. Where do you want your Aunt Cora?
JULIA: On my dresser!
HERMAN: An awful mean woman.
JULIA: Don't get me started on your mama and Annabelle. (*Pause.*)
HERMAN: Julia, why did you move into a backyard?
JULIA: (*Goes to him.*) Another move, another mess. Sometimes I feel like fightin' . . . and there's nobody to fight but you . . .
HERMAN: Open the box. Go on. Open it.
JULIA: (*Opens the box and reveals a small but ornate wedding cake with a bride and groom on top and ten pink candles.*) Ohhh, it's the best one ever. Tassels, bells, roses . . .
HERMAN: . . . Daffodils and silver sprinkles . . .
JULIA: You're the best baker in the world.
HERMAN: (*As he lights the candles.*) Because you put up with me . . .
JULIA: Gawd knows that.
HERMAN: . . . because the palms of your hands and the soles of your feet are pink and brown . . .
JULIA: Jus' listen to him. Well, go on.
HERMAN: Because you're a good woman, a kind, good woman.
JULIA: Thank you very much, Herman.
HERMAN: Because you care about me.
JULIA: Well, I do.
HERMAN: Happy ten years . . . Happy tenth year.
JULIA: And the same to you.
HERMAN: (*Tries a bit of soft barbershop harmony.*)
I love you as I never loved before (JULIA *joins him.*)
When first I met you on the village green
Come to me e'er my dream of love is o'er
I love you as I loved you
When you were sweet—Take the end up higher—
When you were su-weet six-ateen.
Now blow! (*They blow out the candles and kiss through a cloud of smoke.*)
JULIA: (*Almost forgetting something.*) Got something for you. Because you were my only friend when Aunt Cora sent me on a sleep-in job in the white-folks kitchen. And wasn't that Miss Bessie one mean white woman? (*Gives present to* HERMAN.)

HERMAN: Oh, Julia, just say she was mean.
JULIA: Well yes, but she was white too.
HERMAN: A new peel, thank you. A new pastry bag. Thank you.
JULIA: (*She gives him a sweater.*) I did everything right but one arm came out shorter.
HERMAN: That's how I feel. Since three o'clock this morning, I turned out twenty ginger breads, thirty sponge cakes, lady fingers, Charlotte Russe . . . loaf bread, round bread, twist bread and water rolls . . . and—
JULIA: Tell me about pies. Do pies!
HERMAN: Fifty pies. Open apple, closed apple, applecrumb, sweet potato and pecan. And I got a order for a large wedding cake. They want it in the shape of a battleship. (HERMAN *gives* JULIA *ring box.* JULIA *takes out a wide, gold wedding band—it is strung on a chain.*) It's a wedding band . . . on a chain . . . To have until such time as . . . It's what you wanted, Julia. A damn fool present.
JULIA: Sorry I lost your graduation ring. If you'd-a gone to college what do you think you'd-a been?
HERMAN: A baker with a degree.
JULIA: (*Reads.*) Herman and Julia 1908 . . . and now it's . . . 1918. Time runs away. A wedding band . . . on a chain. (*She fastens the chain around her neck.*)
HERMAN: A damn fool present. (JULIA *drops the ring inside of her dress.*)
JULIA: It comforts me. It's your promise. You hungry?
HERMAN: No.
JULIA: After the war, the people across the way are goin' to Philadelphia.
HERMAN: I hear it's cold up there. People freeze to death waitin' for a trolley car.
JULIA: (*Leans back beside him, rubs his head.*) In the middle of the night a big bird flew cryin' over this house—Then he was gone, the way time goes flyin' . . .
HERMAN: Julia, why did you move in a back yard? Out in the country the air was so sweet and clean. Makes me feel shame . . .
JULIA: (*Rubbing his back.*) Crickets singin' that lonesome evenin' song. Any kind-a people better than none a-tall.
HERMAN: Mama's beggin' me to hire Greenlee again, to help in the shop, "Herman, sit back like a half-way gentleman and just take in money."
JULIA: Greenlee! When white-folks decide . . .
HERMAN: People, Julia, people.
JULIA: When people decide to give other people a job, they come up with the biggest Uncle Tom they can find. The *people* I know call him a "white-folks-nigger." It's a terrible expression so don't you ever use it.
HERMAN: He seems dignified, Julia.
JULIA: Jus' 'cause you're clean and stand straight, that's not dignity. Even speakin' nice might not be dignity.
HERMAN: What's dignity? Tell me. Do it.

JULIA: Well, it . . . it . . . It's a feeling—It's a spirit that rises higher than the dirt around it, without any by-your-leave. It's not proud and it's not 'shamed . . . Dignity "Is" . . . and it's never Greenlee . . . I don't know if it's us either, honey.

HERMAN: (*Standing.*) It still bothers my mother that I'm a baker. "When you gonna rise in the world!" A baker who rises . . . (*Laughs and coughs a little.*) Now she's worried 'bout Annabelle marryin' a sailor. After all, Annabelle is a concert pianist. She's had only one concert . . . in a church . . . and not many people there.

JULIA: A sailor might just perservere and become an admiral. Yes, an admiral and a concert pianist.

HERMAN: Ten years. If I'd-a known what I know now, I wouldn't-a let Mama borrow on the house or give me the bakery.

JULIA: Give what? Three broken stoves and all-a your papa's unpaid bills.

HERMAN: I *got* to pay her back. And I can't go to Philadelphia or wherever the hell you're saying to go. I can hear you thinkin', Philadelphia, Philadelphia, Phil . . .

JULIA: (*Jumping up. Pours wine.*) Oh damnation! The hell with that!

HERMAN: All right, not so much hell and damn. When we first met you were so shy.

JULIA: Sure was, wouldn't say "dog" 'cause it had a tail. In the beginnin' nothin' but lovin' and kissin' . . . and thinkin' 'bout you. Now I worry 'bout gettin' old. I do. Maybe you'll meet somebody younger. People do get old, y'know. (*Sits on bed.*)

HERMAN: There's an old couple 'cross from the bakery . . . "Mabel," he yells, "Where's my keys!" . . . Mabel has a big behind on her. She wears his carpet slippers. "All right, Robbie, m'boy," she says . . . Robbie walks kinda one-sided. But they're havin' a pretty good time. We'll grow old together both of us havin' the same name. (*Takes her in his arms.*) Julia, I love you . . . you know it . . . I love you . . . (*After a pause.*) Did you have my watch fixed?

JULIA: (*Sleepily.*) Uh-huh, it's in my purse. (*Getting up.*) Last night when the bird flew over the house—I dreamed 'bout the devil's face in the fire . . . He said "I'm comin' to drag you to hell."

HERMAN: (*Sitting up.*) There's no other hell, honey. Celestine was sayin' the other day—

JULIA: How do you know what Celestine says?

HERMAN: Annabelle invited her to dinner.

JULIA: They still trying to throw that white widow-woman at you? Oh, Herman, I'm gettin' mean . . . jumpin' at noises . . . and bad dreams.

HERMAN: (*Brandishing bottle.*) Dammit, this is the big bird that flew over the house!

JULIA: I don't go anywhere, I don't know anybody, I gotta do somethin'. Sometimes I need to have company—

to say . . . "Howdy-do, pleasant evenin,' do drop in." Sometimes I need

other people. How you ever gonna pay back three thousand dollars? Your side hurt?
HERMAN: Schumann, came in to see me this mornin'. Says he'll buy me out, ten cents on the dollar, and give me a job bakin' for him . . . it's an offer,—can get seventeen hundred cash.
JULIA: Don't do it, Herman. That sure wouldn't be dignity.
HERMAN: He makes an American flag outta gingerbread. But they sell. Bad taste sells. Julia, where do you want to go? New York, Philadelphia, where? Let's try their dignity. Say where you want to go.
JULIA: Well, darlin', if folks are freezin' in Philadelphia, we'll go to New York.
HERMAN: Right! You go and size up the place. Meanwhile I'll stay here and do like everybody else, make war money . . . battleship cakes, cannonball cookies . . . chocolate bullets . . . they'll sell. Pay my debts. Less than a year, I'll be up there with money in my pockets.
JULIA: Northerners talk funny— "We're from New Yor*rr*k."
HERMAN: I'll getcha train ticket next week.
JULIA: No train. I wanta stand on the deck of a Clyde Line boat, wavin' to the people on the shore. The whistle blowin', flags flyin' . . . wavin' my handkerchief . . . So long, so long, look here—South Carolina . . . so long, hometown . . . goin' away by myself— (*Tearfully blows her nose.*)
HERMAN: You gonna like it. Stay with your cousin and don't talk to strangers. (JULIA *gets dress from her hope chest.*)
JULIA: Then, when we do get married we can have a quiet reception. My cut glass punch bowl . . . little sandwiches, a few friends . . . Herman? Hope my weddin' dress isn't too small. It's been waitin' a good while. (*Holds dress in front of her.*) I'll use all of my hope chest things. Quilts, Irish linens, the silver cups . . . Oh, Honey, how are you gonna manage with me gone?
HERMAN: Buy warm underwear and a woolen coat with a fur collar . . . to turn against the northern wind. What size socks do I wear?
JULIA: Eleven, eleven and a half if they run small.
HERMAN: . . . what's the store? Write it down.
JULIA: Coleridge. And go to King Street for your shirts.
HERMAN: Coleridge. Write it down.
JULIA: Keep payin' Ruckheiser, the tailor, so he can start your new suit.
HERMAN: Ruckheiser. Write it down.
JULIA: Now that I know I'm goin' we can take our time.
HERMAN: No, rush, hurry, make haste, do it. Look at you . . . like your old self.
JULIA: No, no, not yet—I'll go soon as we get around to it. (*Kisses him.*)
HERMAN: That's right. Take your time . . .
JULIA: Oh, Herman. (MATTIE *enters through the back gate with* TEETA. *She pats and arranges* TEETA'S *hair.* FANNY *enters from the front entry and goes to* JULIA'S *window.*)

MATTIE: You goin' to Lula's service?
FANNY: A new faith. Rather be a Catholic than somethin' you gotta make up. Girl, my new tenant and her—
MATTIE: (*Giving* FANNY *the high-sign to watch what she says in front of* TEETA.) . . . and her husband.
FANNY: I gotcha. She and her husband was in there havin' a orgy. Singin', laughin', screamin', cryin' . . . I'd like to be a fly on that wall. (LULA *enters the yard wearing a shawl over her head and a red band on her arm. She carries two chairs and places them beside two kegs.*)
LULA: Service time! (MATTIE, TEETA and FANNY *enter the yard and sit down.* LULA *places a small table and a cross.*)
FANNY: (*Goes to* JULIA'S *door and knocks.*) Let's spread the word to those who need it. (*Shouts.*) Miss Julia, don't stop if you in the middle-a somethin'. We who love Gawd are gatherin' for prayer. Got any time for Jesus?
ALL: (*Sing.*) When the roll is called up yonder.
JULIA: Thank you, Miss Fanny. (FANNY *flounces back to her seat in triumph.* JULIA *sits on the bed near* HERMAN.)
HERMAN: Dammit, she's makin' fun of you.
JULIA: (*Smooths her dress and hair.*) Nobody's invited me anywhere in a long time . . . so I'm goin'.
HERMAN: (*Standing.*) I'm gonna buy you a Clyde Line ticket for New York City on Monday . . . this Monday.
JULIA: Monday?
HERMAN: As Gawd is my judge. That's dignity. Monday.
JULIA: (*Joyfully kissing him.*) Yes, Herman! (*She enters yard.*)
LULA: My form-a service opens with praise. Let us speak to Gawd.
MATTIE: Well, I thang Gawd that—that I'm livin' and I pray my husband comes home safe.
TEETA: I love Jesus and Jesus loves me.
ALL: Amen.
FANNY: I thang Gawd that I'm able to rise spite-a those who try to hold me down, spite-a those who are two-faceted, spite-a those in my own race who jealous 'cause I'm doin' so much better than the rest of 'em. He preparest a table for me in the presence of my enemies. Double-deal Fanny Johnson all you want but me 'n' Gawd's gonna come out on top. (ALL *look to* JULIA.)
JULIA: I'm sorry for past sin—but from Monday on through eternity—I'm gonna live in dignity accordin' to the laws of God and man. Oh, Glory!
LULA: Glory Hallelujah! (NELSON *enters a bit unsteadily . . . struts and preens while singing.*)
NELSON: Come here black woman . . . whoooo . . . eee . . . on daddy's knee . . . etc.
LULA: (*Trying to interrupt him.*) We're testifyin . . .
NELSON: (*Throwing hat on porch.*) Right! Testify! Tonight I asked the

prettiest girl in Carolina to be my wife; And Merrilee Jones told me . . . I'm sorry but you got nothin to offer. She's right! I got nothin to offer but a hard way to go. Merrilee Jones . . . workin for the rich white folks and better off washin their dirty drawers than marryin me.
LULA: Respect the church! (*Slaps him.*)
NELSON: (*Sings.*) Come here, black woman (etc.) . . .
JULIA: Oh, Nelson, respect your mother!
NELSON: Respect your damn self, Julia Augustine! (*Continues singing.*)
LULA: How we gonna find a new faith?
NELSON: (*Softly.*) By tellin' the truth, Mamma. Merilee ain't no liar. I got nothin' to offer, just like October.
MATTIE: You keep my husband's name outta your mouth.
NELSON: (*Sings.*) Come here, black woman . . .
FANNY AND CONGREGATION: (*Sing.*)
Ain't gon let nobody turn me round, turn me round, turn me round
Ain't gon let nobody turn me round . . .
HERMAN: (*Staggers out to porch.*) Julia, I'm going now, I'm sorry . . . I don't feel well . . . I don't know . . . (*Slides forward and falls.*)
JULIA: Mr. Nelson . . . won'tcha please help me . . .
FANNY: Get him out of my yard. (NELSON *and* JULIA *help* HERMAN *in to bed. Others freeze in yard.*)

END OF ACT ONE

ACT TWO

SCENE 1

TIME: *Sunday morning.*

SCENE: *The same as Act One except the yard and houses are neater. The clothes line is down. Off in the distance someone is humming a snatch of a hymn. Church bells are ringing.* HERMAN *is in a heavy, restless sleep. The bed covers indicate he has spent a troubled night. On the table* D. R. *are medicine bottles, cups and spoons.* JULIA *is standing beside the bed, swinging a steam kettle, she stops and puts it on a trivet on top of her hope chest.*

FANNY: (*Seeing her.*) Keep usin' the steam-kettle. (HERMAN *groans lightly.*)
MATTIE: (*Picks up scissors.*) Put the scissors under the bed, open. It'll cut the pain.

FANNY: (*Takes scissors from* MATTIE.) That's for childbirth.
JULIA: He's had too much paregoric. Sleepin' his life away. I want a doctor.
FANNY: Over my dead body. It's against the damn law for him to be layin' up in a black woman's bed.
MATTIE: A doctor will call the police.
FANNY: They'll say I run a bad house.
JULIA: I'll tell 'em the truth.
MATTIE: We don't tell things to police.
FANNY: When Lula gets back with his sister, his damn sister will take charge.
MATTIE: That's his family.
FANNY: Family is family.
JULIA: I'll hire a hack and take him to a doctor.
FANNY: He might die on you. That's police. That's the work-house.
JULIA: I'll say I found him on the street!
FANNY: Walk into the jaws of the law—they'll chew you up.
JULIA: Suppose his sister won't come?
FANNY: She'll be here. (FANNY *picks up a tea-cup and turns it upside down on the saucer and twirls it.*) I see a ship, a ship sailin' on the water.
MATTIE: Water clear or muddy?
FANNY: Crystal clear.
MATTIE: (*Realizing she's late.*) Oh, I gotta get Princess so her folks can open their ice cream parlor. Take care-a Teeta.
FANNY: I see you on your way to Miami, Florida, goin' on a trip.
JULIA: (*Sitting on window seat.*) I know you want me to move. I will, Fanny.
FANNY: Julia, it's hard to live under these mean white-folks . . . but I've done it. I'm the first and only colored they let buy land 'round here.
JULIA: They all like you, Fanny. Only one of 'em cares for me . . . just one.
FANNY: Yes, I'm thought highly of. When I pass by they can say . . . "There she go, Fanny Johnson, reppresentin' her race in-a approved manner" . . . 'cause they don't have to worry 'bout my next move. I can't afford to mess that up on account-a you or any-a the rest-a these hard-luck, better-off-dead, triflin' niggers.
JULIA: (*Crossing up Right.*) I'll move. But I'm gonna call a doctor.
FANNY: Do it, we'll have a yellow quarantine sign on the front door . . . "INFLUENZA". Doctor'll fill out papers for the law . . . address . . . race . . .
JULIA: I . . . I guess I'll wait until his sister gets here.
FANNY: No, you call a doctor, Nelson won't march in the parade tomorrow or go back to the army, Mattie'll be outta work, Lula can't deliver flowers . . .
JULIA: I'm sorry, so very sorry. I'm the one breakin' laws, doin' wrong.
FANNY: I'm not judgin' you. High or low, nobody's against this if it's kept quiet. But when you pickin' white . . . pick a wealthy white. It makes things easier.

JULIA: No, Herman's not rich and I've never tried to beat him out of anything.
FANNY: (*Crossing to* JULIA.) Well, he just ought-a be and you just should-a. A colored woman needs money more than anybody else in this world.
JULIA: You sell yours.
FANNY: All I don't sell I'm going to keep.
HERMAN: Julia?
FANNY: (*Very genial.*) Well, well, sir, how you feelin', Mr. Herman? This is Aunt Fanny . . . Miss Julia's landlady. You lookin' better, Mr. Herman. We've been praying for you. (FANNY *exits to* TEETA'S *house.*)
JULIA: Miss Lula—went to get your sister.
HERMAN: Why?
JULIA: Fanny made me. We couldn't wake you up. (*He tries to sit up in bed to prepare for leaving. She tries to help him. He falls back on the pillow.*)
HERMAN: Get my wallet . . . see how much money is there. What's that smell? (*She takes the wallet from his coat pocket. She completes counting the money.*)
JULIA: Eucalyptus oil, to help you breathe; I smell it, you smell it and Annabelle will have to smell it too! Seventeen dollars.
HERMAN: A boat ticket to New York is fourteen dollars—Ohhhh, Kerist! Pain . . . pain . . . Count to ten . . . one, two . . . (JULIA *gives paregoric water to him. He drinks. She puts down glass and picks up damp cloth from bowl on tray and wipes his brow.*) My mother is made out of too many . . . little things . . . the price of carrots, how much fat is on the meat . . . little things make people small. Make ignorance—y'know?
JULIA: Don't fret about your people, I promise I won't be surprised at anything and I won't have unpleasant words no matter what.
HERMAN: (*The pain eases. He is exhausted.*) Ahhh, there . . . All men are born which is—utterly untrue. (NELSON *steps out of the house. He is brushing his army jacket.* HERMAN *moans slightly.* JULIA *gets her dressmaking scissors and opens them, places the scissors under the bed.*)
FANNY: (*To* NELSON *as she nods towards* JULIA'S *house.*) I like men of African descent, myself.
NELSON: Pitiful people. They pitiful.
FANNY: They common. Only reason I'm sleepin' in a double bed by myself is 'cause I got to bear the standard for the race. I oughta run her outta here for the sake-a the race too.
NELSON: It's your property. Run us all off it, Fanny.
FANNY: Plenty-a these hungry, jobless, bad-luck colored men, just-a itchin' to move in on my gravy-train. I don't want 'em.
NELSON: (*With good nature.*) Right, Fanny! We empty-handed, got nothin' to offer.
FANNY: But I'm damn tired-a ramblin' round in five rooms by myself. House full-a new furniture, the icebox forever full-a goodies. I'm a fine

cook and I know how to pleasure a man . . . he wouldn't have to step outside for a thing . . . food, fun and finance . . . all under one roof. Nelson, how'd you like to be my business advisor? Fix you up a little office in my front parlor. You wouldn't have to work for white folks . . . and Lula wouldn't have to pay rent. The war won't last forever . . . then what you gonna do? They got nothin' for you but haulin' wood and cleanin' toilets. Let's you and me pitch in together.
NELSON: I know you just teasin', but I wouldn't do a-tall. Somebody like me ain't good enough for you noway, but you a fine-lookin' woman, though. After the war I might hit out for Chicago or Detroit . . . a rollin' stone gathers no moss.
FANNY: Roll on. Just tryin' to help the race. (LULA *enters by front entry, followed by* ANNABELLE, *a woman in her thirties. She assumes a slightly mincing air of fashionable delicacy. She might be graceful if she were not ashamed of her size. She is nervous and fearful in this strange atmosphere. The others fall silent as they see her.* ANNABELLE *wonders if* PRINCESS *is her brother's child? Or could it be* TEETA, *or both?*)
ANNABELLE: Hello there . . . er . . . children.
PRINCESS: (*Can't resist mocking her.*) Hello there, er . . . children. (*Giggles.*)
ANNABELLE: (*To* TEETA.) Is she your sister? (ANNABELLE *looks at* NELSON *and draws her shawl a little closer.*)
TEETA: You have to ask my mama.
NELSON: (*Annoyed with* ANNABELLE'S *discomfort.*) Mom, where's the flatiron? (*Turns and enters his house.* LULA *follows.* MATTIE *and* CHILDREN *exit.*)
FANNY: I'm the landlady. Mr. Herman had every care and kindness 'cept a doctor. Miss Juliaaaa! That's the family's concern. (FANNY *opens door, then exits.*)
ANNABELLE: Sister's here. It's Annabelle.
JULIA: (*Shows her to a chair.*) One minute he's with you, the next he's gone. Paregoric makes you sleep.
ANNABELLE: (*Dabs at her eyes with a handkerchief.*) Cryin' doesn't make sense a-tall. I'm a volunteer worker at the Naval hospital . . . I've nursed my mother . . . (*Chokes with tears.*)
JULIA: (*Pours a glass of water for her.*) Well, this is more than sickness. It's not knowin' 'bout other things.
ANNABELLE: We've known for years. He is away all the time and when old Uncle Greenlee . . . He's a colored gentlemen who works in our neighborhood . . . and he said . . . he told . . . er, well, people do talk. (ANNABELLE *spills water,* JULIA *attempts to wipe the water from her dress.*) Don't do that . . . It's all right.
HERMAN: Julia?
ANNABELLE: Sister's here. Mama and Uncle Greenlee have a hack down the street. Gets a little darker we'll take you home, call a physician . . .
JULIA: Can't you do it right away?

ANNABELLE: 'Course you could put him out. Please let us wait 'til dark.
JULIA: Get a doctor.
ANNABELLE: Our plans are made, thank you.
HERMAN: Annabelle, this is Julia.
ANNABELLE: Hush.
HERMAN: This is my sister.
ANNABELLE: Now be still.
JULIA: I'll call Greenlee to help him dress.
ANNABELLE: No. Dress first. The colored folk in *our* neighborhood have great respect for us.
HERMAN: Because I give away cinnamon buns, for Kerist sake.
ANNABELLE: (*To* JULIA.) I promised my mother I'd try and talk to you. Now—you look like one-a the nice coloreds . . .
HERMAN: Remember you are a concert pianist, that is a very dignified calling.
ANNABELLE: Put these on. We'll turn our backs.
JULIA: He can't.
ANNABELLE: (*Holds the covers in a way to keep his mid-section under wraps.*) Hold up. (*They manage to get the trousers up as high as his waist but they are twisted and crooked.*) Up we go! There . . . (*They are breathless from the effort of lifting him.*) Now fasten your clothing. (JULIA *fastens his clothes.*) I declare, even a dead man oughta have enough pride to fasten himself.
JULIA: You're a volunteer at the Naval hospital?
HERMAN: (*As another pain hits him.*) Julia, my little brown girl . . . Keep singing . . .
JULIA:
We are climbin' Jacob's ladder, We are climbin' Jacob's ladder,
We are climbin' Jacob's ladder, Soldier of the Cross . . .
HERMAN: The palms of your hands . . .
JULIA: (*Singing.*) Every round goes higher and higher . . .
HERMAN: . . . the soles of your feet are pink and brown.
ANNABELLE: Dammit, hush. Hush this noise. Sick or not sick, hush! It's ugliness. (*To* JULIA.) Let me take care of him, please, leave us alone.
JULIA: I'll get Greenlee.
ANNABELLE: No! You hear me? No.
JULIA: I'll be outside.
ANNABELLE: (*Sitting on bed.*) If she hadn't-a gone I'd-a screamed. (JULIA *stands on the porch.* ANNABELLE *cries.*) I thought so highly of you . . . and here you are in somethin' that's been festerin' for years. (*In disbelief.*) One of the finest women in the world is pinin' her heart out for you, a woman who's pure gold. Everything Celestine does for Mama she's really doin' for you . . . to get next to you . . . But even a Saint wants some reward.
HERMAN: I don't want Saint Celestine.
ANNABELLE: (*Standing.*) Get up! (*Tries to move* HERMAN.) At the Naval

hospital I've seen influenza cases tied down to keep 'em from walkin'. What're we doin' here? How do you meet a black woman?

HERMAN: She came in the bakery on a rainy Saturday evening.

ANNABELLE: (*Giving in to curiosity.*) Yes?

MATTIE: (*Offstage. Scolding* TEETA *and* PRINCESS.) Sit down and drink that lemonade. Don't bother me!

HERMAN: "I smell rye bread baking." Those were the first words . . . Every day . . . Each time the bell sounds over the shop door I'm hopin' it's the brown girl . . . pretty shirt-waist and navy blue skirt. One day I took her hand . . . "little lady, don't be afraid of me" . . . She wasn't . . . I've never been lonesome since.

ANNABELLE: (*Holding out his shirt.*) Here, your arm goes in the sleeve. (*They're managing to get the shirt on.*)

HERMAN: (*Beginning to ramble.*) Julia? Your body is velvet . . . the sweet blackberry kisses . . . you are the night-time, the warm, Carolina night-time in my arms . . .

ANNABELLE: (*Bitterly.*) Most excitement I've ever had was takin' piano lessons.

JULIA: (*Calls from porch.*) Ready?

ANNABELLE: No. Rushin' us out. A little longer, please. (*Takes a comb from her purse and nervously combs his hair.*) You nor Mama put yourselves out to understand my Walter when I had him home to dinner. Yes, he's a common sailor . . . I wish he was an officer. I never liked a sailor's uniform, tight pants and middy blouses . . . but they are in the service of their country . . . He's taller than I am. You didn't even stay home that one Sunday like you promised. Must-a been chasin' after some-a them blackberry kisses you love so well. Mama made a jackass outta Walter. You know how she can do. He left lookin' like a whipped dog. Small wonder he won't live down here. I'm crazy-wild 'bout Walter even if he is a sailor. Marry Celestine. She'll take care-a Mama and I can go right on up to the Brooklyn Navy Yard. I been prayin' so hard . . . You marry Celestine and set me free. And Gawd knows I don't want another concert.

HERMAN: (*Sighs.*) Pain, keep singing.

ANNABELLE: Dum-dum-blue Danube. (*He falls back on the pillow. She bathes his head with a damp cloth.*)

JULIA: (*As* NELSON *enters the yard.*) Tell your mother I'm grateful for her kindness. I appreciate . . .

NELSON: Don't have so much to say to me. (*Quietly, in a straightforward manner.*) They set us on fire 'bout their women. String us up, pour on kerosene and light a match. Wouldn't I make a bright flame in my new uniform?

JULIA: Don't be thinkin' that way.

NELSON: I'm thinkin' 'bout black boys hangin' from trees in Little Mountain, Elloree, Winnsboro.

JULIA: Herman never killed anybody. I couldn't care 'bout that kind-a man.
NELSON: (*Stepping, turning to her.*) How can you account for carin' 'bout him a-tall?
JULIA: In that place where I worked, he was the only one who cared . . . who really cared. So gentle, such a gentle man . . . "Yes, Ma'am," . . . "No, Ma'am," "Thank you, Ma'am . . ." In the best years of my youth, my Aunt Cora sent me out to work on a sleep-in job. His shop was near that place where I worked. . . . Most folks don't have to *account* for why they love.
NELSON: You ain't most folks. You're down on the bottom with us, under his foot. A black man got nothin' to offer you . . .
JULIA: I wasn't lookin' for anybody to do for me.
NELSON: . . . and *he's* got nothin' to offer. The one layin' on your mattress, not even if he's kind as you say. He got nothin' for you . . . but some meat and gravy or a new petticoat . . . or maybe he can give you meriny-lookin' little bastard chirrun for us to take in and raise up. We're the ones who feed and raise 'em when it's like this . . . They don't want 'em. They only too glad to let us have their kin-folk. As it is, we supportin' half-a the slave-master's offspring right now.
JULIA: Go fight those who fight you. He never threw a pail-a water on you. Why didn't you fight them that did? Takin' it out on me 'n Herman 'cause you scared of 'em . . .
NELSON: Scared? What scared! If I gotta die I'm carryin' one 'long with me.
JULIA: No you not. You gon' keep on fightin' me.
NELSON: . . . Scared-a what? I look down on 'em, I spit on 'em.
JULIA: No, you don't. They throw dirty water on your uniform . . . and you spit on me!
NELSON: Scared, what scared!
JULIA: You fightin' me, me, me, not them . . . never them.
NELSON: Yeah, I was scared and I'm tougher, stronger, a better man than any of 'em . . . but they won't letcha fight one or four or ten. I was scared to fight a hundred or a thousand. A losin' fight.
JULIA: I'd-a been afraid too.
NELSON: And you scared right now, you let the woman run you out your house.
JULIA: I didn't want to make trouble.
NELSON: But that's what a fight is . . . trouble.
LULA: (*In her doorway.*) Your mouth will kill you. (*To* JULIA.) Don't tell Mr. Herman anything he said . . . or I'll hurt you.
JULIA: Oh, Miss Lula.
LULA: Anyway, he didn't say nothin'. (HERMAN'S *mother enters the yard. She is a "poor white" about fifty-seven years old. She has risen above her poor farm background and tries to assume the airs of "quality." Her clothes are well-kept-*

shabby. *She wears white shoes, a shirtwaist and skirt, drop earrings, a cameo brooch, a faded blue straw hat with a limp bit of veiling. She carries a heavy-black, oil-cloth bag. All in the yard give a step backward as she enters. She assumes an air of calm well-being. Almost as though visiting friends, but anxiety shows around the edges and underneath.* JULIA *approaches and* HERMAN'S MOTHER *abruptly turns to* MATTIE.)
HERMAN'S MOTHER: How do. (MATTIE, TEETA *and* PRINCESS *look at* HERMAN'S MOTHER. HERMAN'S MOTHER *is also curious about them.*)
MATTIE: (*In answer to a penetrating stare from the old woman.*) She's mine. I take care-a her. (*Speaking her defiance by ordering the children.*) Stay inside 'fore y'all catch the flu!
HERMAN'S MOTHER: (*To* LULA.) You were very kind to bring word ... er ...
LULA: Lula, Ma'am.
HERMAN'S MOTHER: The woman who nursed my second cousin's children ... she had a name like that ... Lu*lu* we called her.
LULA: My son, Nelson.
HERMAN'S MOTHER: Can see that. (MATTIE *and the children exit.* FANNY *hurries in from the front entry. Is most eager to establish herself on the good side of* HERMAN'S MOTHER. *With a slight bow. She is carrying the silver tea service.*)
FANNY: Beg pardon, if I may be so bold, I'm Fanny, the owner of all this property.
HERMAN'S MOTHER: (*Definitely approving of* FANNY.) I'm ... er ... Miss Annabelle's mother.
FANNY: My humble pleasure ... er ... Miss er ...
HERMAN'S MOTHER: (*After a brief, thoughtful pause.*) Miss Thelma. (*They move aside but* FANNY *makes sure others hear.*)
FANNY: Miss Thelma, this is not Squeeze-gut Alley. We're just poor, humble, colored people ... and everybody knows how to keep their mouth shut.
HERMAN'S MOTHER: I thank you.
FANNY: She wanted to get a doctor. I put my foot down.
HERMAN'S MOTHER: You did right. (*Shaking her head, confiding her troubles.*) Ohhhh, you don't know.
FANNY: (*With deep understanding.*) Ohhhh, yes, I do. She moved in on me yesterday.
HERMAN'S MOTHER: Friend Fanny, help me to get through this.
FANNY: I will. Now this is Julia, she's the one ... (HERMAN'S MOTHER *starts toward the house without looking at* JULIA. FANNY *decides to let the matter drop.*)
HERMAN'S MOTHER: (*To* LULA.) Tell Uncle Greenlee not to worry. He's holdin' the horse and buggy.
NELSON: (*Bars* LULA'S *way.*) Mama. I'll do it. (LULA *exits into her house.* FANNY *leads her to the chair near* HERMAN'S *bed.*)
ANNABELLE: Mama, if we don't call a doctor Herman's gonna die.

HERMAN'S MOTHER: Everybody's gon' die. Just a matter of when, where and how. A pretty silver service.
FANNY: English china. Belgian linen. Have a cup-a tea?
HERMAN'S MOTHER: (*As a studied pronouncement.*) My son comes to deliver baked goods and the influenza strikes him down. Sickness, it's the war.
FANNY: (*Admiring her cleverness.*) Yes, Ma'am, I'm a witness. I saw him with the packages.
JULIA: Now please call the doctor.
ANNABELLE: Yes, please, Mama. No way for him to move 'less we pick him up bodily.
HERMAN'S MOTHER: Then we'll pick him up.
HERMAN: About Walter . . . your Walter . . . I'm sorry . . . (JULIA *tries to give* HERMAN *some water.*)
HERMAN'S MOTHER: Annabelle, help your brother. (ANNABELLE *gingerly takes glass from* JULIA.) Get that boy to help us. I'll give him a dollar. Now gather his things.
ANNABELLE: What things?
HERMAN'S MOTHER: His possessions, anything he owns, whatever is his. What you been doin' in here all this time? (FANNY *notices* JULIA *is about to speak, so she hurries her through the motions of going through dresser drawers and throwing articles into a pillow case.*)
FANNY: Come on, sugar, make haste.
JULIA: Don't go through my belongings. (*Tears through the drawers, flinging things around as she tries to find his articles.* FANNY *neatly piles them together.*)
FANNY: (*Taking inventory.*) Three shirts . . . one is kinda soiled.
HERMAN'S MOTHER: That's all right, I'll burn 'em.
FANNY: Some new undershirts.
HERMAN'S MOTHER: I'll burn them too.
JULIA: (*To* FANNY.) Put 'em down. I bought 'em and they're not for burnin'.
HERMAN'S MOTHER: (*Struggling to hold her anger in check.*) Fanny, go get that boy. I'll give him fifty cents.
FANNY: You said a dollar.
HERMAN'S MOTHER: All right, dollar it is. (FANNY *exits toward the front entry. In tense, hushed, excited tones, they argue back and forth.*) Now where's the billfold . . . there's papers . . . identity . . . (*Looks in* HERMAN'S *coat pockets.*)
ANNABELLE: Don't make such-a to-do.
HERMAN'S MOTHER: You got any money of your own? Yes, I wanta know where's his money.
JULIA: I'm gettin' it.
HERMAN'S MOTHER: In her pocketbook. This is why the bakery can't make it.
HERMAN: I gave her the Gawd-damned money!
JULIA: And I know what Herman wants me to do . . .

HERMAN'S MOTHER: (*With a wry smile.*) I'm sure you know what he wants.
JULIA: I'm not gonna match words with you. Furthermore, I'm too much of a lady.
HERMAN'S MOTHER: A lady oughta learn how to keep her dress down.
ANNABELLE: Mama, you makin' a spectacle outta yourself.
HERMAN'S MOTHER: You a big simpleton. Men have nasty natures, they can't help it. A man would go with a snake if he only knew how. They cleaned out your wallet.
HERMAN: (*Shivering with a chill.*) I gave her the damn money. (JULIA *takes it from her purse.*)
HERMAN'S MOTHER: Where's your pocket-watch or did you give that too? Annabelle, get another lock put on that bakery door.
HERMAN: I gave her the money to go—to go to New York. (JULIA *drops the money in* HERMAN'S MOTHER'S *lap. She is silent for a moment.*)
HERMAN'S MOTHER: All right. Take it and go. It's never too late to undo a mistake. I'll add more to it. (*She puts the money on the dresser.*)
JULIA: I'm not goin' anywhere.
HERMAN'S MOTHER: Look here, girl, you leave him 'lone.
ANNABELLE: Oh, Mama, all he has to do is stay away.
HERMAN'S MOTHER: But he can't do it. Been years and he can't do it.
JULIA: I got him hoo-dooed, I sprinkle red pepper on his shirt-tail.
HERMAN'S MOTHER: I believe you.
HERMAN: I have a black woman . . . and I'm gon' marry her. I'm gon' marry her . . . got that? Pride needs a paper, for . . . for the sake of herself . . . that's dignity—tell me, what is dignity—Higher than the dirt it is . . . dignity is . . .
ANNABELLE: Let's take him to the doctor, Mama.
HERMAN'S MOTHER: When it's dark.
JULIA: Please!
HERMAN'S MOTHER: Nightfall. (JULIA *steps out on the porch but hears every word said in the room.*) I had such high hopes for him. (*As if* HERMAN *is dead.*) All my high hopes. When he wasn't but five years old I had to whip him so he'd study his John C. Calhoun speech. Oh, Calhoun knew 'bout niggers. He said, "MEN are not born . . . equal, or any other kinda way . . . MEN are *made*" . . . Yes, indeed, for recitin' that John C. Calhoun speech . . . Herman won first mention and a twenty dollar gold piece . . . at the Knights of The Gold Carnation picnic.
ANNABELLE: Papa changed his mind about the Klan. I'm glad.
HERMAN'S MOTHER: Yes, he was always changin' his mind about somethin'. But I was proud-a my men-folk that day. He spoke that speech . . . The officers shook my hand. They honored me . . . "That boy a-yours gonna be somebody." A poor baker-son layin' up with a nigger woman, a over-grown daughter in heat over a common sailor. I must be payin' for somethin' I did. Yesiree, do a wrong, God'll whip you.

ANNABELLE: I wish it was dark.
HERMAN'S MOTHER: I put up with a man breathin' stale whiskey in my face every night . . . pullin' and pawin' at me . . . always tired, inside and out . . . (*Deepest confidence she has ever shared.*) Gave birth to seven . . . five-a them babies couldn't draw breath.
ANNABELLE: (*Suddenly wanting to know more about her.*) Did you love Papa, Mama? Did you ever love him? . . .
HERMAN'S MOTHER: Don't ask me 'bout love . . . I don't know nothin' about it. Never mind love. This is my harvest . . .
HERMAN: Go home. I'm better. (HERMAN'S MOTHER'S *strategy is to enlighten* HERMAN *and also wear him down. Out on the porch,* JULIA *can hear what is being said in the house.*)
HERMAN'S MOTHER: There's something wrong 'bout mis-matched things, be they shoes, socks, or people.
HERMAN: Go away, don't look at us.
HERMAN'S MOTHER: People don't like it. They're not gonna letcha do it in peace.
HERMAN: We'll go North.
HERMAN'S MOTHER: Not a thing will change except her last name.
HERMAN: She's not like others . . . she's not like that . . .
HERMAN'S MOTHER: All right, sell out to Schumann. I want my cash-money . . . You got no feelin' for me, I got none for you . . .
HERMAN: I feel . . . I feel what I feel . . . I don't know what I feel . . .
HERMAN'S MOTHER: Don't need to feel. Live by the law. Follow the law—law, law of the land. Obey the law!
ANNABELLE: We're not obeyin' the law. He should be quarantined right here. The city's tryin' to stop an epidemic.
HERMAN'S MOTHER: Let the city drop dead and you 'long with it. *Rather* be dead than disgraced. Your papa gimme the house and little money . . . I want my money back. (*She tries to drag* HERMAN *up in the bed.*) I ain't payin' for this. (*Shoves* ANNABELLE *aside.*) Let Schumann take over. A man who knows what he's doin'. Go with her . . . Take the last step against your own! Kill us all. Jesus, Gawd, save us or take us—
HERMAN: (*Screams.*) No! No! No! No!
HERMAN'S MOTHER: Thank Gawd, the truth is the light. Oh, Blessed Savior . . . (HERMAN *screams out, starting low and ever going higher. She tries to cover his mouth.* ANNABELLE *pulls her hand away.*) Thank you, Gawd, let the fire go out . . . this awful fire. (LULA *and* NELSON *enter the yard.*)
ANNABELLE: You chokin' him. Mama . . .
JULIA: (*From the porch.*) It's dark! It's dark. Now it's very dark.
HERMAN: One ticket on the Clyde Line . . . Julia . . . where are you? Keep singing . . . count . . . one, two . . . three. Over there, over there . . . send the word, send the word . . .
HERMAN'S MOTHER: Soon be home, son. (HERMAN *breaks away from the*

men, staggers to MATTIE'S *porch and holds on.* MATTIE *smothers a scream and gets the children out of the way.* FANNY *enters.*)

HERMAN: Shut the door . . . don't go out . . . the enemy . . . the enemy . . . (*Recites the Calhoun speech.*) Men are not born infants are born! They grow to all the freedom of which the condition in which they were born permits. It is a great and dangerous error to suppose that all people are equally entitled to liberty.

JULIA: Go home—Please be still.

HERMAN: It is a reward to be earned, a reward reserved for the intelligent, the patriotic, the virtuous and deserving; and not a boon to be bestowed on a people too ignorant, degraded and vicious . . .

JULIA: You be still now, shut up.

HERMAN: . . . to be capable either of appreciating or of enjoying it.

JULIA: (*Covers her ears.*) Take him . . .

HERMAN: A black woman . . . not like the others . . .

JULIA: . . . outta my sight . . .

HERMAN: Julia, the ship is sinking . . . (HERMAN'S MOTHER *and* NELSON *help* HERMAN *up and out.*)

ANNABELLE: (*To* JULIA *on the porch.*) I'm sorry . . . so sorry it had to be this way. I can't leave with you thinkin' I uphold Herman, and blame you.

HERMAN'S MOTHER: (*Returning.*) You the biggest fool.

ANNABELLE: I say a man is responsible for his own behavior.

HERMAN'S MOTHER: And you, you oughta be locked up . . . workhouse . . . jail! Who you think you are!?

JULIA: I'm your damn daughter-in-law, you old bitch! The Battleship Bitch! The bitch who destroys with her filthy mouth. They could win the war with your killin' mouth. The son-killer, man-killer-bitch . . . She's killin' him 'cause he loved me more than anybody in the world. (FANNY *returns.*)

HERMAN'S MOTHER: Better off . . . He's better off dead in his coffin than live with the likes-a you . . . black thing! (*She is almost backing into* JULIA'S *house.*)

JULIA: The black thing who bought a hot water bottle to put on your sick, white self when rheumatism threw you flat on your back . . . who bought flannel gowns to warm your pale, mean body. He never ran up and down King Street shoppin' for you . . . I bought what he took home to you . . .

HERMAN'S MOTHER: Lies . . . tear outcha lyin' tongue.

JULIA: . . . the lace curtains in your parlor . . . the shirt-waist you wearin'—I made them.

FANNY: Go on . . . I got her. (*Holds* JULIA.)

HERMAN'S MOTHER: Leave 'er go! The undertaker will have-ta unlock my hands off her black throat!

FANNY: Go on, Miss Thelma.

JULIA: Miss Thelma my ass! Her first name is Frieda. The Germans are here . . . in purple paint!

HERMAN'S MOTHER: Black, sassy nigger!
JULIA: Kraut, knuckle-eater, red-neck . . .
HERMAN'S MOTHER: Nigger whore . . . he used you for a garbage pail . . .
JULIA: White trash! Sharecropper! Let him die . . . let 'em all die . . . Kill him with your murderin' mouth—sharecropper bitch!
HERMAN'S MOTHER: Dirty black nigger . . .
JULIA: . . . If I wasn't black with all-a Carolina 'gainst me I'd be mistress of your house! (*To* ANNABELLE.) Annabelle, you'd be married livin' in Brooklyn, New York . . . (*To* HERMAN'S MOTHER.) . . . and I'd be waitin' on Frieda . . . cookin' your meals . . . waterin' that damn red-white and blue garden!
HERMAN'S MOTHER: Dirty black bitch.
JULIA: Daughter of a bitch!
ANNABELLE: Leave my mother alone! She's old . . . and sick.
JULIA: But never sick enough to die . . . dirty everlasting woman.
HERMAN'S MOTHER: (*Clinging to* ANNABELLE, *she moves toward the front entry.*) I'm as high over you as Mount Everest over the sea. White reigns supreme . . . I'm white, you can't change that. (*They exit.* FANNY *goes with them.*)
JULIA: Out! Out! Out! And take the last ten years-a my life with you and . . . when he gets better . . . keep him home. Killers, murderers . . . Kinsmen! Klansmen! Keep him home. (*To* MATTIE.) Name and protection . . . he can't gimme either one. (*To* LULA.) I'm gon' get down on my knees and scrub where they walked . . . what they touched . . . (*To* MATTIE.) . . . with brown soap . . . hot lye-water . . . scaldin' hot . . . (*She dashes into the house and collects an armful of bedding . . .*) Clean! . . . Clean the whiteness outta my house . . . clean everything . . . even the memory . . . no more love . . . Free . . . free to hate-cha for the rest-a my life. (*Back to the porch with her arms full.*) When I die I'm gonna keep on hatin' . . . I don't want any whiteness in my house. Stay out . . . out . . . (*Dumps the things in the yard.*) . . . out . . . out . . . out . . . and leave me to my black self!

BLACKOUT

ACT TWO

Scene 2

TIME: *Early afternoon the following day.*

PLACE: *The same.*

In JULIA'S *room, some of the hope chest things are spilled out on the floor, bedspread, linens, silver cups. The half-emptied wine decanter is in a prominent spot. A table is set up in the yard. We hear the distant sound of a marching band. The excitement of a special day is in the air.* NELSON'S *army jacket hangs on his porch.* LULA *brings a pitcher of punch to table.* MATTIE *enters with* TEETA *and* PRINCESS; *she is annoyed and upset in contrast to* LULA'S *singing and gala mood. She scolds the children, smacks* TEETA'S *behind.*

MATTIE: They was teasin' the Chinaman down the street 'cause his hair is braided. (*To* CHILDREN.) If he ketches you, he'll cook you with onions and gravy.
LULA: (*Inspecting* NELSON'S *jacket.*) Sure will.
TEETA: Can we go play?
MATTIE: A mad dog might bite-cha.
PRINCESS: Can we go play?
MATTIE: No, you might step on a nail and get lockjaw.
TEETA: Can we go play?
MATTIE: Oh, go on and play! I wish a gypsy would steal both of 'em! (JULIA *enters her room.*)
LULA: What's the matter, Mattie?
MATTIE: Them damn fool people at the Merchant Marine don't wanta give me my 'lotment money.
JULIA: (*Steps out on her porch with deliberate, defiant energy. She is wearing her wedding dress . . . carrying a wine glass. She is over-demonstrating a show of carefree abandon and joy.*) I'm so happy! I never been this happy in all my life! I'm happy to be alive, alive and livin for my people.
LULA: You better stop drinkin so much wine. (LULA *enters her house.*)
JULIA: But if you got no feelin's they can't be hurt!
MATTIE: Hey, Julia, the people at the Merchant Marine say I'm not married to October.
JULIA: Getcha license, honey, show your papers. Some of us, thang Gawd, got papers!
MATTIE: I don't have none.
JULIA: Why? Was October married before?
MATTIE: No, but I was. A good for nothin' named Delroy . . . I hate to call his name. Was years 'fore I met October. Delroy used to beat the hell outta

me . . . tried to stomp me, grind me into the ground . . . callin' me such dirty names . . . Got so 'til I was shame to look at myself in a mirror. I was glad when he run off.
JULIA: Where'd he go?
MATTIE: I don't know. Man at the office kept sayin' . . . "You're not married to October" . . . and wavin' me 'way like that.
JULIA: Mattie, this state won't allow divorce.
MATTIE: Well, I never got one.
JULIA: You shoulda so you could marry October. You have to be married to get his benefits.
MATTIE: We was married. On Edisto Island. I had a white dress and flowers . . . everything but papers. We couldn't get papers. Elder Burns knew we was doin' best we could.
JULIA: You can't marry without papers.
MATTIE: What if your husband run off? And you got no money? Readin' from the Bible makes people married, not no piece-a paper. We're together eleven years, that oughta-a be legal.
JULIA: (*Puts down glass.*) No, it doesn't go that way.
MATTIE: October's out on the icy water, in the wartime, worryin' 'bout me 'n Teeta. I say he's my husband. Gotta pay Fanny, buy food. Julia, what must I do?
JULIA: I don't know.
MATTIE: What's the use-a so much-a education if you don't know what to do?
JULIA: You may's well just lived with October. Your marriage meant nothin'.
MATTIE: (*Standing angry.*) It meant somethin' to me if not to anybody else. It means I'm ice cream, too, strawberry. (MATTIE *heads for her house.*)
JULIA: Get mad with me if it'll make you feel better.
MATTIE: Julia, could you lend me two dollars?
JULIA: Yes, that's somethin' I can do besides drink this wine. (JULIA *goes into her room, to get the two dollars. Enter* FANNY, TEETA *and* PRINCESS.)
FANNY: Colored men don't know how to do nothin' right. I paid that big black boy cross the street . . . thirty cents to paint my sign . . . (*Sign reads* . . . GOODBYE COLORED BOYS . . . *on one side; the other reads* . . . FOR GOD AND CONTRY.) But he can't spell. I'm gon' call him a dumb darky and get my money back. Come on, children! (CHILDREN *follow laughing.*)
LULA: Why call him names!?
FANNY: 'Cause it makes him mad, that's why. (FANNY *exits with* TEETA *and* PRINCESS. JULIA *goes into her room. The* BELL MAN *enters carrying a display board filled with badges and flags . . . buttons, red and blue ribbons attached to the buttons . . . slogans . . .* THE WAR TO END ALL WARS. *He also carries a string of overseas caps [paper] and wears one. Blows a war tune on his tin flute.* LULA *exits.*)

BELL MAN: "War to end all wars . . ." Flags and badges! Getcha emblems! Hup-two-three . . . Flags and badges . . . hup-two-three! Hey, Aunty! Come back here! Where you at? (*Starts to follow* LULA *into her house.* NELSON *steps out on the porch and blocks his way.*)
NELSON: My mother is in her house. You ain't to come walkin' in. You knock.
BELL MAN: Don't letcha uniform go to your head, Boy, or you'll end your days swingin' from a tree.
LULA: (*Squeezing past* NELSON *dressed in skirt and open shirt-waist.*) Please, Mister, he ain't got good sense.
MATTIE: He crazy, Mister.
NELSON: Fact is, you stay out of here. Don't ever come back here no more.
BELL MAN: (*Backing up in surprise.*) He got no respect. One them crazies. I ain't never harmed a bareassed soul but, hot damn, I can got madder and badder than you. Let your uniform go to your head.
LULA: Yessir, he goin' back in the army today.
BELL MAN: Might not get there way he's actin.'
MATTIE: (*As* LULA *takes two one dollar bills from her bosom.*) He sorry right now, Mister, his head ain' right.
BELL MAN: (*Speaks to* LULA *but keeps an eye on* NELSON.) Why me? I try to give you a laugh but they say, "Play with a puppy and he'll lick your mouth." Familiarity makes for contempt.
LULA: (*Taking flags and badges.*) Yessir. Here's somethin' on my account . . . and I'm buyin' flags and badges for the children. Everybody know you a good man and do right.
BELL MAN: (*To* LULA.) You pay up by Monday. (*To* NELSON.) Boy, you done cut off your Mama's credit.
LULA: I don't blame you, Mister. (BELL MAN *exits.*)
NELSON: Mama, your new faith don't seem to do much for you.
LULA: (*Turning to him.*) Nelson, go on off to the war 'fore somebody kills you. I ain't goin' to let nobody spoil my day. (LULA *puts flags and badges on punchbowl table.* JULIA *comes out of her room, with the two dollars for* MATTIE—*hands it to her. Sound of Jenkins Colored Orphan Band is heard* [*Record: Ramblin' by Bunk Johnson*].)
JULIA: Listen, Lula . . . Listen, Mattie . . . it's Jenkin's Colored Orphan Band . . . Play! Play, you Orphan boys! Rise up higher than the dirt around you! Play! That's struttin' music, Lula!
LULA: It sure is! (LULA *struts, arms akimbo, head held high.* JULIA *joins her; they haughtily strut toward each other, then retreat with mock arrogance . . . exchange cold, hostile looks . . . A Carolina folk dance passed on from some dimly-remembered African beginning. Dance ends strutting.*)
JULIA: (*Concedes defeat in the dance.*) All right, Lula, strut me down! Strut me right on down! (*They end dance with breathless laughter and cross to* LULA'S *porch.*)
LULA: Julia! Fasten me! Pin my hair.

JULIA: I'm not goin' to that silly parade, with the colored soldiers marchin' at the end of it. (LULA *sits on the stool.* JULIA *combs and arranges her hair.*)
LULA: Come on, we'll march behind the white folks whether they want us or not. Mister Herman's people got a nice house . . . lemon trees in the yard, lace curtains at the window.
JULIA: And red, white and blue flowers all around.
LULA: That Uncle Greenlee seems to be well-fixed.
JULIA: He works for the livery stable . . . cleans up behind horses . . . in a uniform.
LULA: That's nice.
JULIA: Weeds their gardens . . . clips white people's pet dogs . . .
LULA: Ain't that lovely? I wish Nelson was safe and nicely settled.
JULIA: Uncle Greenlee is a well-fed, tale-carryin' son-of-a-bitch . . . and that's the only kind-a love they want from us.
LULA: It's wrong to hate.
JULIA: They say it's wrong to love too.
LULA: We got to show 'em we're good, got to be three times as good, just to make it.
JULIA: Why? When they mistreat us who cares? We mistreat each other, who cares? Why we gotta be so good jus' for them?
LULA: Dern you, Julia Augustine, you hard-headed thing, 'cause they'll kill us if we not.
JULIA: They doin' it anyway. Last night I dreamed of the dead slaves—all the murdered black and bloody men silently gathered at the foot-a my bed. Oh, that awful silence. I wish the dead could scream and fight back. What they do to us . . . and all they want is to be loved in return. Nelson's not Greenlee. Nelson is a fighter.
LULA: (*Standing.*) I know. But I'm tryin' to keep him from findin' it out. (NELSON, *unseen by* LULA, *listens.*)
JULIA: Your hair looks pretty.
LULA: Thank you. A few years back I got down on my knees in the courthouse to keep him off-a the chain gang. I crawled and cried, "Please white folks, yall's everything, I'se nothin, yall's everything." the court laughed—I meant for 'em to laugh . . . then they let Nelson go.
JULIA: (*Pitying her.*) Oh, Miss Lula, a lady's not supposed to crawl and cry.
LULA: I was savin' his life. Is my skirt fastened? Today might be the last time I ever see Nelson. (NELSON *goes back in house.*) Tell him how life's gon' be better when he gets back. Make up what *should* be true. A man can't fight a war on nothin' . . . would you send a man off—to die on nothin'?
JULIA: That's sin, Miss Lula, leavin' on a lie.
LULA: That's all right—some truth has no nourishment in it. Let him feel good.
JULIA: I'll do my best. (MATTIE *enters carrying a colorful, expensive parasol. It is far beyond the price range of her outfit.*)

MATTIE: October bought it for my birthday 'cause he know I always wanted a fine-quality parasol. (FANNY *enters through the back entry,* CHILDREN *with her. The mistake on the sign has been corrected by pasting* OU *over the error.*)
FANNY: (*Admiring* MATTIE'S *appearance.*) Just shows how the race can look when we wanta. I called Rusty Bennet a dumb darky and he wouldn't even get mad. Wouldn't gimme my money back either. A black Jew. (NELSON *enters wearing his Private's uniform with quartermaster insignia. He salutes them.*)
NELSON: Ladies. Was nice seein' you these few days. If I couldn't help, 'least I didn't do you no harm, so nothin' from nothin' leaves nothin'.
FANNY: (*Holds up her punch cup;* LULA *gives* JULIA *high sign.*) Get one-a them Germans for me.
JULIA: (*Stands on her porch.*) Soon, Nelson, in a little while . . . we'll have whatsoever our hearts desire. You're comin' back in glory . . . with honors and shining medals . . . And those medals and that uniform is gonna open doors for you . . . and for October . . . for all, all of the servicemen. Nelson, on account-a you we're gonna be able to go in the park. They're gonna take down the no-colored signs . . . and Rusty Bennet's gonna print new ones . . . Everybody welcome . . . Everybody welcome . . .
MATTIE: (*To* TEETA.) Hear that? We gon' go in the park.
FANNY: Some of us ain't ready for that.
PRINCESS: Me too?
MATTIE: You can go now . . . and me too if I got you by the hand.
PRINCESS: (*Feeling left out.*) Ohhhhh.
JULIA: We'll go to the band concerts, the museums . . . we'll go in the library and draw out books.
MATTIE: And we'll draw books.
FANNY: Who'll read 'em to you?
MATTIE: My Teeta!
JULIA: Your life'll be safe, you and October'll be heroes.
FANNY: (*Very moved.*) Colored heroes.
JULIA: And at last we'll come into our own. (ALL *cheer and applaud.* JULIA *steps down from porch.*)
NELSON: Julia, can you look me dead in the eye and say you believe all-a that?
JULIA: If you just gotta believe somethin', it may's well be that. (*Applause.*)
NELSON: (*Steps up on* JULIA'S *porch to make his speech.*) Friends, relatives and all other well-wishers. All-a my fine ladies and little ladies—all you goodlookin', tantalizin', pretty-eyed ladies—yeah, with your *kind* ways and your *mean* ways. I find myself a thorn among six lovely roses. Sweet little Teeta . . . the merry little Princess. Mattie, she so pretty 'til October better hurry up and come on back here. Fanny—uh—tryin' to help the race . . . a race woman. And Julia—my good friend. Mama—the only mama I got, I wanta thank you for savin' my life from time to time. What's

hard ain't the goin', it's the comin' back. From the bottom-a my heart, I'd truly like to see y'all, each and every one-a you . . . able to go in the park and all that. I really would. So, with a full heart and a loaded mind, I bid you, as the French say, Adieu.

LULA: (*Bowing graciously, she takes* NELSON'S *arm and they exit.*) Our humble thanks . . . my humble pleasure . . . gratitude . . . thank you . . . (CHILDREN *wave their flags.*)

FANNY: (*To the* CHILDREN.) Let's mind our manners in front-a the downtown white people. Remember we're bein' judged.

PRINCESS: Me too?

MATTIE: (*Opening umbrella.*) Yes, you too.

FANNY: (*Leads the way and counts time.*) Step, step, one, two, step, step. (MATTIE, FANNY *and the* CHILDREN *exit.* HERMAN *enters yard by far gate, takes two long steamer tickets from his pocket.* JULIA *senses him, turns. He is carelessly dressed and sweating.*)

HERMAN: I bought our tickets. Boat tickets to New York.

JULIA: (*Looks at tickets.*) Colored tickets. You can't use yours. (*She lets tickets flutter to the ground.*)

HERMAN: They'll change and give one white ticket. You'll ride one deck, I'll ride the other . . .

JULIA: John C. Calhoun really said a mouthful—men are not born—men are made. Ten years ago—that's when you should-a bought tickets. You chained me to your mother for ten years.

HERMAN: (*Kneeling, picking up tickets.*) Could I walk out on 'em? . . . Ker-ist sake. I'm that kinda man like my father was . . . a debt-payer, a plain, workin' man—

JULIA: He was a member in good standin' of The Gold Carnation. What kinda robes and hoods did those plain men wear? For downin' me and mine. You won twenty dollars in gold.

HERMAN: I love you . . . I love work, to come home in the evenin' . . . to enjoy the breeze for Gawd's sake . . . But no, I never wanted to go to New York. The hell with Goddamn bread factories . . . I'm a stony-broke, half-dead, half-way gentleman . . . But I'm what I wanta be. A baker.

JULIA: You waited 'til you was half-dead to buy those tickets. I don't want to go either . . . Get off the boat, the same faces'll be there at the dock. It's that shop. It's that shop!

HERMAN: It's mine. I did want to keep it.

JULIA: Right . . . people pick what they want most.

HERMAN: (*Indicating the tickets.*) I did . . . you threw it in my face.

JULIA: Get out. Get your things and get out of my life. (*The remarks become counterpoint. Each rides through the other's speech.* HERMAN *goes in house.*) Must be fine to *own* somethin'—even if it's four walls and a sack-a flour.

HERMAN: (JULIA *has followed him into the house.*) My father labored in the street . . . liftin' and layin' down cobblestone . . . liftin' and layin' down stone 'til there was enough money to open a shop . . .

JULIA: My people . . . relatives, friends and strangers . . . they worked and slaved free for nothin' for some-a the biggest name families down here . . . Elliots, Lawrences, Ravenals . . . (HERMAN *is wearily gathering his belongings.*)
HERMAN: Great honor, working for the biggest name families. That's who you slaved for. Not me. The big names.
JULIA: . . . the rich and the poor . . . we know you . . . all of you . . . Who you are . . . where you came from . . . where you goin' . . .
HERMAN: What's my privilege . . . Good mornin', good afternoon . . . pies are ten cents today . . . and you can get 'em from Schumann for eight . . .
JULIA: "She's different" . . . I'm no different . . .
HERMAN: I'm white . . . did it give me favors and friends?
JULIA: . . . "Not like the others" . . . We raised up all-a these Carolina children . . . white and the black . . . I'm just like all the rest of the colored women . . . like Lula, Mattie . . . Yes, like Fanny!
HERMAN: Go here, go there . . . Philadelphia . . . New York . . . Schumann wants me to go North too . . .
JULIA: We nursed you, fed you, buried your dead . . . grinned in your face—cried 'bout your troubles—and laughed 'bout ours.
HERMAN: Schumann . . . Alien robber . . . waitin' to buy me out . . . My father . . .
JULIA: Pickin' up cobblestones . . . left him plenty-a time to wear bedsheets in that Gold Carnation Society . . .
HERMAN: He never hurt anybody.
JULIA: He hurts me. There's no room for you to love him and me too . . . (*Sits.*) it can't be done—
HERMAN: The ignorance . . . he didn't know . . . the ignorance . . . mama . . . they don't know.
JULIA: But *you* know. My father was somebody. He helped put up Roper Hospital and Webster Rice Mills after the earthquake wiped the face-a this Gawd-forsaken city clean . . . a fine brick-mason he was . . . paid him one-third-a what they paid the white ones . . .
HERMAN: We were poor . . . No big name, no quality.
JULIA: Poor! My Gramma was a slave wash-woman bustin' suds for free! Can't get poorer than that.
HERMAN: (*Trying to shut out the sound of her voice.*) Not for me, she didn't!
JULIA: We the ones built the pretty white mansions . . . for free . . . the fishin' boats . . . for free . . . made your clothes, raised your food . . . for free . . . and I loved you—for free.
HERMAN: A Gawd-damn lie . . . nobody did for me . . . you know it . . . you know how hard I worked—
JULIA: If it's anybody's home down here it's mine . . . everything in the city is mine—why should I go anywhere . . . ground I'm standin' on—it's mine.

HERMAN: (*Sitting on foot of the bed.*) It's the ignorance . . . Lemme be, lemme rest . . . Ker-ist sake . . . It's the ignorance . . .
JULIA: After ten years you still won't look. All-a my people that's been killed . . . It's your people that killed 'em . . . all that's been in bondage—your people put 'em there—all that didn't go to school—your people kept 'em out.
HERMAN: But I didn't do it. Did I do it?
JULIA: They killed 'em . . . all the dead slaves . . . buried under a blanket-a this Carolina earth, even the cotton crop is nourished with hearts' blood . . . roots-a that cotton tangled and wrapped 'round my bones.
HERMAN: And you blamin' me for it . . .
JULIA: Yes! . . . For the one thing we never talk about . . . white folks killin' me and mine. You wouldn't let me speak.
HERMAN: I never stopped you . . .
JULIA: Every time I open my mouth 'bout what they do . . . you say . . . "Ker-ist, there it is again . . ." Whenever somebody was lynched . . . you 'n me would eat a very silent supper. It hurt me not to talk . . . what you don't say you swallow down . . . (*Pours wine.*)
HERMAN: I was just glad to close the door 'gainst what's out there. You did all the givin' . . . I failed you in every way.
JULIA: You nursed me when I was sick . . . paid my debts . . .
HERMAN: I didn't give my name.
JULIA: You couldn't . . . was the law . . .
HERMAN: I shoulda walked 'til we came to where it'd be all right.
JULIA: You never put any other woman before me.
HERMAN: Only, Mama, Annabelle, the customers, the law . . . the ignorance . . . I honored them while you waited and waited—
JULIA: You clothed me . . . you fed me . . . you were kind, loving . . .
HERMAN: I never did a damn thing for you. After ten years look at it—I never did a damn thing for you.
JULIA: Don't low-rate yourself . . . leave me something.
HERMAN: When my mother and sister came . . . I was ashamed. What am I doin' bein' ashamed of us?
JULIA: When you first came in this yard I almost died-a shame . . . so many times you was nothin' to me but white . . . times we were angry . . . damn white man . . . times I was tired . . . damn white man . . . but most times you were my husband, my friend, my lover . . .
HERMAN: Whatever is wrong, Julia . . . not the law . . . *me*; what I didn't do, with all-a my faults, spite-a all that . . . You gotta believe I love you . . . 'cause I do . . . That's the one thing I know . . . I love you . . . I love you.
JULIA: Ain't too many people in this world that get to be loved . . . really loved.
HERMAN: We gon' take that boat trip . . . You'll see, you'll never be sorry.
JULIA: To hell with sorry. Let's be glad!

HERMAN: Sweetheart, leave the ignorance outside . . . (*Stretches out across the bed.*) Don't let that doctor in here . . . to stand over me shakin' his head.
JULIA: (*Pours water in a silver cup.*) Bet you never drank from a silver cup. Carolina water is sweet water . . . Wherever you go you gotta come back for a drink-a this water. Sweet water, like the breeze that blows 'cross the battery.
HERMAN: (*Happily weary.*) I'm gettin' old, that ain' no joke.
JULIA: No, you're not. Herman, my real weddin' cake . . . I wanta big one . . .
HERMAN: Gonna bake it in a wash-tub . . .
JULIA: We'll put pieces of it in little boxes for folks to take home and dream on.
HERMAN: . . . But let's don't give none to your landlady . . . Gon' get old and funny-lookin' like Robbie m'boy and . . . and . . .
JULIA: And Mable . . .
HERMAN: (*Breathing heavier.*) Robbie says "Mable, where's my keys" . . . Mable— Robbie— Mable—(*Lights change, shadows grow longer.* MATTIE *enters the yard.*)
MATTIE: Hey, Julia! (*Sound of carriage wheels in front of the main house.* MATTIE *enters* JULIA'S *house. As she sees* HERMAN.) They 'round there, they come to get him, Julia. (JULIA *takes the wedding band and chain from around her neck, gives it to* MATTIE *with tickets.*)
JULIA: Surprise. Present.
MATTIE: For me?
JULIA: Northern tickets . . . and a wedding band.
MATTIE: I can't take that for nothing.
JULIA: You and Teeta are my people.
MATTIE: Yes.
JULIA: You and Teeta are my family. Be my family.
MATTIE: We your people whether we blood kin or not. (MATTIE *exits to her own porch.*)
FANNY: (*Offstage.*) No . . . No, Ma'am. (*Enters with* LULA. LULA *is carrying the wilted bouquet.*) Julia! They think Mr. Herman's come back. (HERMAN'S MOTHER *enters with* ANNABELLE. *The old lady is weary and subdued.* ANNABELLE *is almost without feeling.* JULIA *is on her porch waiting.*)
JULIA: Yes, Fanny, he's here. (LULA *retires to her doorway.* JULIA *silently stares at them, studying each* WOMAN, *seeing them with new eyes. She is going through that rising process wherein she must reject them as the molders and dictators of her life.*) Nobody comes in my house.
FANNY: What kind-a way is that?
JULIA: Nobody comes in my house.
ANNABELLE: We'll quietly take him home.
JULIA: You can't come in.

HERMAN'S MOTHER: (*Low-keyed, polite and humble simplicity.*) You see my condition. Gawd's punishin' me . . . Whippin' me for somethin' I did or didn't do. I can't understand this . . . I prayed, but ain't no understandin' Herman's dyin'. He's almost gone. It's right and proper that he should die at home in his own bed. I'm askin' humbly . . . or else I'm forced to get help from the police.

ANNABELLE: Give her a chance . . . She'll do right . . . won'tcha? (HERMAN *stirs. His breathing becomes harsh and deepens into the sound known as the "death rattle."* MATTIE *leads the* CHILDREN *away.*)

JULIA: (*Not unkindly.*) Do whatever you have to do. Win the war. Represent the race. Call the police. (*She enters her house, closes the door and bolts it.* HERMAN'S MOTHER *leaves through the front entry.* FANNY *slowly follows her.*) I'm here, do you hear me? (*He tries to answer but can't.*) We're standin' on the deck-a that Clyde Line Boat . . . wavin' to the people on the shore . . . Your mama, Annabelle, my Aunt Cora . . . all of our friends . . . the children . . . all wavin' . . . "Don't stay 'way too long . . . Be sure and come back . . . We gon' miss you . . . Come back, we need you" . . . But we're goin' . . . The whistle's blowin', flags wavin' . . . We're takin' off, ridin' the waves so smooth and easy . . . There now . . . (ANNABELLE *moves closer to the house as she listens to* JULIA.) . . . the bakery's fine . . . all the orders are ready . . . out to sea . . . on our way . . . (*The weight has lifted, she is radiantly happy. She helps him gasp out each remaining breath. With each gasp he seems to draw a step nearer to a wonderful goal.*) Yes . . . Yes . . . Yes . . . Yes . . . Yes . . . Yes . . .

CURTAIN

END OF PLAY

What the Butler Saw

Joe Orton

Within the space of an all too brief four year period between the acceptance of his first play for publication in 1963 and the year that he was murdered by his mentally unstable lover in 1967, Joe Orton produced a small but influential body of work which includes, *The Ruffian on the Stairs, Entertaining Mr. Sloane, The Good and Faithful Servant, Loot, The Erpingham Camp, Funeral Games,* and *What the Butler Saw.* Given the quality of his output, Orton showed enormous promise as a playwright and social provocateur. Without a doubt, the theatre world lost a very gifted comic writer when he died.

Toward the end of his life the Beetles sought out Orton to write a film script in which they might star. The project may well have been realized if their manager had not been scandalized by Orton's damaging portrayal of "the boys" in his preliminary draft. After his death Orton's own life was the subject of a major motion picture entitled, "Prick Up Your Ears," based on John Lahr's biography of the same name.

What the Butler Saw was Orton's final and certainly his most important work. It appeared in London's West End to mixed critical reviews principally because the moral values of all its characters shocked the conservative sensibilities of the day. Critics were not accustomed to Orton's iconoclastic portrayal of British society. Not since the English Restoration in 1660 had an English playwright so boldly set out to ruffle the feathers of audiences by clinically addressing their pretensions.

Orton was among the first openly gay playwrights in the western world. His concern for cross-gender issues, the excesses of psychology, and the interference of government in the functioning of social institutions, are positively modern in tone. *What the Butler Saw* is distinguished for its brittle language and wit, its vividly drawn characters, and its carefully crafted dramatic action which gallops along at a breathtaking pace, concluding with a surprising deus ex machina reminiscent of those in some classical comedies of ancient Greece, Rome and neo-classical France. In many ways the play is unrivaled as a farce in any period perhaps explaining why it is still popularly produced today throughout the English speaking world.

Production History

The first London production of *What the Butler Saw* was given at the Queen's Theatre by Lewenstein-Delfont Productions Ltd. and H.M. Tennent Ltd. on 5 March 1969. It was directed by Robert Chetwyn and designed by Hutchinson Scott. The cast, in order of appearance, was as follows:

Dr. Prentice	Stanley Baxter
Geraldine Barclay	Julia Foster
Mrs. Prentice	Coral Browne
Nicholas Beckett	Hayward Morse
Dr. Rance	Ralph Richardson
Sergeant Match	Peter Bayliss

What the Butler Saw opened officially in New York City on Monday, May 4, 1970, at the McAlpin Rooftop Theater, McAlpin Hotel, after 8 previews. It was produced by Charles Woodward and Michael Kasdan by arrangement with Lewenstein-Delfont Productions Ltd. and H.M. Tennent Ltd. It was directed by Joseph Hardy. The production was designed by William Ritman with costumes by Ann Roth. The cast, in order of appearance, was as follows:

Dr. Prentice	Laurence Luckinbill
Geraldine Barclay	Diana Davila
Mrs. Prentice	Jan Farrand
Nicholas Beckett	Charles Murphy
Dr. Rance	Lucian Scott
Sergeant Match	Tom Rosqui

Place

The consulting room of an exclusive, private psychiatric clinic.

Time

A spring day.

Characters

DR. PRENTICE
GERALDINE BARCLAY
MRS. PRENTICE
NICHOLAS BECKETT
DR. RANCE
SERGEANT MATCH

What the Butler Saw by Joe Orton

From The Complete Plays of Joe Orton. Copyright © 1969, 1976 by Estate of Joe Orton. Used by permission of Grove/Atlantic, Inc.

THE PLAY

WHAT THE BUTLER SAW

ACT ONE

The consulting room of an exclusive, private psychiatric clinic. A spring day. Doors lead to main hall U. R., *the wards and dispensary* D. R. *Double doors* U. L. *lead to a hall and the garden off stage. Open closet with hangers and hooks* D. L. *above proscenium and just off stage. Desk, chairs, consulting couch upstage with curtains.*

DR. PRENTICE *enters briskly from the hall.* GERALDINE BARCLAY *follows him.*

PRENTICE: Take a seat. Is this your first job?
GERALDINE: Yes, Doctor.
PRENTICE: (*Puts on a pair of spectacles, stares at her. He opens a drawer in the desk, takes out a notebook. Picking up a pencil.*) I'm going to ask you a few questions. (*He hands her a notebook and pencil.*) Write them down. In English, please. (*He returns to his desk, sits, smiles.*) Who was your father? Put that at the head of the page. (GERALDINE *crosses her legs, rests the notebook upon her knee and makes a note.*) And now the reply immediately underneath for quick reference.
GERALDINE: I've no idea who my father was.
PRENTICE: (*Is perturbed by her reply although he gives no evidence of this. He gives her a kindly smile.*) I'd better be frank, Miss Barclay. I can't employ you if you're in any way miraculous. It would be contrary to established practice. You did have a father?
GERALDINE: Oh, I'm sure I did. My mother was frugal in her habits, but she'd never economize unwisely.
PRENTICE: If you had a father why can't you produce him?
GERALDINE: He deserted my mother. Many years ago. She was the victim of an unpleasant attack.
PRENTICE: (*Shrewdly.*) She was a nun?
GERALDINE: No. She was a chambermaid at the Station Hotel.

PRENTICE: (*Frowns, takes off his spectacles and pinches the bridge of his nose.*) Pass that large, leather-bound volume, will you? I must check your story. To safeguard my interests, you understand? (GERALDINE *lifts the book from the bookcase and takes it to* DR. PRENTICE. *Consulting the index.*) The Station Hotel? (*Opening the book, running his finger down the page.*) Ah, here we are! It's a building of small architectural merit built for some unknown purpose at the turn of the century. It was converted into a hotel by public subscription. (*Nods, wisely.*) I stayed there once myself as a young man. It has a reputation for luxury which baffles the most undemanding guest. (*Closes the book with a bang and pushes it to one side.*) Your story appears, in the main, to be correct. This admirable volume, of course, omits most of the details. But that is only to be expected in a publication of wide general usage. (*Puts on his spectacles.*) Make a note to the effect that your father is missing. Say nothing of the circumstances. It might influence my final decision. (GERALDINE *makes a jotting in her notebook.* DR. PRENTICE *takes the leather-bound volume to the bookcase.*) Is your mother alive? Or has she too unaccountably vanished? That is a trick question. Be careful—you could lose marks on your final scoring.
GERALDINE: I haven't seen my mother for many years. I was brought up by a Mrs. Barclay. She died recently.
PRENTICE: I'm so sorry. From what cause?
GERALDINE: An explosion, due to a faulty gas-main, killed her outright and took the roof off the house.
PRENTICE: Have you applied for compensation?
GERALDINE: Just for the roof.
PRENTICE: Were there no other victims of the disaster?
GERALDINE: Yes. A recently erected statue of Sir Winston Churchill was so badly injured that the special medal has been talked of. Parts of the great man were actually found embedded in my stepmother.
PRENTICE: Which parts?
GERALDINE: I'm afraid I can't help you there. I was too upset to supervise the funeral arrangements. Or, indeed, to identify the body.
PRENTICE: Surely the Churchill family did that?
GERALDINE: Yes. They were most kind.
PRENTICE: You've had a unique experience. It's not everyone who has their stepmother assassinated by a public utility. (*Shakes his head, sharing the poor girl's sorrow.*) Can I get you an aspirin?
GERALDINE: No, thank you, sir. I don't want to start taking drugs.
PRENTICE: Your caution does you credit, my dear. (*Smiles in a kindly fashion.*) Now, I have to ask a question which may cause you embarrassment. Please remember that I'm a doctor. (*Pause.*) What is your shorthand speed?
GERALDINE: I can manage twenty words a minute with ease, sir.
PRENTICE: And your typing speed?
GERALDINE: I haven't mastered the keyboard. My money ran out, you see.

PRENTICE: (*Takes the notebook and puts it aside.*) Perhaps you have other qualities which aren't immediately apparent. (*Pulls aside the curtains on the couch.*) Kindly remove your stockings. I wish to see what effect your stepmother's death had upon your legs.
GERALDINE: Isn't this rather unusual, Doctor?
PRENTICE: Have no fear, Miss Barclay. What I see before me isn't a lovely and desirable girl. It's a sick mind in need of psychiatric treatment. The body is of no interest to a medical man. A woman once threw herself at me. I needn't tell you that this is spoken in confidence. She was stark naked. She wished me to misbehave myself. And, d'you know, all I was conscious of was that she had a malformed navel? That's how much notice I take of women's bodies.
GERALDINE: Please forgive me, Doctor. I wasn't meaning to suggest that your attentions were in any way improper. (*Takes off her shoes and stockings.* DR. PRENTICE *runs a hand along her legs and nods, sagely.*)
PRENTICE: As I thought. You've a febrile condition of the calves. You're quite wise to have a check-up. (*Straightens and takes off his spectacles.*) Undress. (*Turns to the desk and takes off his coat.*)
GERALDINE: I've never undressed in front of a man before.
PRENTICE: I shall take account of your inexperience in these matters. (*Puts his spectacles on the desk and rolls back his cuffs.*)
GERALDINE: I couldn't allow a man to touch me while I was unclothed.
PRENTICE: I shall wear rubber gloves, Miss Barclay.
GERALDINE: (*Is worried and makes no attempt to conceal her growing doubts.*) How long would I have to remain undressed?
PRENTICE: If your reactions are normal you'll be back on your feet in next to no time.
GERALDINE: I'd like another woman present. Is your wife available?
PRENTICE: Mrs. Prentice is attending a more than usually lengthy meeting of her coven. She won't be back until this evening.
GERALDINE: I could wait until then.
PRENTICE: I haven't the patience, my dear. I've a natural tendency to rush things . . . something my wife has never understood. But I won't trouble you with the details of my private life till you're dressed. Put your clothes on this. Lie on that couch.

(GERALDINE *unzips and removes her dress and shoes.* DR. PRENTICE *puts dress on hanger and hangs it in* D. L. *closet. Puts shoes on closet floor.*)

GERALDINE: What is Mrs. Prentice like, Doctor? I've heard so many stories about her. (*Stands in her panties and bra.*)
PRENTICE: My wife is a nymphomaniac. Consequently, like the Holy Grail, she's ardently sought after by young men. I married her for her money and, upon discovering her to be penniless, I attempted to throttle her . . . a mental aberration for which I've never forgiven myself. Needless to say, our relationship has been delicate ever since.

GERALDINE: (*With a sigh.*) Poor Dr. Prentice. How trying it must be for you. (*Climbing on to the couch.*) I wish there were something I could do to cheer you up. (*Closes the curtains.*)
PRENTICE: (*Puts on a white surgical coat.*) Well, my dear, if it'll give you any pleasure you can test my new contraceptive device.
GERALDINE: (*Looks through the curtain and smiles sweetly.*) I'll be delighted to help you in any way I can, Doctor.
PRENTICE: (*With an indulgent, superior smile.*) Lie on the couch with your hands behind your head and think of the closing chapters of your favorite work of fiction. The rest may be left to me.

(GERALDINE *disappears behind the curtain.* DR. PRENTICE *goes to the drawer in his desk. Starts to unzip his trousers.* MRS. PRENTICE *enters from the hall. She is wearing a coat.*)

MRS. PRENTICE: Who are you talking to?
PRENTICE: (*Is surprised and angry at his wife's unexpected appearance. Flushing, guilty.*) I must ask you not to enter my consulting room without warning. You're interrupting my studies.
MRS. PRENTICE: (*Stares about the room.*) Well, who were you talking to? There's no one here. Have you taken up talking to yourself?
PRENTICE: I was dictating a memo to the head nurse. She's worried about her inability to control her bladder.
MRS. PRENTICE: Can urine be controlled by thinking of one's favorite work of fiction? Hers is *Tess of the d'Urbervilles*, you know?
PRENTICE: Whose?
MRS. PRENTICE: The head nurse.
PRENTICE: My theory is still in the planning stages. I'd rather not discuss it. Why have you returned so soon?

(DR. PRENTICE *turns his back and zips up his trousers.*)

MRS. PRENTICE: I arrived at my meeting to find the hall in an uproar. Helen Duncanon had declared herself to be in love with a man. And, as you know, the coven is primarily for Lesbians. I myself am exempt from the rule because you count as a woman. We expelled Helen and by that time it was so late that I spent the night at the Station Hotel. It's so difficult being a woman.
PRENTICE: Well, I'm sure you're the best judge of that. (*A BUZZER sounds from the wards.*) It's an emergency in Ward B. They need me in Ward B. I trust you'll have left by the time I return. (*He goes.*)
MRS. PRENTICE: You can come in now. (NICHOLAS BECKETT *enters. He is a hotel page and wears a page boy's uniform.*) I'm not asking for my handbag back, or for the money you've stolen, but unless my dress is returned I shall file a complaint with your employer. You have until lunchtime.

NICK: I've already sold the dress for a lump sum. I could get it back at a price. I've also found someone to take an option on the photographs.
MRS. PRENTICE: (*Stares.*) What photographs?
NICK: I had a camera concealed in the room.
MRS. PRENTICE: When I gave myself to you the contract didn't include cinematic rights.
NICK: I'd like a hundred for the negatives. You've got until lunchtime.
MRS. PRENTICE: I shall complain to the manager.
NICK: It will do you no good. He took the photographs.
MRS. PRENTICE: Oh, this is scandalous! I'm a married woman.
NICK: You didn't behave like a married woman last night.
MRS. PRENTICE: I was upset. A Lesbian friend of mine had just announced her engagement to a Member of Parliament.
NICK: You must be more careful in your choice of friends. Look, I could reconsider. I'd like to get out of the indecent photograph racket. It's so wearing on the nerves. Can you find me a worthwhile job? I had a hard boyhood.
MRS. PRENTICE: What kind of job do you want?
NICK: I'm an expert typist. I was taught by a man in the printing trade.
MRS. PRENTICE: (*Firmly.*) I'm willing to pay for the photographs, but I can't possibly recommend your typing.
NICK: I want a hundred for the negatives and the job of secretary to your husband!
MRS. PRENTICE: You put me in an impossible position.
NICK: No position is impossible when you're young and healthy.
PRENTICE: (*Enters.*) Who is he?
MRS. PRENTICE: I neglected to mention that having lost my handbag at the Station Hotel this young man was kind enough to drive me home on his motor bike.
PRENTICE: I see. Drinking so early? You'll be sodden before lunch.
NICK: Have you a family, sir?
PRENTICE: No. My wife said breast-feeding would spoil her shape. Though, from what I remember, it would've been improved by a little nibbling. She's an example of in-breeding among the lobelia-growing classes. A failure in eugenics, combined with a taste for alcohol and sexual intercourse, makes it most undesirable for her to become a mother.
MRS. PRENTICE: (*Quietly.*) I hardly ever have sexual intercourse.
PRENTICE: You were born with your legs apart. They'll send you to the grave in a Y-shaped coffin.
MRS. PRENTICE: (*With a brittle laugh.*) My trouble stems from your inadequacy as a lover! That's the reason for my never having an orgasm.
PRENTICE: How dare you say that! Your book on the climax in the female is largely autobiographical. (*Pause. He stares.*) Or have you been masquerading as a sexually responsive woman?

MRS. PRENTICE: My uterine contractions have been bogus for some time! (*She exits into hall.* NICK *follows her out.*)
PRENTICE: (*Looking after her.*) What a discovery! Married to a mistress of the fraudulent climax. It's no good. . . . It's no good lying there, Miss Barclay. My wife has returned.
GERALDINE: Will she be able to help with your examination?
PRENTICE: The examination is canceled until further notice. Get dressed!
MRS. PRENTICE: (*Re-entering.*) Has your new secretary arrived?
PRENTICE: (*Holds the underwear behind his back.* GERALDINE *is concealed by the curtain.*) Yes. I've got her particulars somewhere. (*Unable to conceal the underclothes behind his back, he drops them into a wastepaper basket.*)
MRS. PRENTICE: Have you ever given thought to a male secretary?
PRENTICE: A man could never get used to the work.
MRS. PRENTICE: My father had a male secretary. My mother said he was much better than a woman.
PRENTICE: I couldn't ask a young fellow to do overtime and then palm him off with a lipstick or a bottle of Yardley's. It'd be silk suits and Alfa Romeos if I so much as breathed on him.
MRS. PRENTICE: Try a boy for a change. You're a rich man. You can afford the luxuries of life.
PRENTICE: I can't possibly. I've already given Miss Barclay a preliminary interview. (*Takes* GERALDINE'S *dress from the closet and tries to sneak it over the top of the curtains.*)
MRS. PRENTICE: (*Turns and sees him with the dress.*) You must explain . . . (*In a surprised tone.*) What are you doing with that dress?
PRENTICE: (*Pause.*) It's an old one of yours.
MRS. PRENTICE: Have you taken up transvestism? I'd no idea our marriage teetered on the edge of fashion.
PRENTICE: Our marriage is like the peace of God—it passeth all understanding.
MRS. PRENTICE: Give me the dress. I need it.
PRENTICE: (*Reluctant.*) May I have the one you're wearing in exchange?
MRS. PRENTICE: I'm not wearing a dress. (*Slips off her coat. Under it she is dressed only in a slip.*)
PRENTICE: (*Cannot conceal his surprise.*) Why aren't you wearing a dress?
MRS. PRENTICE: (*Putting on* GERALDINE'S *dress.*) I'll tell you frankly and with complete candor. Please listen carefully and save your comments for later. (*Zips up the dress.*) My room at the hotel was small, airless and uncomfortable. A model of its kind. When I turned down the bed I noticed that the sheets were none too clean. I went to the linen closet, which I knew to be on the second floor, hoping to find a chambermaid. Instead I found a page boy, the one in fact who was just here. He enticed me into the closet and then made an indecent suggestion. When I repulsed him he attempted to rape me. I fought him off but not before he'd stolen my handbag and dress.

PRENTICE: It doesn't sound like the kind of behavior one expects at a four-star hotel.
MRS. PRENTICE: The boy has promised to return my dress. He's sold it to a friend who probably intends using it at sex orgies.
PRENTICE: Do you realize what would happen if your adventures became public? I'd be ruined. The doors of society would be slammed in my face. Did you inform the authorities of this escapade?
MRS. PRENTICE: No.
PRENTICE: Why not?
MRS. PRENTICE: I saw in the boy a natural goodness that had all but been destroyed by the pressures of society. I promised to find him employment.
PRENTICE: What qualifications has he got?
MRS. PRENTICE: He can type.
PRENTICE: There aren't many jobs for male typists.
MRS. PRENTICE: Exactly. He's been depressed by his failure in business. That's why he took to rape.
PRENTICE: How do you hope to employ him? Is there a market for illegal entrance?
MRS. PRENTICE: I don't propose to lead him into a dead-end job. I want you to hire him as your secretary. He'll be back soon. You can check his credentials at your leisure. Where is Miss Barclay?
PRENTICE: She's upstairs.
MRS. PRENTICE: I shall inform her that the position is no longer vacant.
PRENTICE: Could I borrow one of your dresses for a while, my dear?
MRS. PRENTICE: I find your sudden craving for women's clothing a dull and, on the whole, a rather distasteful subject. (*Exits into the garden.*)
PRENTICE: Miss Barclay—the situation is fraught—my wife is under the impression that your dress belongs to her.
GERALDINE: (*Looks through the curtain.*) Can't we explain, as tactfully as possible, that she has made a mistake?
PRENTICE: I'm afraid that is impossible. You must be patient for a little longer.
GERALDINE: Doctor—I'm naked! You do realize that, don't you?
PRENTICE: Indeed I do, Miss Barclay. I'm sure it must cause you acute embarrassment. I'll set about finding you suitable clothing.

> (*He turns to the wastepaper basket, and is about to remove the underclothing when* DR. RANCE *enters from the hall.* DR. PRENTICE *drops the clothing into the basket and puts the basket down.* GERALDINE *ducks behind the curtain out of sight.*)

RANCE: Good morning. Are you Dr. Prentice?
PRENTICE: Yes. Do you have an appointment?
RANCE: No. I never make appointments. I represent our government, your immediate superiors in madness.

PRENTICE: Which branch?
RANCE: The mental branch.
PRENTICE: Do you cover asylums proper or just houses of tentative madness?
RANCE: My authority is unlimited. I have the power to close your clinic on a moment's notice should I find it necessary. I'd even have sway over a rabbit hutch if the inmates were mentally disturbed.
PRENTICE: You're obviously a force to be reckoned with.
RANCE: Indeed I am, but I hope our relationship will be a pleasant one. I'd like to be given full details of your clinic. It's run, I understand, with the full knowledge and permission of the local hospital authorities. (*He looks behind the curtains.*) You specialize in the complete breakdown and its by-products?
PRENTICE: Yes, but it's highly confidential. My files are never open to strangers.
RANCE: You may speak freely in front of me, Prentice. Remember I represent the government. Now, is this your consulting room?
PRENTICE: Yes.
RANCE: What's down this corridor?
PRENTICE: The first door on the right is the dispensary and the doors at the end of the hall lead to the wards.
RANCE: Is your couch regulation size? It looks big enough for two.
PRENTICE: I do double consultations. Toddlers are often terrified of a doctor. So I've taken to examining their mothers at the same time.
RANCE: Has the theory received much publicity?
PRENTICE: I don't approve of scientists who publicize their theories.
RANCE: I must say I agree with you. I wish more scientists would keep their ideas to themselves. (*A piece of paper flutters from under the curtain. Picking up the paper.*) Is this something to do with you?
PRENTICE: It's a prescription, sir.
RANCE: (*Reading.*) "Keep your head down and don't make a sound?" (*Pause.*) Do you find your patients react favorably to such treatment?
PRENTICE: I can claim to have had some success with it.
RANCE: Your ideas, I think, are in advance of the times. Why is there a naked woman behind there?
PRENTICE: She's a patient, sir. I'd just managed to calm her down when you arrived.
RANCE: You were attacked by a naked woman?
PRENTICE: Yes.
RANCE: Well, Prentice, I don't know whether to applaud your daring or envy you your luck. I'd like to question her.
PRENTICE: (*Goes to the curtains.*) Miss Barclay, a gentleman wishes to speak to you.
GERALDINE: (*Looking through the curtain.*) I can't meet anyone without my clothes on, Doctor.

PRENTICE: (*Coolly, to* DR. RANCE.) Notice the obstinacy with which she clings to her suburban upbringing.
RANCE: Have you tried shock treatment?
PRENTICE: No.
RANCE: How long has she been a patient?
PRENTICE: The committal order hasn't yet been signed.
RANCE: Fill it out. I'll sign it.
PRENTICE: That's not my usual procedure, sir, to certify someone before examining them.
RANCE: The government requires certification before examination. Young woman, why did you take your clothes off? Did it never occur to you that your psychiatrist might be embarrassed by your behavior?
GERALDINE: I'm not a patient. I'm from the Friendly Faces Employment Bureau.
RANCE: (*Over his shoulder to* DR. PRENTICE.) When did these delusions first manifest themselves?
PRENTICE: (*Returning with a document.*) I've been aware of them for some time, sir.
RANCE: (*To* GERALDINE.) Do you imagine that any businessman would tolerate a naked typist in his office?
GERALDINE: (*Smiles and, in a reasonable manner, attempts to explain.*) Dr. Prentice asked me to undress in order that he might discover my fitness for the tasks ahead. There was no suggestion of my working permanently without clothing.
RANCE: (*To* DR. PRENTICE.) I shall take charge of this case. It appears to have all the bizarre qualities that make for a fascinating thesis. (*Signs the document.*) Make the necessary entry in your register and alert your staff of my requirements. (DR. PRENTICE *tears the document in half as he exits to the dispensary.* DR. RANCE *turns to* GERALDINE.) Young lady, is there a history of mental illness in your family?
GERALDINE: (*Primly.*) I find your questions irrelevant. I refuse to answer them.
RANCE: I've just certified you insane. You know that, don't you?
GERALDINE: What right have you to take such high-handed action?
RANCE: Every right. You've had a nervous breakdown.
GERALDINE: I'm quite sane!
RANCE: Pull yourself together. Why have you been certified if you're sane? Even for a madwoman she's unusually dense. (DR. PRENTICE *enters from the dispensary, wheeling a hospital trolley. On it are a rubber mattress, a pillow and a sheet. Over his arm,* DR. PRENTICE *carries a white hospital nightgown.* DR. RANCE *takes this from him. He throws it over the curtain to* GERALDINE.) Put that on!
GERALDINE: (*To* DR. RANCE.) Oh, thank you. It will be a great relief to be clothed again.

RANCE: (*Draws* DR. PRENTICE *aside.* GERALDINE *puts on the nightgown.*) What is the background of this case? Has the patient any family?
PRENTICE: No, sir. Her stepmother died recently after a remarkably intimate involvement with Sir Winston Churchill.
RANCE: What of the father?
PRENTICE: He appears to have been an unpleasant fellow. He made her mother pregnant at her place of employment.
RANCE: Was there any reason for such conduct?
PRENTICE: The patient is reticent on the subject.
RANCE: I find that strange. And very revealing. Prepare a sedative.
GERALDINE: Please call a taxi, sir. I wish to return home. I haven't the qualities required for this job.
RANCE: Lie on that trolley. You're slowing down your recovery rate, Miss Barclay.

(DR. PRENTICE *forces* GERALDINE *to take a pill and he lifts her onto the trolley. He covers her with the sheet. She gasps and bursts into tears.*)

GERALDINE: This is intolerable! You're a disgrace to your profession! I shall ring the medical association after lunch.
RANCE: Accept your condition without tears and without abusing those placed in authority.
GERALDINE: Am I mad, Doctor?
PRENTICE: No.
GERALDINE: Are you mad?
PRENTICE: No.
GERALDINE: Is this "Candid Camera"?
PRENTICE: There is a perfectly rational explanation for what has taken place. Keep calm. All will be well.

(MRS. PRENTICE *enters from the garden.*)

MRS. PRENTICE: (*Anxious.*) Miss Barclay is nowhere to be found.
RANCE: She's under strong sedation and on no account to be disturbed.
PRENTICE: (*Nervous, gives a fleeting smile in* DR. RANCE'S *direction.*) My wife is talking of my secretary, sir. She's been missing since this morning.
GERALDINE: I'm Geraldine Barclay. Looking for part-time secretarial work. I've been certified insane.
RANCE: (*To* MRS. PRENTICE.) Ignore these random reflections, Mrs. Prentice. They're an essential factor in the patient's condition. (*To* DR. PRENTICE.) Does she have the same name as your secretary?
PRENTICE: She's taken my secretary's name as her "nom-de-folie." Although morally reprehensible, there's little we can do legally, I'm afraid.

RANCE: (*Drying his hands.*) It seems a trifle capricious, but the insane are famous for their wild ways.

MRS. PRENTICE: I shall contact the employment agency. Miss Barclay can't have vanished into thin air. (*Goes into the hall.*)

PRENTICE: My wife is unfamiliar with the habits of young women, sir. I've known many who could vanish into thin air. And some who took a delight in doing so.

RANCE: In my experience young women vanish only at midnight and after a heavy meal. Were your relations with your secretary normal?

PRENTICE: Yes.

RANCE: Well, Prentice, your private life is your own affair. I find it shocking nonetheless. Did the patient know of your liaison with Miss Barclay?

PRENTICE: She may have.

RANCE: I see. A definite pattern is beginning to emerge. (*Returns to the trolley and stands looking down at* GERALDINE. *Takes a white coat from* DR. PRENTICE.) Under the influence of the drug you've just—oh, thank you—administered to Miss Barclay, she will be relaxed and unafraid. I'm going to ask you some questions which I want answered in a clear non-technical style. (*To* DR. PRENTICE.) She'll take that as an invitation to use bad language. (*To* GERALDINE.) Who was the first man in your life?

GERALDINE: My father.

RANCE: Did he assault you?

GERALDINE: No!

RANCE: (*To* DR. PRENTICE.) She may mean "Yes" when she says "No." It's elementary feminine psychology. (*To* GERALDINE.) Was your mother aware of your love for your father?

GERALDINE: I lived in a normal family. I had no love for my father.

RANCE: (*To* DR. PRENTICE.) I'd take a bet that she was the victim of an incestuous attack. She clearly associates violence and the sexual act. Her attempt, when naked, to provoke you to erotic response may have deeper significance. (*To* GERALDINE.) Did your father have any religious beliefs?

GERALDINE: I'm sure he did.

RANCE: (*To* DR. PRENTICE.) Yet she claims to have lived in a normal family. The depth of her condition can be measured from such a statement. (*To* GERALDINE.) Did your father's church sanction rape? (*To* DR. PRENTICE.) Some religions will turn a blind eye to anything as long as it's kept within the family circle. (*To* GERALDINE.) Was there a church service before you were assaulted?

GERALDINE: I can't answer these questions, sir. They seem pointless and disgusting.

RANCE: I'm interested in rape, Miss Barclay, not the aesthetics of cross-examination. Answer me, please! Were you molested by your father?

GERALDINE: (*With a scream of horror.*) No, no, no!

RANCE: The vehemence of her denials is proof positive of guilt. It's a textbook case!
PRENTICE: It's fascinating, sir, and the questions are cleverly put together. Do they tie in with known facts?
RANCE: That need not cause us undue anxiety. Civilizations have been founded and maintained on theories which refused to obey facts. As far as I'm concerned this child was unnaturally assaulted by her own father. I shall base my future actions upon that assumption.
PRENTICE: Perhaps there's a simpler explanation for the apparent complexities of the case, sir.
RANCE: Simple explanations are for simple minds. I've no use for either. I shall supervise the cutting of the patient's hair. (*Wheels* GERALDINE *into the wards.*)

(DR. PRENTICE'S *glance falls on to the wastepaper basket. He shakes out* GERALDINE'S *underclothes, takes her shoes from the closet.* MRS. PRENTICE *enters from the hall.* DR. PRENTICE *swings round, turns his back on her and walks away, bent double in an effort to conceal the clothing and shoes.*)

MRS. PRENTICE: The young man is here.
PRENTICE: Ohhhh.
MRS. PRENTICE: (*Alarmed by his strange conduct.*) What's the matter? (*She approaches.*) Are you in pain?
PRENTICE: (*His back to her, strangled.*) Yes. Get me a glass of water.

(MRS. PRENTICE *hurries into the dispensary.* DR. PRENTICE *stares about him in desperation. He sees a tall vase of roses. He removes the roses and stuffs the underclothing and one shoe into the vase. The second shoe won't go in. He pauses, perplexed. He is about to replace the roses when* MRS. PRENTICE *enters carrying a glass of water.* DR. PRENTICE *conceals the shoe under his coat.* MRS. PRENTICE *stares. He is holding the roses. He gives a feeble smile and presents them to her with a flourish.* MRS. PRENTICE *is surprised and angry.*)

MRS. PRENTICE: Here you are. Put them back at once!
PRENTICE: Ohhhh. (*The shoe slips and* DR. PRENTICE, *in an effort to retain it, doubles up.*)
MRS. PRENTICE: Should I call a doctor?
PRENTICE: No. I'll be all right.
MRS. PRENTICE: (*Offering him the glass.*) Here. Drink this.
PRENTICE: (*Backs away, still holding the roses and the shoe.*) I wonder if you'd get another glass? That one is quite the wrong shape.
MRS. PRENTICE: (*Puzzled.*) The wrong shape?
PRENTICE: Yes, the wrong shape.

(MRS. PRENTICE *stares hard at him, then goes into the dispensary.* DR. PRENTICE *tries to replace the roses in the vase. They won't go in. He picks up a pair of scissors from his desk and cuts the stalks down to within an inch or so of the heads. He puts the roses into the vase. He looks for somewhere to conceal the second shoe. He shoves it between the space on top of the books on the lower shelf of the bookcase. He sees the stalks on the floor and kneels down to clean them up.* MRS. PRENTICE *enters carrying another glass. She stops and stares.*)

MRS. PRENTICE: What are you doing now?
PRENTICE: (*Lifting his hands.*) Praying.
MRS. PRENTICE: This puerile behavior ill accords with your high academic standards. Here, drink this. The young man I wish you to engage as your secretary has arrived.
PRENTICE: Perhaps he'd call back later. I'm not up to seeing anyone just now.
MRS. PRENTICE: I'll see what he says. He's an impatient young man.
PRENTICE: Is that why he took to rape?

(*She hurries away into the hall.* DR. RANCE *enters from the ward.*)

RANCE: You'll have no trouble recognizing the patient, Prentice. I've clipped her hair within an inch of the scalp.
PRENTICE: (*Shocked.*) Was it quite wise to do that, sir? Is it in accord with the present enlightened approach to the mentally sick?
RANCE: Perfectly in accord. As a matter of fact I've published a monograph on the subject. I wrote it while studying at the psychic institute. My tutor advised it. A remarkable man. Having failed to achieve madness himself, he took to teaching it to others.
PRENTICE: And you were his prize pupil?
RANCE: There were some more able than I.
PRENTICE: Where are they now?
RANCE: In mental institutions.
PRENTICE: Running them?
RANCE: For the most part.

(MRS. PRENTICE *enters from the hall.*)

MRS. PRENTICE: (*To* DR. PRENTICE.) The young man insists upon punctuality. He'll give you five minutes.
PRENTICE: A prospective employee, sir. I'm afraid you must excuse me. He'll give me five minutes.
RANCE: Very well.
PRENTICE: It's useless to claim that Socialism has had no effect.
RANCE: Mrs. Prentice, is there no news of Miss Barclay?
MRS. PRENTICE: None. She's still missing. I've checked with the Employ-

ment Bureau. Their clients have strict instructions to call them immediately after an interview. Miss Barclay has failed to do so.
RANCE: A search party must be organized. (*To* DR. PRENTICE.) What have you in the way of dogs?
MRS. PRENTICE: A spaniel and a miniature poodle.
RANCE: Let them be unleashed! Geraldine Barclay must be found or the authorities informed.
MRS. PRENTICE: I'll contact the warden. He has charge of the gate and will know whether she left the building. (*Turns to go.*)
PRENTICE: No—don't do that. Miss Barclay is quite safe. I've just remembered. She's in the therapy workshop.
RANCE: (*Pause, surprised.*) Why did you keep the fact from us?
PRENTICE: It'd slipped my memory.
RANCE: Have you suffered from lapses of memory before?
PRENTICE: I can't remember.
RANCE: Your memory plays you false even on the subject of its own inadequacy?
PRENTICE: I may have had a blackout. I don't recall having one on any other occasion.
RANCE: You might have forgotten. You admit your memory isn't reliable.
PRENTICE: I can only state what I know, sir. I can't be expected to remember things I've forgotten.
MRS. PRENTICE: What's Miss Barclay doing in the therapy workshop?
PRENTICE: She's making white tarbabies for sale in color-prejudice trouble-spots.

(DR. RANCE *and* MRS. PRENTICE *exchange startled looks.*)

RANCE: You claim, Prentice, that you forgot your secretary was manufacturing these monstrosities?
PRENTICE: Yes.
RANCE: I can hardly credit it. Once seen, a white tarbaby is not easily forgotten. What was the object in creating these nightmare creatures?
PRENTICE: I hoped it might promote racial harmony.
RANCE: These hellish white mutations must be put out of their misery. I order you to destroy them before their baleful influence can make itself felt.
PRENTICE: (*Wearily.*) I'll get Miss Barclay to carry out your orders, sir. (*He goes out to the wards.*)
RANCE: The man's a second Frankenstein.
MRS. PRENTICE: I don't believe we've been introduced.
RANCE: I represent our government. The mental branch. I'm here to investigate your husband's clinic and I find his behavior gives me cause for grave disquiet. Are you convinced that his methods can result in the lessening of tension between the sane and the insane?

MRS. PRENTICE: The purpose of my husband's clinic isn't to cure, but to liberate and exploit madness.

RANCE: In this he appears to succeed only too well. Never have I seen matters conducted as they are in this house. Read that.

MRS. PRENTICE: (*Reading.*) "Keep your head down and don't make a sound?" (*Handing it back.*) What does it mean?

RANCE: It's a prescription of your husband's. He's using dangerously unorthodox methods in his treatment of the insane.

MRS. PRENTICE: I must confess that only this morning my husband prescribed the reading of Thomas Hardy to cure a disorder of the bladder.

RANCE: Now, you see what I mean. Have there been other schemes besides this tarbaby scandal?

MRS. PRENTICE: Endless ones. His letters to the newspapers are legion. From his first letter at the age of 12 speculating on the nature and extent of Nazi propaganda, to his latest published a month ago, in which he calls gentlemen's lavatories the last stronghold of male privilege. What do you think, Doctor? Is he a genius or just a highly strung fool?

RANCE: As a psychiatrist your husband seems not only ineffective but also undesirable.

MRS. PRENTICE: (*Discovers* GERALDINE'S *shoe and looks at it in amazement.*) Oh!

RANCE: (*Pause.*) What is it?

MRS. PRENTICE: A shoe.

RANCE: Is it yours?

MRS. PRENTICE: No.

RANCE: Let me see it. (*She hands him the shoe. He turns it over in his hand. Looking up, after a pause.*) I must ask you to be honest with me, Mrs. Prentice. Has Dr. Prentice at any time given you cause to doubt his own sanity?

MRS. PRENTICE: (*Gives a quick gasp of fear, rising to her feet.*) He's a respected member of his profession. His work in all fields has been praised by numerous colleagues.

RANCE: Let me remind you, Mrs. Prentice, that radical thought comes easily to the lunatic.

MRS. PRENTICE: (*Pause.*) You're quite right. I've known for some time that all was not well. I've tried to convince myself that my fears were groundless. All the while I knew I was deceiving myself.

RANCE: (*Quietly.*) What first aroused your suspicions?

MRS. PRENTICE: His boorish attitude towards my mother. He used to call her up on the telephone and suggest painful ways of committing suicide. Worn out at last by his pestering, she took his advice.

RANCE: And more recently, say from this morning, has there been an increase in his condition?

MRS. PRENTICE: Oh, yes. Quite definitely, Doctor. He had no sympathy for me when I complained of being assaulted by a page boy at the Station Hotel.

RANCE: What was the object of the assault?

MRS. PRENTICE: The boy wanted to rape me.

RANCE: Did he succeed?

MRS. PRENTICE: No.

RANCE: (*Shaking his head.*) The service in these hotels is dreadful.

MRS. PRENTICE: And now he has developed a craving for women's clothes.

RANCE: (*Picking up* GERALDINE'S *shoe.*) This confirms your story. I can't doubt that what you've told me has great significance. We must also take into account his admitted lapse of memory, and the attempts to create alien forms of life. Say nothing of our suspicions. Fancies grow like weeds in the unhealthy soil of a sick brain. (DR. PRENTICE *enters Turning to him.*) Have you carried out my instructions?

PRENTICE: Yes.

RANCE: You guilty scientists will destroy the world with your shameful secrets. (*Takes* GERALDINE'S *shoe.*) Does this belong to your secretary?

PRENTICE: No. (*Pause.*) It's mine.

RANCE: (*Heavily, with irony.*) Are you in the habit of wearing women's footwear?

PRENTICE: (*Quickly, desperate.*) My private life is my own. Society must not be too harsh in its judgments. (*Tries to grab shoe from* RANCE. RANCE *won't let it go.*)

RANCE: Where is this secretary of yours? I've a few questions I'd like to put to her.

PRENTICE: I can't allow you to disturb her. She has work to do.

RANCE: I don't think you quite appreciate your position, Prentice. The powers vested in me by the government give the right to interview any member of your staff should occasion demand. (RANCE *dislodges shoe from* PRENTICE. *Thrusts it into his case.*) Where is Geraldine Barclay?

PRENTICE: She's in the garden.

RANCE: Ask her to step this way.

PRENTICE: She's making a funeral pyre for the tarbabies. It would be wrong to disturb her.

RANCE: Very well. I shall seek her out myself. You may be sure, Prentice, your conduct won't go unreported! (*Goes to the garden.*)

PRENTICE: (*Turns on his wife.*) What've you told him?

MRS. PRENTICE: Nothing but the truth.

PRENTICE: You've been spreading it around that I'm a transvestite, haven't you?

MRS. PRENTICE: There was a woman's shoe hidden in the bookcase. What was it doing there?

PRENTICE: Why were you rooting among my books?

MRS. PRENTICE: I was looking for the clippings file. I showed it to Dr. Rance.

PRENTICE: You'd no right to do that.
MRS. PRENTICE: Are you ashamed of the fact that you write to strange men?
PRENTICE: There's nothing suspect about my relationship with the editor of *The Times*.
MRS. PRENTICE: Dr. Rance and I are trying to help you. We're not satisfied with your condition.
PRENTICE: Neither am I. It's impossible and you're to blame.
MRS. PRENTICE: (*Turns on* DR. PRENTICE *resentfully*.) Whose fault is it if our marriage is on the rocks? You're selfish and inconsiderate.
PRENTICE: (*He backs her against the desk and begins to unzip her dress.*) Your irresponsible behavior causes me untold anxiety. Your nymphomania knows no bounds.
MRS. PRENTICE: You've no psychological understanding of the difficulties I face.
PRENTICE: (*Her dress is off her shoulders.*) Unless you're very careful you'll find yourself in a suitcase awaiting collection!
MRS. PRENTICE: These veiled threats confirm the doubts I already have of your sanity.

(NICK *enters from the hall, carrying a dress on a hanger.*)

NICK: I'm tired of waiting, madam. I believe this is yours. Do you want it?
MRS. PRENTICE: (*With delight.*) My dress!
PRENTICE: A dress? I'll take that. (*Grabs the dress and hanger from* NICK.)
MRS. PRENTICE: I shall inform Dr. Rance of your theft of one of my dresses.
PRENTICE: Don't raise your voice.
NICK: If you'll hand over the money, madam, I'll let you have the photos. However, some guarantee of employment must be given before I part with the negatives.
PRENTICE: What's he talking about?
MRS. PRENTICE: He has in his possession a series of pornographic studies of me. He took them last night without my knowledge.
PRENTICE: I suppose I shall have to turn pederast to get you out of this mess. Take a biscuit from the barrel and retire to your room. (*He chases her out the hall door.*)
NICK: I'm sorry if my behavior last night caused your wife undue anxiety, but I've a burning desire to sleep with every woman I meet.
PRENTICE: That's a filthy habit and, in my opinion, very injurious to the health.
NICK: It is, sir. My health's never been the same since I went off stamp collecting.
PRENTICE: We have an overall moral policy in this clinic from which even I am not exempt. While you're with us as my secretary I shall expect you to show an interest in no one's sexual organs but your own.

NICK: I would miss a lot of fun that way.
PRENTICE: That is the purpose of the exercise.

(DR. RANCE *enters from the garden.*)

RANCE: I can find no trace of your secretary. I might add, Prentice, that my patience is all but exhausted. Unless I discover her whereabouts within the next few minutes you'll find yourself in serious trouble. (*Exits to the wards.*)
MRS. PRENTICE: (*Enters from the hall.*) They've called from the front desk. A policeman is in the hall. He wishes to speak to some member of the household.
PRENTICE: Ask him to wait. Tell him I'll see him in a moment.

(MRS. PRENTICE *goes into the hall.* NICK *stands and appeals to* DR. PRENTICE, *emotional.*)

NICK: Oh, sir! They've come to arrest me!
PRENTICE: This paranoia is uncalled for. The officer has probably called to ask me for the hand of my cook in marriage.
NICK: You're wrong, sir! They'll give me five years if I'm caught.
PRENTICE: Why are you in danger of arrest?
NICK: Well, sir, as your wife has already told you, I attempted last night to misbehave myself with her. I didn't succeed.
PRENTICE: I'm sure you didn't. Despite all appearances to the contrary, Mrs. Prentice is harder to get into than the reading room of the British Museum.
NICK: Undeterred I took the elevator to the third floor of the hotel where a party of schoolgirls were staying. Oh, sir, what lonely and aimless lives they lead! I did what I could to bring them some happiness.
PRENTICE: (*With a frown.*) Was there no mistress in attendance?
NICK: She occupied a room across the corridor.
PRENTICE: Did you disturb her?
NICK: No. And she'll never forgive me for it. It was she who reported the incident to the police. Oh, sir! Don't turn me over to the law.

(DR. RANCE *enters from the dispensary.*)

RANCE: I warn you, Prentice, unless you're prepared to cooperate in finding Miss Barclay I shall call upon you to account for her disappearance. If you're unable to do so the police must be informed. (*Goes into the garden.*)
PRENTICE: (*Turns to* NICK, *an idea dawning. Abruptly.*) Take your clothes off.
NICK: (*Pause.*) Are you going to fool around with me, sir?
PRENTICE: Certainly not! Is that what usually happens when men ask you to take your clothes off?

NICK: Yes. They usually give me money.
PRENTICE: How much? Oh, never mind. Strip! I want you to impersonate my secretary, Geraldine Barclay. It will solve both our problems. (*Gives* NICK *the dress.*) It's of particular importance to convince that man that you're my secretary. You should encounter no real difficulties there. He's an elderly man. I don't suppose he's checked with the original lately. That done, plead illness and leave the house. I'll be waiting with your own clothes. The operation completed, you'll be given a sum of money and a ticket for any destination you choose. If you run into trouble I shall deny all knowledge of you. Put this on. (*Hands* NICK *the dress.*)

(MRS. PRENTICE *enters from the hall. She stops in horror, seeing* NICK *only in his shorts.*)

MRS. PRENTICE: The policeman is still waiting. What devilry are you up to now?
PRENTICE: I'm carrying out a medical examination.
MRS. PRENTICE: But you're a psychiatrist. Why do you need the child undressed?
PRENTICE: (*Smiling, with enormous patience.*) My investigations upon his clothed body would be strictly "unscientific" and, inevitably, superficial. In order to assure myself that he's going to be of use to me I must examine him fully. And skin-wise.
MRS. PRENTICE: You ogre! Never, in my whole life, have I heard anything so lame and stupid. This folly will get you struck off the Medical Register. (*Picking up* NICK'S *uniform.*) Come with me, dear. (*Takes the uniform into the garden.*)
NICK: What do we do now, sir? If that policeman comes in I can't even make a run for it.
PRENTICE: Dress in there. (*Shoves him toward the dispensary. Then goes to the hall and calls in friendly tones.*) Would you like to step this way, officer? I'm sorry to have kept you waiting.
NICK: Shoes, sir!

(DR. PRENTICE *swings round in alarm.*)

PRENTICE: Shoes! (*Takes* GERALDINE'S *shoe from* DR. RANCE'S *brief case and throws it to* NICK. *He goes to the vase and lifts the roses quickly. He puts a hand into the vase, searching for the other shoe.* SERGEANT MATCH *enters from the hall.* NICK *darts back into the dispensary.* DR. PRENTICE *holds the roses. In cold tones:*) Would you mind not entering my consulting room without permission?
MATCH: (*A little put out.*) You asked me to come in, sir.
PRENTICE: I don't believe I did. Wait outside.

(SERGEANT MATCH *leaves the room.* DR. PRENTICE *takes the roses and shakes* GERALDINE'S *shoe from the vase.* MRS. PRENTICE *enters from the garden.* PRENTICE, *caught with the flowers, hides the shoe behind his back and offers the roses to her. She steps back in amazement.*)

MRS. PRENTICE: What have you done with that boy? Why do you keep giving me flowers?
PRENTICE: It's because I'm very fond of you, my dear.
MRS. PRENTICE: Your actions grow wilder with every passing moment. Why were you rude to the policeman?
PRENTICE: He barged in without so much as a by-your-leave.
MRS. PRENTICE: But he said you asked him to come in. Had you forgotten?
PRENTICE: Yes. (*Pause.*) My memory isn't what it was. Tell him I'll see him now.

(MRS. PRENTICE *goes into the hall.*)

GERALDINE: Dr. Prentice. (*Enters from the dispensary. Her hair has been cut short. She is wearing the hospital nightdress.* NICK *enters just behind her; takes the shoe from* PRENTICE *and darts back into the dispensary.*)
PRENTICE: Miss Barclay! What are you doing here?

(SERGEANT MATCH *enters from the hall,* PRENTICE *shields* GERALDINE *from* MATCH *with his body.*)

MATCH: Sorry for the misunderstanding, sir.
PRENTICE: (*Turning, abrupt.*) Please remain outside. I think I made myself plain.
MATCH: (*Pause.*) You don't wish to see me?
PRENTICE: No.
GERALDINE: Nothing would induce me to remain on your staff a moment longer, Doctor. I wish to give notice.
PRENTICE: Your disclosures could ruin me. Give me a chance to get us out of this mess.
GERALDINE: You must put matters right by telling the truth.
PRENTICE: (*Pulls curtains round couch.*) Hide behind here. Nothing unpleasant will happen. You have my word as a gentleman.
GERALDINE: We must tell the truth!
PRENTICE: That's a thoroughly defeatist attitude. (*Bundles her behind the curtain.*)
GERALDINE: (*Looking through the curtain.*) At least give me back my clothes. I feel naked without them.

(DR. PRENTICE *offers the vase with the underwear in it.* GERALDINE *takes out underclothes and retreats behind curtains. As* PRENTICE *stands with roses in his hands and the vase,* MRS. PRENTICE *and* SERGEANT MATCH *enter from the hall.* MRS. PRENTICE *clutches* MATCH'S *arm.)*

MRS. PRENTICE: Oh, if he presents me with those flowers again I shall faint! (*They watch in silence as* DR. PRENTICE *replaces the roses with an air of confidence. Without* GERALDINE'S *clothes under them the stalks are too short. The flowers vanish into the vase.* MRS. PRENTICE *cries out in surprise.*) Oh, he's cut the stalks off! His lunacy is beyond belief.
PRENTICE: Excuse my wife's hysteria. A man tried to molest her last night. Her recovery is far from complete.
MATCH: I understand that Mrs. Prentice introduced the young man to you, sir?
PRENTICE: Yes, but we won't prefer charges.
MATCH: I believe your wife to be ill-advised in not repeating her experiences before a judge and jury. However, as it happens, I'm not concerned with this case. I'm interested in the youth's movements between midnight and seven A.M. During that period he is alleged to have misconducted himself with a party of schoolchildren.
MRS. PRENTICE: How vile and disgraceful!
MATCH: Yes, ma'am. After carrying out a medical examination our lady doctor is up in arms. She can't wait to meet this fellow face to face.
PRENTICE: Well, Sergeant, he isn't on the premises. If he turns up you'll be informed.
MRS. PRENTICE: (*Shocked.*) How dare you give misleading information to the police? (*To* SERGEANT MATCH.) He was here. I have his clothes upstairs.
MATCH: Very wise of you to confiscate his clothing, ma'am. If more women did the same the number of cases of rape would be halved.
PRENTICE: (*At the desk.*) Or doubled.
MRS. PRENTICE: Disregard anything my husband says. I'll get the clothing. (*Goes into the garden.*)
MATCH: (*Turns to* DR. PRENTICE.) I'm also anxious, sir, to trace the whereabouts of a young woman called Barclay. (DR. PRENTICE *coughs.*) Can you help in my inquiries?
PRENTICE: Why do you wish to see Miss Barclay?
MATCH: It's a matter of national importance. Miss Barclay's—
PRENTICE: Shh! I must ask you to lower your voice. I specialize in patients who are allergic to sound. . . . They've been known to become violent at the merest whisper.
MATCH: Miss Barclay's stepmother, a woman of otherwise unblemished character, died recently. Shortly before her death her name had been linked in a most unpleasant way with that of Sir Winston Churchill. Mrs. Barclay's association with the great man gave offense in some circles. However, the local council, composed by and large of no-nonsense men and women in their sixties, decided in view of his war record to overlook Sir Winston's moral lapse. Under expert guidance he was to be reintegrat-

ed into society. The task accomplished, it became clear that the great man was incomplete. The council decided to sue the heirs of Mrs. Barclay for those parts of Sir Winston which an army-type medical had proved to be missing. The council's lawyers obtained an exhumation order. Early this morning Mrs. Barclay's coffin was opened in the presence of the Lord Mayor and Lady Mayoress of this borough. Fainting women were held back as the official in charge searched high and low for council property. His efforts were not crowned with success. Mrs. Barclay had taken nothing with her to the grave except those things which she ought to have done. That is when the matter came to the attention of the police.
PRENTICE: You suspect my secretary of having stolen certain parts of Sir Winston Churchill?
MATCH: Yes.

(MRS. PRENTICE *enters, with* NICK'S *uniform, from the garden.*)

MRS. PRENTICE: Sergeant, here is proof that the young man was in this room.
MATCH: He can't get far without clothing.
PRENTICE: His progress without clothing last night was enviable.
MATCH: (*To* DR. PRENTICE.) You still claim, sir, that you have no knowledge of the youth's whereabouts?
PRENTICE: Yes.
MATCH: And what has become of Miss Barclay?
PRENTICE: I've no idea.
MRS. PRENTICE: You told Dr. Rance she was burning the tarbabies. (SERGEANT MATCH looks from one to the other in amazement.) Was that a lie?
PRENTICE: It may have been. I can't remember.
MRS. PRENTICE: (*Gives an impatient toss of her head.*) You must talk to Dr. Rance, Sergeant. He's from the government. He may be able to account for my husband's unusual behavior pattern. Please tell him that his specialized knowledge is urgently required.
MATCH: Where would the doctor be?
MRS. PRENTICE: In the garden. (SERGEANT MATCH *goes into the garden.*) Now, darling, try to remember why you damaged the flowers in this vase. It may have a direct bearing on the case. (*Exits to the garden with the vase.*)
GERALDINE: (*Pokes her head through the curtain.*) Tell the truth, sir. All your troubles spring from a lack of candor.
PRENTICE: My troubles spring from a misguided attempt to seduce you.
GERALDINE: (*With a gasp.*) You never told me you were seducing me. You said you were interested in my mind.

(SERGEANT MATCH *appears from the garden.* GERALDINE *ducks behind the curtain.*)

MATCH: Are you sure that Dr. Rance is out here, sir?
PRENTICE: Yes.
MATCH: Where would he be then?
PRENTICE: In the shrubbery. We've a naked elf on a birdbath. We often have trouble with Peeping Toms.
MATCH: I'd like you to accompany me, sir.

(DR. PRENTICE *shrugs and follows* SERGEANT MATCH *into the garden.* GERALDINE *steps down from the couch. She is wearing her panties and bra. She carries the nightgown. She picks up* NICK'S *uniform. She hurries to the dispensary. She retreats at once dropping the nightgown. She scurries to the hall, checks herself and scuttles back to the couch. She climbs behind the curtains. As* NICK *enters from the dispensary, dressed in women's clothing,* MRS. PRENTICE *enters from the garden with the roses in a small vase.*)

MRS. PRENTICE: Are you Geraldine Barclay?
NICK: Yes.
MRS. PRENTICE: Where have you been?
NICK: (*Primly.*) I've been attending to the thousand and one duties that occupy the average secretary during her working hours.
MRS. PRENTICE: It doesn't take the whole morning to file your nails, surely?
NICK: I had to lie down. I was sick.
MRS. PRENTICE: Are you pregnant?
NICK: I can't discuss my employer's business with you.
MRS. PRENTICE: What was your last job?
NICK: I was a hostess at the "One, Two, Three" Club.
MRS. PRENTICE: (*Purses her lips in disapproval.*) It's obvious that you're unsuited to the work here. I shan't recommend you for employment. (DR. PRENTICE *and* SERGEANT MATCH *enter from the garden. To* SERGEANT MATCH.) Ah, Sergeant. This is Geraldine Barclay. She'll be happy to help you in your inquiries.
MATCH: (*To* NICK.) Miss Barclay, I must ask you to produce, or cause to be produced, the missing parts of Sir Winston Churchill.
NICK: What do they look like?
MATCH: You're claiming ignorance of the shape and structure of the objects sought?
NICK: I'm in the dark.
MATCH: You handled them only at night? We shall draw our own conclusions.
NICK: I'm not the sort of girl to be mixed up in that kind of thing. I'm an ex-member of the Brownies.
MATCH: Are you concealing unlawful property about your person?
NICK: No.

MATCH: I'll have to call medical evidence to prove your story, miss. You must be thoroughly looked into.
PRENTICE: I'm a qualified doctor.
MATCH: Only women are permitted to examine female suspects.
PRENTICE: Doesn't that breed discontent in the force?
MATCH: Among the single men there's a certain amount of bitterness. Married men who are familiar with the country are glad to be let off extra map-reading.
MRS. PRENTICE: Sergeant, I'll examine Miss Barclay. That will solve all our problems. Come along, Miss Barclay.
MATCH: Thank you, ma'am. I accept your kind offer.

(MRS. PRENTICE *leads* NICK *into the garden. A siren sounds from the wards; then a buzzer.* DR. RANCE *enters from the wards.*)

RANCE: Prentice! The patient has escaped. I've sounded the alarm.
MATCH: How long has the patient been gone, sir?
RANCE: Only a few minutes. This is her gown. She must be naked then.
MATCH: Any steps you feel may be necessary to recover your patient may be taken, sir. (DR. RANCE *crosses, hurries into the hall.*) She must've come through this room. You and I were in the garden. Mrs. Prentice was upstairs. Escape would be out of the question. She must still be in this room. (*Turns to* DR. PRENTICE *in triumph.*) Only one hiding place is possible. (*Pulls the curtain on the couch aside.* GERALDINE *is revealed. She is wearing* NICK'S *uniform, his hat. Taking in the picture at a glance.*) Are you from the Station Hotel?
GERALDINE: (*Answers in a scared voice.*) Yes.
MATCH: I want a word with you, my lad. (*Takes out his notebook. The siren and buzzer wail.*)

BLACKOUT

CURTAIN

ACT TWO

Continuous. The siren and buzzer. They stop. EVERYONE *is as they were at the end of* ACT ONE.

MATCH: Are you from the Station Hotel?
GERALDINE: Yes.
MATCH: I want a word with you, my lad. You're under arrest.
GERALDINE: (*To* SERGEANT MATCH.) You've no idea how glad I am to be arrested.
MATCH: Why?
GERALDINE: I'm in great danger.
MATCH: Who from?
GERALDINE: Dr. Prentice. His conduct is scandalous. Take me to the police station. I shall prefer charges.
MATCH: (*To* DR. PRENTICE.) Have you anything to say, sir?
PRENTICE: Yes. What this young woman claims is a tissue of lies.
MATCH: (*Pause.*) This is a boy, sir. Not a girl. If you're baffled by the difference it might be as well to approach both with caution. (*To* GERALDINE.) Let's hear what you've got to say for yourself.
GERALDINE: I came here for a job. On some pretext the doctor got me to remove my clothes. Afterwards he behaved in a strange manner.
MATCH: (*Glances at* DR. PRENTICE *in disapproval.* MATCH *turns to* GERALDINE. *Quietly.*) Did he, at any time, attempt to interfere with you?
PRENTICE: You'll be disappointed, Sergeant, if you imagine that that boy has lost his virginity.
MATCH: I hope he'll be considerably more experienced before he loses that, sir. What reason had you for taking off his clothes?
PRENTICE: I wished to assure myself of his unquestioning obedience. I give a prize each year.
MATCH: Have you been in trouble of this kind before?
PRENTICE: I'm not in trouble.
MATCH: You must realize this boy is bringing a serious charge against you?
PRENTICE: Yes. It's ridiculous. I'm a married man.
MATCH: Marriage excuses no one the freak's roll-call.
PRENTICE: I'm a respected member of my profession. Your accusations are absurd.
MATCH: It's not for me to bring accusations in a matter I don't fully understand.
PRENTICE: The boy has an unsavory reputation. Last night requires explaining before this morning.
GERALDINE: I had nothing to do with the disgraceful happenings at the Station Hotel.

MATCH: You deny that on the night of Thursday last you did behave in an obscene manner with a section of the Priory Road School for Girls?
GERALDINE: Yes.
MATCH: Nicholas Becket, I warn you that anything you say will be taken down and may be used in evidence against you.
GERALDINE: My name is not Nicholas Beckett.
MATCH: (*Pause, with a frown.*) Then why d'you suppose I'd wish to arrest you?
GERALDINE: To safeguard my interests?
PRENTICE: You imagine you'll be safe from acts of indecency in a police station?
GERALDINE: Of course.
PRENTICE: I wish I shared your optimism.
RANCE: (*Enters from the hall.*) Full security arrangements are in force. No one is to leave the clinic without written permission. Prentice, get your secretary to issue warrants to every member of the staff.
PRENTICE: I'll do that, sir, as soon as she's ready to resume her normal duties.
MATCH: Are you Dr. Rance?
RANCE: Yes.
MATCH: (*To* DR. RANCE.) Would you help us clear up a spot of trouble, Doctor? It's a matter of some urgency. Last night this young man assaulted a number of female schoolchildren. This morning he was assaulted in his turn.
RANCE: (*With a shrug.*) What can I say? It's a case of "be done by as you did."
MATCH: The boy has made a serious charge against Dr. Prentice. He claims he was forced to strip and lie on a couch.
RANCE: (*To* DR. PRENTICE.) A complete list of your indiscretions would make a best seller. Have you behaved in an unseemly manner?
PRENTICE: No! It's just that my nerves are on edge.
RANCE: You should consult a qualified psychiatrist.
PRENTICE: I am a qualified psychiatrist.
RANCE: You're a fool. That isn't quite the same thing. Though, in your case, the two may have much in common. (*To* SERGEANT MATCH.) Has the boy come to your notice before?
MATCH: Not on a case of this kind. That's why we have to be careful. As the doctor rightly says, he has an unsavory reputation. It may be that he bears Dr. Prentice a grudge.
RANCE: (*To* DR. PRENTICE.) Perhaps this accusation springs from disappointment. It might have been wiser if you hadn't rejected the young fellow's blandishments.
PRENTICE: Unnatural vice can ruin a man.
RANCE: Ruin follows the accusation, not the vice. Had you committed the act you wouldn't now be facing the charge.

PRENTICE: I couldn't commit the act. I'm a heterosexual.
RANCE: I wish you wouldn't use these Chaucerian words. It's most confusing. (*To* SERGEANT MATCH.) How do you propose to get to the bottom of this affair?
MATCH: A reputable person must examine the lad.
GERALDINE: I refuse to be examined!
MATCH: You can't refuse. You're under arrest.
GERALDINE: I'm not Nicholas Beckett. I want to be taken to prison.
MATCH: If you aren't Nicholas Beckett you can't go to prison. You're not under arrest.
GERALDINE: (*Pause, biting her lip.*) I am Nicholas Beckett.
MATCH: Then you're under arrest. You'll submit to a medical examination.
RANCE: And I shall conduct it. The mind of the victim of this kind of assault must be considered equally with the body.
GERALDINE: I haven't been assaulted.
RANCE: Then why make such a foul accusation?
GERALDINE: I didn't accuse anyone. The sergeant made the accusation.
RANCE: (*To* SERGEANT MATCH.) Has Dr. Prentice assaulted you too? (*To* DR. PRENTICE.) Is it policemen or young boys you're after? At your age it's high time you came to a decision. (*To* SERGEANT MATCH.) Wait outside. I shall examine the boy and make my report. Afterwards I'll take a look at you, too.
MATCH: (*Stunned.*) At me?
RANCE: Yes. We can't be too careful.
MATCH: It seems a bit unusual, sir.
RANCE: You're in a madhouse. Unusual behavior is the order of the day.
MATCH: Only for patients.
RANCE: We've no privileged class here. We practice democratic lunacy. (SERGEANT MATCH *goes into the hall.*) Take your clothes off, sonny. Lie on the couch.
GERALDINE: I shouldn't've behaved as I did, sir. I wasn't harmed.
RANCE: You enjoyed the experience? Would you enjoy normal intercourse?
GERALDINE: No. I might get pregnant—(*Realizes her mistake and attempts to cover up.*)—or be the cause of pregnancy in others.
RANCE: (*Quick to notice the error, turns to* DR. PRENTICE.) He's just given away a vital piece of information. (*Advances on* GERALDINE.) Do you think of yourself as a girl?
GERALDINE: No.
RANCE: Why not?
GERALDINE: I'm a boy.
RANCE: (*Kindly.*) Do you have the evidence about you?
GERALDINE: (*Her eyes flashing an appeal to* DR. PRENTICE.) I must be a boy. I like girls.
RANCE: (*Stops and wrinkles his brow, puzzled. Aside, to* DR. PRENTICE.) I can't quite follow the reasoning there.

PRENTICE: Many men imagine that a preference for women is, ipso facto, a proof of virility.
RANCE: (*Nodding, sagely.*) Someone should really write a book on these folk myths. (*To* GERALDINE.) Take your trousers down. I'll tell you which sex you belong to.
GERALDINE: (*Backing away.*) I'd rather not know!
RANCE: You wish to remain in ignorance?
GERALDINE: Yes.
RANCE: I can't encourage you in such a self-indulgent attitude. You must face facts like the rest of us. (*Forces* GERALDINE *back to the couch.*)
PRENTICE: You're forcing the boy to undergo a repetition of a traumatic experience, sir. He might go insane.
RANCE: This is a mental home. He couldn't choose a more appropriate place. (*To* GERALDINE.) Undress. My time is valuable.
GERALDINE: (*Unable to stand the ordeal any longer, cries out to* DR. PRENTICE *in anguish.*) I can't go on, Doctor! I must tell the truth. (*To* DR. RANCE.) I'm not a boy! I'm a girl!
RANCE: (*To* DR. PRENTICE.) Excellent. A confession at last. He wishes to believe he's a girl in order to minimize the feelings of guilt after homosexual intercourse.
GERALDINE: (*Wild-eye, desperate.*) I pretended to be a boy. I did it to help Dr. Prentice.
RANCE: How does it help a man if a girl pretends to be a boy?
GERALDINE: Wives are angry if they find their husbands have undressed and seduced a girl.
RANCE: But boys are fair game? I doubt whether your very personal view of society would go unchallenged.

(*Provoked beyond endurance,* GERALDINE *flings herself into* DR. RANCE'S *arms and cries hysterically.*)

GERALDINE: Undress me then, Doctor! Do whatever you like, only prove that I'm a girl.
RANCE: (*Pushes away and turns, frigidly, to* DR. PRENTICE.) If he's going to carry on like this he'll have to be strapped down.

(MRS. PRENTICE *enters from the garden.*)

MRS. PRENTICE: (*To* DR. RANCE.) Dr. Rance, would you take a look at Miss Barclay? She refuses to undress in front of a woman.
RANCE: How about in front of a man?
MRS. PRENTICE: I haven't sounded her on the subject.
RANCE: I wonder if I could tempt her. I'll give it a try. She may be a nymphomaniac. (*To* DR. PRENTICE.) If this boy becomes foul-mouthed keep him on the boil till I return. (*Goes to the garden, followed by* MRS. PRENTICE. GERALDINE *pulls herself together.*)

GERALDINE: I'll go through the garden, Doctor. I can get a taxi home.
PRENTICE: That isn't possible. Dr. Rance has arranged for strict security precautions to be in force until the patient is recaptured.
GERALDINE: When the patient is recaptured can I go?
PRENTICE: No.
GERALDINE: Why not?
PRENTICE: You *are* the patient.

(GERALDINE *gives a little cry of distress.* DR. RANCE *reenters.*)

RANCE: Prentice, your secretary is standing on a table fighting off any attempt to undress her. She seems incapable of conducting herself in a proper manner.
PRENTICE: She's given me no cause for complaint.
RANCE: But you expect a secretary to misbehave herself. It's a condition of employment. (*Faces* DR. PRENTICE, *candidly.*) Do you realize the woman uses a razor?
PRENTICE: I see nothing remarkable in that. Mrs. Prentice has occasion sometimes to remove unwanted hair.
RANCE: From her chin? There are two sexes. The unpalatable truth must be faced. Your attempts at a merger can end in heartbreak.

(MRS. PRENTICE *enters from the garden, a syringe in her hand, leading a chastened* NICK *by the hand.*)

MRS. PRENTICE: Miss Barclay is calmer now, Doctor. I've given her a sedative.
RANCE: (*Turning to* NICK, *shaking his head.*) What an absorbing picture of the mind in decay. Why won't you allow Mrs. Prentice to undress you?
MRS. PRENTICE: Her objections appear to be religious. She claims to be at one with God.
RANCE: Come here, sonny. Were you present when Dr. Prentice used this youth unnaturally?
NICK: What is unnatural?
RANCE: (*To* MRS. PRENTICE.) How disturbing the questions of the mad can be.
MRS. PRENTICE: (*Nodding to* GERALDINE.) Has my husband misbehaved with that boy?
RANCE: It's impossible to say with any degree of accuracy. He refuses to cooperate with a medical examination.
MRS. PRENTICE: (*To* DR. PRENTICE.) What happened to the other boy?
RANCE: Which boy?
MRS. PRENTICE: The one my husband undressed.
RANCE: This is the boy he undressed.
MRS. PRENTICE: No. He undressed the boy who made a nuisance of himself to me.

RANCE: (*Pause.*) Isn't this the same one?
MRS. PRENTICE: No.
RANCE: (*Staring, perplexed.*) There's another boy?
MRS. PRENTICE: He was being interviewed for a secretarial post. My husband made him undress.
RANCE: (*Coldly, to* DR. PRENTICE.) How long have you been a pervert?
PRENTICE: I'm not a pervert!
RANCE: How would you describe a man who mauls young boys, importunes policemen and lives on terms of intimacy with a woman who shaves twice a day?
PRENTICE: I'd say the man was a pervert.
RANCE: I'm glad you're beginning to face the realities of the situation. (*To* GERALDINE.) Who are you if you're not Nicholas Beckett?

(GERALDINE *looks to* DR. PRENTICE *and bites her lip.*)

PRENTICE: His name is Gerald Barclay.
RANCE: (*Indicating* NICK.) Is he this young woman's brother?
PRENTICE: No.
RANCE: What happened then to Nicholas Beckett?
PRENTICE: He left an hour ago to resume his duties at the Station Hotel.
MRS. PRENTICE: He can't have! I took his uniform. He'd be naked.
PRENTICE: From what one hears of the Station Hotel the uniform is optional.
RANCE: (*Shaking his head, worried.*) I hope we haven't lost another one. We'll be alone with our miracle drugs if many more go. (*To* MRS. PRENTICE.) Find out whether the boy has returned to the hotel.
MRS. PRENTICE: I'll call immediately. (*Goes into the hall.*)
RANCE: (*Turns to* DR. PRENTICE.) Prepare the necessary papers. I'm certifying these two.

(*Cries of alarm come from* NICK *and* GERALDINE.)

NICK: Can't you do something about him, sir? He's off his head.
RANCE: (*Sternly.*) I am a representative of order, you of chaos. Unless that fact is faced, I can never hope to cure you. (*To* DR. PRENTICE.) Make out the committal orders for me to sign.
PRENTICE: (*Upset and angry.*) I can't agree to such drastic action. We've no evidence of insanity. These children are no more ill than I am.
RANCE: But your condition is worse than hers.
PRENTICE: I can't accept that.
RANCE: No madman ever accepts madness. Only the sane do that. I'm relieving you of your post as head of the clinic. You'll do as I say from now on.
PRENTICE: I resent your handling of this affair, sir. I shall make my views known to the commissioners.

RANCE: I doubt whether the views of a madman will carry much weight with the commissioners.
PRENTICE: I'm not mad. It only looks that way.
RANCE: Your actions today could get the Archbishop of Canterbury declared non-compos.
PRENTICE: I'm not the Archbishop of Canterbury.
RANCE: That will come at a later stage of your illness.
PRENTICE: Your interpretation of my behavior is misplaced and erroneous. If anyone borders on lunacy it's you yourself!
RANCE: Bearing in mind your abnormality, that is a normal reaction. The sane appear as strange to the mad as the mad to the sane. Take two of these. (*Takes red pillbox from pocket.*)
PRENTICE: (*Looking at the pillbox.*) What are they?
RANCE: Dangerous drugs intended to relieve your pathologically elevated mood. Be careful not to exceed the stated dose. I shall return shortly. All of you remain here. (*Exits to the wards.*)
NICK: Why is he wearing my uniform?
GERALDINE: Why is she wearing my shoes?
PRENTICE: He isn't a boy. He's a girl. She isn't a girl. She's a boy. And we'll all be sharing the same cell at this rate.
NICK: If we changed clothes, sir, we could get things back to normal.
PRENTICE: We'd then have to account for the disappearance of my secretary and the page boy.
GERALDINE: But they don't exist!
PRENTICE: When people who don't exist disappear the account of their departure must be convincing.
NICK: (*Pause.*) Is the policeman corruptible?
PRENTICE: Why?
NICK: I must have his uniform.
PRENTICE: For what reason?
NICK: To arrest Nicholas Beckett.
PRENTICE: But you're Nicholas Beckett.
NICK: Once I've arrested myself you can write me off.
GERALDINE: Aren't you multiplying our problems instead of dividing them?
NICK: (*To* DR. PRENTICE.) Some glib pretext will get her out of the way. Then she and I can change clothes.

(DR. RANCE *enters from the wards.*)

RANCE: I'm putting this youth into a padded cell. Rampant hermaphroditism must be discouraged.
PRENTICE: Quite right.
GERALDINE: (*With a sob.*) Twice declared insane in one day! And they said I'd be working for a cheerful, well-spoken crowd. Oh, I'm glad my parents are dead. This would've killed them. (DR. RANCE *takes her to the wards.*)

PRENTICE: (*To* NICK.) I'll get the sergeant to undress so you can have his uniform. I'm suspected of the offense, I might as well commit it. We'll need something to calm him down. A mild tranquilizer wouldn't harm him, I suppose. You'll find a box of anti-depressants in the top right-hand drawer of my desk. (NICK *goes to the desk and takes a square, white pillbox from the drawer.* DR. PRENTICE *opens the hall door. Calling, friendly.*) Would you step this way, Sergeant? (*To* NICK.) Hide in there.

(NICK *hands* DR. PRENTICE *the white pillbox and hides in the closet.* SERGEANT MATCH *enters from the hall.*)

MATCH: You wish to speak to me, Doctor?
PRENTICE: Yes. Dr. Rance has asked me to examine you. I'd like you to undress and lie on that couch.
MATCH: (*Pause.*) I haven't been interfered with.
PRENTICE: Never mind about that. Strip down to your underwear.
MATCH: (*Sitting on couch, unlacing boots.*) If you make any attempt to arouse me, Doctor, I shall call for help.
PRENTICE: It's easy to see why you've never been interfered with. You place too many obstacles in the way. Come along. Come along. Speed is essential.

(SERGEANT MATCH *takes off his boots.* NICK *appears from the closet.* DR. PRENTICE *hands him the boots.* SERGEANT MATCH *takes off his tunic and hands it to* DR. PRENTICE. DR. PRENTICE *throws tunic to* NICK *who retreats.* SERGEANT MATCH *drops his trousers.* MRS. PRENTICE *enters from the hall. Seeing the* SERGEANT *without his trousers, she screams loudly. Shocked and embarrassed,* SERGEANT MATCH *pulls up his trousers.*)

MRS. PRENTICE: (*Icily.*) What were you doing with your trousers down, officer?
MATCH: The doctor is going to examine me.
MRS. PRENTICE: Why?
MATCH: There's reason to suppose that I had a nasty experience a short time ago.
MRS. PRENTICE: What kind of experience?
PRENTICE: He was meddled with.
MRS. PRENTICE: By whom?
PRENTICE: Me.
MRS. PRENTICE: And why are you examining him?
PRENTICE: To find out whether his story is true.
MRS. PRENTICE: Don't you know?
PRENTICE: No. I didn't feel a thing.
MRS. PRENTICE: (*With a toss of her head.*) Where is Dr. Rance?
PRENTICE: He's just certified the hotel page. He's putting him in a padded cell.

MRS. PRENTICE: I must speak to him. Things are getting out of control. (*Hurries into the ward.*)
PRENTICE: (*Turns to* SERGEANT MATCH.) Remove your trousers, Sergeant, and we'll continue. (SERGEANT MATCH *takes off his trousers and hands them to* DR. PRENTICE. *He is naked except for his underpants and socks. With a flourish* DR. PRENTICE *takes the red pillbox from his pocket and hands it to the* SERGEANT. *Smiling.*) Swallow these. Take as many as you like. They're quite harmless. (*The* SERGEANT *accepts the box.*) Now I want you to lie on this couch and concentrate on the closing chapters of your favorite work of fiction. (SERGEANT MATCH *lies on the couch.* DR. PRENTICE *pulls the curtain around him and hurries to the closet with the trousers. He meets* NICK *in the doorway.* NICK *carries the* SERGEANT'S *uniform.* DR. PRENTICE *hands him the trousers. To* NICK.) In the garden you'll find a little summerhouse. You won't be disturbed in there. (NICK *goes into the garden with the clothes.* DR. PRENTICE *goes to the desk.* NICK *reappears, without the uniform.*)
NICK: The helmet, sir!
PRENTICE: (*Hurries to the couch.*) The helmet, Sergeant!
MATCH: (*From behind the curtain.*) In the hall, sir.
PRENTICE: (*To* NICK.) Miss Barclay's clothes are in the closet.

(NICK *hurries into the hall, with the uniform to get the helmet.* MRS. PRENTICE *enters from the ward.* NICK *re-enters from the hall, wearing only underpants and the helmet. Upon seeing him,* MRS. PRENTICE *shrieks and follows* NICK *into the garden.* DR. PRENTICE *ducks under the desk and runs into the hall with the dress [the one* NICK *has just changed out of] and* GERALDINE'S *shoes [which* NICK *has also just left there].*)

MRS. PRENTICE: (*Re-enters alone.*) This place is like a madhouse!
RANCE: (*Enters from the wards.*) Where is Dr. Prentice?
MRS. PRENTICE: I don't know. When I returned from telephoning the Station Hotel he was undressing the sergeant.
RANCE: How would you describe his relations with the sergeant?
MRS. PRENTICE: Strange and, in many ways, puzzling. He's called him into this room on several occasions and then abruptly dismissed him.
RANCE: Playing the coquette, eh? Well, well, it adds spice to a love affair. What news of the missing patient?
MRS. PRENTICE: None.
RANCE: And what's the report from the Station Hotel?
MRS. PRENTICE: They state that they have no page called Gerald Barclay on their register. The youth you've certified insane must be an imposter.
RANCE: And what of Nicholas Beckett—the real page boy?
MRS. PRENTICE: He hasn't returned to the hotel. And when he disappeared his uniform was in my possession.
RANCE: (*Greatly concerned.*) Two young people—one mad and one sexually insatiable—both naked—are roaming this house. At all costs we must

prevent a collision. Oh, this is incredible. When I publish it, I'll make my fortune. My "documentary type" novelette will go into twelve record-breaking reprints. I'll be able to leave the service of the government and bask in the attentions of those who, like myself, find other people's iniquity puts money in their purse. (DR. RANCE *picks up red pillbox from floor in front of couch.*) What's this? The pills I gave your husband? It's empty. He's taken an overdose! We have here terrible evidence of conflict. His tormented mind, seeking release, has led him to attempt to destroy himself.
MRS. PRENTICE: (*Gasps with shock and amazement.*) Suicide? This is so unexpected.
RANCE: Just when one least expects it, the unexpected always happens. We must find him before it's too late.

(*They both exit into the hall.* DR. PRENTICE *and Nick enter simultaneously from the dispensary and the garden.* DR. PRENTICE *carries the shoes and dress.* NICK *is wearing the* SERGEANT'S *uniform.*)

PRENTICE: Miss Barclay has escaped from the padded cell! (*A sound from behind the curtains. They part the curtains of the couch and* SERGEANT MATCH *tumbles forward drugged into insensibility.* DR. PRENTICE *and* NICK *react to the* SERGEANT'S *condition and catch him. They place him in a sitting position in a chair.* DR. PRENTICE *feels in his pocket and pulls out the square white pillbox. His eyes widen. He clutches his throat.*) My God! I've poisoned him! (DR. PRENTICE *puts the dress down and attempts to drag* SERGEANT MATCH *to his feet. The* SERGEANT *moans, stares about him in a stupor and shivers uncontrollably.*)
NICK: (*Holding the* SERGEANT'S *pulse.*) He's frozen, sir.
PRENTICE: The effect of the drug. We find the same process at work in corpses. He'll be all right if we get him in the open air so he can sleep it off.
NICK: Get some clothes on him and dump him outside. (*He picks up the dress.*)
PRENTICE: (*Wringing his hands.*) How will I explain the presence in my garden of the drugged police sergeant?
NICK: (*Putting the dress onto* SERGEANT MATCH.) You're guilty. You don't have to explain. Only the innocent do that.
PRENTICE: (*Puts* GERALDINE'S *shoes in his pants pockets. He and* NICK *carry* SERGEANT MATCH *to the garden in the chair.*) Oh, if this ever gets out I'll be reduced to casting horoscopes.

(MRS. PRENTICE *enters from the hall, followed immediately by* DR. RANCE. *They look at each other for an instant. She exits to the garden,* RANCE *to the wards. They both re-enter immediately.*)

MRS. PRENTICE: Dr. Rance, I've just seen my husband carrying a woman into the shrubbery.

RANCE: Was she struggling?
MRS. PRENTICE: No.
RANCE: Then a new and frightening possibility presents itself. The drugs in this box—(*He lifts up the bright red pillbox.*)—may not have been used for suicide, but for murder. Your husband has made away with his secretary!
MRS. PRENTICE: Isn't that a little melodramatic, Doctor?
RANCE: Lunatics *are* melodramatic. The subtleties of drama are wasted on them. Everything is now clear. The final chapters of my book are knitting together: incest, buggery, outrageous women and strange love-cults catering to depraved appetites. All the fashionable bric-a-brac. (*To* MRS. PRENTICE.) My "unbiased account" of the case of the infamous sex-killer Prentice will undoubtedly add a great deal to our understanding of such creatures. Society must be made aware of the growing menace of pornography. The whole treacherous avant-garde movement will be exposed for what it is—an instrument for inciting decent citizens to commit bizarre crimes against humanity and the state! (*He pauses, a little overcome, and wipes his brow.*) You have, under your roof, my dear, one of the most remarkable lunatics of all time. We must institute a search for the corpse. As a transvestite, fetishist, bisexual murderer Dr. Prentice displays considerable deviation overlap. We may get necrophilia too. As a sort of bonus. (DR. PRENTICE *enters from the garden with an empty chair; replaces it by the desk. He still has the shoes in his pockets. Turning, and giving a disdainful stare:*) Would you confirm, Prentice, that your wife saw you carrying a body into the shrubbery?
PRENTICE: Yes. I have an explanation for my conduct.
RANCE: I'm not interested in your explanations. I can provide my own. Where is your secretary?
PRENTICE: I've given her the sack. (*Puts shoes on the desk.*)
RANCE: (*Aside to* MRS. PRENTICE.) He killed her and wrapped her body in a sack. The word association is very clear.
PRENTICE: I haven't killed anyone!
RANCE: Your answer is in accord with the complex structure of your neurosis.
PRENTICE: The person my wife saw wasn't dead. They were asleep.
RANCE: (*To* MRS. PRENTICE.) He hopes for a resurrection. We've a link here with primitive religion. (*To* DR. PRENTICE.) Why have you turned your back on the God of your fathers?
PRENTICE: I'm a rationalist.
RANCE: You can't be a rationalist in an irrational world. It isn't rational. (*Pointing to the shoes.*) Was it your intention to wear these shoes for auto-erotic excitement?
PRENTICE: No, I'm a perfectly normal man.
RANCE: (*To* MRS. PRENTICE.) His belief in normality is quite abnormal. (*To* DR. PRENTICE.) Was the girl killed before or after you took her clothes off?
PRENTICE: He wasn't a girl. He was a man.

MRS. PRENTICE: He was wearing a dress.
PRENTICE: He was a man for all that.
RANCE: Women wear dresses, Prentice, not men. I won't be a party to the wanton destruction of a fine old tradition. Did you change clothes with your victim before it died?
PRENTICE: Nobody died! The person you saw me with was a policeman who'd taken an overdose of narcotics.
MRS. PRENTICE: Why was he dressed as a woman?
PRENTICE: He was naked when I found him. The dress was readily to hand.
MRS. PRENTICE: Where were his own clothes?
PRENTICE: A boy had stolen them. (DR. RANCE *draws* MRS. PRENTICE *aside, his face a mask of disapproval.*)
RANCE: Mrs. Prentice, the time has come to call a halt to this Graeco-Roman hallucination. Is there a strait jacket in the house?
MRS. PRENTICE: Modern methods of treatment have rendered the strait jacket obsolete.
RANCE: I'm well aware of that. We still use them nonetheless. Have you one here?
MRS. PRENTICE: The porter has a few.
RANCE: We can take no chances with your husband in his present condition. Keep him occupied until I return. (*He goes.*)
PRENTICE: Is this another of your plots to undermine my reputation for sound judgment, you treacherous harpy?
MRS. PRENTICE: (*Gently.*) Dr. Rance believes that you've caused a poor girl's death, darling. You may be called upon to accept a period of restraint.
PRENTICE: Miss Barclay isn't dead!
MRS. PRENTICE: Produce her then and your difficulties will be over.
PRENTICE: I can't.
MRS. PRENTICE: Why not?
PRENTICE: You're wearing her dress. (*With a shrug of resignation.*) You surprised me this morning when I was attempting to seduce her.
MRS. PRENTICE: (*Smiles a smile of disbelief.*) If we're to save our marriage, my dear, you must admit that you prefer boys to women.
PRENTICE: (*Is stunned by her suggestion. He rounds on her in a fury.*) I won't have you making scandalous allegations about a matter of which you know nothing.
MRS. PRENTICE: (*Tossing her head.*) The page at the hotel accused you of behaving in an indecent manner.
PRENTICE: That wasn't a boy. It was a girl.
MRS. PRENTICE: Admit that you prefer your sex to mine. I've no hesitation in saying that I do.
PRENTICE: You filthy degenerate! Take your clothes off! (*He unzips her dress.*)

MRS. PRENTICE: (*Eagerly.*) Are you going to beat me? Do if you wish. Your psychotic experiences are immensely valuable to you and should be encouraged rather than thwarted or repressed. (*Gasping as he slaps her.*) Oh, my darling! This is the way to sexual adjustment in marriage. (RANCE *enters from the hall with two strait jackets, a witness to the final moment.* PRENTICE *picks up the dress, throws it over his arm; and with the shoes he exits proudly into the garden.*)
RANCE: What are you doing?
MRS. PRENTICE: Oh, Doctor, during your absence my husband became violent and struck me.
RANCE: Did you enjoy it?
MRS. PRENTICE: At first. But the pleasures of the senses quickly pall.
RANCE: We must lose no time in putting Dr. Prentice under restraint. We'll need help in the enterprise. Have you no brawny youth upon whom you can call in time of stress?
MRS. PRENTICE: I'm a married woman, Doctor! Your suggestion is in the worst of taste.

(NICK *enters from the garden dressed in the* SERGEANT'S *uniform.*)

NICK: Doctor, I'd like a word with you about my brother, Nicholas Beckett. I've just arrested him.
RANCE: Why?
NICK: He'd broken the law.
RANCE: And because of that he's to be treated as a common criminal? What's happened to the Anglo-Saxon love of fair play? Did you see Dr. Prentice in the garden?
NICK: No.
RANCE: We must find him. We have reason to believe he has killed his secretary.
NICK: (*Horrified.*) He can't have. He's got the Order of the Garter.
RANCE: These cabalistic signs are of no more use in warding off evil than the moons and stars on a sorcerer's hat. We shall need your help in tracking down that mindless killer.
NICK: (*With a groan.*) Oh, Doctor, I'm sick of all this. I have to make a confession.
RANCE: You must call for an appointment. I can't listen to confessions off the cuff.
NICK: I am Nicholas Beckett. (*Takes off his helmet.*) I dressed as Geraldine Barclay at the doctor's request, never imagining that I was unwittingly assisting a psychopath. (*To* MRS. PRENTICE.) That's why I objected to being undressed. It would've embarrassed me.
RANCE: Have you aided other men in their perverted follies?
NICK: During my last term at school I was the slave of a corporal in the Army.

RANCE: Were you never warned of the dangers inherent in such relationships?
NICK: When he was sent overseas he left me a copy of "The Way to Healthy Manhood."
RANCE: (*Drily, to* MRS. PRENTICE.) A case of opening the barn door after the horse is in. (*To* NICK. *He picks up the strait jacket.*) This is a strait jacket. I require your help in persuading Dr. Prentice to put it on. There may be violence. His body has a mind of its own. (*To* MRS. PRENTICE.) Have you any guns?
MRS. PRENTICE: Guns?
RANCE: (*Opens a drawer in the desk and takes out two guns.*) Oh, here. There are two. Take one.
MRS. PRENTICE: You will make sure before you fire that my husband isn't waving an olive branch?
RANCE: An olive branch can be used as an offensive weapon. I'm loath to certify a fellow psychiatrist. It causes such bad feelings within the profession. (*Goes into the garden.*)
MRS. PRENTICE: (*To* NICK.) Take no chances. Call for help the minute you see Dr. Prentice. (*Goes to the hall door, waving the gun. She goes into the hall.*)

(NICK *opens the strait jacket.* DR. PRENTICE *enters from the garden, carrying the dress taken from* MRS. PRENTICE.)

PRENTICE: Oh, there you are. Miss Barclay is nowhere to be found. Have you seen her? I want you to cooperate with me in getting things back to normal in this house.
MATCH: (*Enters from the garden swaying unsteadily.*) I'm ready to be examined when you are, Doctor. (*He stumbles into the wards. As he crosses,* PRENTICE *slaps his helmet on his head.*)
GERALDINE: (*Wearing* NICK'S *uniform, staggers in from the garden.*) They're combing the grounds for us, Doctor! They've got guns. What shall we do?
PRENTICE: It would help me considerably if you'd take your clothes off. You must lose no time in getting undressed. Both of you.
NICK: (*Pause.*) If I do that, sir, will you put this on? (*He holds up the jacket.*)
PRENTICE: (*Angry, losing patience.*) Of course not! That's a strait jacket. I won't be a party to kinky capers. You've lived too long at the Station Hotel to know how decent people behave. Now do as I say and undress!
GERALDINE: (*Tearful, beating him away.*) You're behaving like a maniac!
NICK: He is a maniac. He's murdered a woman and hidden her body somewhere.
PRENTICE: Who is responsible for these vile stories?
NICK: Dr. Rance is having you certified. (*Waving the jacket.*) I've got to get you into this! (*He leaps upon* DR. PRENTICE *and attempts to put him into the strait jacket.*)
MATCH: (*Enters from the wards—retreats immediately.*) I'm ready when you are, Doctor!

PRENTICE: (*To* NICK.) Put that down. Take your clothes off. Don't you know the penalty for impersonating a sergeant? Put on your own clothing. Give this youth that tunic and put on this dress and all our problems will be solved.

(NICK *takes off his uniform.* GERALDINE *pulls down her trousers.* NICK *is now naked except for his underpants.* GERALDINE *exits into wards.* MRS. PRENTICE *enters from the hall in her underwear, waving a gun. She advances on* DR. PRENTICE.)

MRS. PRENTICE: (*Waving gun at him.*) Come with me and lie down!
PRENTICE: The woman is insatiable.
MRS. PRENTICE: Unless you make love to me I shall shoot you.
PRENTICE: No husband can be expected to give his best at gun point. (*He backs away and exits into the garden. She shoots at him.*)

(*Hearing the shot,* NICK, *who has crouched behind the desk to hide from* MRS. PRENTICE, *runs into the hall.* A SECOND SHOT. GERALDINE *enters from the wards, sees* MRS. PRENTICE *and retreats back into the wards.* THIRD SHOT. MATCH *enters from wards, sees* MRS. PRENTICE *and exits running into the garden.* FOURTH SHOT. NICK *enters from the hall and exits running into the garden.* MRS. PRENTICE *follows after him, then re-enters immediately as* DR. RANCE *enters from the hall.*)

MRS. PRENTICE: Doctor Rance! Doctor Rance! The world is full of naked men running in all directions!
RANCE: When did these delusions start?
MRS. PRENTICE: Just now.
RANCE: It's not difficult to guess what's on your mind, my dear. Are you having marital troubles?
MRS. PRENTICE: Well, yes. My husband refuses to prescribe anything.
RANCE: A man shouldn't have to drug his wife to achieve a happy union.
MRS. PRENTICE: I don't want drugs. I want account taken of my sexual nature.
RANCE: Where do you keep your tranquilizers? (GERALDINE *runs out from the wards. She has taken off the uniform and wears her own panties and bra.*) At last we've caught the patient! Get the strait jacket! (*Takes one from the chair.*)
GERALDINE: I'm not a patient. I'm telling the truth!
RANCE: It's much too late to tell the truth. (*Ties* GERALDINE *down.*) These final harrowing scenes will be lavishly illustrated with graphs showing the effect of her downfall upon her poor tortured mind. Meanwhile, in his temple of love, the hideous Dr. Prentice and his acolyte are praying to their false gods, unaware that the forces of reason have got their measure. (MRS. PRENTICE *steps back.*) Fetch a syringe. (MRS. PRENTICE *goes into the wards.*)

GERALDINE: (*Trussed up, unable to move.*) What have I done to deserve this? I've always led such a respectable life.
RANCE: Where is the body?
GERALDINE: I don't know.
RANCE: Are you under the seal of the confessional? What black rites were you initiated into by that foul priest of the Unknown? (GERALDINE *sobs, unable to speak.* DR. RANCE *abruptly throws himself on to her and holds her in his arms.*) Let me cure your neurosis! It's the only thing I want out of life.

(MRS. PRENTICE *enters from the dispensary, carrying a hypodermic syringe and bowl.*)

MRS. PRENTICE: What is the meaning of this exhibition?
RANCE: (*Breaking away from* GERALDINE.) It's a new and hitherto untried type of therapy. I think it's viable under the circumstances.
MRS. PRENTICE: Your treatment seems designed to plunge the patient deeper into lunacy rather than achieve any lasting cure.
RANCE: Someone whose unconscious is as quirky as your own could hardly be expected to understand my methods.
MRS. PRENTICE: What do you mean by that?
RANCE: I'm referring to those naked men you encounter with an increasing degree of frequency.
MRS. PRENTICE: You've seen them too.
RANCE: What does that prove? Merely that you've given me your wretched disease. Give me that! (*He takes the hypodermic from her.*)
MRS. PRENTICE: Shouldn't I swab the patient's arm?
RANCE: You don't imagine I'm wasting this stuff on her, do you? (*He rolls back his sleeve.*) For what it costs an ounce, it would be criminal. (*He gives himself an injection.*) Go and call the police. (*Puts the hypodermic aside.*)
MRS. PRENTICE: There's a policeman outside, naked in the center of the garden.
RANCE: If he is, indeed, naked, how do you dare to presume he is a policeman?
MRS. PRENTICE: He's wearing his helmet.
RANCE: The bounds of decency have long been overstepped in this house. Your subconscious cannot be encouraged in its skulduggery. Remain where you are. I'll call the police. (RANCE *exits to wards.*)

(NICK *appears from the garden.*)

MRS. PRENTICE: Oh, I'm losing my mind!
GERALDINE: (*Calls to* NICK.) Help me!
NICK: Why are you tied up?
GERALDINE: Dr. Rance did it. He says I'm mad.

NICK: He's a psychiatrist, he must know. He wouldn't put you in a strait jacket if you were sane. He'd have to be mad.
GERALDINE: He is mad!
NICK: (*To* GERALDINE.) Is she mad?
GERALDINE: She thinks she is. She imagines you're a figment of her imagination.
NICK: (*To* MRS. PRENTICE, *nodding to* GERALDINE.) Mrs. Prentice, she can see me. Doesn't that prove I'm real?
MRS. PRENTICE: No. She's mad.
NICK: If you think I'm a phantom of your subconscious you must be mad.
PRENTICE: Why were you chasing me with a gun? Do you think I'm mad?
MRS. PRENTICE: (*With a hysterical giggle.*) I am mad! (NICK *grabs her gun.*)
PRENTICE: (*Entering from the garden as* DR. RANCE *is putting* MRS. PRENTICE *into a strait jacket.*) Are you all mad? Stop! A husband must be allowed to put his own wife into a strait jacket. It's one of the few pleasures left in modern marriage. (*Grabs gun from* NICK.) Stand away! Doctor Rance! Your conduct today has been a model of official irresponsibility and I'm going to certify you.
RANCE: (*Quietly, with dignity.*) No. I am going to certify you.
PRENTICE: I have the weapon. You have the choice. What is it to be? Madness or death, neither of which would enable you to continue to be employed by the Government.
RANCE: That isn't true. The higher reaches of the civil service are recruited entirely from corpses or madmen. Your deterrent is useless. Put it down. (DR. RANCE *takes out his own gun and points it at the astonished* DR. PRENTICE. *Holding* DR. PRENTICE *at bay with the gun.*) I'll have you in a jacket within the hour.
PRENTICE: Is that a record for you?
RANCE: By no means. I once put a whole family into a communal strait jacket.
PRENTICE: How proud your mother must've been.
RANCE: She wasn't, I'm afraid. It was my own family, you see. I've a snapshot of the scene at home. My foot placed squarely upon my father's head. I sent it to Sigmund Freud and had a charming postcard in reply.

(SERGEANT MATCH *enters from the garden.*)

MATCH: (*To* RANCE.) I'm still ready to be examined, Doctor.
RANCE: (*To* PRENTICE, *in a firm voice.*) What have you done with Geraldine Barclay?
GERALDINE: (*Feebly.*) I'm here.
MATCH: (*To* GERALDINE, *with all the dignity he can muster.*) Will you kindly produce, or cause to be produced, the missing part of Sir Winston Churchill?

PRENTICE: Stop! All of you! (*Grabs gun from* RANCE.) We are now approaching what our racier novelists term the climax. Release my wife and the young woman, too. The story you're about to hear is concerned solely with the heart: the mind and its mysteries could not have been further from my thoughts when, early this morning, in what must be the most ill-timed attempt at seduction ever, I persuaded that young woman to take her clothes off.
GERALDINE: (*To* DR. RANCE.) Mrs. Prentice mistook my dress for her own and, by an oversight, you mistook me for a patient. Dr. Prentice asked me to keep quiet in order to protect his good name. What could I do? I was terrified of exposure.
MRS. PRENTICE: You were naked at the time?
GERALDINE: Yes. Under duress I agreed to help the doctor. I've never ceased reproaching myself. The whole day has been spent fighting to retain my self-respect.
PRENTICE: Oh, if I live to be ninety, I'll never again attempt sexual intercourse.
RANCE: I'd be willing to stake my professional reputation upon the fact that this girl has been the victim of an incestuous attack. I won't go back upon my diagnosis. My publishers will sue me for loss of royalties.
GERALDINE: (*Stepping from the couch.*) I'm sure my shorthand speed has been affected by what I've suffered today. (*Tearful, to* DR. PRENTICE.) And I wish to report the loss of my lucky elephant charm.
RANCE: (*Takes a brooch from his pocket.*) Is this the piece of jewelry to which you refer? I removed it from your neck when I cut your hair.
GERALDINE: Yes. It has great sentimental value. (DR. RANCE *passes brooch to* MRS. PRENTICE *who gives it to* GERALDINE.)
NICK: Look. I've got one like that. (*Shows* GERALDINE *a brooch.*)
MRS. PRENTICE: A single brooch can be made of these two fragments. Oh, my heart is beating like a wild thing!

(DR. RANCE *examines the brooch.*)

NICK AND GERALDINE: It's true!
MATCH: Two elephants carrying a richly engraved howdah in which is seated a young and beautiful woman—perhaps a princess of the royal line—magnificent example of oriental craftsmanship. (*To* MRS. PRENTICE.) How did you know this was a single piece?
MRS. PRENTICE: It belonged to me once. Many years ago, when I was a young woman, I was raped in a linen closet on the second floor of the Station Hotel. As the man left me he pressed that brooch into my hands in part payment.
MATCH: How did these children come to be in possession of the separate halves?
MRS. PRENTICE: I paid for my misdemeanor by conceiving twins. It was

impossible for me to keep them—I was by then engaged to be married to a promising young psychiatrist. I decided to abandon them to their fate. I broke the brooch in half and pinned a separate piece to each babe. I then placed them at either end of the small country town in which I was resident. Some kind people must've brought the children up as their own. (*Hugging* NICK *and* GERALDINE.) Oh, children! I am your mother! Can you ever forgive me for what I did?

NICK: What kind of mother must you have been to stay alone at the Station Hotel?

MRS. PRENTICE: I was employed as a chambermaid. I did it for a joke shortly after the war. The effect of a Labour Government on the middle classes had to be seen to be believed.

GERALDINE: Was our father also employed by the Station Hotel?

MRS. PRENTICE: I never saw your father. The incident occurred during a power failure. I became pregnant as I waited for normal services to be resumed.

PRENTICE: You'll find an inscription on the back of the brooch, sir—"To Lillian from Avis. Christmas 1939." I found that brooch many years ago. It was on the pavement outside a large department store.

RANCE: Who were Lillian and Avis?

PRENTICE: I've no idea. It fell from the collar of a Pekinese. Lillian and Avis may have been the creature's owners. (*He stares about him in shame.*) I haven't seen it since I pressed it into the hand of a chambermaid whom I debauched shortly before my marriage.

MRS. PRENTICE: (*With a cry of recognition.*) I understand now why you suggested that we spend our wedding night in a linen closet!

PRENTICE: I wished to recreate a moment that was very precious to me. My darling, we have been instrumental in uncovering a number of remarkable peccadilloes today.

RANCE: (*To* PRENTICE, *with wild delight.*) If you are this child's father my book can be written in good faith—she *is* the victim of an incestuous attack!

MRS. PRENTICE: And so am I, doctor! My son has a collection of photographs which prove beyond doubt that he attempted to seduce me in the same hotel—indeed in the same linen closet where his conception took place.

RANCE: Double incest is even more likely to produce a best-seller than murder—and this is as it should be for love must bring greater joy than violence.

DR. PRENTICE: Come, let us put on our clothes and face the world. (*They all turn to the audience and bow crisply and formally.*)

BLACKOUT

THE CURTAIN FALLS

END OF PLAY

Yankee Dawg You Die

Philip Kan Gotanda

Philip Kan Gotanda is one of a growing number of Asian American playwrights working in the contemporary theatre. Like so many other minority writers he struggles to get his plays produced and to develop an audience for his particular voice. *Yankee Dawg You Die* concerns the struggles of Asian American artists for recognition, dignity, and a place at the table in the predominately white male entertainment establishment.

Yankee Dawg You Die has only two characters. A young, pro-active Asian American actor and an older established Asian American actor who has made compromises with his racial heritage by playing stereotypical Asian roles in B rated movies. The play is written as a series of short vignettes in which the two characters first meet, study and work together, eventually becoming friends. By the end of the play they have virtually exchanged identities and values.

Woven throughout the episodic progress of their relationship are references to Hollywood films many of which serve as a backdrop and often an integral part of their view of the world. In the opening interlude of the play Gotanda introduces a Japanese soldier who speaks with a stereotypical Japanese accent, ala 1940s Hollywood movies. He pretends to address an imaginary American prisoner whom he guards. The brief speech contrasts sharply in tone to the next scene in which the two actors first meet. Gotanda subtitles this scene, "You Looked Like a Fucking Chimpanzee." It is to such parodies of Asian Americans that the title of the play eventually refers.

The world that emerges from the play is one which is narrowly proscribed for Asian Americans, one which it appears they may never escape and in which they may eventually go on endlessly exchanging roles forever.

Production History

Yankee Dawg You Die was presented by Playwrights Horizons (Andre Bishop, Artistic Director) in New York City, in April, 1989. It was directed by Sharon Ott; the set design was by Kent Dorsey; the costume design was by Jess Goldstein; the lighting design was by Dan Kotlowitz; the music and sound design was by Stephen LeGrand and Eric Drew Feldman; the production stage manager was Robin Rumpf and the production manager was Carl Mulert. The cast was as follows:

Vincent Chang	Sab Shimono
Bradley Yamashita	Stan Egi

Yankee Dawg You Die received its world premiere at the Berkeley Repertory Theatre (Sharon Ott, Artistic Director; Mitzi Sales, Managing Director) in Berkeley, California, in February 1988. The production was subsequently moved to the Los Angeles Theatre Center in May of 1988. It was directed by Sharon Ott; the set and lighting design was by Kent Dorsey; the costume design was by Lydia Tanji; the sound design was by James LeBrecht; original music was by Stephen LeGrand and Eric Drew Feldman; the assistant director was Phyllis S.K. Look and the stage manager was Michael Suenkel. In the Los Angeles Theatre Center production, the co-lighting designer was Douglas Smith. The cast was as follows:

Vincent Chang . . . . Sab Shimono
Bradley Yamashita . . . . Kelvin Han Yee

Set

Minimal with a hint of fragmentation and distortion of perspective to allow for a subtle dream-like quality. Upstage, high-tech shoji screens for title and visual projections. Set should allow for a certain fluidity of movement. Allow for lights to be integral in scene transitions. Suggested colors-black with red accents.

Lighting

Fluid. Interludes should use cross-fades. Dream sequences might experiment with color and shafts of light cutting at askew angles, film-noirish.

Music

Minimal instrumentation. Classical in feel.

Characters

VINCENT CHANG, ACTOR. MID TO LATE 60S. FORMER HOOFER.
BRADLEY YAMASHITA, ACTOR. MID TO LATE 20S.

Yankee Dawg You Die by Philip Kan Gotanda

Copyright © by Philip Kan Gotanda. Reprinted by permission of Joyce Ketay Agency.

THE PLAY

YANKEE DAWG YOU DIE

INTRODUCTION

Darkness. Filmic music score enters. Then, on the projection screens upstage we see emblazoned the following titles:

"[Name of Producing Theatre] PRESENTS . . ."

"VINCENT CHANG . . ."

Vincent lit in pool of light, staring pensively into the darkness. The music dips and we hear the faint beating of a heart. A hint of blood red washes over Vincent as he lightly touches his breast near his heart area. Fade to black.

"AND INTRODUCING . . ."

"BRADLEY YAMASHITA"

Bradley lit in pool of light. Restless, shifting his weight back and forth on his feet. The music dips and we hear the light rustling of large wings. As he looks skyward, a large shadow passes over head. Fade to black.

"IN . . ."

"YANKEE DAWG YOU DIE . . ."

The entire theater—stage as well as audience area—is gradually inundated in an ocean of stars. Hold for a moment, then a slow fade to black.

INTERLUDE 1

Lights come up. Vincent portraying a "Jap soldier." Lighting creates the mood of an old 40's black and white movie. Thick Coke-bottle glasses, holding a gun. Acts in an exaggerated, stereotypic—almost cartoonish manner.

Sergeant Moto pretends to be falling asleep while guarding American prisoners. The snake-like lids of his slanty eyes drooping into a feigned slumber. Suddenly Moto's eyes spitting hates and bile, flash open, catching the American prisoners in the midst of their escape plans.

VINCENT: (*As Moto.*) You stupid American G.I. I know you try and escape. You think you can pull my leg. I speakee your language. I graduate UCLA, Class of '34. I drive big American car with big-chested American blond sitting next to . . . Heh? No, no, no, not "dirty floor." Floor clean. Class of '34. No, no, not "dirty floor." Floor clean. Just clean this morning. 34. No, no, not "dirty floor." Listen carefully. Watch my lips. (*He moves his lips but the words are not synched with them ala poorly-dubbed Japanese monster movie.*) 34. 34! 34!!! (*Pause. Return to synched speaking.*) What is wrong with you? You sickee in the head? What the hell is wrong with you? Why can't you hear what I'm saying? Why can't you see me as I really am? (*Vincent as Sergeant Moto dims to darkness.*)

END OF INTERLUDE

ACT ONE

Scene One

"You Looked Like A Fucking Chimpanzee"

Night. Party. House in Hollywood Hills. Vincent Chang, a youthful, silver-maned man, in his late 60's, stands on the back terrace balcony sipping on a glass of red wine. Stares into the night air. Bradley Yamashita, 27, pokes his head out from the party and notices Vincent. Stops, losing his nerve. Changes his mind again and moves out on the terrace next to Vincent. Bradley holds a cup of club soda.

Silence. Vincent notices Bradley, Bradley smiles, Vincent nods. Silence. They both sip on their drinks.

BRADLEY: Hello. (*Vincent nods.*) Nice Evening. (*Silence.*) God. What a night. Love it. (*Silence. Looking out.*) Stars. Wow, would you believe. Stars, stars, stars. (*Pause.*)
VINCENT: Orion's belt. (*Bradley doesn't follow his comment. Vincent points upwards.*) The constellation. Orion the Hunter. That line of stars there forms his belt. See?
BRADLEY: Uh-huh. (*Pause. Sips his drink. Vincent points to another part of the night sky.*)
VINCENT: And of course, the Big Dipper.
BRADLEY: Of course.
VINCENT: And, using the two stars that form the front of the lip of the dipper as your guide, it leads to the . . .
BRADLEY: The North Star.
VINCENT: Yes. Good. Very good. You will never be lost. (*Both quietly laugh.*)
BRADLEY: Jeez, it's a bit stuffy in there. With all of them. It's nice to be with someone I can feel comfortable around. (*Vincent doesn't understand.*) Well, I mean, like you and me. We're—I mean, we don't exactly look like . . . (*Nods towards the people inside.*)
VINCENT: Ahhh. (*Bradley laughs nervously, relieved that Vincent has understood.*) Actually, I had not noticed. I do not really notice, or quite frankly care, if someone is Caucasian of oriental or . . .
BRADLEY: (*Interrupts, correcting Asian. Vincent doesn't understand.*) It's Asian, not oriental. (*Vincent still doesn't follow. Bradley, embarrassed, tries to explain.*) Asian, oriental. Black, negro. Woman, girl. Gay, homosexual . . . Asian, oriental.
VINCENT: Ahhh. (*Pause.*) Orientals are rugs? (*Bradley nods sheepishly.*) I see. (*Vincent studies him for a moment, then goes back to sipping his red wine.*) You don't look familiar.
BRADLEY: First time.
VINCENT: You haven't been to one of these parties before? (*Bradley shakes his head.*) Hah! You're in for a wonderful surprise. Everyone here is as obnoxious as hell.
BRADLEY: I noticed.
VINCENT: (*Laughs, extends his hand.*) Vincent Chang . . .
BRADLEY: (*Overlapping.*) Chang! (*Bradley grabs Vincent's hand and manipulates it through the classic "right-on" handshake. Vincent watches it unfold.*) You don't have to tell me. Everybody knows who you are. Especially in the community. Not that you're not famous—I mean, walking down the street they'd notice you—but in the community, whew! Forget it.
VINCENT: Ahhh. And you?
BRADLEY: What?
VINCENT: Your name.

BRADLEY: Oh. Bradley Yamashita. (*Pronounced "Yamasheeta" by him. Bradley shakes his hand again. Vincent repeats name to himself, trying to remember where he's heard it. He pronounces the name correctly.*) This is an amazing business. It really is. It's an amazing business. One moment I'm this snotty nose kid watching you on TV and the next thing you know I'm standing next to you and we're talking and stuff and you know . . . (*Silence. Sips drinks. Looks at stars.*) Mr. Chang? Mr. Chang? I think it's important that all of us know each other. Asian American actors. I think the two of us meeting is very important. The young and the old. We can learn from each other. We can. I mean, the way things are, the way they're going, Jesus. If we don't stick together who the hell is going—
VINCENT: (*Interrupts, waving at someone.*) Ah, Theodora. Hello!
BRADLEY: Wow . . .
VINCENT: Theodora Ando. The *Asian-American* actress.
BRADLEY: God, she's gorgeous.
VINCENT: (*Coldly.*) Don't turn your back on her. (*Bradley doesn't follow. Vincent mimes sticking a knife in and twisting it.*)
BRADLEY: (*Staring after a disappearing Theodora.*) Oh . . . (*Silence. They sip and stare out into the darkness. Bradley begins to turn and smile at Vincent in hopes that Vincent will recognize his face. Vincent does not.*) New York. Jesus, what a town. Do you spend much time out there? (*Vincent shrugs.*) Yeah. I've been out in New York. That's where they know me most. Out in New York. I come from San Francisco. That's where I was born and raised. Trained—ACT. But I've been out in New York. I just came back from there. A film of mine opened. New York Film Festival. Guillaume Bouchet, the French critic loved it.
VINCENT: (*Impressed.*) Guillaume Bouchet.
BRADLEY: Uh-huh. Called it one of the 10 best films of the year.
VINCENT: It's your film? You . . . directed it? (*Bradley shakes his head.*) Wrote it?
BRADLEY: No, no, I'm in it. I'm the main actor in it.
VINCENT: (*Mutters under his breath.*) An actor . . .
BRADLEY: It's a Matthew Iwasaki film.
VINCENT: I have heard of him, yes. He does those low-budget . . .
BRADLEY: (*Interrupts, correcting.*) Independent.
VINCENT: Ahhh. *Independent movies* about . . .
BRADLEY: (*Interrupts, correcting again.*) Films. Independent films, they play in art houses.
VINCENT: Ahhhh. *Independent films* that play in *art houses* about people like . . . (*Nods to Bradley and to himself.*)
BRADLEY: Uh-huh
VINCENT: I see. Hmmm.
BRADLEY: I'm in it. I star in it. Eugene Bickle . . .
VINCENT: (*Interrupts.*) Who?

BRADLEY: Eugene Bickle, the film critic on TV. You know, everybody knows about him. He used to be on PBS and now he's on the networks with that other fat guy. He said I was one of the most "watchable" stars he's seen this year.
VINCENT: Really?
BRADLEY: He said he wouldn't mind watching me no matter what I was doing.
VINCENT: *Really?*
BRADLEY: Well, that's not exactly—I'm sort of paraphrasing, but that's what he meant. Not that he'd wanna watch me doing anything—you know, walking down the street. But on the screen. In another movie.
VINCENT: Film.
BRADLEY: What?
VINCENT: You said "another movie."
BRADLEY: Film.
VINCENT: Ahh.
BRADLEY: My agent at William Morris wanted me to come to L.A. I have an audition on Monday. One of the big theatres.
VINCENT: (*Impressed, but hiding it.*) William Morris?
BRADLEY: (*Notices that Vincent is impressed.*) Uh-huh. (*Pause.*) Who handles you?
VINCENT: Snow Kwong-Johnson.
BRADLEY: Oh. (*Pause.*) I hear they handle mainly . . .
VINCENT: (*Interrupts.*) She.
BRADLEY: Oh, yes. *She* handles mainly . . . (*Motions to Vincent and himself.*)
VINCENT: Yes. Mainly . . . (*Motions to Bradley and to himself.*)
BRADLEY: Ahhh, I see. Well. (*Silence.*)
VINCENT: It's a bit warm tonight.
BRADLEY: I feel fine, just fine. (*Vincent takes a cigarette out and is about to smoke. Bradley begins to steal glances at Vincent's face. Vincent remembers to offer one to Bradley.*) I don't smoke. (*The mood is ruined for Vincent. He puts the cigarette away. About to take a sip of his red wine. Bradley notices Vincent's drink.*) Tanins. Bad for the complexion. (*Holds up his drink.*) Club soda.
VINCENT: I imagine you exercise, too?
BRADLEY: I swim three times a week. Do you work out?
VINCENT: Yes. Watch. (*Lifts drink to his lips and gulps it down. Pause. Vincent notices Bradley looking at his face. Bradley realizes he's been caught, feigns ignorance, and looks away. Vincent touches his face to see if he has a piece of food on his cheek, or something worse on his nose. Vincent's not sure of Bradley's intent. Perhaps he was admiring his good looks. Vincent's not sure.*) Bradley? Was there something? You were . . . looking at me? (*Vincent motions gracefully towards his face. Pause. Bradley decides to explain.*)
BRADLEY: This is kind of personal, I know. I don't know if I should ask you. (*Pause.*) Ok, is that your real nose?

VINCENT: What?
BRADLEY: I mean, your original one—you know, the one you were born with?
VINCENT: (*Smile fading.*) What?
BRADLEY: Someone once told me—and if it's not true just say so—someone once told me you hold the record for "noses." (*Barely able to contain his giggling.*) You've had all these different noses. Sinatra, Montgomery Clift, Troy Donahue—whatever was *in* at the time. Sort of like the "7 Noses of Dr. Lao . . ." (*Notices Vincent is not laughing.*) That's what they said. I just thought maybe I would ask you about . . .
VINCENT: (*Interrupts.*) Who told you this?
BRADLEY: No one.
VINCENT: You said someone told you.
BRADLEY: Yes, but . . .
VINCENT: (*Interrupts.*) Someone is usually a person. And if this person *told you* it means he probably has lips. Who is this person with *big, fat, moving* lips.
BRADLEY: I don't know, just someone. I forget—I'm not good at remembering lips.
VINCENT: No. (*Bradley doesn't follow.*) No, it is *not* true. This is my natural nose. As God is my witness. (*Silence. Vincent sipping drink. Turns to look at Bradley. Repeating the name to himself.*) Yamashita . . . Ya-ma-shita . . . You worked with Chloe Fong in New York? (*Bradley nods.*) Ahhh.
BRADLEY: What? (*Vincent ignores Bradley's query and goes back to staring out at the night sky. Occasionally, glances at Bradley knowingly.*) What? (*Pause.*)
VINCENT: Now this is kind of personal. And tell me if I am wrong. I heard you almost got fired in New York.
BRADLEY: Who said that—what?
VINCENT: You are the fellow who was out in that play in New York, correct? With Chloe?
BRADLEY: Yeah, so?
VINCENT: I heard—and tell me if I am wrong, rumors are such vicious things—I heard they were not too happy with you, your work.
BRADLEY: What do you mean, "not happy with me?"
VINCENT: Now, this is probably just a rumor—I do not know—But, that is what I . . .
BRADLEY: (*Interrupts.*) That's not true. That's not true at all. I was a little nervous, so was everybody. And I never, "almost got fired." Did Chloe say that?
VINCENT: No, no, no.
BRADLEY: Cause I was OK. Once I got comfortable I was good. You ask Chloe. The director came up afterwards and congratulated me he liked my work so much. White director.
VINCENT: Ah, rumors.

BRADLEY: (*Mutters under his breath.*) Bull shit . . . (*Silence. Vincent takes a cigarette out, lights it and takes a deep, satisfying drag.*)
VINCENT: Ahhh. I needed that. (*Pause.*)
BRADLEY: Who said I almost got fired? Was it Chloe? She wouldn't say something like that. I know her. (*Beat.*) Was it her?
VINCENT: It is just a rumor. Take it easy. Just a rumor. Remember this? (*Taps his nose.*) Dr. Lao? It comes with the terrain. You must learn to live with it. It happens to everyone. Sooner or later. *Everyone.* You are walking along, minding your own business, your head filled with poems and paintings—when what do you see coming your way? Some ugly "rumor," dressed in your clothes, staggering down the street impersonating you. And it is not you but no one seems to care. They want this impersonator—who is drinking from a brown paper bag, whose pant zipper is down to here and flapping in the wind—to be you. Why? They like it. It gives them glee. They like the lie. And the more incensed you become, the more real it seems to grow. Like some monster in a nightmare. If you ignore it, you rob it of its strength. It will soon disappear. (*Beat.*) You will live. We all go to bed thinking, "The pain is so great, I will not last through the night." (*Beat.*) We wake up. Alive. C'est dommage. (*Pause.*) Have you seen my latest film? It has been out for several months.
BRADLEY: Was this the Ninja assassin one?
VINCENT: No, that was 3 years ago. This one deals with life after the atomic holocaust and dramatizes how post-nuclear man must deal with what has become, basically, a very very hostile environ . . .
BRADLEY: (*Interrupts.*) Oh, the one with the mutant monsters—they moved all jerky, Ray Harryhausen stuff—and the hairy guys eating raw meat? You were in that film? I saw that film.
VINCENT: I got billing. I got . . .
BRADLEY: You were in it?
VINCENT: . . . the box.
BRADLEY: I'm sure I saw that film. (*Looking at Vincent's face.*)
VINCENT: I came in after everyone signed so my name is in the square box. My name . . .
BRADLEY: Nah, you weren't in it. I saw that film.
VINCENT: . . . is in all the ads. There is a big marquee as you drive down Sunset Boulevard with my name in that box.
BRADLEY: (*Staring at Vincent's face, it's coming to him.*) Oh, oh . . . You were the husband of the woman who was eaten by the giant salamander? (*Bradley is having a hard time suppressing his laughter.*)
VINCENT: (*Shrugging.*) It was a little hard to tell, I know. The make-up was a little heavy. But it was important to create characters that in some way reflected the effects . . .
BRADLEY: (*Overlapping, can no longer contain himself and bursts out laughing.*) Make-up a little heavy? Jesus Christ, you had so much hair on your face

you looked like a fucking chimpanzee! (*Bradley stops laughing as he notices Vincent's pained expression. Awkward silence. Vincent smokes his cigarette. Bradley sips on his soda. Bradley occasionally steals a glance at Vincent. Vincent watches the North Star. Dim to darkness.*)

END OF SCENE

Scene Two

"Win One For The Nipper"

Audition waiting room at a theater. Vincent seated, reading a magazine. Bradley enters, carrying script.

BRADLEY: (*Calls back.*) Yeah, thanks, ten minutes. (*Bradley sees Vincent, cautiously seats himself. Vincent pretends not to notice Bradley and turns away from him, still buried in his magazine. They sit in silence. Breaking the ice.*) Mr. Chang, I'm sorry. I really didn't mean to laugh . . .
VINCENT: (*Interrupts.*) Excuse me young man, but do I know you?
BRADLEY: Well, yes . . . we met at that party over the weekend in the Hollywood Hills . . .
VINCENT: (*Interrupts.*) What did you say your name was?
BRADLEY: Bradley. Bradley Yamashita.
VINCENT: And we met at that party?
BRADLEY: Yeah. On the balcony. (*Vincent stares intently at Bradley who is becoming uncomfortable.*)
VINCENT: You look familiar. You must forgive me. I go to so many parties. Did I make a fool of myself? I do that sometimes. I drink too much and do not remember a thing. That makes me an angel. You see, angels have no memories. (*Vincent smiles and goes back to reading.*)
BRADLEY: Look, whether you want to remember or not, that's your business. But I'm sorry, Mr. Chang. I sincerely apologize. I can't do more than that. I shouldn't have laughed at you. (*Silence.*)
VINCENT: You say your name is Bradley? Bradley Yamashita? (*Bradley nods.*) Which part in the play are you reading for?
BRADLEY: The son.
VINCENT: They want me for the part of the father. I am meeting the director. We could end up father and son. It might prove to be interesting.
BRADLEY: Yeah.
VINCENT: Then again, it might not. (*Silence. Awkward moment. Vincent studies Bradley.*) Maybe they will cast Theodora Ando. As your sister. Make it a *murder* mystery. (*Vincent mimes stabbing with a knife and twisting the blade. Bradley recalls Vincent's earlier reference to Theodora at the party and laughs. Vincent laughs, also. Pause.*)

BRADLEY: You know, Mr. Chang, when I was growing up you were sort of my hero. No, really, you were. I mean, I'd be watching TV and suddenly you'd appear in some old film or an old Bonanza or something. And at first something would always jerk inside. Whoo, what's this? This is weird, like watching my own family on TV. It's like the first time I made it with an Asian girl—up to then only white girls. They seemed more outgoing—I don't know—more normal. With this Asian girl it was like doing it with my sister. It was weird. Everything about her was familiar. Her face, her skin, the sound of her voice, the way she smelled. It was like having sex with someone in my own family. That's how it was when you'd come on the TV. You were kind of an idol. (*Pause.*)

VINCENT: You know who I wanted to be like? You know who my hero was? Fred Astaire. (*Noticing Bradley's look.*) Yes, Fred Astaire.

BRADLEY: You danced?

VINCENT: (*Nods.*) Un-huh.

BRADLEY: I didn't know that.

VINCENT: Yes, well . . . (*Awkward pause. Both want to pursue conversation but unsure how to. Vincent starts to go back to script.*)

BRADLEY: What kind of dancing did you do? I mean, Fred Astaire kind of dancing or Gene Kelly-like, or, or, like the Nicholas Brothers—flying off those risers, landing doing the splits—ouch!

VINCENT: (*Laughs.*) You know who the Nicholas Brothers are?

BRADLEY: Yeah, sure, of course. And Fred Astaire—Jesus, so smooth. I loved him in *Silk Stockings*. And Cyd Charisse was great.

VINCENT: No, no, Ginger Rogers, *Top Hat*. The two of them together, Ahhh. (*Silence.*)

BRADLEY: Would you show me something? (*Vincent doesn't follow.*) Some dance moves.

VINCENT: Now? Right here?

BRADLEY: Yeah, come on, just a little.

VINCENT: No, no, I haven't danced in years.

BRADLEY: Come on, Vincent. I'd love to see you . . .

VINCENT: (*Overlapping.*) No, no, I can't.

BRADLEY: . . . dance. No one's around. Come on, Vincent, I'd love to see it.

VINCENT: Well. Alright. (*He gets up.*) A little soft-shoe routine . . . (*Vincent does a small sampling of some dance moves ending with a small flourish.*)

BRADLEY: (*Applauds.*) Great! That was great!

VINCENT: Back then you did everything. Tell jokes, juggle, sing—The Kanazawa Trio, great jugglers. Oh, and Jade Wing, a wonderful, wonderful, dancer. The Wongettes—like the Andrews Sisters. On and on, all great performers. We all worked the Chop Suey Circuit.

BRADLEY: Chop Suey Circuit?

VINCENT: In San Francisco you had of course, Forbidden City, Kubla Kan, New York's China Doll—some of the greatest oriental acts ever to go down. That's my theater background. (*Vincent tries to catch his breath.*) See,

there was this one routine that Jade—Jade Wing, she was my partner—and I did that was special. We had developed it ourselves and at the end we did this spectacular move where I pull her up on my shoulders, she falls back, and as she's falling I reach under, grab her hands and pull her through my legs thrusting her into the air . . . And I catch her! Tadah! We were rather famous for it. This one night we performed it—we were in town here, I forget the name of the club—and as the audience began to clap, these two people at one of the front tables stood up, applauding enthusiastically. Everyone followed. It was an amazing feeling to have the whole house on their feet. And then we saw the two people leading the standing ovation. We couldn't believe our eyes—Anna Mae Wong, the "Chinese Flapper" herself, and Sessue Hayakawa. The two most famous oriental stars of the day. They invited us to their table, Hayakawa with his fancy French cigarettes and his thick accent. It was a good thing that I spoke Japanese.
BRADLEY: You speak Japanese?
VINCENT: A little, I speak a little. But Anna Mae Wong spoke impeccable English. In fact, she had an English accent, can you believe that? "Vincent, you danced like you were floating on air." We nearly died then and there. Jade and I sitting at the same table with Anna Mae and Sessue.
BRADLEY: God, wasn't Anna Mae gorgeous.
VINCENT: Yes. But not as pretty as Jade Wing. I think Anna Mae Wong was a little jealous of all the attention Sessue was paying to Jade. God, Jade was beautiful. She was 23 when I met her. I was just 19. She was a burlesque dancer at the Forbidden City.
BRADLEY: What? Did you two have a thing going on or something?
VINCENT: For a while. But things happen. You are on the road continuously. She wanted one thing, I wanted another. I was pretty wild in those days. There were things about me she just could not accept. That was a long, long time ago.
BRADLEY: What happened to her?
VINCENT: I do not know. I heard she ended up marrying someone up in San Francisco who owned a bar in Chinatown. I forget the name of the bar—"Gumbo's" or some such name. I always meant to go and see her.
BRADLEY: I've been there a couple of times. There's . . .
VINCENT: (*Overlapping.*) I think she may have passed away. She was . . .
BRADLEY: . . . this old woman who runs it, a grouchy old bitch . . .
VINCENT: . . . so beautiful . . . (*Awkward pause. Vincent had heard Bradley speak of the old woman.*) Remember this? (*Re-enacting a scene from his most famous role.*) "A sleep that will take an eternity to wash away the weariness that I now feel."
BRADLEY: I know that, I know that . . . *Tears of Winter,* opposite Peter O'Toole. You were nominated for best supporting actor! It's out on video, I have it. I know it by heart. (*Vincent feels good. Decides to launch into the whole scene. Saki is mortally wounded.*)

VINCENT: (*As Saki.*) Death is a funny thing Master Abrams. You spend your entire life running from its toothless grin. Yet, when you are face to face with it, death is friendly. It smiles and beckons to you like some long lost lover. And you find yourself wanting, more than anything in the world, to rest, to sleep in her open inviting arms. A sleep that will take an eternity to wash away the weariness that I now feel. (*Vincent stumbles towards Bradley.*)
BRADLEY: Vincent? (*Vincent collapses into Bradley's unexpecting arms. They tumble to the ground. Vincent, cradled in Bradley's arms, looks up at him.*) You surprised me.
VINCENT: Don't speak.
BRADLEY: What?
VINCENT: Don't speak. That's your line, Peter O'Toole's line. *Don't speak.*
BRADLEY: Oh-oh. Don't speak, Saki. You must save your strength. We did the best we could. All is lost my little "nipper." The dream is dead. (*Saki is fading fast. Starts to close eyes. Then suddenly.*)
VINCENT: *No!* A dream does not die with one man's death, Master. Think of all the women, children, and babies who will suffer if we are defeated. You must smash the enemy! You must win! (*Pause. Coughs up blood. Continues with heroic efforts.*) Then I can sleep the final sleep with only one dream, the most important dream to keep me company on my journey through hell. (*Vincent nudges Bradley to feed him his line.*)
BRADLEY: What dream is that Saki?
VINCENT: The dream of *victory!* (*Saki gasps for life.*) Master . . .
BRADLEY: Yes?
VINCENT: Win one for the . . . Nipper. (*Saki dies in his master's arms.*)
BRADLEY: Saki? Saki? (*He bows his grief-stricken head in Saki's breast. Then, recovering.*) Oh, you were great in that film. Great.
VINCENT: You weren't so bad yourself. (*Bradley helps Vincent to his feet.*) I'm ready for the director now.
BRADLEY: Can I run my audition piece for you? This is the first Asian American play I ever saw. Characters up there talking to me, something inside of me, not some white guy. I'd never experienced anything . . .
VINCENT: (*Interrupts.*) Just do it, do it. Don't explain it away. (*Bradley stands in silence. Closes eyes. Shrugs, fidgets, clears throat. Opens eyes, finally, and begins.*)
BRADLEY: It was night. It was one of those typical summer nights in the Valley. The hot dry heat of the day was gone. Just the night air filled with swarming mosquitoes, the sound of those irrigation pumps sloshing away. And that peculiar smell that comes from those empty fruit crates stacked in the sheds with their bits and pieces of mashed apricots still clinging to the sides and bottom. They've been sitting in the moist heat of the packing sheds all day long. And by evening they fill the night air with that unmistakable pungent odor of sour and sweet that only a summer night, a summer night in the San Joaquin Valley can give you. And that night, as with every night, I was lost. And that night, as with every night of my life,

I was looking for somewhere, someplace that belonged to me. I took my Dad's car 'cause I just had to go for a drive. "Where you going son? We got more work to do in the sheds separating out the fruit." "Sorry, Dad . . ." I'd drive out to the Yonemoto's and pick up my girl, Bess. Her mother'd say, "Drive carefully and take good care of my daughter—She's Pa and me's only girl." "Sure, Mrs. Yonemoto . . ." And I'd drive. Long into the night. Windows down, my girl Bess beside me, the radio blasting away . . . . But it continued to escape me—this thing, place, that belonged to me . . . And then the DJ came on the radio, "Here's a new record by a hot new artist, 'Carol' by Neil Sedaka!" Neil who? Sedaka? Did you say, "Sedaka." (*Pronunciation gradually becomes Japanese.*) Sedaka. Sedaka. Sedaka. *Sedaakaa.* As in my father's cousin's brother-in-law's name, Hiroshi Sedaka? What's that you say—the first Japanese American rock 'n roll star! Neil Sedaka. That name. I couldn't believe it. Suddenly everything was alright. I was there. Driving in my car, windows down, girl beside me—with a goddamned Buddhahead singing on the radio . . . Neil Sedaakaa! I knew. I just knew for once, where ever I drove to that night, the road belonged to me. (*Silence.*)

VINCENT: Bradley? Neil Sedaka is not Japanese.

BRADLEY: Yes, I know.

VINCENT: I have met him before. He's Jewish, or was it Lebanese. Very nice fellow. But definitely not Japanese.

BRADLEY: Yes, yes, I know. It's by Robinson Kan, the sansei playwright. It shows the need we have for legitimate heroes. And how when you don't have any, just how far you'll go to make them up.

VINCENT: Yes, yes. Well . . . (*Awkward pause.*) Say, do you sing?

BRADLEY: "Scoshi", a little.

VINCENT: Do you know the musical I was in, *Tea Cakes and Moon Songs?* Sure you do. Let's do Charlie Chop Suey's love song to Mei Ling. I'll play Charlie the Waiter and you play Mei Ling.

BRADLEY: Mei Ling?

VINCENT: (*Dragging Bradley about.*) Your part is easy. All you have to do is stand there and sing, "So Sorry, Charlie." You hit the gong. (*Standing side by side. Vincent provides classic sing-songey intro.*) Da Da Da Da - Dah Dah Dah Dah Dah Da Da Da Dah Dah DAH! (*Vincent looks expectantly at Bradley who doesn't have a clue and is feeling ridiculous.*) You hit the gong. You hit the gong. (*Vincent demonstrates, then quickly hums intro and starts the song. Bradley feels awkward but is swept along by the enthusiasm of Vincent. Vincent singing.*)

> Tea cakes and moon songs
> June bugs and love gongs
> I feel like dancing with you.
> Roast duck and dao fu
> Lop chong and char siu
> Strolling down Grant Avenue

Chorus: Da Da Da Da—Dah Dah Dah Dah Dah
So Solly Cholly.
(*As they dance around, Bradley coquettishly hiding behind a fan, Vincent urges him to make his voice more female sounding.*) Higher, make your voice higher! Da Da Da Da—Dah Dah Dah Dah Dah.
BRADLEY: (*Struggling to go higher.*) So Solly Cholly!
VINCENT: Higher! Higher!
BRADLEY: (*Falsetto.*) So Solly Cholly! (*They are whirling around the stage. Vincent singing and tap dancing with Bradley in tow singing in a high pitched falsetto. Both are getting more and more involved, acting out more and more outrageous stereotypes. Bradley slowly starts to realize what he's doing.*) Wait, wait, wait, what is this—WAIT! What am I doing? What is this shit? (*Then accusingly to Vincent who has gradually stopped.*) You're acting like a Chinese Steppin Fetchit. That's what you're acting like. Jesus, fucking Christ, Vincent. A *Chinese Steppin Fetchit.* (*Bradley exits. Vincent glares in the direction of his exit.*)

END OF SCENE

INTERLUDE 2

Vincent lit in pool of light accepting an award.

VINCENT: This is a great honor. A great honor, indeed. To be recognized by my fellow Asian American actors in the industry. I have been criticized. Yes, I am aware of that. But I am an actor. Not a writer. I can only speak the words that are written for me. I am an actor. Not a politician. I cannot change the world. I can only bring life, through truth and craft, to my characterizations. I have never turned down a role. Good or bad, the responsibility of an actor is to do that role well. That is all an actor should or has to be concerned about. Acting. Whatever is asked of you, do it. Yes. But do it with dignity. I am an actor. (*Vincent dims to darkness. Flash! Bradley lit in pool of light. Holding a camera that has just flashed. Wearing stereotypic glasses. He is at an audition for a commercial.*)
BRADLEY: What? Take the picture, then put my hand like this—in front of my mouth and *giggle*? Yeah, but Japanese men don't giggle. How about if I shoot the picture and like this . . . Just laugh. (*Listens.*) I'm sorry but I can't do that. Look, it's not truthful to the character. Japanese men don't giggle. What? (*Listens. Turns to leave.*) Yeah, well the same to you Mr. Ass-hole director. (*Dim to darkness on Bradley. We hear a glitzy, Las Vegas version of* Tea Cakes and Moon Songs. *Vincent lit in a pool of light. Wearing a big cowboy hat.*

He is the master of ceremonies at a huge Tupperware convention in Houston. Holding mike.)

VINCENT: Howdy! Howdy! It is good to be here in Houston, Texas. In case you don't know me, I'm Vincent Chang. *(Applause.)* Thank you, thank you. And if you do not know who I am, shame on you! And, go out and buy a copy of *Tears of Winter*. It is out on video now I understand. Hey, you know what they call Chinese blindfolds? *Dental Floss! (Laughter.)* And I would especially like to thank Tupperware for inviting me to be your master-of-ceremonies at your annual national—no, I take that back—your *international* convention. *(Applause, and more applause.)* Yeah! Yeah! What's the word? *(Holds mike out to audience.)* TUPPERWARE! Yeah! What's the word? *(Vincent holds mike out to the audience. Black-out on Vincent. Bradley lit talking to his Asian actor friends.)*

BRADLEY: I can't believe this business with the Asian American awards. I mean it's a joke—there aren't enough decent roles for us in a year. What? An award for the best Asian American actor in the role of Vietnamese killer. *(Mimicking sarcastically.)* And now in the category of "Best Actress with 5 lines or Less . . ." That's all we get. Who're we kidding. This business. This goddamned fucking business. And I can't believe they gave that award to Vincent Chang. *Vincent Chang.* His speech—"I never turned down a role." Shi-it! *(Dim to darkness.)*

END OF INTERLUDE

Scene Three

"THEY EDITED IT OUT"

After an acting class. Vincent is upset. Bradley packing his duffle bag.

VINCENT: You do not know a thing about the industry. Not a damn thing. Who the hell . . .
BRADLEY: *(Interrupts, calling to someone across the room.)* Yeah, Alice—I'll get my lines down for our scene, sorry.
VINCENT: *(Attempts to lower his voice so as not to be heard.)* Who the hell are you to talk to me that way. Been in the business a few . . .
BRADLEY: *(Interrupts.)* Look, if I offended you last time by something I said I'm sorry. I like your work, Mr. Chang. You know that. I like your . . .
VINCENT: *(Interrupts.)* A "Chinese Steppin Fetchit"—that is what you called me. A "Chinese Steppin Fetchit." Remember?
BRADLEY: I'm an angel, OK, I'm an angel. *No memory.*
VINCENT: And you do not belong in this class.
BRADLEY: My agent at William Morris arranged for me to join this class.
VINCENT: This is for *advanced* actors.
BRADLEY: I've been acting in the theatre for 7 years, Mr. Chang.

VINCENT: 7 years? 7 years? 7 years is a wink of an eye. An itch on the ass. A fart in my sleep my fine, feathered friend.
BRADLEY: I've been acting at the Theatre Project of Asian America in San Francisco for 7 years—acting, directing, writing . . .
VINCENT: Poppycock, Cockypoop, bullshit. Theatre Project of Asian America—"Amateur Hour."
BRADLEY: "Amateur hour?" Asian American theaters are where we do the real work, Mr. Chang.
VINCENT: The business, Bradley, I am talking about the business, the industry. That Matthew Iwasaki movie was a fluke, an accident . . .
BRADLEY: (*Interrupts.*) Film, Mr. Chang.
VINCENT: *Movie!* And stop calling me Mr. Chang. It's Shigeo Nakada. "Asian American consciousness." Hah. You can't even tell the difference between a Chinaman and a Jap. I'm Japanese, didn't you know that? I changed my name after the war. Hell, I wanted to work . . .
BRADLEY: (*Mutters.*) You are so jive, Mr. Chang . . .
VINCENT: You think you're better than I, don't you? Somehow special, above it all. The new generation. With all your fancy politics about this Asian American new-way-of-thinking and 7 long years of paying your dues at Asian Project Theater or whatever it is. You don't know shit my friend. You don't know the meaning of paying your dues in this business.
BRADLEY: The business. You keep talking about the business. The industry. Hollywood. What's Hollywood? Cutting up your face to look more white? So my nose is a little flat. Fine! Flat is beautiful. So I don't have a double-fold in my eyelid. Great! No one in my entire racial family has had it in the last 10,000 years. My old girlfriend used to put scotch tape on her eyelids to get the double fold so she could look more "cau-ca-sian." My new girlfriend—she doesn't mess around, she got surgery. Where does it begin? Vincent? All that self hate, *where does it begin?* You and your Charley Chop Suey roles . . .
VINCENT: You want to know the truth? I'm glad I did it. Yes, you heard me right. I'm glad I did it and I'm not ashamed, I wanted to do it. And no one is ever going to get an apology out of me. And in some small way it is a victory. Yes, a victory. At least an oriental was on screen acting, being seen. We existed.
BRADLEY: But that's not existing—wearing some god-damn monkey suit and kissing up to some white man, that's not existing.
VINCENT: That's all there was, Bradley. That's all there was! But you don't think I wouldn't have wanted to play a better role than that bucktoothed, groveling waiter? I would have killed for a better role where I could have played an honest-to-god human being with real emotions. I would have killed for it. You seem to assume "Asian Americans" always existed. That there were always roles for you. You didn't exist back then buster. Back then there was no Asian American consciousness, no Asian American actor, and no Asian American theaters. Just a handful of "orientals" who

for some god forsaken reason wanted to perform. *Act.* And we did. At church bazaars, community talent night, and on the Chop Suey Circuit playing Chinatowns and Little Tokyos around the country as hoofers, jugglers, acrobats, strippers—anything we could for anyone who would watch. You, you with that holier than thou look, trying to make me feel ashamed. You wouldn't be here if it weren't for all the crap we had put up with. We built something. We built the mountain, as small as it may be, that you stand on so proudly looking down at me. Sure, it's a mountain of Charley Chop Suey's and slipper-toting geishas. But it is also filled with forgotten moments of extraordinary wonder, artistic achievement. A singer, Larry Ching, he could croon like Frank Sinatra and better looking, too. Ever heard of him? Toy Yet Mar—boy, she could belt it out with the best of them. "The Chinese Sophie Tucker." No one's ever heard of her. And Dorothy Takahashi, she could dance the high heels off of anyone, Ginger Rodgers included. And, who in the hell has ever heard of Fred Astaire and Dorothy Takahashi? Dead dreams, my friend. Dead dreams, broken backs and long forgotten beauty. I swear sometimes when I'm taking my curtain call I can see this shadowy figure out of the corner of my eye taking the most glorious, dignified bow. Who remembers? *Who appreciates?*

BRADLEY: See, you think every time you do one of those demeaning roles, the only thing lost is *your* dignity. That the only person who has to pay is you. Don't you see that every time you do that millions of people in movie theaters will see it. Believe it. Every time you do any old stereotypic role just to pay the bills, someone has to pay for it—and it ain't you. *No.* It's some Asian kid innocently walking home. "Hey, it's a Chinaman gook!" "Rambo, Rambo, Rambo!" You older actors. You ask to be understood, forgiven, but you refuse to change. You have no sense of social responsibility. Only me . . .

VINCENT: (*Overlapping.*) No . . .

BRADLEY: . . . me, me. Shame on you. I'd never play a role like that stupid waiter in that musical. And . . .

VINCENT: You don't know . . .

BRADLEY: . . . I'd never let them put so much make-up on my face that I look like some goddamn chimpanzee on the screen.

VINCENT: (*Overlapping.*) You don't know . . .

BRADLEY: I don't care if they paid me a million dollars, what good is it to lose your dignity. I'm not going to prostitute my soul just to . . .

VINCENT: (*Overlapping.*) There's *that* word. I was wondering when we'd get around to that word. I hate that word! I HATE THAT WORD!

BRADLEY: . . . see myself on screen if I have to go grunting around like some slant-eyed animal. You probably wouldn't know a good role if it grabbed you by the balls!

VINCENT: I have played many good roles.

BRADLEY: Sure, waiters, Viet Cong killers, chimpanzees, drug dealers, hookers—
VINCENT: (*Interrupts.*) I was the first to be nominated for an Academy Award.
BRADLEY: Oh, it's pull-out-the-old-credits time. But what about some of the TV stuff you've been doing lately. Jesus, TV! At least in the movies we're still dangerous. But TV? They fucking cut off our balls and made us all house boys on the evening soaps. (*Calls out.*) "Get your very own neutered, oriental houseboy!"
VINCENT: I got the woman once. (*Bradley doesn't understand.*) In the movie. I got the woman.
BRADLEY: Sure.
VINCENT: And she was *white*.
BRADLEY: You're so full of it.
VINCENT: And I kissed her!
BRADLEY: What, a peck on the cheek?
VINCENT: ON THE LIPS! ON THE LIPS! *I GOT THE WOMAN*.
BRADLEY: Nah.
VINCENT: Yes.
BRADLEY: Nah?
VINCENT: *YES*.
BRADLEY: (*Pondering.*) When was this? In the 30's. Before the war?
VINCENT: (*Overlapping.*) No.
BRADLEY: Because that happened back then. After the war forget it. Mr. Moto even disappeared and he was played by Peter Lorre.
VINCENT: No, no. This was the 50's.
BRADLEY: Come on, you're kidding.
VINCENT: 1959. A cop movie. (*Correcting himself.*) Film. *The Scarlet Kimono*. Directed by Sam Fuller. Set in L.A. 2 police detectives, one Japanese American and one Caucasian. And a beautiful blond, they both love.
BRADLEY: Yeah . . . I remember. And there's this violent kendo fight between you two guys because you both want the woman. (*Realizing.*) And you get the woman.
VINCENT: See, I told you so. (*Pause. Bradley seated himself.*)
BRADLEY: Except when I saw it you didn't kiss her. I mean I would have remembered something like that. An Asian man and a white woman. You didn't kiss her.
VINCENT: TV?
BRADLEY: Late Night. (*Bradley nods. Vincent making the realization.*)
VINCENT: They edited it out. (*Silence. Vincent is upset. Bradley watches him. Dim to darkness.*)

END OF SCENE

INTERLUDE 3

Darkness. Bradley lit in pool of light. Silently practicing "tai-chi," with dark glasses on. His movements are graceful, fluid. Stops. Poised in silence like a statue. Suddenly breaks into savage kung-fu kicks with the accompanying Bruce Lee screams. Stops. Silence. Bradley shakes himself as if trying to release pent-up tension. Quietly begins the graceful "tai-chi" movement. Bradley dims to darkness and Vincent lit in pool of light.

VINCENT: (*On the phone to Kenneth.*) I can not. You know why. Someone might see us together. (*Listens.*) You do not know. People talk. Especially in this oriental community and then what happens to my career. I am a leading man. (*Kenneth hangs up on him.*) I am a leading man. (*Dim to darkness.*)

END OF INTERLUDE

Scene Four

"The Look In Their Eyes"

After acting class, Vincent and Bradley in a crowded, noisy bar having a drink. They play a raucous verbal game.

BRADLEY: Mr. Chang, it's a . . .
VINCENT: (*Interrupts, calls to a waitress.*) Excuse me! Tanquery martini, straight up with a twist. Dry.
BRADLEY: (*Pretending to be a casting agent making an offer.*) Mr. Chang, it's a 2 day contract.
VINCENT: (*No accent, straight, not much effort.*) Yankee dog, you die.
BRADLEY: (*Trying to suppress his laughter.*) Mr. Chang, it's a "1 week" contract. And don't forget the residuals when this goes into syndication.
VINCENT: (*Big "oriental" accent. Barely able to contain his laughter.*) Yankee dawg, you die!
BRADLEY: Mr. Chang, it's a "3 month shoot" on location in the "Caribbean Islands." Vincent, we're talking a cool 6 figures here. You can get your condo in Malibu, your silver mercedes, you'll . . .
VINCENT: (*Overlapping. An outrageous caricature, all the while barely containing his laughter.*) YANKEE DAWG YOU DIE! YANKEE DAWG YOU DIE! YANKEE DAWG YOU DIE!
BRADLEY: . . . BE LYING ON SOME BEACH IN ST. TROPEZ, GETTING A TAN, HAVING A GOOD OLE TIME! . . .
VINCENT: My drink . . . (*Both calm down.*)
BRADLEY: I talked my agent into getting me an audition. It's that new lawyer series. He was very reluctant, the role wasn't written for an Asian. I

said, "Jason, just get me in there." I showed up for the audition. I said, "I can do it, I can do it." They said, "No, the character's name is Jones." I said, "I can play a character named Jones." They said, "No." "I was adopted." "No." "I married a women and gave up my name." "No." Hell, if some white guy can play Chan, some yellow guy can play Jones. (*Pause. Sipping drinks.*)

VINCENT: Do you remember that film, *Bad Day At Black Rock*?
BRADLEY: (*Remembering.*) Yeah, yeah . . .
VINCENT: That role, that role that Spencer Tracy plays?
BRADLEY: Yeah, but it's about some Nisei 442 vet, right?
VINCENT: That's who the story revolves around but he does not appear. He's dead. Got killed saving Tracy's life in Italy. After the war Tracy goes to the dead soldier's home town to return a war medal to his Issei parents. Only they don't appear either. Their farm is burned down, they are missing, and therein lies the tale. I should have played that role.
BRADLEY: Whose role? Spencer Tracy's?
VINCENT: It's about a Nisei.
BRADLEY: Yeah, but none appear.
VINCENT: But he could have been a Nisei, Tracy's character. And I have always felt I should have played it.
BRADLEY: Me. Robert De Niro, Taxi Driver. "You talking to me? You talking to me?"
VINCENT: *Harvey.*
BRADLEY: Keitel?
VINCENT: No, no. The film with Jimmy Stewart.
BRADLEY: With the rabbit? The big fucking rabbit nobody can see?
VINCENT: God, Stewart's role is wonderful. Everyone thinks he is mad, but he is not. He is not. Original innocence.
BRADLEY: Mickey Rourke in Pope of Greenwich Village. "Hit me again—see if I change."
VINCENT: James Dean, East of Eden, Salinas, a farm boy just like me. (*As Vincent enacts a scene from the movie, Bradley appears quiet and momentarily lost in thought.*)
BRADLEY: (*Interrupts.*) Forget what I said about Mickey Rourke. He's an ass-hole—he did that *Year of the Dragon*. I hated that film.
VINCENT: Not that film again. It is . . . just a "movie." (*Calls after waitress who seems to be ignoring him.*) My drink! (*They sip in silence. Bradley reaches into his bag and pulls out a script.*)
BRADLEY: Vincent? Want to work on something together?
VINCENT: We already are taking the same class . . .
BRADLEY: (*Interrupts.*) No, no, over at the Asian American Theater. The one here in town.
VINCENT: No, no, all those orientals huddling together, scared of the outside world—it is stifling to an actor's need for freedom.

BRADLEY: It's a workshop production, a new play by Robinson Kan—a sci-fi, political drama about . . .
VINCENT: (*Interrupts.*) You should be out there doing the classics, Bradley. It is limiting, seeing yourself just as an Asian. And you must never limit yourself. Never. (*Bradley reaches into his bag and pulls out a small Godzilla toy.*)
BRADLEY: It's got Godzilla in it.
VINCENT: Godzilla? (*Moving it playfully.*) Godzilla. Aahk. (*Calling to waitress.*) My drink, *please.*
BRADLEY: You can do and say whatever you want there.
VINCENT: An actor must be free. You must understand that. *Free.*
BRADLEY: And they will never edit it out. (*Awkward silence. Sipping.*) I was in a theater in Westwood. I was there with a bunch of Asian friends. And then that "movie" starts. Rourke struts into this room of Chinatown elders like he's John Wayne and starts going on and on, "Fuck you, fuck you. I'm tired of all this Chinese this, Chinese that. This is America." And then these young teenagers sitting across from us start going, "Right on, kick their butts." I started to feel scared. Can you believe that? "Right on Mickey, kick *their* asses!" I looked over at my friends. They all knew what was happening in that theater. As we walked out I could feel people staring at us. And the look in their eyes. I'm an American. Three fucking generations, *I'm an American.* And this goddamn movie comes along and makes me feel like I don't belong here. Like I'm the enemy. *I belong here.* I wanted to rip the whole goddamn fucking place up. Tear it all down. (*Silence. Vincent picks up Godzilla.*)
VINCENT: Godzilla? Robinson Kan, a workshop production? (*Bradley nods.*) Well. "I never turn down a role." (*They both laugh. Vincent picks up script.*) Let's see what we have here. (*Dim to darkness.*)

END OF SCENE

Scene Five

"Godzilla . . . Aahk!"

Darkness. Godzilla-like theme music. High tension wires crackle across the projection screens.

VINCENT: (*V.O.*) I can't believe I let you talk me into this!
BRADLEY: (*V.O.*) Take it easy, take it easy.
VINCENT: (*V.O.*) I should have never let you talk me into this Asian American thing! And this costume . . .
BRADLEY: (*V.O. Interrupts.*) We're on! (*Bradley lit in pool of light D.R. He plays a reporter out of the 50's. He wears a hat and holds one of those old-style announcer microphones.*) Good evening Mr. and Mrs. America and all the ships at sea. Flash! Godzilla!

VINCENT: (*On tape.*) AAHK!
REPORTER: A 1957 TOHO production. Filmed in Tokyo, to be distributed in Japan *AND* America. Starring Kehara Ken, the scientist who develops the anti-oxygen bomb that wipes out Godzilla . . .
GODZILLA: (*On tape.*) AAHK!
REPORTER: . . . and Raymond Burr, an American actor who was so popular as Perry Mason that he just might be the drawing card needed to bring in those American audiences. Godzilla! . . .
GODZILLA: (*On tape.*) AAHK!
REPORTER: Rising, rising from the depths. In Japan it's released as *Gojira*. In America, it's Anglicized and marketed as *Godzilla!* . . . (*Vincent, dressed up in a Godzilla outfit, bursts through the projected high-tension wires as the projection screens turn to allow him to enter. Smoke and flashing lights.*)
GODZILLA: AAHK! (*During the following, Godzilla acts out what the Reporter is describing.*)
REPORTER: It breaks through the surface just off the shores of San Francisco. SPPLAASSHH!!! It's swum the entire Pacific Ocean underwater and is about to hyperventilate. It staggers onto the beach and collapses. It looks like a giant zucchini gone to seed. A huge capsized pickle with legs.
VICTOR: (*Struggling to get up.*) Bradley! Bradley, I'm stuck! (*Bradley helps Victor up.*)
REPORTER: 5 days later—refreshed and revived, it continues its trek inland. It takes the Great Highway up to Geary Boulevard, hangs a right on Gough and follows that sucker right onto the Bay Bridge. It pays no toll. Cars screech, children cry, mothers with babies scream. The men don't. They're "manly." Godzilla! . . .
GODZILLA: AAHK! (*Godzilla strolls over to the Reporter/Bradley, takes the hat and mike and now he becomes the Reporter. Bradley, in turn, now becomes the Little Boy acting out what is said by Vincent.*)
REPORTER/GODZILLA/VINCENT: A little boy. A little boy watching TV. A little boy watching TV on Saturday night and it's "Creature Features" on Channel 2. Tonight the feature is "Godzilla . . ." (*Reporter momentarily becomes Godzilla.*) AAHK! (*Back to reporting.*) . . . And a little boy watching, watching, has a hunger, a craving for a hero, for a symbol, for a secret agent to carry out his secret deeds . . . Godzilla!
GODZILLA/LITTLE BOY: AAHK! (*Bradley grabs the hat and mike back and becomes the Reporter once again. Vincent as Godzilla acts out the blow by blow account.*)
REPORTER: . . . In its anger it lashes out. It gouges out eyes of people who stare, rips out the tongues of people who taunt! Causes blackouts of old World War II movies! Godzilla! . . .
GODZILLA: AAHK!
REPORTER: It takes the 580 turn off and continues to head inland into the San Joaquin Valley. And there in the distance . . . STOCKTON! Stockton, a small aggie town just south of Sacramento, population 120,000 and the

home of a little boy. A little boy who knows, understands, and needs Godzilla . . .

GODZILLA: AAHK!

REPORTER: And who Godzilla . . .

GODZILLA: AAHK!

REPORTER: . . . with his pea-sized brain, regards with supreme affection and would do anything the little boy asked it to do. And this is what the little boy asked . . . (*Bradley puts hat and mike aside and becomes the Little Boy.*)

BRADLEY/LITTLE BOY: Godzilla, ya know Sammy Jones. She's this little fancy pants girl. She said she was watching this old war movie last night and that there was this female nurse—the *only* female in the whole entire army—and that a Japanese sniper shot her dead in the first 10 minutes of the movie. Then she said I was the enemy. And *then* she called me a "dirty Jap." (*Godzilla looks appalled, then angry.*) You know what to do. (*Godzilla turns, picks up a 'Sammy Jones' doll, looks down, and then dramatically stomps his foot down as if he were crushing a bug.*) OH BOY! OH BOY! (*End of Scene. Bradley and Vincent laughing. They had a good time together. They do a "right on" handshake. Godzilla-like music swells. Dim to darkness.*)

END OF ACT ONE

ACT TWO

INTERLUDE 4

Vincent lit in a pool of light. Body microphone. Visual projections.

VINCENT: I have this dream. In this dream there is a man. And though this man is rich, successful, famous—he is unhappy, so very unhappy. He is unhappy because the love around him, the love in the hearts of those he cared for most, was beginning to shrivel and wither away. And this, in turn, made his own heart begin to grow in order to make up for the love that was disappearing around him. And the more the love in the hearts of those around him shriveled up, the bigger his own heart grew in order to make up for the growing emptiness that he now began to feel. So the love kept withering away and his heart kept growing bigger. Until one day there was so little love around him and his own heart so big—it burst into a thousand red petals that filled the sky and fell slowly, so very slowly, to the earth. And the people, his friends, the ones who had withheld their love, began to swallow the petals, these remains of the man's glorious heart as they fell from the sky. Hungrily, they fed. Greedily they swallowed. They pushed and shoved each other, gorging themselves on these petals because they felt then, they too, would become like the man. Rich, famous, beautiful, lonely . . . (*Vincent dims to darkness.*)

END OF INTERLUDE

Scene One

"We Went To See The Movie"

Bradley reading from a Shakespeare book. Rehearsing. Vincent coaching.

BRADLEY: Or art thou but
a dagger of the mind, a false creation,
Proceeding from the heat-oppressed—
(*Vincent entering, correcting.*)
VINCENT: Oppres-sed. Oppres-sed. (*Bradley, frustrated continues.*)
BRADLEY: . . . heat oppres-sed brain?
I see thee yet, in form as palpable
As this which I now draw.
(*Bradley draws a knife. Uncomfortable holding it.*)
VINCENT: (*Overlapping towards end of Bradley's speech.*) . . . which now I draw.
BRADLEY: . . . now I draw, now I draw.
VINCENT: You should be elated you are doing Shakespeare. This is a great opportunity for you.
BRADLEY: (*Holding up a script.*)But this is Macbeth. I'm doing "Romeo and Juliet", Vincent—I'm doing Romeo.
VINCENT: (*Holding his book up.*) You must learn them all while you are still young. "Is this a dagger which I see before me, the handle toward my hand? Come, let me clutch thee." There is music to its language and you must know its rhythm so you can think clearly within its verse. I studied Shakespeare when I was younger. And I was—all modesty aside—the best Shakespearean actor in my class. But the only role I got was carrying a spear. And here you are with a gem of a role and you don't want to work. Come on, come on, let's hear it. (*Bradley puts his script aside and reads from his book.*)
BRADLEY: Is this a dagger which I see before me,
The handle toward my hand? Come, let me clutch thee.
I have thee not and yet I see thee still
Art thou not, fatal vision, sensible
To feeling as to sight, or art thou but
A dagger of the mind, a false creation,
Proceeding from the heat-oppres-sed brain?

I see thee yet, in form as palpable
As this which now I draw.

VINCENT: Thou marshal'st me the way that I was going— (*Bradley lowers his knife. Vincent notices.*) Grip it. Hold it. You must be able to imagine it, feel it. Know the experience from the inside. Of course, you may not have wanted to kill someone. You must know the feeling.

BRADLEY: (*Overlapping after "kill someone".*) I'm having trouble with this one, Vincent. I just can't. I can't. OK.

VINCENT: This is ridiculous. You're too tense, way too tense. Lie on the floor. (*Bradley resists.*) Lie on the floor. (*While speaking Vincent lights up a cigarette. He needs a break and can do this role. Not paying attention to Bradley sprawled out on the ground, trying out different shapes.*) Become a . . . rock. You are a rock. Find your shape. Are you big, small, flat, oblong? Keep looking until you find your own particular shape. (*Bradley slowly gets up into an upright position. Vincent puffing, doesn't notice.*) Got it?

BRADLEY: Yeah.

VINCENT: What do you feel? (*Vincent turns to see the standing Bradley.*)

BRADLEY: Alive. Conscious. But there is no hunger, no wanting. And no sense of time. It is now. Yes, that's it. Everything is *now*.

VINCENT: A rock that stands. With no appetite.

BRADLEY: No, no really I know. This is what a rock feels.

VINCENT: I have no reason not to believe.

BRADLEY: I have been a rock before.

VINCENT: Now I have a reason.

BRADLEY: I have. On acid. LSD. The first time I dropped acid I walked into a forest in the Santa Cruz mountains and became a rock.

VINCENT: Why did you do this?

BRADLEY: I was in college.

VINCENT: Alright. Let's work with it. Since we finally have something. (*Putting out cigarette.*) Go with it Bradley. Relive the experience. Relive it moment by moment. Pebble by pebble. (*Suppressing giggle.*) I'm sorry.

BRADLEY: I am walking. There is a tightness I feel in the back of my neck—I guess it's the acid coming on. With each step I go deeper into the forest. And with each step I can feel the civilized part of me peeling away like an old skin. Whoo, my mind is beginning to cast aside whole concepts. God, the earth is breathing. I can feel it. It's like standing on someone's tummy. And this rock. This big, beautiful rock. Our consciousnesses are very similar. I do a Vulcan Mind-meld. (*Touching the rock.*) "I am waiting for nothing. I am expecting no one." (*Releases Vulcan Mind-meld.*) It is beautiful in its own rockness.

VINCENT: Good. OK, let us work with . . .

BRADLEY: I began walking again.

VINCENT: OK.

BRADLEY: Thoughts of great insight float in and out of my mind like pretty butterflies. Skin holds the body together. And the head holds the brain together. But what holds the mind together? *What holds the mind together?* I panic! I feel my mind beginning to drift away. There in nothing to hold my mind together. Soon bits and pieces of my consciousness will be scattered across the universe. I'll NEVER GRADUATE! What? What's this? Cows. 10, 20, 60, hundreds. Hundreds and hundreds of cows. Where did they come from? They spot me. They see that I am different. One cow steps forward. He is the leader. He wears a bell as a sign of his authority. He approaches me cautiously, studying me. This head cow nods in approval. He knows I am no longer a civilized human, but somehow different, like them. He turns and signals the others. They all begin to move towards me. Soon I am surrounded in a sea of friendly cows. Hello, hi—It's like old home week. Suddenly I hear a noise coming from far away. It tugs at something inside me. I turn to see where the noise is coming from. I see . . . I recognize . . . Jeffrey. My best friend. Calling my "name." I look at the cows. They are waiting to see what I will do. I look at Jeffrey, his voice ringing clearer and clearer, my name sounding more and more familiar. I look at the cows—They are beginning to turn away. Should I stay and run wild and free with the cows? Or, should I return to the dorms on campus? "HOWDY JEFFREY!" As I run back to see, the cows are once again pretending to be cows. They slowly lumber away, stupid and dumb. Moo, moo. (*Bradley notices Vincent staring at him.*) It's a true story.

VINCENT: Cows?
BRADLEY: Yes.
VINCENT: Cows that have a double life? (*Bradley nods.*) The dumb facade they show to the outside world and their true cow selves that they show to one another when they are alone? Moo, moo? Well, back to the real world. Perhaps. Anyway, to the task at hand. The role you are playing. Let me rethink this. (*Holding book.*) "Is this a dagger which I see before me, the handle towards my hand? Come, let me clutch thee . . ."
BRADLEY: (*Quietly.*) I killed someone.
VINCENT: What?
BRADLEY: I think I killed someone.
VINCENT: Like in a person? A human being? (*Bradley nods.*) My God.
BRADLEY: I'm not sure. I may have. But I'm not sure. It was stupid. So stupid. I was about 16. I used to hang around a lot with some Chinatown boys, gangs and that sort of thing. I was walking down Jackson Street with my girlfriend, we were going to see the movies, when these two guys—they must have been college students come to gawk at all the Chinese people—turned the corner. Well, as they walked passed, one of them looked at my girlfriend and said, "Hey, look at the yellow pussy." So I walked over to the one guy, "What did you say? What did you say?" He just laughed at me. So I pulled a knife and stabbed him. (*Shocked silence.*)
VINCENT: What happened then?
BRADLEY: We went to see the movie. (*Pause.*) I don't know. Sometimes it

just builds up. The anger. (*Pause.*) That was over 10 years ago. I hope he's OK. I hope with my heart he's OK. (*Dim to darkness.*)

END OF SCENE

INTERLUDE 5

Darkness. Over house speakers we hear: "Un Bel Di Vedremo" from Madame Butterfly. *Vincent lit in pool of light. He relaxes at home, wearing a velvet bathrobe. He is seated, looking at himself in a mirror.*

VINCENT: (*Repeated 2 times with different interpretations.*) "You will cooperate or I will kill you." (*Pause.*) "You will cooperate or I will kill you." I will take my moment. They expect me to just read my lines and get the hell out of there, another dumb North Vietnamese general. "You will cooperate or I will kill you." Yes, I will take my moment. And I am not going to let the director know. I won't tell Robert. I am just going to do it. (*Pause. Smiling to himself.*) Yes, I will take my moment. Vincent Chang is an actor. (*Vincent dims to darkness. Music lowers in volume. Bradley lit in a pool of light.*)
BRADLEY: (*On the phone.*) But why? I don't understand, Jason. I thought we had an agreement, an understanding. I know the series fell through, but I'm going to get other roles. I'm a leading man. You told me so yourself. How many young Asian American leading men are there? (*Beat.*) I'm not *like* the rest of them. What? (*Listening.*) Yeah . . . I've heard of Snow Kwong Johnson. (*Bradley dims to darkness. Music up. Vincent lit in a pool of light.*)
VINCENT: Why do you keep threatening to do it? I hate that. You know you won't do it. Besides I am not going to change my mind. (*Pause.*) We can still see each other. (*Beat.*) As friends. (*His eyes follow someone out of the room. Music fades. Vincent dims. Music out. Bradley lit in a pool of light. He is talking to a friend.*)
BRADLEY: That's not true. Who said that about me? That's not true at all. What? I was an "ex-con?" I was a "hit-man" for the *what*? (*Pause. Butterfly's suicide aria in.*) Who told you this? Huh? Who told you this? (*Music swells and peaks as lights go down on Bradley.*)

END OF INTERLUDE

Scene Two

"... Hit Man For The Chinese Mafia ..."

Vincent's apartment. Bradley has stormed in. Vincent is trying to put on his coat and pack a small duffle bag at the same time.

VINCENT: (*Putting things back into bag.*) I cannot talk now. I cannot. Now, please.
BRADLEY: (*Angry.*) Who else could have told them, Vincent? You're the only one who knows.
VINCENT: (*In a great hurry.*) Can't we talk about this later. I have to go somewhere. (*Pushing Bradley out of the way, continuing to pack.*)
BRADLEY: I told you in confidence. Haven't you heard of "confidentiality?" What do they call it, what do they call it—"privilege." Doctor-patient privilege. Lawyer-client privilege. *Actor-acting teacher privilege.* (*Vincent is all packed. Trying to get his coat on which has been dangling off his left shoulder.*)
VINCENT: I have to go Bradley. I have a very important appointment.
BRADLEY: (*Interrupts.*) Fuck your audition! What about *my* career? You told him, didn't you. Goddamn it. You told everybody I was an ex-con, a hit-man for the *Chinese Mafia!* (*Pause.*) What if the casting agencies hear about it? Huh? Think they'll want to hire me?
VINCENT: (*Quietly.*) My friend is dying ...
BRADLEY: (*Not hearing.*) What happens to my ...
VINCENT: (*Interrupts.*) My friend is dying! (*Silence.*) He over-dosed. Took a whole bottle of pills. I have to go to the hospital. Now, get out of my way, Bradley. (*Pushing a stunned Bradley aside.*) There are some things in this world more important than *your* career ... What has happened to you Bradley? What the hell has happened to you?
BRADLEY: (*Quietly.*) I just wanted to know. That's all. If you told him. I haven't gotten a call lately and I thought you know ... (*Pause. Vincent feels badly about his remarks.*)
VINCENT: Look. I am sorry ...
BRADLEY: You better go Vincent, your friend ...
VINCENT: (*Starts to leave, stops.*) He always does this. My friend is just ... lonely. He wants me to come running.
BRADLEY: You said he took a whole bottle of sleeping pills?
VINCENT: Last time it was a whole bottle of laxatives. One week in the hospital. He was so happy. He lost 15 pounds. (*Pause.*) Maybe I did. (*Bradley doesn't follow his comment.*) Mention it. About what happened in Chinatown. Just to a few people. I just never had someone tell me they killed ...
BRADLEY: (*Overlapping.*) He's probably OK, now. I'm sure the guy's fine.
VINCENT: ... someone before. I had to tell somebody. And I never said you were a hit-man for the Chinese Mafia, or whatever ... (*Pause.*) I am sorry, Bradley. Remember? (*Taps his nose.*) Dr. Lao? I have to go. The

nurses may need some help with the bed pans. (*Notices Bradley.*) We all go through these periods when the phone does not ring. I, too, have had them. Of course, far and few between, but I, too. Try some "ochazuke" with some "umeboshi"—it's on the stove. My mother used to make me eat it when I was upset. Soothes the nerves. (*Vincent turns to exit.*)
BRADLEY: Vincent? I was going to kick your ass. I was. (*Vincent stops. Stares at Bradley.*) I just sit in my room, waiting for the phone to ring. Why won't the phone ring, Vincent? Huh? Why won't the goddamn phone ring? (*Dim to darkness.*)

END OF SCENE

INTERLUDE 6

> *Darkness. We hear Bradley's voice. Gradually lights are brought up as he speaks. Up stage area, lit in a pool of light. Body microphone. Visual projections.*

BRADLEY: I have this dream. In this dream, I'm lying on a park bench. I wear only a very ragged black overcoat. Then, I fall asleep. My mouth wide open. It is a kind of perfect sleep. No hunger, no desire . . . no dreams. My heart stops beating. The blood comes to rest in my veins. (*Noticing.*) It's quite pleasureful. The whispering of warm breezes through my hair. Big, colorful maple leaves of red and orange that flutter down and cover my eyes like coins. Ahh . . . What's this? 2 dark clouds circling high above. Now they swoop down, down, towards my sleeping corpse. I see what they are. Two magnificent vultures. I think of something to offer. "Here, here, take my fingers. Yes, yes . . . don't be afraid. Here, take the rest of my hand." That should be enough. No. They want more . . . They've jumped on my chest. They're beginning to rip me open. It feels . . . so . . . so . . . (*Dim to darkness.*)

END OF INTERLUDE

Scene Three

"I See Myself 35 Years Ago"

> *Thunder. Bradley seated on a bench in a small outdoor shelter. Raining. Umbrella on ground. Vincent runs to the shelter holding 2 cups of hot coffee.*

VINCENT: (*Hands coffee to Bradley.*) Black, right? (*Bradley nods, takes coffee. Sips, watches rain.*)

BRADLEY: I finally got a call. I just came from an audition. It was for one of those evening soaps, everybody was there. Butler gig, glorified extra. I didn't get the role. I walked outside and I started crying. And I was crying, not because of the humiliation. But because, *I wanted the role.* I keep thinking, if I got it, the part, could I go through with it? I mean, actually show up and do that stuff?

VINCENT: When you walk on that set and there is all that expectation from everyone—the director, the writer, the other actors to be that way, it is so . . . I was watching TV last week. They had on this story about Martin Luther King. He was picked up by some night riders. Drove him to the outskirts of town, dragged him out of the car and surrounded him. And that night he felt something inside he never felt before—impotent, like the slave, willing to go along, almost wanting to comply. After that, he realized he had to fight not only the white man on the outside, but that feeling, the slave inside of him. It is so easy to slip into being the "ching-chong-chinaman." (*Vincent looks at Bradley, knowingly.*) Moo, moo.

BRADLEY: It's still raining pretty hard. I felt kind a bad about last time. That's why I called you up. Your friend OK? (*Vincent nods. Pause.*)

VINCENT: I love the rain. It is like meditating. It seems to quiet all the distractions around you so you can better hear the voice of your own heart. The heart. A mysterious thing. Kind. Cruel. At times you would like to rip it out. It feels too much, gives you too much pain. And other times—aah, the ecstasy. You wish it were a huge golden peach so that everyone might taste of its sweetness. (*Pause. Thinks.*) It is also like a mirror. Yes, a mirror. And if one is brave enough to gaze into it, in it is reflected the truth of what we really are. Not as we would like to be, or as we would like the world to see us. But as we truly are. (*Vincent looks at Bradley intently.*) Would you like to know what I see? (*Bradley motions to himself, questioningly. Vincent nods.*)

BRADLEY: That's OK, I'd rather you didn't tell me. An egomaniac, right? A selfish, arrogant, insecure actor.

VINCENT: No, no, quite the contrary. I see a sensitive, shy and compassionate soul. (*Pause.*) And I see a driven, ambitious, self-centered asshole. In other words, I see myself 35 years ago. (*They laugh quietly.*)

BRADLEY: I know this sounds kind of silly. I've never told anyone. You know how, everyone has these secret goals. You know what mine were? OOT. Obie, Oscar, Tony. (*They quietly laugh.*)

VINCENT: I was so cocky after my Oscar nomination. No more of those lousy chinaman's parts for me anymore. This was my ticket out of there. Hell, I might even call my own shots. My agent kept warning me though. " 'Vincent, you're an oriental actor. It's different for you.' I said, 'No way. Not anymore. From now on only good roles are coming my way.'

BRADLEY: Did the offers for good roles come in?

VINCENT: No." I have this dream. I am standing in the * middle of a room

with all these people staring at me. At first I think they are friendly towards me. Then I think, no, they are evil people out to get me. Then suddenly again, I think this is exactly where I want to be, it feels wonderful. Then I am seized with a strange fear and I feel I must get the hell out of there. A spotlight flashes on me. I am disoriented. Someone hands me a script. (*Vincent glances at the lines.*) "Why do I have to do this?" Then this warm, soothing voice says, "Is there a problem Vincent? All we want you to do is fuck yourself. Take all the time you want. We'll get the most expensive lubricant if you need. Vincent, is there a problem? We hear Sly Stallone's doing it, so it must be OK. OK?" "Read the lines this way." (*Pause.*) I know what is going on, Bradley. I am not stupid. I know what I am doing. That is the problem. (*They sip their drinks in silence. Watch the rain.*)
BRADLEY: Maybe you should call Gumbo's, that bar in San Francisco. Right now. Come on, let's be crazy!
VINCENT: What? And find out that my beautiful memory of Jade Wing has turned into—what did you say? A grouchy old bitch? No. I could not bear to kill any more of my dreams.
BRADLEY: That was probably just the bartender. Jade is probably rich, still beautiful, living in some expensive home in Pacific Heights, wondering this very instant, "What ever happened to Shig Nakada?" (*Vincent sadly shakes his head.*)
VINCENT: We were married. Jade and I. No one ever knew that. Just us. We were so young. (*Pause.*) She left me one night. Never saw her again. I don't blame her. She caught me in bed with someone.
BRADLEY: Vincent.
VINCENT: Actually, she did not mind the idea of me playing around. Or rather she minded but she could live with it. What she could not stomach was who I was playing around with. (*Pause.*) Well. It is getting late. And the rain seems to have finally abated. (*Both get up.*) Bradley? Would you like to come over to my place? For a drink? (*Awkward pause.*)
BRADLEY: No, Vincent. No, I can't.
VINCENT: Right. Well. Good night. (*Pause.*)
BRADLEY: It's OK. (*Vincent doesn't follow.*) It's OK, Vincent. It doesn't matter to me.
VINCENT: I do not know what you are talking about.
BRADLEY: It doesn't matter, Vincent. People don't care nowadays.
VINCENT: I do not know what you are talking about Bradley. I do not. It is late. Good-bye.
BRADLEY: Good night, Vincent. (*Bradley sadly watches Vincent exit. Dim to darkness.*)

END OF SCENE

---

* Dialogue based on a scene from the film, *Yuki Shimoda* by John Esaki and Amy Kato.

INTERLUDE 7

Bradley lit in pool of light, sitting.

BRADLEY: (*Bragging.*) They want me to play this Chinese waiter. I'll go, OK, take a look. I get there and look at the script. Jesus. I read the lines straight. No accent, no nothing. They say, "No, no, we need an accent." You know, THE accent. I told my agent—What? No, I quit them—if they pay me twice the amount of the offer, OK. I'll do it anyway they want. Otherwise forget it. They paid it. The dumb shits. They paid it. (*Laughing smugly.*) On top of it, they liked me. Yeah, they liked me. (*Cross fade to an empty pool of light. The aria from* Madame Butterfly *softly underscoring this scene. Vincent enters dancing. He is wearing headphones with a walkman and is practicing one of his old routines. Gradually the TV light and sound are brought up. We hear the Sergeant Moto monologue. Vincent stops dancing, takes off headphones and watches the TV light. Upset. Reaches for the phone and dials for his agent.*)

VINCENT'S VOICE ON TV: You stupid American G.I. I know you try and escape. You think you can pull my leg. I speakee your language. I graduate UCLA, Class of 34. I drive big, American car with big chested American blond sitting next to—Heh? No, no, not "dirty floor." Floor clean. Class of 34. No, no, not "dirty floor." Floor clean, just clean this morning. 34. No, no, not "dirty floor." Listen carefully. Watch my lips. 34. 34! 34!!! What is wrong with you? You sickee in the head? What the hell is wrong with you? Why can't you hear what I'm saying? Why can't you see me as I really am? (*Dim to darkness on Vincent dialing the phone.*)

END OF INTERLUDE

Scene Four

"Ahhh . . . The North Star"

Six months later. Party at the same home in the Hollywood Hills. Balcony. Night. Vincent sips on a drink and stares into the night sky. Bradley appears. Walks over and stands beside him. They watch stars in silence.

VINCENT: (*Notices Bradley's drink.*) Tanins are bad for your complexion. (*They both laugh, clink glasses and sip.*) It's been a while. What, 6 months or so? I tried calling your service.

BRADLEY: It's been a little hectic. My girlfriend moved down from San Francisco.

VINCENT: Oh, I didn't know. I've been seeing more of my friend . . . Kenneth.

BRADLEY: Ahh, Kenneth. (*Pause.*)

VINCENT: You look good. Different. (*Looking closer at Bradley.*) What is it? Your hair? Your nose?
BRADLEY: Oh, yeah. I was having a sinus problem, so I thought, you know, while they were doing that they might as well . . .
VINCENT: Ahhh. It looks good.
BRADLEY: You look good.
VINCENT: Always.
BRADLEY: God. The night air. Ahhh. It was getting a bit stuffy in there.
VINCENT: I thought you liked being around Asians.
BRADLEY: Yeah, but not a whole room full of them. (*They both laugh.*) No way I can protect my back side. (*Mimes jabbing a knife.*)
VINCENT: Ahhh. (*Awkward pause. Bradley embarrassed that Vincent didn't laugh at the knife joke. Vincent looks up at the night sky.*) Pointing The Big Dipper. Follow the two stars that form its lip and . . .
BRADLEY: The North Star.
VINCENT: Voila! You will never be lost, my dear friend. Never. (*Silence. They sip their drinks.*) Something interesting happened to me last week. I was offered a very well paying job in that new film everyone is talking about, *Angry Yellow Planet*.
BRADLEY: I read for that movie, too.
VINCENT: Playing "Yang, the Evil One."
BRADLEY: Yang! Hah! I read for the part of Yang's number one son. We could be father and son. Might be interesting.
VINCENT: Yes.
BRADLEY: Then again it might not. (*Both laugh at the old joke.*) You know what, Vincent? You won't believe this . . .
VINCENT: I turned it down. (*No response.*) I just could not do it. Not this time. (*Pause.*) It feels . . . It feels good. Almost. I turned it down to be in Emily Sakoda's new film. It is about a Japanese American family living in Sacramento before the war. Just like my childhood. 16mm, everyone deferring pay. And my role, it's wonderful. I get to play my father. (*Mimics father.*) "Urusai, yo!" That. It's my father. And this . . . "So - ka?" I mean, it's so damn exciting, Bradley. I had forgotten what it feels like. What it is supposed to feel like. Do you know what I mean?
BRADLEY: I took it. (*Vincent doesn't follow.*) I took *it*. The role.
VINCENT: Oh . . .
BRADLEY: I took the role of Yang's number one son. He's half Chinese and half rock.
VINCENT: I see.
BRADLEY: It's a science fiction movie.
VINCENT: Ahhh.
BRADLEY: I figure once I get there I can change it. I can sit down with the producers and writers and explain the situation. Look, if I don't take it then what happens? Some other jerk takes it and plays it like some goddamned geek.

VINCENT: Yes. Well.
BRADLEY: I'll sit down and convince them to change it. I will. Even if it's a bit. Just a small change, it's still something. And, even if they don't change it, they'll at least know how we feel and next time, maybe next time . . .
VINCENT: Yes.
BRADLEY: And in that sense. In a small way. It's a victory. Yes, a victory. (*Pause.*) Remember this? (*Sings.*) Tea cakes and moon songs . . . (*They both laugh. Pause. Bradley looks at Vincent.*) Moo, moo. (*Muttering to himself.*) Fucking cows.
VINCENT: Remember this? (*Starts Sergeant Moto monologue with the same stereotypic reading as in the opening Interlude, but quickly loses accent. And, ultimately, performs with great passion.*) You stupid American G.I. I know you try to escape. You think you can pull my leg. I speakee your language. (*Accent fading.*) I graduated from UCLA, the Class of 1934. I had this big car . . . (*Accent gone.*) What? No, no, not "dirty floor." The floor is clean. Class of 34. No, no, not "dirty floor." I had it cleaned this morning. How many times do I have to tell you. 34. Class of 34. No, no, not "dirty floor." Listen carefully and watch my lips. 34. 34! 34!! What is wrong with you? What the hell is wrong with you? I graduated from the University of California right here in Los Angeles. I was born and raised in the San Joaquin Valley and spent my entire life growing up in California. Why can't you hear what I'm saying? Why can't you see me as I really am? (*Vincent stops. Bradley is truly moved. Bradley quietly applauds his performance. They smile at each other. They turn to look out at the night sky. They are now lit in a pool of light. Bradley points to the lip of the Big Dipper and moving his hand traces a path to the North Star.*) Ahhh. The North Star. (*Vincent and Bradley begin a slow fade to black. At the same time, the theater is again filled with a vast array of stars. The music swells in volume. As Vincent and Bradley fade to black, the stars hold for a beat. Then, surge in brightness for a moment. Then, blackout. Screen: "THE END". Screen darkens.*)

END OF PLAY